Concept Formation in Global Studies

GLOBAL EPISTEMICS

In partnership with the Centre for Global Knowledge Studies (*gloknos*)

Series Editor: Inanna Hamati-Ataya (University of Groningen)

Global Epistemics is a transdisciplinary book series established in partnership with the Centre for Global Knowledge Studies (gloknos), that aims to foster, promote, and disseminate empirically grounded and theoretically ambitious research on knowledge as a cultural and natural phenomenon. The series welcomes innovative contributions that serve its mission, regardless of their methodologies, conceptual frameworks, levels of analysis, temporal scope, or specific objects of investigation. Learn more about the series at tinyurl.com/GlobalEpistemics | https://tinyurl.com/RLgloknos.

Titles in the Series:

Imaginaries of Connectivity: *The Creation of Novel Spaces of Governance*, edited by Luis Lobo-Guerrero, Suvi Alt, and Maarten Meijer

Mapping, Connectivity, and the Making of European Empires, edited by Luis Lobo-Guerrero, Laura Lo Presti, and Filipe dos Reis

Invisible Labour in Modern Science, edited by Jenny Bangham, Xan Chacko, and Judith Kaplan

Scientific Freedom: The Heart of the Right to Science, by Sebastian Porsdam Mann, Maximilian Martin Schmid, Peter Vilmos Treit, and Helle Porsdam

Epistemologies of *Land*, edited by Felix Anderl

An Invitation to Non-Hegemonic World Sociology, edited by Stéphane Dufoix and Eric Macé

Concept Formation in Global Studies: Post-Western Approaches to Critical Human Knowledge, by Gennaro Ascione

Concept Formation in Global Studies

Post-Western Approaches to Critical Human Knowledge

Gennaro Ascione

ROWMAN & LITTLEFIELD
Lanham • Boulder • New York • London

Published by Rowman & Littlefield
An imprint of The Rowman & Littlefield Publishing Group, Inc.
4501 Forbes Boulevard, Suite 200, Lanham, Maryland 20706
www.rowman.com

86-90 Paul Street, London EC2A 4NE

British Library Cataloguing in Publication Information Available

Library of Congress Cataloging-in-Publication Data

Names: Ascione, Gennaro, author.
Title: Concept formation in global studies : post-Western approaches to critical human knowledge / Gennaro Ascione.
Description: Lanham : Rowman & Littlefield, [2024] | Series: Global epistemics | Includes bibliographical references and index.
Identifiers: LCCN 2024005872 (print) | LCCN 2024005873 (ebook) | ISBN 9781538178423 (cloth ; alk. paper) | ISBN 9781538178430 (ebook)
Subjects: LCSH: Knowledge, Sociology of. | Epistemology. | Social sciences--Philosophy.
Classification: LCC HM651 .A83 2024 (print) | LCC HM651 (ebook) | DDC 306.4/2--dc23/eng/20240223
LC record available at https://lccn.loc.gov/2024005872
LC ebook record available at https://lccn.loc.gov/2024005873

™ The paper used in this publication meets the minimum requirements of American National Standard for Information Sciences—Permanence of Paper for Printed Library Materials, ANSI/NISO Z39.48-1992.

"By the help of translation, all Science had its offspring"

Giordano Bruno, il Nolano

Oxford, 1583

Contents

Series Editor's Note ix

Introduction: From a Two-Faced Janus to a Many-Headed Hydra 1

Chapter 1: The Racial Foundations of Premodern Epistemology 19

Chapter 2: Giordano Bruno and the Decolonial Construction of the Renaissance 63

Chapter 3: Teratologic Concept Formation 115

Chapter 4: The Global as the Unit of Analysis 165

Chapter 5: Conceptualization: The Operational Language of Theoretical Praxis 211

Conclusion: Limits and Concerns 247

Index 253

About the Author 269

Series Editor's Note

The fact that the social sciences emerged from particular sociopolitical contexts that have constituted and oriented them as fields of knowledge is no longer a contested truth among their practitioners. But after decades of sustained critique targeting every aspect of the sociological enterprise, there remains little else to be said about the historicity and social-situatedness of thought, and much to be done to redefine the foundations of knowing.

In this book, Gennaro Ascione takes a difficult and bold step in this direction. Drawing and extending on the critical traditions of historical epistemology, the sociology of knowledge, and postcolonial and decolonial studies, *Concept Formation in Global Studies* takes the task of reconstruction just as seriously as it does the task of critique. The stakes are high as the field of global studies is confronted with the challenge of delineating a nonhegemonic, nonethnocentric vantage point on the global—an object historically subordinated to the geopolitics of asymmetrical civilizational encounters but irresistibly elevated by humanist aspirations for emancipatory unity.

Turning to concept formation as the most crucial act in the performance of theoretical thought, Ascione deploys a reflexive methodology that unravels our unconscious inheritances while bringing multiple world perspectives to bear on the construction of meaning in global studies analysis. The exercise is demanding but the argument is clear: if we are to build knowledge anew, its building blocks themselves need to be carved out of a different material and shaped by different tools.

The readers who believe the destination is worth the trouble will appreciate the journey and may well want to dwell a bit longer in that creative space before theory closes in on the wondering mind.

Inanna Hamati-Ataya

(Groningen, December 14, 2023)

Introduction

From a *Two-Faced Janus* to a *Many-Headed Hydra*

Social science acts as a two-faced Janus. One face looks at the world as the space of homogenization where interactions among geocultural regions and social groups occur, producing an increasing convergence toward one world. The other face looks at the world as the space where the multiplicity of knowledges and forms of human organization tend to transform heterogeneity into many, often irreconcilable, worlds. This permanent opposition inherits the dialectics between universalism and particularism that has marked social science since its genesis in the nineteenth century: universalism belonged to Europe and, by extension, to the West, which was considered the exclusive repository of the conditions of possibility to construct one single world; particularism set the boundaries wherein each non-Western articulation of knowledge, form of social organization, or subaltern worldview is relegated to compose the mosaic of the many worlds. This spatial articulation corresponds to the dualism between modernity and tradition that constitutes the backbone of the dominant notion of temporality in the colonial modern world. Such a dualism forces social science to oscillate between Eurocentrism and its Western-centric avatar, on the one hand, and epistemological relativism, on the other hand (Tickner and Smith 2020).

Global studies tackles this impasse and promises to create an *n*-dimensional spacetime between uniformity and difference. Yet it is my contention that this *n*-dimensional spacetime should not merely configure a condition of hybridization. It should rather allow for multiplex, non–mutually exclusive, and unexpected possibilities of dialogue, coexistence, conflict, and negotiation but also reciprocal untranslatability between different sources of knowledge, theoretical perspectives, and applied methodologies. To allow for such a possibility of worlds, this book puts in dialogue the critical approaches of the sociology of knowledge, historical epistemology, global historical sociology, conceptual history, and postcolonial and decolonial studies with a variety of epistemics produced by multiplex social groups with their different conceptual vocabularies. Such epistemics open global studies to nonbinary/nondual logics of theorization. They move across fields of knowledge that social science uses to conceive of them as reciprocally distant within the spectrum of knowledge and its presumed hierarchy of validity: Indigenous epistemologies from the Andean region; topological geometry; Aboriginal approaches to statistics; translation studies of ancient Greek knowledge through Arabic language; critical studies in Gnostic mythologies; Renaissance studies on hermetic astrology; the Afrocentric philosophy of *ubuntu*; Zoroastrian mathesis; theologies from premodern pagan, Muslim, Christian, and Jewish sources; nonhuman semiosis; Aymara cosmovisions; feminist perspectives on the "Māori Renaissance"; heretic natural philosophy from the Italian Renaissance; ancient Persian language; the Indian tradition of *Advaita*, the Chinese *Tianxia*, or the Japanese *muri*; Afrofuturism; and queer standpoint methodologies of monstrosity.

These existing alternatives transfigure the ethnocentric, two-faced Janus brain of social science into the many-headed post-Western Hydra of global studies. The historians of Atlantic piracy Peter Linebaugh and Marcus Rediker (2000) used the mythological metaphor of this amphibious creature to narrate the counterhistory of the modern colonial world from the perspective of sailors, slaves, corsairs, laborers, market women, indentured servants, and other dispossessed or subalterns coming from disparate places but united in their diversities, untold histories, and unpredictable futures, who conjoined their forces to appropriate the tools of power managed and deployed by dominant groups. Like a Hydra in the ocean of human knowledge, global studies is against Eurocentrism because it prevents thought and research from creating the concrete possibility that multiple social agencies at multiple scales with their own rationalities can dialogue and interact in different languages within the unitarian spacetime of the planet, according to more egalitarian ways to analyze and face the long-term and large-scale transformations the world is undergoing. A monstrous, not normalized, not pacified, uncanny Hydra, who lives with its heads as plural sources for making sense of a world in which no one can arrogate to themselves the right to speak for all the others; endorsing different logics moved by noncoincidental needs, expressed through polyphonic voices; oriented by divergent or convergent glances that look simultaneously in multiple directions, thereby questioning the notion of trajectory in space and linearity in time; relating either to other-than-them or among each other, yet tied to one single living body bound to inhabit the same planet. Interstate war escalation, genocide, ethnic cleansing, ecological devastation, humanitarian crises, forced diasporas, extreme socioeconomic polarization, state violence, mass health and migratory catastrophes: all need collective views as well as shared actions both respectful of diversities and concerned with fragility rather than the abuse of brutal force or unilateral display of power to which Western hegemony has accustomed global human society through colonialism, imperialism, and neocolonialism.

But ethnocentrism in human and social science is rooted in epistemological depths that are often hidden and invisible. Samir Amin (1988, 166, 187) effectively defined this problem in his early definition of Eurocentrism:

> Eurocentrism is not, properly speaking, a social theory, which integrates various elements into a global and coherent vision of society and history. It is rather a prejudice that distorts social theories. It draws from its storehouse of components, retaining one or rejecting another according to the ideological needs of the moment. . . . The Eurocentric dimension of the dominant ideology constitutes a veritable paradigm of Western social science which, as Thomas Kuhn observes about all paradigms, is internalized to the point that it most often operates without anyone noticing it. This is why many specialists, historians, and intellectuals can reject particular expressions of the Eurocentric construct without being embarrassed by the incoherence of the overall vision that results.

Two elements stand out in this general definition. First, the metatheoretical level at which ethnocentrism resides makes it an epistemological architecture rather than a theoretical bias. Second, the self-transforming ability of Eurocentrism enables it to respond to changing organizational needs, thereby preserving its capacity to inform knowledge production. The former explains why ethnocentrism exists in global studies even though several perspectives orient criticisms against specific aspects, narratives, or theories within the field. The second explains how ethnocentrism reshapes its own ideological attributes in order to resurface even in non-Western geohistorical and subaltern cultural locations that, consciously or not, reinforce the pillars of such an epistemological architecture. Immanuel Wallerstein (1997, 31–32) further specifies Amin's definition by focusing on the palingenesis Eurocentrism in anti-Eurocentric critiques:

> The critics fundamentally make, however, three different (and somewhat contradictory) kinds of claims. The first is that whatever it is that Europe did, other civilizations were also in the process of doing it, up to the moment that Europe used its geopolitical power to interrupt the process in other parts of the world. The second is that whatever Europe did is nothing more than a continuation of what others had already been doing for a long time, with the Europeans temporarily coming to the foreground. The third is that whatever Europe did has been analysed incorrectly and subjected to inappropriate extrapolations, which have had dangerous consequences for both science and the political world.

The constant recombination between the two elements that Amin enunciated constitutes the generative grammar for the argumentative language spoken by the three avatars of Eurocentrism that Wallerstein stigmatized. Amitav Acharya and Barry Buzan (2016, 228) have more recently proposed to move beyond this anti-Eurocentric Eurocentrism and enlarge the theoretical base of international relations theory (IRT) by "bringing the non-Western in" in a resolute manner:

> This perspective also resonates with the view noted above that the world is returning to a culturally and politically polycentric form reminiscent, though certainly not a mere re-creation, of the several centers of civilization during ancient and classical times. Now, of course, all these civilizations are much more sharply aware of each other than they were before the expansion of the West, though it is fair to say that the non-Western societies are still much more aware of the West than the West is of them. The powerful, sustained and often deeply intrusive Western penetration of the non-West also means that "non-Western" societies are no longer pristine. All have been deeply changed by the encounter with the West, and to a lesser extent by the encounter with each other mediated through the West. Not the least significant of the ideas universalized by the West has been nationalism, a doctrine that encourages cultures to draw identity from their history, and to use history and identity for political purposes. As just suggested, this may well have profound significance for the type of IRT that gets developed in the non-West. It can be argued that much of Western IRT is fundamentally Eurocentric in the way it uses history, though for the most part this ethnocentrism is unacknowledged and hidden underneath assumptions of universality.

As far as the "non-Western" is concerned, what imaginable theoretical strategy could avoid fetishizing the supposed authenticity of alternative perspectives rooted in the precolonial or even colonial past and defined on geohistorical, civilizational, or cultural bases? The geopolitics of knowledge is radically transforming in this age of transition, and several geohistorical locations put pressures on the existing conceptual archive of social science to make their own voices heard and their words understood. Yet this wide space of theoretical production is not homogeneous. It is hierarchical, organized according to asymmetries in geopolitical power. On the one hand, rising economic and political powers such as India, China, Turkey, or Russia and their structures of knowledge production enjoy increasing relevance (Chu 2022), for their voice is stronger within the interstate system. On the other hand, subaltern or Indigenous knowledges from the Global South or belonging to discriminated and marginalized social groups across intersectional dislocations often remain unheard. Yet the conceptual shifts their intervention is able to produce are as relevant as those of the rising global powers (Layug and Hobson 2022). Therefore, the intersection between non-Western and nonhegemonic epistemologies designs the *n*-dimensional spacetime of global studies wherein new concepts and words connected to the post-Western approaches they put forward, elaborate, or rediscover take momentum.

The genealogy of this *problematique* that connects Acharya and Buzan, Wallerstein, and Amin sets the terms of the theoretical problem at stake in this book: global studies has effectively mobilized non-Western international relations theory, critical race and gender studies, and postcolonial and decolonial theories, as well as global historical sociology and critical globalization studies, to dismantle *why* Eurocentrism raises constant and reiterated challenges. Yet they have proven less effective in elaborating *how* the social sciences should cope with multiplex challenges coming from heterogeneous geohistorical as well as epistemological standpoints located in different positions within the hierarchy of human knowledges, in order to unleash their universalist potential for pluriversality that would become a common theoretical and practical language, and how to do so without falling into the trap of essentialism.

During the last forty years, in fact, a vast intellectual movement has fruitfully metabolized both the logics of anti-ethnocentrism (Ascione 2016) and the critique of positivism (Steinmetz 2005). Such a collective transnational movement has insistently looked at manifold sources of alternative knowledge to find a way out of the fundamental cul-de-sac where the social sciences have ended up. But four decades of radical criticisms against Eurocentrism manifest today through a side effect: the idiosyncrasy to elaborate a more adequate methodology enabling global studies to cope with the multiplex social knowledges coming from heterogeneous geohistorical as well as epistemological standpoints. The task of elaborating new methodological parameters is urgent, even though it remains inexplicit, for it solicits the automatic suspicion of neopositivist "conspiracies" or a "neocolonialism" of knowledge when scrutinized from postcolonial, decolonial, or non-Western perspectives. In turn, these same critical perspectives do not acknowledge their own inability to elaborate an appropriate methodology out of a pressing demand: to struggle against the prejudice that the instances they express are in fact exclusively confined to provincial, exotic, or solipsistic particularisms, therefore, never as universalistic as the dominant ones. Such a contradiction needs a working formulation of the core methodological problem that this book addresses. The problem is enunciated as follows: once it is agreed upon that the world is a single yet multilayered spacetime of analysis, how should research about large-scale/long-term processes of social change advance in order to cope with the asymmetrical power relations that materialize colonial history through hierarchies of class, gender, race, ethnicity, culture, knowledge, cosmology, and ecology?

To answer this question, this book addresses one particular issue among the many that this formulation raises: concept formation. This means to elaborate a new methodology of concept formation that works either as a way to draw notions from data and histories to which the modern Western hegemonic conceptual archive remains blind and deaf, or as a way to allow for a cross-cultural translation of concepts across the linguistic, philosophical, and civilizational divides that form the geocultural cartography of the world. In what follows, I introduce protocols and integrated techniques, either to confront existing concepts with their own intrinsic limits or to propose different techniques to think, rethink, or unthink existing notions; to create concepts and possibility in different languages; to even thoughtfully abandon existing concepts because they are inadequate, obsolete, or misleading. This methodology discloses a path to enlarge and deepen the conceptual tools of the historical social sciences to words and lemmas in non-European languages that are able to form a new conceptual archive in order to move from the limits of inadequacy of the historical social sciences to the possibility of the more inclusive and planetary field of global studies.

PROVINCIALIZING CONCEPT FORMATION

The globalization of concepts modeled upon European history has encountered insurmountable limits in its ability to explain, narrate, or represent non-Western contexts and experiences, and has often proven inadequate in expressing nondominant instances and standpoints (Burawoy 2005, 2008; Hartsock 2019). At the same time, the intrusive presence of Eurocentrism in the production of knowledge impedes dialogue among non-Western epistemologies and mortifies their ability to carve out a space for their autonomy that would be relatively independent from dominant Western knowledges. Yet, between the specific inquiry into concept formation and the emerging field of global studies, there exists a space still undertheorized. Those who work systematically on the way concept formation occurs in social science in relation to specific theoretical frameworks underrate the problem of the cross-cultural articulation of existing categories in non-Western worlds (Kontopoulos 1993; Marradi 2012). Those who work on non-Western or subaltern knowledges and their contribution to social thinking do not move beyond the discourse on single notions to engage directly with the formalization of alternative ways of designing concepts and assessing their adequacy (Akiwowo 1988, 1999; Alatas 2006; Mignolo and Walsh 2018; Querejazu 2016). Therefore, the debate over the methodology of concept formation does not cross the line traced between two sharable premises: the constitutive relevance of conversations between perspectives that arise in different places at different times, on the one hand, and on the other, the effort to work for a common language of the social sciences informed by a common set of values and concerns (Ersche 2014). There follows that an alternative, more advanced proposal is needed to avoid reductionist classificatory schemas, but, at the same time, this proposal has to transgress the boundaries of existing cross-cultural frames of conceptual translation (Bachmann-Medick 2014; Braidotti 2006; Runciman 1983, 1989, 1997). Such a path consists in the systematic effort to introduce, explain, and apply new protocols of conceptualization that contribute to a dialogue between the social sciences and the epistemological richness characterizing the vastness of knowledges that colonial modernity suppressed, ignored, or deemed irrelevant, though prove crucial for understanding historical social change. This effort is systematic to the extent that it does not consider methodological issues as a circumscribed set of isolable procedures but rather as a constitutive dimension of knowledge production inextricably intertwined with the overall epistemological *problematique*.

The act of putting in place the qualification of such a systematicity interferes *in se* and *per se* with the rigidity of the triad ontology-epistemology-methodology. This tripartite architecture owes its cohesion to an infrastructural logic according to which alternative ontologies determine competing epistemologies; this serves to legitimate corresponding methodologies wherein the gamut of methods draws the conditions of possibility of its own applicative forms of operationalization. Nevertheless, as far as the global is assumed as the relevant unit of analysis for large-scale and long-term processes of knowledge production as well as circulation, and the entanglement of social hierarchies in power configurations is exposed, an alternative infrastructural logic emerges. By means of this alternative logic, epistemology results as both inevitably historically determined and ethnocentric—whose prefix *ethnos* ethymologically refers to the sociological concept of *group*—thereby existing as the driving force that overdetermines either ontology or methodology. Epistemology shapes the anthropic landscape of knowledge. To the extent this alternative infrastructural logic remodulates the relation between epistemology and ontology, the latter materializes into the fortress upon whose threshold epistemological assertions about truth are transmuted into a set of postulates about the infinite essence of what reality is and is not. This set is manufactured according to the transient horizon of certitude the group establishes as predominant over competing others and is eventually stored, preserved, and guarded in the form of axiomatics kept in theological or philosophical coffers. To the extent this different infrastructural logic remodulates the relation between epistemology and methodology, instead, the latter becomes the in-becoming map where epistemological assertions about certitude transmute into finite ways (*method* from ancient Greek: *meta*=beyond; *hodós*=to walk. *Dao* in Chinese; *Dharma* in Hindi). *Way* conveys a two-fold meaning, which is literally equivocal (from Latin, *aequus*=equivalent; *vox*=voice). Way means both paths and modes. Ways are walkable in two opposite directions. In one direction, ways signal how to go from one place to another according to given methodological directives, and expand, redesign, or amend delineate the borders of the map representing the anthropic landscape wherein epistemology transforms the historically determined organizational needs of the social group into knowledge. But in the opposite direction, ways simultaneously signal the viable routes throughout the epistemological landscape that the *ethnos* designed, and release the appropriate linguistic code for understanding what infrastructural logic is in place beyond those signs (methodology = method + *logos*). Reading methodology in such a reverse mode suggests the way to recursively unveil the entire path and enter the fortress where lies the possibility of questioning the ultimate authority of established truths. By making the infrastructural logic understandable, and replicable, the discourse on methods forces the gateways of knowledge to remain ajar, while urging the gatekeepers to remain vigilant, since the possibility of transforming the entire architecture of knowledge endures. This is why, four centuries ago, Descartes entrusted his diriment worldview to an overarching program for knowledge production, which, on the one hand, concealed its author behind the anonymity while, on the other hand, showed off its unequivocal taxonomy: *Discourse on the Method of Rightly Conducting One's Reason and of Seeking Truth in the Sciences*.

In social science, the last attempt to address concept formation in a systematic manner remains William Outhwaite's now-classic *Concept Formation in Social Science*, published four decades ago. In his opening paragraph, Outhwaite formulates the overall *problematique* of concept formation as follows:

> Since the early 1960s there has been a growing interest in examining the concepts used by scientists in general and social scientists in particular. . . . The notion that concepts, assumptions, measurement techniques and so on are linked together in a limited set of frameworks is only too familiar in the social sciences, where representatives of alternative traditions have characteristically ignored each other or talked past each other. The fact that differences such as these can be assimilated with apparent ease to traditional philosophical oppositions such as those between individualism and holism or between empiricism and conventionalism may lead the social scientist to see them as irresolvable and therefore to avoid any serious examination of them. . . . For if social scientists are inevitably pushed into taking serious notice of semantic aspects of their own practice, they are also compelled to adopt positions in the philosophy of meaning and science. They must, for example, support their choice of concepts and the ways in which they choose to specify them (by definition or otherwise), by metatheoretical reflections on the relation between scientific terminology and ordinary language, on the legitimacy or illegitimacy of stipulative definitions, and so

> on. More precisely, they can hardly avoid rejecting the more vulgar positivist positions on these issues—for example extreme empiricism or operationalism. (Outhwaite 1983, 1)

Outhwaite scrutinized the positivist, hermeneutic, rationalist, and realist traditions and developed the implications of these traditions for what *definition* means accordingly. In his methodology, the notion of definition was pivotal since the adherence to the way each of the paradigms sets the boundaries of the semantic fields of each concept became a measure of the ability of each theory to come to terms with the complexity of the processes of social change it aimed to understand and represent. Looking at the extent to which Outhwaite's thinking was entrenched within its coeval epistemological horizon four decades later makes immediately clear how his book remains constrained within the historically determined limits of Eurocentrism. Today, this horizon is enlarged: from the paradigms in the philosophy of science to the worlds of global epistemics. Here, the semantic boundaries of the notion of definition become permeable to a variety of words, lemmas, sintagmas, and conceptual structures whose anthropological richness creates an unprecedented gnoseological effervescence whose generative potential remains largely latent.

To define what science *is* against what it *is not* was the crucial *problematique* of what Immanuel Kant named the "demarcation problem" (Jackson 2010). The multiple possible definitions within the Western traditions gave birth to alternative paradigms. The rigidity of the notion of paradigm poses the problem of adopting a more open framework wherein the possibility of post-Western approaches to human knowledge can fully express their potential, and this is the reason why the notion paradigm does not apply to the epistemological resources mobilized in this book: paradigms and global epistemics are incommensurable. Paradigms were the historical by-product of internal differentiation within the hegemonic structures of knowledge of the modern world. And even though the substance of several stances and perspectives that characterized the paradigms that Outhwaite brings into consideration are analogous to the philosophical content of many alternative non-Western philosophical traditions or epistemologies, global epistemics encapsulate those contents into radically different visions and cosmovisions, languages and worldviews, ecologies and ethics that exceed and often oppose hegemonic modern Western paradigms, blurring the boundaries between ontology, epistemology, and methodology. Global epistemics is rather a multiverse where the many forms of knowledge of non-Western or subaltern social groups, which the dominant epistemologies destroyed, canceled, silenced, or transformed into exotic oddities, find their theoretical citizenship. These knowledges do not remain confined in the apartheid of particularism where the Western hegemonic universalism has kept them. They call for a pluriversality that lies outside the historical horizon of Western thinking that dominated epistemology before the long-term and large-scale outcomes that the process of decolonization produced in the global structures of knowledge.

One way of honoring the groundbreaking work of Outhwaite consists in reframing the *problematique* of concept formation beyond the Western ethnocentrism of Outhwaite's reflexive approach and compensate its lack of historiographical depth into the emergence of the epistemological configuration of knowledge production he analyzed without questioning its foundations. This movement is not an exploration into exotic continents to mine knowledge heritages, nor back into remote regions of time in search for mythical origins, but rather a dynamic repositioning that enables global studies to listen and learn from elsewhere in spacetime. It is a dialogue with difference among differences.

STRUCTURE OF THE BOOK

The argumentative logic of this book resembles Outhwaite's. Being a new methodology, it elaborates its own tools along the route that it incrementally designs to eventually become a modular protocol with a set of applied techniques. Even the structure of the book resembles that of Outhwaite's. It is organized into five chapters. Among these five chapters, one focuses on a particular intellectual figure: Outhwaite devoted one chapter to the twentieth-century German sociologist Max Weber; I devote chapter 2 to the sixteenth-century Neapolitan intellectual and migrant Giordano Bruno, burned to death in Campo de' Fiori by the Roman inquisition at the beginning of the jubilee year 1600. The main differences between this book and its illustrious predecessor consist in the fact that I ground my methodological *problematique* on historiographical bases and that I engage with a variety of non-Western and nonhegemonic epistemologies, as well as with several disciplines beyond philosophy and the social sciences. My argument is articulated around two historiographical hypotheses, which form the first two chapters, and my methodological stance is formulated in the remaining three chapters.

Chapter 1 begins the dismantling of the modern Western dogma of the separation between ontology and epistemology, which is fully completed in chapter 5. The separation between ontology and epistemology originates in the racialization of knowledges coming from the east and the south, which occurred in the Latin premodern Mediterranean as a by-product of the political, cultural, and institutional struggles that the dominant Christian groups fought from a fragile position of power against Muslim/Arabic rulers leading the multiple political entities that formed the cartography of the thirteenth-century Maghreb and Southeastern Mediterranean. I expose the conjunctural path, neither linear nor incremental, that led to the racialization of alterity in the context of the dialogue and negotiation between different trends in knowledge production. The transmission of Aristotle's and other Greek and Hellenistic thinkers' work to Latin Christian erudite strata through Arabic translations dismantles the taken-for-granted notions of Western and Eastern civilizations and shows how this construction served immediate political needs instead of expressing an essentialist core that historically would manifest the inner divergences of alternative and irreconcilable political religions and gnoseologies.

Chapter 2 focuses on the Renaissance from a historical and theoretical perspective. It puts in dialogue well-established historiographical trends about the Italian Renaissance with decolonial studies in order to question the assumption of the continuity between the Renaissance and the Enlightenment, which postcolonial and decolonial studies share with the Western hegemonic master narrative of modernity. It proposes to rethink the Renaissance as an epistemological rupture in space and time. In space, it engages with Mignolo's influential interpretation of the "darker side" of the Renaissance and the early modern period, in order to disarticulate the conflation of the Spanish Renaissance with the Renaissance in Italy, where the latter becomes an epistemic space of connection with non-Western knowledges for the generative grammar of monstrosity to emerge. In time, it draws from Eugenio Garin and its epigones to question the historiography that appropriated and deformed the cultural phenomenon of the Renaissance during the late eighteenth and nineteenth centuries, from the French encyclopedists to the romantics. It presents sixteenth-century heretic philosopher and southern Italian migrant Giordano Bruno, his concepts of *temporality* and *infinite universe*, his pioneering anticolonial critique, and his theory of knowledge as alternative resources for a post-Western theory of concept formation. This restitution of complexity to the Renaissance discloses a different horizon of theorization where non-Western, heretic, and silenced knowledges ally against Western hegemonic epistemology, functioning as a syntonizer for a variety of forms of knowledge, across the past, present, and future, and across east(s), west(s), north(s) and south(s).

Chapter 3 formulates the methodological proposal of assuming monstrosity as the generative grammar of a new holistic approach to concept formation, which enables the sociological imagination to cocreate new and more adequate linguistic tools and notions to think the world and make global studies an open, inclusive, and more egalitarian space of knowledge production. Once the teratologic approach to concept formation is deployed, an alliance is possible between different forms of human knowledge that dominant thinking in the social sciences has neglected. The literary figure of Shakespeare's

Caliban, approached through the decolonial lens of the Cuban literary critic Roberto Fernàndez Retamar, is pivotal in this context. I put Caliban in dialogue with the juvenile work of the Hungarian philosopher Imre Lakatos. The forms of knowledge that teratology puts in dialogue move across the human and natural sciences, beyond Eurocentrism and speciesism, including international relations theory; political economy; critical geography; philology and etymology; postcolonial, decolonial, or post-Western perspectives; late medieval scholasticism; medieval and Renaissance art; literary criticism; cultural studies; and anthropology. Teratological concept formation is propaedeutic to the techniques explained in chapter 5.

Chapter 4 directly addresses the methodological issue of assuming the global as a meaningful unit of analysis as far as global studies is concerned. It focuses on five aspects of the construction of "the global" that are systematically neglected. The first is the emergence of modernization theories as a response to the embryonic forms of the decolonization of theory in the immediate aftermath of World War II, rather than the latter being a reaction to the hegemony of the former. The second is the assessment of world systems analysis in the tradition of American sociology and its attempt to turn global since the 1960s. The third is the disentanglement of relationalism from holism that the irruption of the colonial difference into the realm of theory production has provoked since the 1980s. The fourth concerns the methodological upshots of the multiple ways of conceiving relationalism as a way out of the impasse of critical globalization theories that developed since the early 1990s and mobilizes the historiographical approaches of connected histories to affirm the possibility of conceiving the global as a unit of analysis through the conceptual tension emerging among the concepts of *connectedness*, *borders*, and *assemblages*. The fifth consists in the entanglement of the global with the notion of the "planetary," where the latter stands as the figurative creative pathway toward the transitional adequacy of our available notion of the global itself.

Chapter 5 proposes techniques of conceptualization within the methodological option of assuming the space of tension between the global and the planetary as a meaningful unit of analysis. Conceptualization stands as the operational dimension of concept formation in its ability to shape reality according to alternative worldviews as well as to produce critical knowledge learning from post-Western approaches. It sets out the possibility of a new generative grammar for conceptualization that addresses the problem of translation across geocultural, linguistic, or epistemological borders. The notion of *translatability* drawn from Antonio Gramsci provides a way out of the impasse of methodologically conceiving cross-cultural dialogue as a specific theoretical praxis. It introduces and explains the strategy of semantic spatialization for concept formation. Such a strategy applies to two fundamental notions situated at a higher level of abstraction that provides necessary categories of thought to form concepts: *relation* and *concept* itself. Both are usually taken for granted. Yet their cogency is questioned by means of Silvia Rivera Cusicanqui's interpretation of Aymara theory of knowledge and Renaissance heretic epistemologies in order to argue for the generative power of the tension between *relation* and *vinculum*, as well as the tension between *concept* and *intention*. Eventually, eight styles of concept formation are introduced that transcend the logical and epistemological binaries upon which the architecture of knowledge production characteristic of the hegemonic western thinking is based, together with six possible, non–mutually exclusive, methodological directives. These methodological directives offer manifold open-ended operational protocols, whose concrete deployment I show throughout the chapter by means of examples of conceptualizations across linguistic and geocultural divides, applied to several major concepts. Among these are the concepts of *capital*, *incorporation*, *nation-state*, and *human*.

The conclusion addresses limits and concerns. It discusses the possible impact of demography on concept formation and the notion of hegemony.

SITUATING RESEARCH

This work involves self-reflection about the situatedness of the research presented in the following pages. The Mediterranean, more specifically Southern Italy, and the city of Naples in particular, occupies a particular place in the world history of the structures of knowledge. In Naples, exactly eight hundred years ago, on June 5, 1224, the emperor Frederick II founded the first secular university in the world, named after him, taking as an example the university of Al-Qarawiyyīn, in Fez, Morocco, which opened in 859. Universities, or *studii*, existed in Europe since the eleventh century. The *studium* in Bologna, for example, dates back to 1088. These, however, were ecclesiastical institutions wherein teachers belonged to the Christian clergy. The first secular university, instead, wanted to challenge the monopoly of expert knowledge that had been in the hands of religious authorities for centuries. This challenge was perceived by the Christian Church for what it actually was: a fatal threat to its authority in establishing what true knowledge was and what were the limits that human knowledge could not question. In a modern formulation: it challenged the monopoly of epistemology. This struggle for the control of knowledge flared up for four centuries until it was pacified in the seventeenth century, when the anti-ecclesiastic stances that modern science launched against the authority of the Church found an accommodation that set the separation of the search for truth from the search for beauty and the search for justice (Wallerstein 1997). Before this unstable synthesis, though, that struggle fostered by the circulation of knowledge from the east and from the south of the Mediterranean, produced new powerful heterodoxies. These heterodoxies enlarged the human horizons of understanding, but they also produced—as a reaction—a new brutal authoritarian system of repression: inquisition, that Pope Innocent III institutionalized in the first decade of the thirteenth century. Heresies, to be sure, had emerged in late antiquity during the early centuries of Christianity. Inquisition became an official institution of the Church in 1189, in a period of profound crisis of both secular and religious authority that I investigate in chapter 1.

This historically determined social relation globalized as it reached its apogee during the sixteenth-century Renaissance. It is part and parcel of the colonization and evangelization of the Americas that came together with the imposition of the most detrimental forms of capitalist exploitation, depredation, dispossession, and racial hierarchization of the global workforce (Quijano 2007). Inquisition backed up the conquistadores in the colonies and extended to Indigenous knowledge producers the tools of repression and torture against idolatry and disbelief it had forged in the struggle against heresy, political opponents, and intellectual heterodoxy influenced by the circulation of Arabic translations of major ancient Greek knowledge to which Latin Christian erudite strata had remained oblivious until the twelfth century. The Italian peninsula at the time was economically and culturally fragmented. Southern Italy, unlike the rest of the peninsula, was also the subaltern Mediterranean periphery of the Castilian Empire. The missionaries returning from the Americas called it *las Indias de por acà* (Huamanchumo de la Cuba 2021), that is, "the Indies of this side (of the world)." The inhabitants of the most inner areas appeared to them as savage, illiterate, and idolaters as the human groups on the other side of the Atlantic or in the Indian Ocean they were beginning to refer to in terms of *indio* (Pagden 1987). For this reason, a counterfactual question lies underneath the surface of the methodological issues that this book raises: what forms of knowledge would emerge if the more radical heretical cosmovisions from the subaltern Arabic/Muslim/pantheistic/naturalist/Latin Mediterranean spacetime could dialogue with non-Western, African, Asian, South and Central American Indigenous epistemologies and philosophies of knowledge? To answer this question without fetishizing the past and the elsewhere, an alternative, new, and fascinating understanding of spacetime and the relation it entails with knowledge becomes necessary, as the reader will discover through the pages that follows.

Now I am aware that heretics and the planetary survivors to the colonial epistemological genocides of colonial modernity are formidable allies. My contribution consists in materializing this alliance through a pathbreaking methodology of concept formation that looks to the possibility of working collectively in the future to endow global studies with a planetary conceptual vocabulary. The awareness that such a possibility is concrete has grown along the way of writing. It looked tight as a water trickle at the beginning and then became a river flowing into the sea. Listening to the Indigenous women's voices from the so-called Māori Renaissance as a way to decolonize methodology and elaborate a methodology of the oppressed, I have learned that what for me would be a "river" is better conceptualized in terms of *Ki uta ki tai* (Fisher 2022; Sandoval 2000; Smith 1999). *Ki uta ki tai* does not translate as "course of water" or alike. It literally means "from the mountains to the sea," that is, a dynamic ecological, human and spiritual system of integrating relations that provides the spacetime coordinates within which I can locate my position in the limited course of my mundane life, but also the human group I was born within and the ethnocentrism that connotes its relations with other groups in terms of people, culture, social structures, and living beings, including nonhuman and supernatural beings, all of them coexisting in connection along the path going from the mountain to the sea, and back to the mountain once again. A river is a tie between identity, history, natural constraints, forms of knowing, ways of living, and modes of being. It is a system of meanings that partakes in the process of knowledge production about the world, from an unstable place in space during a transient moment in time. The production, elaboration, transmission, sharing, and constant critique of such knowledge is a form of gratitude, responsibility, and care toward the expanded, planetary system of human and nonhuman relations through which I am able to try to make sense of the world in the struggle for a more just global human society.

BIBLIOGRAPHY

Acharya Amitav and Buzan Barry, eds. 2016. *Non-Western International Relations Theory: Perspectives on and Beyond Asia*. London: Routledge.

Akiwowo, Akinsola. 1999. "Indigenous Sociologies. Extending the Scope of the Argument." *International Sociology* 14, no. 2: 115–38.

Alatas, Farid. 2006. *Alternative Discourses in Asian Social Science: Responses to Eurocentrism*. New York: SAGE.

Alatas, Syed Hussein. 2006. "The Autonomous, the Universal and the Future of Sociology." *Current Sociology* 54, no. 1: 7–23.

———. ed. 2017. "Ibn-Khaldun: Theory and Methodology." *Journal of Historical Sociology* 30, no. 4.

Amin, Samir. 1988. *Eurocentrism: Modernity, Religion, and Democracy: A Critique of Eurocentrism and Culturalism*. New York: Monthly Review Press.

Ascione, Gennaro. 2016. *Science and the Decolonization of Social Theory: Unthinking Modernity*. London: Palgrave.

Bachmann-Medick, Doris, ed. 2014. *The trans/national study of culture: a translational perspective. Vol. 4*. Berlin: Walter de Gruyter, 2014

Braidotti, Rosi. 2006. *Transpositions: On nomadic ethics*. New York: Polity.

Burawoy, Michael. 2005. "Provincializing the Social Sciences." In *The Politics of Method in the Human Sciences: Positivism and Its Epistemological Others*, edited by George Steinmetz, 508–25. Chapel Hill, NC: Duke University Press.

———. 2008. "Open the Social Sciences: To Whom and for What?" *Portuguese Journal of Social Science* 6, no. 3: 137–46.

Chu, Sinan. 2022. "Fantastic Theories and Where to Find Them: Rethinking Interlocutors in Global IR." *Millennium: Journal of International Studies* 50, no. 3: 700–29.

Cohen, Robert S., and Marx W. Wartofsky, eds. 1983. *Epistemology, methodology, and the social sciences*. New York: Springer.

Ersche, Christian, et al., eds. 2014. *Global knowledge production in the social sciences: made in circulation*. Dublin: Ashgate Publishing.

Fisher, Karen. 2022. "Decolonizing Rivers in Aotearoa New Zealand." In *Indigenous Women's Voices: 20 Years on from Linda Tuhiwai Smith's Decolonizing Methodologies*, edited by Emma Lee and Jennifer Evans, 1–31. London: Bloomsbury.

Hartsock, Nancy. 2019. *The Feminist Standpoint Revisited, And Other Essays*. New York: Routledge.Huamanchumo de la Cuba, Ofelia. 2021. "Las 'Indias de por acá' en el discurso italiano de la época de la Contrarreforma." In *Rutas Atlánticas. Redes narrativas entre América Latina y Europa*, edited by Simone Ferrari y Emanuele Leonardi, 73–84. Milan: Milan University Press.

Kontopoulos, Kyriakos M. 1993. *The Logics of Social Structure*. New York: Cambridge University Press.

Jackson, Patrick Thaddeus. 2010. *The Conduct of Inquiry in International Relations: Philosophy of Science and Its Implications for the Study of World Politics*. London: Routledge.

Layug, A., and John M. Hobson, eds. 2022. *Globalizing International Theory: The Problem with Western IR Theory and How to Overcome It*. London: Routledge.

Linebaugh, and Marcus Rediker. 2000. *The Many-Headed Hydra: Sailors, Slaves, Commoners, and the Hidden History of the Revolutionary Atlantic*. Boston: Beacon Press.

Marradi, Alberto. 2012. "The Concept of Concept: Concepts and Terms." *Knowledge Organization* 39: 29–54.

Mignolo, Walter D., and Catherine E. Walsh. 2018. *On Decoloniality: Concepts, Analytics, Praxis*. Durham, NC: Duke University Press.

Outhwaite, William. 1983. *Concept Formation in Social Science*. London: Routledge.

Querejazu, Amaya. 2016. "Encountering the Pluriverse: Looking for Alternatives in Other Worlds." *Revista Brasileira de Política Internacional* 59, no. 2: 1–16.

Pagden, Anthony. 1987. *The Fall of Natural Man. The American Indian and the Origins of Comparative Ethnology*. London: Cambridge University Press.

Quijano, Anibal. 2007. Coloniality and Modernity/Rationality, *Cultural Studies*, 21:2–3, 168–178.

Robinson, William, I. 2005. "What Is a Critical Globalization Studies? Intellectual Labor and Global Society." In *Critical Globalization Studies*, edited by Richard P. Appelbaum and William I. Robinson, 11–18. New York: Routledge.

Runciman, Walter Garrison. 1997. *A treatise on social theory. Vol. 3*. London: Cambridge University Press.

———. 1989. *A treatise on social theory. Vol. 2*. London: Cambridge University Press.

———. 1983. *A treatise on social theory. Vol. 1*. London: Cambridge University Press, 1983.

Sandoval, Chela. 2000. *Methodology of the Oppressed*. Minneapolis: Minnesota University Press.

Smith, Linda Tuhiwai. 1999. *Decolonizing Methodologies: Research and Indigenous People*. London: Zed Books.

Steinmetz, George, ed. 2005. *The Politics of Method in the Human Sciences: Positivism and Its Epistemological Others*. Chapel Hill, NC: Duke University Press.

Tickner, Arlene B., and Karen Smith, eds. 200. *International Relations from the Global South: Worlds of Difference*. London: Routledge.

Wallerstein, Immanuel. 1997. "Eurocentrism and its Avatars: The Dilemmas of Social Science." *Sociological Bulletin* 46, no. 1: 21–39.

Chapter 1

The Racial Foundations of Premodern Epistemology[1]

ONTOLOGY-EPISTEMOLOGY-METHODOLOGY THROUGH THE WHIRLPOOLS OF TIME

The separation between ontology, epistemology, and methodology took place in the *longue durée*, and its legitimacy is a problem of historiographical inquiry. This tripartite architecture is problematic from a post-Western perspective even though alternative, non-Western, or nonhegemonic knowledges replicate it: such a replication is one among the multiple forms of the palingenesis of Western domination in contemporary human knowledge. Nonetheless, the social sciences have inherited this tripartite architecture; it remains relevant because of the effects of reality it produces. It conceals two substantial conditions for the production of knowledge that become evident when this same architecture is under scrutiny from long-term and large-scale perspectives on global historical social change. First, even though such a tripartite architecture presupposes that ontology precedes epistemology and epistemology precedes methodology, it is epistemology—that is, what a specific social group means by knowledge—that creates and legitimates the remaining two, thereby projecting its own understanding of what knowledge is into the other two imaginatively separated realms concerning what reality is (ontology) and how to produce true knowledge (methodology). Second, epistemology intimately connects with politics and geopolitics, that is, with power structures across the inner or outer boundaries of the institutional landmarks defining the spacetime of existence of a human group. Therefore, any epistemology is literally ethnocentric, where the prefix *ethnos*, refers to the sociological concept of *group* rather than the superimposed layer of racialization to which the social sciences have exposed both expert knowledge and the common sense.

The presumed impossibility of conceiving truth outside modern Eurocentric universalism without ceding to its fragmentation and dissolution into radical relativism configures the argumentative structure of the logical barriers surrounding the epistemological bastion that western hegemonic thought constructed to intellectually legitimate and impose its world domination. Michael Adas' pathbreaking analysis exposes a crucial historical aspect of this process:

> In the Early years of European expansion, European travellers and missionaries took pride in the superiority of their technology and their understanding of the natural world. . . . Still, throughout pre-industrial period, scientific and technological accomplishments remained subordinate among the standards by which Europeans judged and compared non-Western cultures. Religion, physical appearance, and social patterns dominate accounts of the areas explored and colonized. . . . Europeans sense of superiority was anchored in the conviction that because they were Christian, they best understood the transcendent truths. Thus, right thinking on religious questions took precedence over mastery of the mundane world in setting the standards by which human cultures were viewed and compared. The Scientific Revolution did not end the relevance of Christian standards. (1989: 6–7)

To the extent increasingly trustworthy networks of professional, intellectual, and material exchanges intensified the circulation of knowledge, ideas, and theories, techniques and worldviews, customs and manners, goods of consumption and art crafts, collective self-perceptions and attributive identities for otherness were shaped in the colonial expansion. The White, male, Christian, heterosexual, bourgeoisie strata of western Eurasian population raised to the position of a point zero to look at the entire world from a top-down perspective (Castro-Gomez 2005). Modern scientific knowledge they supported, and took advantage from, progressively concealed its historical emergence as a new geocultural worldview, by affirming its universality and objectivity. This view of superiority was affected by a certain strabismus: it looked simultaneously towards peoples constructed as savages, and towards geopolitical entities to which the status of civilization was ascribed by means of orientalist criteria (Anievas, Manchanda, Shilliam 2014). Yet, this narrative and epistemological framework for European superiority was not new, in the sense that it was not self-generated in the conjuncture of the colonization of the Americas.

On a more general sociological level, this means that the relative success in convincing other groups that one's own epistemology is valid is a measure of the power that the hegemonic social group enjoys in the military, economic, social, political, and cultural spheres. Even though the structures of knowledge transform in the *longue durée*, their configuration can emerge from contingent organizational needs rather than stemming out from inner properties. They do not necessarily develop along an incremental path; therefore, any teleological interpretation of their development belongs to a superimposed *ex post* logic of historical thinking transmuted into a self-explaining logical inference. And this is a common trait of, either the canonical Western-centric master-narratives such as Shmuel Eisenstadt's (2000) multiple modernities culminating in the clash of civilizations thesis *à la* Samuel Huntington (1993), or the varieties of critical counter-narratives of the emergence of the modern western dominant civilization, ranging from Cedric J. Robinson's (1983) late antiquity origins of racialized capitalist mode of production, to André Gunther Frank and Barry Gill's (1994) 5000 years-long perspective on world history, up to John M. Hobson's (1998) Eastern origins of Western civilization theses.

Differently from these views, this chapter explains that the social ethnocentric form we know as premodern Western epistemology is based on racial foundations. It does so by elaborating on the history of late medieval configuration of expert knowledge production across the Mediterranean spacetime, and, further, by exposing such racial foundations of premodern Western epistemology as the ideological by-product of the political, cultural, and institutional struggles that Christian dominant groups faced during a particular historical conjuncture where they found themselves in a fragile position of power. They fought inward against dissenters and outward against rival powers during late medieval times in the Mediterranean context of premodern global historical social change. This conjuncture overlaps with the birth of the modern university and its spread in several European cities. Even though the first *studii* existed already since the eleventh century, during the thirteenth century there occurred three transformations: first, the circulation of some of Aristotle's texts via Arabic commentators stimulated unorthodox thinking among students and teachers in medieval arts faculties; second, the newly founded Christian orders of the Dominicans and Franciscans established their presence in the universities; and third, the first state-supported institution of higher education and research, the University of Naples, was founded by the emperor Frederick II in 1224, on the model of the University of Al-Qarawiyyīn, in Fez, Morocco, opened in 859.

In modern Western thinking, there exist structural barriers to conceive epistemology in different terms. That is, there exists a taken-for-granted separation between ontology, epistemology, and methodology. Yet this separation is neither neutral nor universal. It is not neutral because it derives its legitimacy from a historically determined racialization of the different ways to conceive and produce knowledge. It is not universal because it reifies either the boundary between East and West or that between the forms of knowledge that within Western thinking itself became dominant against those that were confined into the realms of anachronism, inutility, speculation, magic, folklore, and nonscience. This taxonomy was implemented three centuries later, from the sixteenth century onwards, to manage, domesticate, or eradicate those knowledges that did not conform to what Western hegemonic thinking came to establish as reliable during the colonization of the world. The construction of this separation is not an incremental, linear path preparing the transition to the modern configuration of knowledge production within the master-narrative of the "breakthrough to modernity." It is a historical-social process with syncopated rhythms and inhomogeneous intensity.

The racialization of competing knowledge systems is entrenched with the geopolitics of the late medieval Mediterranean spacetime. This is why, in order to enrich the humus for a new methodology of concept formation to grow, the entanglement between ontology (what reality is), epistemology (what can be known), and methodology (how to produce true knowledge) needs to be explored anew: revisited.

A preliminary remark on the conduct of inquiry: the possible paths for the exploration of such tripartite architecture of knowledge production are multiplex. Nonetheless, they all belong to two species: logical and historical. A logical path presumes the possibility of addressing the issue on the abstract level of pure reasoning. In the Western tradition, this path refers to the sophistic way of reasoning, which accorded to the *logos* the inner properties of self-resolution. In modern times, such a position assumes the label of theoretical logocentrism, with pejorative meaning. From Descartes to Kant, the tripartite architecture became hegemonic and Hegelian idealism pushed it toward the limit of a totalizing way of conceiving history: the entire destiny of human history converged into the history of the modern West. The emergence of the social sciences is located within this trajectory. In fact, Weberian sociology epitomizes this view, as the fundamental way to interrogate global social change in the social sciences is to ask why a certain phenomenon took place in the West and not elsewhere (Bala 2006), thereby constructing the non-Western in terms of intrinsic deficiency.

Besides its intrinsic ethnocentrism, the pristine logical path assumes that ideas freely flow in the abstract realm of thinking. To be sure, Karl Marx agreed with the Hegelian teleology of historical time and the destiny of Western civilization. Nonetheless, he questioned this self-referential logocentrism through his materialistic view on the history of ideas. In a sense Louis Althusser (1972, 166) grasped this specificity when he extolled Marx's "discovery" of an entire continent: the continent of History. Marx contributed from within the Western tradition to envisioning the path toward thinking about ideas historically. This path allows us to enter the cross-cultural and civilizational dialogue across the different geohistorical locations interacting among themselves in the wide spacetime connecting the European Far West of Gibraltar to the Far East of China after the reconfiguration of planetary civilizations since what Karl Jaspers (1950) called the Axial Age (between 900 and 200 BCE).

This second path is rather logical-historical. It excludes *a priori* even the notion that ideas are meaningful exclusively within the historical context of their emergence, therefore limiting their semantics to philological dilemmas of exact textual exegesis. The logical-historical path instead assumes that ideas do not exist in a vacuum but rather respond to organizational needs. The configuration of the relation between ideas and organizational needs is not fixed in space and time; therefore, the recombination of historiographical and conceptual analysis is a viable path to explore the contemporary and future relevance of alternative epistemological resources. The organizational needs at stake in late medieval Mediterranean consist of pressing geopolitical circumstances far more complex than what modern Western thought is ready to accept and include in its intellectual self-biography. By thinking ideas geopolitically, the abstract and sophistic level of reasoning melts into the living tissue of organizational needs articulated by human groups and their respective ethnocentrism on a geocultural level. Concepts express societal needs of the human group that endorses them. Social groups do not simply express alternative ethnocentrisms in the *longue durée*: their existence cannot be projected backward from the geohistorical entity that modern Western thought produced by means of its essentialist glance—there was no such Europe, for instance, in the twelfth century, as Max Weber imagined it looking backward from the first decades of the twentieth century. Moreover, the groups producing knowledge are not monolithic blocks: they belong in a social stratification of power layers whose dominant strata are in charge of producing expert knowledge, and they use to strenuously defend this prerogative against both rival intellectual views and against the extension of the possibility of subaltern social groups to autonomously produce knowledge. This is why Catholic authorities in Western Europe violently stood against the freedom of usage that the invention of the mobile-type press unleashed, during many decades after its introduction. On the one hand, in 1455 Johannes Gutenberg was celebrated for having printed the Holy Bible in Latin as the first sample art craft of its press machine. On the other hand, in 1536, the doctrinal reformer William Tyndale was burned alive as heretic in the Castle of Vilvorde, near Brussels, because ten years before, in the German city of Worms, he had clandestinely printed and exported to Britain the first six thousand copies of his translation of the New Testament and the Pentateuch in English, that is, in a "vernacular" idiom.

The tripartite architecture of ontology-epistemology-methodology is the modern Western hegemonic lens through which the history of human knowledge is currently read, and it places itself as a more advanced configuration, extending its view over all other human ways of imagining the relation between the *what*, *why,* and *how* of concept formation. In fact, such architecture presupposes that ontology is a precondition for epistemology and methodology. According to this hegemonic view, methodology is nothing but a derivative space within the territories of possibilities that epistemology designs. The long-term process of definition of the boundaries between ontology, epistemology, and methodology took its current shape in three major moments, where the density and intensity of the transformations in the long-term structures of knowledge production took the metaphorical shape of whirlpools in the flow of historical time.

During the global history of the last two millennia, these spacetime whirlpools corresponded to late antiquity (from the third to the seventh century CE), late medieval times/late scholasticism (from the eleventh to the thirteenth century), and the Renaissance (the fifteenth and sixteenth centuries). The definition of these three periods does not imply homogeneous criteria of taxonomic classification, yet any practitioners in the human and social sciences can easily grasp the historical locations they claim to signify. The chronology from which these three historical moments draw legitimacy is Eurocentric, not simply because of the notation that confirms the usage of the Gregorian calendar centered around the divide before and after Christ: such a notation is easily commutable into other calendar systems. More relevantly, it is Eurocentric because, from other geocultural perspectives—as it will become clearer—this chronology is open to reformulation and even to resignification, particularly when related to the emergence of modern Western epistemology after the Enlightenment.

The borders of ontology-epistemology-methodology are strictly patrolled, since the knowledge at stake is expert knowledge: that is, knowledge that directly relates to power, where power materializes into institutions. Institutions are historical configurations of power that organize the collective and individual activities of humans (Wallerstein 2003). In other words, expert knowledge is produced by social groups that occupy dominant positions within their own context of action and confront other dominant groups at the geocultural level. Therefore, the transformations in structures devoted to the production of expert knowledge intimately connect with complex political and geopolitical settings. This is why the transformations in knowledge production that foregrounded the emergence of modern Western epistemology relate to hegemonic transitions in geopolitical scenarios, which occurred in a long-standing network of world-systems linking the multiple regions of the planet well before modern capitalism was born (Abu-Lughod 1991; Frank 1990).

The premodern Mediterranean is the spacetime where the racial foundations of Western epistemology appeared. Some complex intellectual movements in late antiquity anticipated them. The intellectual movements in late antiquity emerged first as a long-term inheritance of the Hellenistic period, when the eastern Mediterranean became a space of great exchanges of ideas after Alexander the Great connected it with India through the Caucasus in the fourth century BCE (Blum 1991). When the Roman Empire flourished between the first and third centuries BCE, the circulation of ideas from the East regularly flowed from Buddhist monasteries and Hindu communities to meet ancient wisdoms such as Zoroastrianism, Chaldean astrology, Greek philosophy, Judaic cabalist texts, Egyptian mathematics, hermeticism, and early Christian theology (Couliano 1992).

During late antiquity, the interaction between Greek thought, Eastern philosophies and astrologies, as well as monotheistic religions such as Judaism and Christianity produced two new main perspectives of thought: Gnosticism and Neoplatonism. Gnosticism was an extremely rich and complex intellectual movement that combined multiple intellectual traditions to give birth to different initiatory practices. These practices were prompted by heterodox interpretations of religious, philosophical, and scientific texts circulating thanks to cross-cultural translations. Neoplatonism was a new interpretation of the Platonic understanding of reality, according to which knowledge corresponded to higher levels of abstraction in search for proximity with the purity of ideas. Both Gnosticism and Neoplatonism shared an antisomatic approach to knowledge production where the possibility of knowing corresponded to a progressive disembodiment of intellectual activities. Therefore, the human senses stayed at the lowest level of possible understanding. The senses being betrayers of human possibility to know the world, both Gnosticism and Neoplatonism put an emphasis on the correct interpretations of texts. Texts were the repositories of wisdom. More specifically, fundamental texts—not only the Bible, but even Plato's dialogues or Aristotle's writings, as well as the *Corpus Hermeticum* circulating since the third century AD—were supposed to keep true wisdom. Historians of religion agree that such texts were already a by-product of thick cross-cultural exchanges across East, South, and West, rather than being pristine productions of a single culture (Eliade 1983). In extreme synthesis, the relevance given to texts as ultimate sources of knowledge and the relative distrust in sensorial knowledge turned into a form of obsessive textual analysis. The doctrinal diatribes around textual exegesis assured the main methodology of research. The outcome of such a wide exegetic movement consisted in the fragmentation of authority over the possibility of establishing what true knowledge is. And the more political power became in need of new sources of religious control over society, the more doctrinal battles became relevant to establish whose legitimacy the problem of truth was about: both spiritual and material. These intellectual moves underlay thinking in the Christian European Middle Ages for about seven centuries. Contrary to what became commonsensical in Western European thinking since the seventeenth century, these centuries were not intellectually stagnant, even though knowledge production and circulation was predominantly Christian, enclosed within the so-called *scholae cahedrales* (namely, cathedral schools): therefore, Scholasticism. The activity of teaching for the learned elite, or for whoever accessed higher education, took place in cathedrals, abbeys, or monasteries. In the meanwhile, from the seventh century onward, the Islamic cultural space of the Mediterranean flourished.

Even in the multiple Arabic/Muslim Mediterranean contexts, higher education took place in religious structures, such as mosques, but often teaching and debate were public, as in Fez (Saliba 2007). Equally important, scholars, intellectuals, and practitioners engaged directly with what would become the classics of Greek philosophy in the West, which had remained unknown to Christian thinkers until the twelfth century, when the Arabic translations of Aristotle, among others texts, circulated widely and produced groundbreaking movements in premodern Western Christian Scholasticism (Bianchi 1993).

The debate within premodern Scholasticism both in the Arab/Muslim and Latin/Christian worlds gave birth to alternative ways of producing knowledge in response to the geopolitical needs of the dominant elites in the Mediterranean space, where the religious and ethnic struggle materialized in the war between Christian and Muslim states provoked by the quest for dominion over the Holy Land: the Crusades. By the end of the thirteenth century, these alternative ways of conceiving knowledge silently moved into the background for about two centuries pushed by the denigration of rival epistemological views associated with geopolitical opposite sides, finally resurfacing in the fifteenth century after the collapse of the Eastern Roman Empire in 1453, with the fall of Constantinople. This reemergence gave birth to the controversial (and partly misunderstood) cultural phenomenon named the Renaissance, to which chapter 2 is devoted. In the history of science, the idea according to which the Renaissance was a consequence of the politics of knowledge established by western European elites in the thirteenth century has been largely debated. According to Pierre Duhem's now-classical interpretation of the Scientific Revolution, the condemnation of Aristotle's teaching at the Sorbonne in Paris in 1270 and 1277 buried the speculative approach to nature of the Middle Ages and produced the paradigmatic shift toward experimentalism, which fully developed in the seventeenth century. This simplistic view does not correspond to the more accurate historiographical analysis (Emery and Speer 2001). Nonetheless, it remains influential, especially in fields of knowledge such as the social sciences, which proved recalcitrant to confront part of the global history of modern science that questions the nineteenth-century foundations it relies upon (Cohen 1994; Shapiro 1998; Bala 2016).

From the emerging perspective of global studies, there exists a missing link between the historiographical interpretative theses and the ongoing processes of global social change of the time. This link is the geopolitical relevance of the theories of knowledge that confronted each other in premodern times. In order to visualize this missing historical link, it is necessary to be acquainted with the landscape of the alternative views that animated debates in late Scholasticism during premodern times. And these alternative views were so powerful that Christian Latin ruling elites perceived them as a fatal threat. Therefore, the protocols for knowledge production they established as valid and legitimate were a reaction to the possibilities that these alternative views were creating, disseminating within the Christian world, their intellectuals, students, and learned strata. As such, premodern epistemology is based on racial foundations that were conceived as a counterrevolution against the heterodoxies that the encounter with Eastern and southern knowledges generated through the Arabic translation of unknown Greek and Hellenistic texts from late antiquity.

WORDS AND MEANINGS IN TIME AND SPACE

Epistemology means "theory of knowledge." It aims at defining what knowledge is, separating what is true knowledge from what is not. Epistemology designates which objects are knowable and analyzes how the subject can know the object, thereby establishing what modes of knowledge production are legitimate and valid. As such, the language wherein epistemology is articulated informs the content of epistemology itself. The modern term *epistemology*, which is current in the global English-speaking world, was absent in premodern Europe. Scottish philosopher James Frederick Ferrier introduced the term in the nineteenth century: it corresponds to a premodern transversal field of knowledge, wider than the one this term designates in modern philosophy. In the Latin-speaking world, from late antiquity to late medieval times, such a wider space extended across philosophy, natural science, ethics, and metaphysics and was inextricably related to theology. The configuration of knowledge production that had stabilized during the seven centuries from the Augustinian synthesis between faith and reason to the twelfth century underwent transformations in response to the mobilization of institutional racism by European Christian elites, due to political, geopolitical, and ideological reasons. In the Mediterranean, between the twelfth and fifteenth centuries, four factors of instability intervened in shaping the historical context for the racialization of nondominant ideas that constitutes the emergence of premodern epistemology: first, the shifting balance of power between Christendom and Islam due to the alternate military fortunes in the Crusades; second, the challenge to the secular power of the Church raised by the Latin Christian empire and kingdoms; third, the mounting threat that heretic movements launched to the established doctrinal orthodoxy of the Church; and fourth, the circulation of Aristotle's texts through Arab commentaries, whose existence and relevance the Christian intelligentsia had ignored for centuries. These four factors of instability conspired to lead the Roman Church to produce a different hierarchical system of racial classification for people, their cultures, and their knowledges, in the Mediterranean world as well as beyond it.

This system was grounded on the stigmatization of whatever ideas were associated with Eastern, Arabic, or Muslim intellectual influences. Epistemology was the pillar of such a system, which proved less cosmopolitan and flexible than the Christian philosophy in use since late antiquity (that is, Augustinian theology) as well as its late medieval reformulation (that is, late Scholasticism). Both Augustinian theology and Scholasticism had attempted to accommodate ancient knowledges and cultures in a nonconflictual way with Christendom: "pagan" knowledges before Christ, such as Greek philosophy or Babylonian astrology, enjoyed respect even though they were considered less true than revealed truth. At the turn of the twelfth century, missing texts from the *Corpus Aristotelicum* were translated into Latin from Greek through the Arabic language, but Christian religious authorities opposed their diffusion to learned elites through universities, even though with syncopated timing.

Within Latin Christendom, Thomas Aquinas (1225–1274) elaborated the most sophisticated version of the attempt to find an equalizing balance between faith and reason in the mid-1250s, but even his Scholasticism began to fall under political and ideological attack to the extent that it no longer, or not adequately, served the political needs of Christian Latin elites. New needs emerged, organized around the principle of affirming white, Christian, Western absolute primacy over whatever form of knowledge was forcedly put under the rubric of "Eastern influences." Eastern influences were labeled *Arabism* in a pejorative fashion and associated with heresy. Religious authorities at the Sorbonne in Paris thus prohibited them first in 1270 and then 1277. Following this racializing reactionary path that run across the borders between politics and knowledge, premodern epistemology moved to set forth the superiority of faith over reason and the ultimate supremacy of *revelatio* (revelation) over *scientia* (knowledge), thereby ideologically and unilaterally setting the universal boundaries that the human mind should not trespass and the questions human beings should not ask.

When in 1854 Ferrier introduced the term *epistemology* (from the Greek *ἐπιστήμη*, meaning "scientific knowledge," and *λόγος*, meaning "discourse") he referred to the discourse about knowledge. He meant it as the critical inquiry into the logical structure and the methodology of the sciences, their foundations, questions, and limits.[2] Premodern epistemology, however, is a wider notion than modern epistemology: as I mentioned earlier, it covers a general set of issues that run through cosmology, theology, metaphysics, philosophy, mathematics, the natural sciences, ethics, economics, and law (as in Aquinas's Scholasticism). Modern epistemology instead conveys a more technical, strictly philosophical meaning (as in Kant's critiques of reason). Epistemology, in this sense, is also quintessential in marking a separation between modern and premodern times, where science—and hence also the way of doing science—comes to perceive itself as an endeavor distinctly different from, and superior to, all the other fields of knowledge, now considered as rival.

Since the eighteenth century, Western thinking assumed the sixteenth-century "European Renaissance" as the threshold between modern and premodern approaches to knowledge. The Renaissance supposedly was the cultural movement led by European geniuses, which inaugurated the time when humanity progressively abandoned the speculative approach to nature and embraced the scientific method. This entire way of making sense of the transition from premodern to modern epistemology, however, is controversial. Since the second half of the twentieth century, the now-commonsensical notion according to which there exists a strict cause-effect nexus between the European Renaissance and the Scientific Revolution, at the turn of the sixteenth century, has been radically contested from a historiographical point of view (Cohen 1994; Poovey 1998). And the presumption of the pristine modern European character of the birth of modern science is deeply destabilized since core elements of modern epistemology either date back to late medieval times or are not pristinely European (Bala 2006; Gheverghese Joseph 2011; Raj 2007). The way premodern epistemology relates to modern epistemology is not simply a move from a lower to a higher degree of certitude fostered by the improvement of the scientific method. Modern and premodern epistemology are not autonomous from changing historical contexts, institutional political projects, ideologies, power relations, religious beliefs, and metaphysical premises. Therefore, to the extent epistemology perceives itself as autonomous from extra-epistemological factors it fails at acknowledging the historical and social needs of the dominant groups it responds to. In fact, during modernity, epistemology was encapsulated into the myth of progress according to which White, Western man guided the whole of humanity to conquer the secrets of nature. The premise of this view was that White man epitomized a superior civilization. There followed that the West was morally legitimate to rule over the rest of the world. Epistemology underpinned the modern edifice of knowledge wherein the less a culture could attain an acceptable degree of scientific credibility in terms of what the West established as truth, the lower level of the civilizational ladder the human group associated with that culture occupied. The weaker the position of a human group, the more abuses the human group suffered in the global colonial modern world. Thus, modern epistemology safeguarded the assumptions thanks to which white colonial rule transformed the mosaic of human differences into a racialized system of naturalized hierarchies.

From this point of view, modern epistemology and premodern epistemology originated from the same social need but under very different historical circumstances: they both served the elite project of reconfiguring power in a transforming world scenario; they both mobilized race as an ideological premise; they both enacted racism in the realm of knowledge production. Yet premodern epistemology was part of the political project to resist the instability that Latin Christian Europe suffered because of Arabs, Mongols, and heretics, in the context of ongoing social transformations that periodically produced peasant revolts. Instead, modern epistemology was part of the political project of western European states to colonize the world.

The modern usage of the term *race* conveys a content that was current also in premodern times, albeit under different terminologies (Heng 2018). The words *natio* and *genus* convey meanings analogous to the modern *race*, which basically establishes that specific attitudes and behavior, together with physical and aesthetic characteristics, are genetic and transmitted inevitably through blood across successive generations (Bethencourt 2013). *Race* and its synonyms define a set of stereotypes concerning hereditary features that would correspond to certain identities, ascribed both in cultural and biological traits, and naturalize them. The term *racism*, in contrast, emerged in the nineteenth century and defines a set of active institutional and social practices of discrimination against selected groups (Hobson 2012). Whereas stereotypes were commonsensical to make sense of the differences among human groups since antiquity, at least, and every organized society or civilization implemented stereotypes to map the other human groups, European dominant strata actively pursued the racialization of anthropological and ethnic differences in late medieval times as a means to strengthen their collective identity: us against them. This move responded to a political strategy. The strategy consisted in responding to the condition of geopolitical weakness that Latin Christendom faced in the late medieval Mediterranean scenario as well as the disempowerment of the Roman Church's secular authority in continental

Europe and also in controlling the internal threats of heresy and social turmoil. The Church's intelligentsia was pivotal in constructing the racial ideology that came to inform premodern epistemology: the association of certain specific ideas with racialized otherness became a hallmark of exclusion, the reason for censorship and the legitimation of persecution.

THE PAGAN-ISLAMIC-CHRISTIAN MEDITERRANEAN SPACETIME

From late antiquity to the thirteenth century, Augustinian theology was the official doctrine of the Church. It provided theological and philosophical foundations for the coexistence of different religious beliefs. Through the notion of "pagan" knowledge, Augustine of Hippo (354–430 CE) had theorized a nonconflictual space for classic texts and knowledges coming from other civilizations and peoples who were not Christians yet provided useful or relevant knowledges. Therefore, ancient Greek philosophy was considered a formidable source of knowledge even though it was produced in a polytheistic context. Augustinian theology consisted in the convergence of Neoplatonism with a limited awareness of Aristotle's writings, as Latin Christendom knew only a few of the texts that form the *Corpus Aristotelicum*. Neoplatonism disdained natural knowledge because it considered the body as irreparably compromised with matter. Matter was the most corrupted form of being in the descending hierarchy of Being. Therefore, efforts to understand the secrets of nature tended to be neglected, because such an activity diverted man from prayer and contemplation. Faith was the only way to salvation and truth. In contrast with this view, medieval Scholasticism, which involved several divergent orientations, located the potentials and also the limits of natural philosophy in the logics of the deductive ability to infer necessary conclusions from theological, revealed, unquestionable, but still rationalizable assumptions of faith. It followed that philosophy and religion were not separated, but connected: philosophy had sensible knowledge as organizing principle; theology had revealed truth. The former set a condition of possibility for other cultures to produce knowledge through reason; the latter set Christendom's superiority on the basis of an epistemological incommensurability. This incommensurability between the Christian faith based on revelation and the other religions took the form of a master narrative: after the Revelation, Christendom represented the most advanced historical achievement of human understanding about God and nature.

This epistemological architecture underpinned the idea of Europe as a geohistorical and cultural entity before the sense of belonging that Europe enjoyed, according to modern Western thinking. Within the Christian medieval world, what in modern terms would be the distinction between Europe and the Others was limited to the distinction between Christians and non-Christians.

In order to assess the intricate relation between "Europe" as a hyperreal construct and Christianity as a geopolitical and theopolitical space, Chester Jordan (2002, 74) has suggested that

> the first issue that needs to be addressed is terminological. People who thought about toponymy at all, even mapmakers who thought about it all the time, rarely used the word Europe (Latin, *Europa*) to describe the geographical or cultural entity we now call Europe. The word of choice among the dominant groups in society, at least from the eleventh century on, was *Christianitas* (Christendom). We may learn a great deal from this fact. Europe was where Latin Christians—Roman Catholic Christians—dominated the political and demographic landscape. A profound divide, symbolized by the mutual excommunication of pope and patriarch of Constantinople in 1054 and made unbridgeable by westerners' occupation of Constantinople (1204–61) following the Fourth Crusade, separated Catholics from Greek or Orthodox Christians in Russia, the Balkans, and the Greek peninsula and archipelago. Regions in North Africa and the Near East, once ruled by Christians and still having substantial sectarian Christian populations (Copts in Egypt, for example), had come under the political and demographic dominance of Muslims.

To the extent that identity and difference were constructed by means of a definitional protocol of religious belonging, the ways hierarchization was produced can be organized around a main divide: refusal versus accommodation. Refusal corresponded to the construction of difference in terms of irreconcilable alterity between what was superior and what was inferior, with the latter being a threat to the former; accommodation corresponded to the construction of difference in terms of superiority among other civilizations and cultures that left space for translation and reformulation of otherness within the coordinates of the presumed superior system of knowledge. Franklin Perkins (2006, 2–3) converges with Jordan when he affirms that

> into the Christian, medieval world, the distinction between Europe and non-Europe is less clear and relevant than that between Christian and non-Christian, as non-Christian cultures became the "other" to Western Christian identity. This complex relationship of indebtedness and distance had a determinative impact on Western thought, as it partly drove the attempt to distinguish philosophy from theology. Medieval thinkers from Augustine to Aquinas took philosophy as that enterprise developed in its highest form by Greeks. For them, the attempt to validate and circumscribe philosophy was at the same time the attempt to validate and circumscribe pagan thought. Later, whenever the thought of other cultures is encountered, the very same distinctions—between

> philosophy and theology or natural and revealed theologies—are deployed, as will be seen in Europe's reaction to Confucianism. [Thus] *the separation of theology and philosophy is a peculiarity of a culture which defines itself by faith in certain texts that contradict reason*. In other words it results from the need to create a space for pagan thought.

This accommodation was made necessary by the obtrusive presence of Greek philosophy: Greek thinkers had developed the highest form of philosophy possible before the Revelation. But historically, the Scholastic way emerged in the eleventh century after the rediscovery of Aristotle by Latin Christianity thanks to Arabic-speaking Muslim thinkers, after centuries of Christian oblivion and partial ignorance (Brams 2003). The Christian intelligentsia, both within the Church and in secular institutions, was aware of the debt that Latin Christendom owed to non-Christian cultures, especially Greek as well as Hellenistic knowledges. Even Augustinian theology was itself in fact a historical by-product of the encounter between East and West in the Eastern Mediterranean during the fifth century. For this reason, premodern epistemology emerged as the result of the attempt to ground in legitimate bases the distinction between philosophy and theology. For medieval thinkers, from Augustine to Thomas Aquinas, Greek philosophy was thus an obtrusive presence because it called for a constant work of accommodation. Therefore, premodern epistemology consisted in the systematic endeavor to validate and circumscribe those knowledges that could be reached through reason because this intellectual endeavor coincided, culturally and politically, with the attempt to locate, define, accommodate, and control the overall pagan thought and all the peoples that this label connoted. In so doing, premodern epistemology responded to the logic of placing Christianity on top of a geocultural ladder without necessarily denigrating other knowledges that preceded Christianity or rejecting other peoples and cultures that cohabited in the Mediterranean. Yet, after the turn of the twelfth century, premodern epistemology's boundaries came to be designed by the mounting political need of the Church to affirm the prevalence of faith over reason when reason contradicted faith in the form written in the texts that the Church itself had established as the canonical repository of the ultimate truth.

This transition corresponded to a racialization of those non-Christian ideas that created a tension in premodern epistemology: Christian religious authorities systematically impeded the circulation of concepts and theories from Arabic/Muslim thinkers among Latin learned strata, associating these ideas in an overall cultural construction of inferiority and danger by which they connoted the hierarchy of anthropological difference they built as a response to the contingent military and political confrontation with the rival states across the Mediterranean. The turning point in this process of racialization was the condemnation of Aristotle's teaching at the Sorbonne in 1270 and 1277 by the bishop of Paris, Tempière. This racialization cannot be understood without bringing into consideration the impact of the circulation and transmission of Aristotle's texts among Latin intellectuals by means of the process of rethinking and rewriting that Arabic and Muslim scholars had been engaged in for four centuries. Between the eleventh and thirteenth centuries, the cultural movement of *translatio studii* (transfer of learning) involved highly learned scholars in Latin Christendom (Budick and Isen 1996; Gertz 2009). Until the eleventh century, Latin Christendom was almost entirely oblivious of fundamental Greek texts that Muslim thinkers had in the meantime studied and reelaborated (Saliba 2007). Before the Mongols opened the terrestrial route toward the East, the spacetime of Christendom was the Mediterranean, where it interacted with Arabic Islamic worlds, which acted as the only intermediary for the circulation of knowledge, along with capital and goods, via the maritime routes.

The coordinates of the debate around the relation between faith and reason in the Mediterranean were set by the theoretical controversies that constituted the Arabic-Muslim historical and philological genealogy of *translatio studii*. The translation of Greek texts in Arabic language had begun in the eighth century CE. This body of knowledge was made essential by the Abbasid rulers to manage the access of bureaucrats to the highest echelons of the administration after they defeated the Umayyad dynasty in Persia in 750 (Saliba 2007). The beginning of the opus of translations of Greek texts from the eighth century onward was the outcome of the competition among different communities of bureaucrats following the defeat of the Umayyads, whose structures of knowledge production were informed by other sources such as Zoroastrianism. From this original effort of translation, together with the political developments of the Islamic caliphates from the eighth century to the Mongol invasion of Baghdad in 1256, the production of knowledge in the Arabic-Islamic world was connected to the ideological role ideas played in the systems of governance deployed in the established ruling social groups that governed the different and autonomous political entities that resulted from the territorial and administrative fragmentation of the Abbasid empire.

From a history of philosophy perspective, Mohammed Abed Al-Jabri (2004) provides an interesting entry point into the subject as he depicts the vastly heterogeneous articulation between ideology, knowledge, and religion in the political entities after the collapse of the Abbasid empire during the late medieval period. He maintains that Arabic thought, to which he refers to in terms of "Arab thinking," conflates a cognitive dimension (that is, what theories says about the knowledge they produce and how it should be produced) and an ideological dimension (that is, the content that thought carries, or the ideological, sociopolitical function to which the cognitive dimension fulfills or seeks to fulfill). The complexification of the orientalist image of a unitary canon for Islamic thought implies either the dialogical reconstruction of the different strains of criticism within the Arabic/Muslim world, since the timespace of premodern Mediterranean world-system, or the appraisal of existing interconnections between analogous perspectives across the presumedly impenetrable border that would separate these strains of Islamic erudite knowledge production from their equally diverse Latin/Christian, then Western/Hegemonic, counterparts (Sehlikoglu and Kurt 2014).

The genealogy of the debate over Greek knowledge connects major intellectual figures in the Muslim world: Al-Kindi (801–872) from Basra (Iraq), Al-Farabi (872–951) from Damascus (Syria), Ibn-Sina (980–1037) from Mazar-i-Sharif (Afghanistan), Al-Ghazali (1058–1111) from Tus (Iran), and Ibn-Rushd (1128–1198) from Seville (Andalucía). Arabic-Islamic natural knowledge, astronomy, and theology were not reducible to a transmission of Greek and Hellenistic ideas. Arabic thinkers, in fact, interpreted those ideas through a complex and rich theoretical apparatus whose historical production derived from the interplay of Persian, Indian, and Syrian interventions. This global cross-genealogy of knowledge had endowed them with refined techniques for conceptual elaboration that they deployed in their commentaries on ancient Greek knowledge (Coccia 2005). In the process of appropriation of Ptolemy's *Almagest* or Euclid's *Elements*, besides Aristotle's works, they were producing new, unprecedented insights. During these four centuries, these scholars interpreted, translated, commented on, and publicly debated Aristotle's texts that Latin Christian scholars ignored. To be sure, a few Aristotelian works had already been translated into Latin by Boethius in the fifth century CE, yet only Aristotelian *Logic* was studied and known in Latin Christendom.

This complexity proves that the late medieval Mediterranean has been limitedly understood through the binarism Christianity/Islam or West/East. In Robert Moore's (1987, 599) influential narrative, the birth of Europe as a Eurasian phenomenon derives from the

> essential continuity in European history from the eleventh to the eighteenth century (whether these centuries are to be called a prolonged medieval period or a precocious early modern one) is that there was no caesura between, on the one hand, the establishment of a dominant high culture, with its accompaniments of social differentiation and administrative intensification, at the cosmopolitan or "civilization" level which is so obvious in the eleventh and twelfth centuries, and on the other, the emergence within it of the ethnicity based polities to which man directs attention, already in some important respects well under way in the thirteenth.

If Moore admits that the cosmopolitan attitude of the eleventh and twelfth centuries reversed in the thirteenth, John Hobson (2004: 25) overlooks it and narrates that the West emerged in a millennium-long linear path determined by the construction of otherness against Islam, from the fifth to the fifteenth century:

> During the early medieval period the Europeans came to define themselves negatively against Islam. This was vital to the construction of Christendom, which in turn enabled the consolidation countering the Eurocentric myth of the feudal economic and political system as it emerged around the end of the first millennium CE. It was also this identity that led on to the Crusades. Subsequently, European Christian identity prompted the so-called "voyages of discovery"—or what I call the "second round" of medieval Crusades—led by Vasco da Gama and Christopher Columbus.

This inflationary theory of historical development locates the preamble of "the breakthrough to modernity" in the global scenario of Eurasia. This view has been substantiated from a global economy perspective by, *inter alia*, Alexander Anievas and Kerem Nisancioglu (2013, 82), who address "the extra-European geopolitical conditions conducive to capitalism's emergence as a distinctive mode of production." Drawing on Abu-Loghud's analysis of the impact of Mongol expansionism in the thirteenth-century Mediterranean space, Anievas and Nisancioglu (2013, 87) affirm that

> up until at least the mid-13th century, the social formations making up "Europe" were the least developed region of a "world system" of increasing economic integration and cultural contacts between "East" and "West." Arising late on the periphery of this world system, European development had the most to gain from the new intersocietal links being forged, particularly through the diffusion of new technologies and "resource portfolios" spreading from East to West. The principles of mathematics, navigational inventions, arts of war and significant military technologies all originated in the more advanced East before eventually passing to the backward West.

The idea that Christianity as a geocultural space would be an adequate unit of analysis, wherein it is correct to locate the transformations in premodern epistemology that were considered responsible for the eventual emergence of modern Western scientific rationality, forces sociological imagination into the narrowness of success/failure narratives. In so doing, it falls under the rubric of the anti-Eurocentric Eurocentrism that Wallerstein (1997, 33) warned against:[3]

> Most of the critics pursuing this line of argument are more interested in explaining how Europe interrupted an indigenous process in their part of the world than in explaining how it was that Europe was able to do this. Even more to the point, by attempting to diminish Europe's credit for this deed, this presumed "achievement," they reinforce the theme that it was an achievement. The theory makes Europe into an "evil hero"—no doubt evil, but also no doubt a hero in the dramatic sense of the term, for it was Europe that made the final spurt in the race and crossed the finish line first. And worse still, there is the implication, not too far beneath the surface, that, given half a chance, Chinese, or Indians, or Arabs not only could have, but would have, done the same—that is, launch modernity/capitalism, conquer the world, exploit resources and people, and play themselves the role of evil hero.

New counterhistories of global science as well as the history of science in East and South Asia confute this incremental notion of historical development and provide alternative cross-cutting readings about the way long-term processes of emergence of specific regimes for the production of knowledge are entangled with conjunctural global phenomena and sociopolitical and ideological transformations (Goonatilake 1999). Elman's history of Chinese science (2005, 160–69) explains that eighteenth-century scientific knowledge in China did not follow the Western path to modern science by imitating the West, not because it was unable to do so due to its traditional epistemological architecture, but rather because China responded to needs and pressures that were locally determined, both socially and politically, by its own historical path. Among these pressures, the Chinese Rites controversy occupies a singular place.[4] After the Jesuits were obliged by Rome to abandon their conciliatory approach to the evangelization of China, which allowed for saving Chinese rituals and looser rules to translate Christian beliefs into Chinese terms, the Chinese elite changed its behavior toward Western knowledge and turned to classics. But while Western historiography has constructed around the Chinese Rites controversy a narrative of opposed civilizational worldviews between China and Europe, and between East and West, Elman demonstrates how the Chinese Rites controversy was mainly an intestine struggle within the different orders of the Catholic Church that was encapsulated into a wider and complex geocultural and geopolitical scenario (Giovannetti-Singh 2022). This explanatory approach is better positioned than Hobson's binary relational definition of Christendom and Islam to understand the racialization of non-Christian ideas in premodern Western epistemology after the crisis of Aquinas's Scholasticism in the second half of the thirteenth century, after the Condemnation in 1277.

For Hobson (2004, 25), the so-called Islamic clause is invoked in Western narratives to dismiss "the Eastern input on the grounds that these [Aristotelian] texts were in fact pure Greek works and that the Muslims had added nothing of intellectual value—all they did was return the original Greek works to the Europeans." Hobson is right, but his reevaluation of Eastern contributions to global modernity remains trapped within a frame that considers macroaggregate constructions such as East and West as explanatory models when retrospectively projected from modernity backward. The cultural and political construction of the presumed Greek purity of classical philosophical texts from the Arabic/Muslim/Islamic world into Latin Christendom was a far more complex process of adaptation, modification, rejection, and translation that does not designate a linear historical development from the sixth century to the threshold of the sixteenth century. The presumed continuity of this long-term geocultural configuration as an incremental trend fails to question its own orientalist presumptions, since it occludes the discrete and synchronic coexistence of multiple threads within an integrated and relational Mediterranean spacetime. Hobson can reduce such a heterogeneity to the master narrative of the breakthrough to modernity only through a deterministic *ex post* civilizational logic of cumulative causation wherein civilization becomes an overarching category of historical interpretation for long-term and large-scale processes of social change.

When looking deeper into the premodern epistemological configuration, the circulation of scientific knowledge happened within the articulated space of late medieval scholasticism that, as José Ignacio Cabezòn (1998) demonstrates, was both an Arabic and Christian approach to knowledge production. This intertwined epistemological generative space was located within the global space connecting the Mediterranean world with Asia. A global space that Marshall Hodgson (1993) referred to as *Ouekumene*, whose literal meaning refers to cohabiting the same place. Its meaning recalls the possibility of sociocultural coexistence that can be considered as an interpretative frame to narrate and configure the multiple perspectives of thought both within the Latin/Christian and the Arabic/Muslim worlds (Makdisi 2019). Rather than a long-term construction of civilizational alterity, the heterogeneity of this integrated and integrating spacetime configures the reciprocal interaction between the supposedly adverse two sides of aforementioned binarisms, together with the awareness that the same approach to human knowledge that in the context of a specific political unity is useful to dominant strata can produce a threat to power in a different political unity. Parthasarathi (2011) proposes this methodological strategy to rethink the relation between India and Europe in the eighteenth century, in order to reframe the global coproduction of what economic historians call the Great Divergence between West and East.

From a methodological perspective, the analysis of this large-scale, long-term interaction moves from what Philip McMichael (2016) defined as incorporated comparison to the heuristics of circulation. This means that the two differential entities that Hobson calls East and West are mutually constructed and simultaneously disaggregated since their presumed singular homogeneity is an essentialization overdetermined by the presumption of adequacy of the crystallized, Orientalist, Eurocentric notion of world civilization. According to the Chinese historian of science Fa-ti Fan (2004, 2), this binary cartography is to be questioned by concepts that

> do not presuppose rigid, inflexible, demarcating cultural boundaries between the parties that came into contact while noting the existence of differences. There were boundaries, of course, but we cannot take them for granted. . . . Nor do they privilege conventional binary categories such as Chinese/Western culture or civilization in explaining the contacts between the parties. Nor do they, moreover, essentializes power relations. On the contrary, they mark out a space for human actors as agents of historical change. They enable us to see mingling, interaction, accommodation, hybridization, and confluence as well as conflicts across borders of many kinds.

Analogously, the Indian historian Kapil Raj (2013) insists that when the history of ideas and practices is rethought as occurring within trading zones, made of circulation or acted by go-betweens,

> it is in the asymmetry in negotiation processes that the power relationship resides, and it can be brought to light in its specificity only through a rigorous analysis of these processes, instead of being raised to the status of an explanatory category. . . . Of course, not everything circulates, and the term could suggest a blindly optimistic vision of books, ideas, practices, people, and material flowing smoothly between different cultures, communities, and geographical spaces. . . . These conditions could depend on the exchange of favors, patronage, friendship, obligation, or just economic exchange, to name but a few possibilities.

So, in the form of complex dispositional identities, geocultural constructs do permeate social action even though they simultaneously offer a set of practicable alternatives in the space of cross-cultural interaction. These interactions involve hierarchies of power, so the possibility and the limits they offer and the permeability they show to be transformed are heterogeneously distributed according to social stratification. As Wang Hui (2010) remarks, the cogency of geocultural constructions depends on the way they are produced and implemented within a complex articulation of power historically determined, where particular significance is attributed to elite discourses, and the shifting meaning dominant groups attach to geocultural constructs according to the political usage they need to mobilize.

According to this view, the Mediterranean appears as a heterogeneous landscape where analogous theoretical problems coexisted and reciprocally informed each other across the multiple boundaries of cross-cultural and political differences. The main cultural cleavage, as regards the circulation of knowledge, was not religion or culture. It was language. Hence the relevance of those agents whose translations, commentaries, teachings and controversies made circulation possible. The first translations happened to be from Greek into Latin through Arabic. This process took place in two areas. The first was Andalucia in southern Spain, which the Arabic-Berber rulers had started to conquer in 711 CE, in the wake of the uprisings that Abd ar-Raḥmān ibn Muḥammad Ibn-Khaldun (1332–1406) explained in terms of the dialectics between nomadism and sedentarism as a part of his *al-Muqaddima*, which is today recognized as a pioneering transdisciplinary work in sociology, anthropology, and political science *ante litteram* (Alatas 2014). The second was Sicily, where the Normans had defeated Muslim rulers starting in 1061 CE. Regardless of the military outcome, the Normans allowed learned Muslims to preserve their own language and use it publicly (Menocal 2002). Both in Sicily and Al-Andalus, Arabic Muslim scholars managed to have at their disposal Arabic translations of Aristotle and other "pagan" texts. Here, prominent Latin scholars who perfectly knew Hebrew and Arabic started to translate some of the cornerstone of Greek knowledge: Adelardus Bathensis in the eleventh century translated the astronomic tables by al-Khwārizmī and the *Introduction to Astrology* of Abū Ma'shar, together with Euclid's *Elements*. In the twelfth century, Enrico Aristippo translated Aristotle's *De Anima* and *De Generatione*; Domenico Gundissalino, *De Mundo* and *Ethica*; Michele Scoto, *De Coelo* and *Physica*; Gerardo da Cremona, *Methaphysica* and *Metereologica*. During the same decades, major works from Arabic-speaking thinkers were also translated into Latin: Avicenna's *Sufficientiae*, the comments on Aristotle's *Methaphysica* by Al-Ghazali and by Averroes, and most of all the comments on *De Anima* by Averroes.

Meanwhile, Arabic thought was undergoing a schismatic configuration between East and West that became evident to the Latin Christian intelligentsia in the twelfth and thirteenth centuries, together with the translations they handled. What happened in the Arabic parts of the Mediterranean was happening in the Christian ones, too. Across the Islam/Christendom divide there existed at least three approaches to knowledge that diverged around the nature of the Greek/Hellenistic heritage and what was the appropriate usage of this heritage. On both sides, there existed a threefold space of ideological tension. A first trend gave priority to Aristotle's *Metaphysics* as a powerful tool to make reason and faith complementary and reciprocally legitimizing; Avicenna and Thomas Aquinas championed this position. A second trend read Aristotle through a Neoplatonic lens and chose the esoteric way as a path to true knowledge and enlightenment; the Persian aristocracy under the Abbasid caliphate, as well as conservative Augustinian Christian thinkers such as Bonaventure, safeguarded this attitude. A third trend did not give priority to Aristotle's *Metaphysicas*, but rather to other aspects of the Stagirite teachings, such as physics, mathematics, logics, economics, and law. This reorientation was a by-product of the institutional, political, and ideological closure that the learned elites and dominant strata of al-Andalus imposed over the intellectual influence of Eastern Arabic thought as they constructed their own intellectual and political autonomy, also stressing their alterity in regard to the esoteric and mystic interpretation of Aristotle that was dominant among the ruling elite of the other Arabic and Muslim south and eastern ruling elites in the states and caliphates in the Mediterranean (Al-Jabri 2004). The jurists of al-Andalus provided a favorable institutional framework for the study of Aristotle that emphasized physics, mathematics, and economics over metaphysics, and this gave a different imprint to the politics of knowledge production, which provided the cultural context for the complex theoretical system that Averroes elaborated, at the intersection of the translation and the commentaries on Aristotle. Averroes inaugurated this trend, followed by Christian scholars, the so-called Latin Averroists.

HISTORICAL SOCIAL CHANGE AND THE GEOPOLITICS OF CONTRIVED CIVILIZATIONS

The ideas forming this tripartite constellation were not free-floating, like in Plato's hyperuranion. They responded to conflicting political interests and profound social transformations. The fact that the thirteenth century was the crossroads of a period of profound reconfiguration in the socioeconomic base of power for western Europe's dominant groups is solid documented historiographic evidence that automatically confutes, *in se*, narratives of immobilism in historical interpretation according to which the Middle Ages were predominantly stagnant (as the non-Western world was as well).

Wallerstein (1999, 46) explains that the income of the Western Eurasian ruling strata was squeezed:

> They were involved in exceptional high level of internecine struggle, which negatively affected their wealth, their authority, and their lives. . . . In a period of economic tightness, the internecine warfare of the ruling strata for the declining global revenues was reflected in increasing conflict between the Church and the temporal rulers, and by great struggles within the Church itself. Even more important was the social conflictuality that was generating mounting uprisings among the peasants, much before the diffusion of the plague in the

> XIV century created the scarcity of wage-labour that provided workers with a temporary counter-power against feudal lords. As a secular power, since the XI century, the Church and its apparatuses were constantly engaged in providing and ideological legitimation for social hierarchies they ruled, so the global pressures socio-economic and cultural change put on how the ideational order of the spatially defined societal formations the Church controlled called for a deep redefinition that disclosed further internecine political divergence, coded in the theoretical idiom of theological battle.

The population growth that serial demographic data register as culminating in the thirteenth century overwhelms technological change as an explanatory factor for what the historiography of the 1990s had labeled the *mutation féodale* (feudal mutation). This mutation forced the Church to attempt to codify these ongoing transformations by means of the delegitimation of the doctrine of the three orders, according to which society was peacefully tripartite between *laboratores* (laborers), *bellatores* (knights), and *oratores* (clerics). As Mathieu Arnoux (2012) systematizes, the framework of the three orders as a social and institutional arrangement was collapsing because of its inability to cope simultaneously with two aspects of the transformation that European society was undergoing during the late Middle Ages. The first was the ambiguous social and political collocation of the figure of the bishop. The bishops occupied an intermediate hierarchical position between knights and clerics, and they enjoyed differential degrees of discretion over the land they governed. Therefore, they played the role of a dynamic yet disaggregating force generating political and social instability. Second was the growing disagreement within the Church hierarchy itself about the acceptance of such a social model, which presented the clergy as one among other orders of society, with no priority or special dignity.

The awareness of such a structural dynamism in feudal society partly contradicts those who, like Hobson, do not take the crisis of the trifunctional order in European late medieval society into consideration and subsumes the global projection of the emerging European ideological system of hierarchization of anthropological difference under the logic of the clash of civilization between Christianity and Islam for the control of the Holy Land. It is true, as Hobson (2004, 51) reminds, that Pope Innocent III (1161–1216) described the Prophet Muhammad as the "Beast of the Apocalypse" in his crusading appeal of 1213. Yet analogous words were used to describe Genghis Khan and the hordes of nomadic Mongol invaders as well as, with even much more insistence, the Cathars, the other heretics (Ginzburg 1974), and also the workers accused of social turmoil after the repression of strikes (Zamboni 2015).

Such an overwhelming understanding of civilization is accordingly totalizing as it falls short of correctly locating the ideological role of the Crusades within the collapse of the three orders doctrine as the ideological architecture of Christian governance. The call for the unity of Christendom against Islam was the desperate attempt to establish a position of power in a hostile configuration—a configuration where geopolitics, culture, and social change were intimately intertwined—rather than the expression of solidity related to that presumed position.

The intellectual cartography of the Mediterranean overlaps with the geopolitical one. Late medieval Europe was part of a complex Mediterranean geohistorical region, which stood as the periphery of the global world-system whose center was China. Professing the Christian faith was the main common identity for Western elites, and the Roman Church embodied the main institutional authority for this fragile identity forged by the perception of geopolitical and political pressures. Geopolitically, Christian elites suffered Muslim expansionism from the south, the Middle East and even the western state of al-Andalus; from the Far East, they feared the rising power of the Mongol empire that reached the Caucasus and the Balkans and arrived to conquer Baghdad in 1258. The Mediterranean was the stage where the Christian rulers engaged in confrontation with the caliphates, following a syncopate timing and discontinuous intensity. The nature of this confrontation was multiplex: theological, intellectual, military, and economic. Theologically, it consisted in reciprocal accusations of infidelity. Intellectually, it concerned the contested heritage of the ancient Greeks' knowledges that for centuries had been forgotten among Christian intellectuals while largely circulated among Arabic thinkers. Militarily, it exploded around the occupation of the Holy Land and mobilized great human and financial resources. Economically, it involved the control of long-distance commercial routes for luxury goods and precious metals from and toward the East. The latter was the result of two factors. First, Arab and Muslim merchants ruled over the maritime route through the Indian Ocean. Second, the Mongols came to disclose and control the terrestrial route from Beijing to Baghdad. Thus, Latin Christendom experienced a fragile position in the global world: the religious center, the Holy Land, was located in the House of Islam (Dar al-Islam); the economic center—that is, where the supply of highly remunerative goods came from—was located in China; the geographical center of the Mediterranean system was in Egypt. This fragility combined with a twofold political unease for the Church. The first was that Christian secular rulers gained importance, autonomy, and military effervescence; the second was the spread of strong heretical movements. These movements spread through European kingdoms, building seditious churches that created strong territorial ties, developed new means of control over proselytes, managed to acquire properties and material goods, challenged the customary norms and beliefs of social rule, and questioned Christian doctrinal supremacy.

The response of the Roman Church to such a geopolitical and political condition of fragility consisted in a regressive turn that merged doctrinal orthodoxy with the racialization of innovative and heterodoxical ideas that the circulation of texts from Arabic/Muslim thinkers was stimulating among the Christian learned strata. This process started in 1204 and culminated with the condemnation of Aristotle's writing in Paris at the Sorbonne in 1270 and 1277. This turn was regressive because it questioned the cosmopolitanism that had connoted European dominant strata's culture since the beginning of the eleventh century. It was racial because it mobilized ideological arguments to stigmatize ideas that challenged on a rational basis the dominant ideology of the Church through the political device of ethnicity: the notions or doctrines deriving from the Arabic influence were associated with infidelity, inferiority, and danger, replicating in the realm of knowledge production the same mechanism of racialization that was used to dehumanize enemies in the wartime of the Crusades. This racialization of nonhegemonic knowledge buttressed a new hostile ideology of civilizational supremacy to sustain the project of establishing the Catholic Church's rule on more solid grounds and create the conditions for expansionism. The more the awareness of fragility emerged among the Catholic intelligentsia, the harsher the supremacist rhetoric became. Yet this claim of superiority was undermined by the ubiquitous awareness of a certain degree of inconsistency involved in this self-portrait, both in terms of power and in terms of knowledge. If there existed a long-term pattern of collective religious identity that defined Latin Christendom, then there also existed an equivalently shared long-term perception that within the changing structures of power in the Mediterranean and in the Eurasian space, this identity corresponded to an unstable power position. In this construction of belonging, the eastern and southern frontiers of what had been the *Mare Nostrum* before the fragmentation that succeeded the fall of the Western Roman Empire in 1056 were still inhabited by "dreadful" peoples, and these peoples were powerful and organized: either violent and barbarian or sophisticated and erudite, possessing desirable wisdoms. More often, "the others" got materialized in recombining concrete historical configurations of these prejudices and stereotypes.

Premodern epistemology was integral to this political project of ideological racialization. This process began under the pontificate of Innocent III (1198–1216) and it is coterminous with the emergence of European identity (Sayers 1994). Its turning point is the year 1204, when three significant events took place: the Albigensian Crusade, the Fourth Crusade, and the first academic censorship of Aristotle in Paris. The Albigensian Crusade and the Fourth Crusade, taken together, mark the creation of a double border, internal and external, that defined Christian European identity. In 1204, the Albigensian Crusade against Cathar heretics of the city of Albi, in the French region of Languedoc, designated the internal border; the Fourth Crusade, which never reached Jerusalem but ended with the sack of Byzantium, marked the external one. As a result, heretics, Jews, Moors, and other minorities were racialized as irreconcilable "Others." This process forged a rigid European Christian identity.

As Bernard Hamilton (2008, 164) remarks, a subtle though strong tie connects the Fourth Crusade and the Albigensian Crusade against the Cathars:

> Innocent III considered them [the Cathars] an international threat. In the first year of his reign [1198] the Cathar supporters were accused of assassinating his *podestà* of Orvieto in the Papal States, and the pope was informed that the ruler of Christian Bosnia, with many of his subjects, had professed the dualist faith. Although in 1203 Bosnia returned to the Roman obedience in response to Hungarian pressure, Innocent became aware of the true extent of Balkan dualism in 1204 when the Bulgaria Church acknowledged the papal primacy, and the Fourth Crusade set up a Latin patriarch in Constantinople.

On the external border, the Fourth Crusade, promoted through the usual call for reconquering the Holy Land, came to be governed by conjunctural but decisive episodic circumstances, which diverted the military expedition from its original target, Jerusalem; troops of knights and soldiers of fortune moved across the Balkans to finally end up in the sack of Constantinople. The destruction of Byzantium that followed the siege recomposed temporarily the orthodox schism of 1056. It violently reunified western and eastern Europe under Latin Christian rule, pushing towards the Urals the external border of Latin Christendom, thereby creating a direct contact with the Mongol Empire and the "peoples of the steppes." The Mongols incarnated the worst nightmare in the Latin Christian European anthropological imagery of the unknown people living in the eastern regions of Eurasia. Their nomadic culture became the antithesis of the emerging European identity, particularly for those peoples and kingdoms the invasions of the Tartars. The aristocratic Christianized elite of Hungary epitomized the need to strongly reaffirm its new European identity in order to stress the social transition that had transformed the nomadic Magyar tribes who, two centuries before, had spread terror in the Christian world, into the subjects of the Kingdom of Hungary (Makkai 1994).

On the internal border, the defeat of the Cathars (which came two decades later) mortified several political insurgencies against the papacy. The outcome of the protracted condemnation and slaughter of these heretics was double: in terms of practical devices of control and repression, the machinery of the Inquisition was introduced and implemented from patrimonial expropriation against discriminated subjects or groups to the confinement of specific social groups in particular occupational positions, from the selective inclusion into the polity to the limitation of access to different kinds of political resources (Moore 2007). In terms of ideology, the struggle against heresy legitimized the doctrine of papal primacy as supreme political and spiritual authority on Earth (Pennington 1976). The doctrine, named *plenitudo potestatis*, was finally declared with the Fourth Lateran Council in 1215 (Cipollone 1992; Watt 2008).

The repression of heresy changed in emphasis. Therefore, it needed more adequate and up-to-date theological support. Augustinian theology, which had dominated previous centuries, provided the theological foundations for the coexistence of different religious beliefs (that had found more adequate synthesis in *The Confessions*) but was now anachronistic. Its logic of coexistence in an (*ante litteram*) multicultural environment vacillated in front of the papacy's strategic need to radicalize the existing lines of demarcation between Christendom and its others (Nicolle 2011). Otherness needed to be constructed as unquestionably inferior to Latin Christendom in order to justify the papal universalistic claim to submission of whomever it needed to subdue: pagans, atheists or heretics, soldiers, kings, or peasants. Otherness came to be increasingly constructed as irreconcilable alterity and exteriority. Being conducted also against Catholic princes who did not align themselves and their subjects with the papacy, the political and military endeavor of the Fourth and the Albigensian Crusade irreversibly pushed the frontiers of the meaning of *crusade* far beyond the consolidated idea of reconquering the Holy Land, namely, *sacrum sepolcrum*. Crusade became a flexible notion in an extended imagery that included claims of expansion under the flag of Latin Christendom (Phillips 2004).

The pontificate of Innocent III is often acknowledged as a foundational moment in European identity. In fact, it was Innocent III who reinforced and legitimated on more solid grounds the doctrine of papal *plenitudo potestatis* against all other secular and spiritual powers on Earth. Yet this does not mean that he succeeded in such a universalizing project: more radical divergences and strong political tensions arose between the papacy and the other secular kingdoms in Latin Christendom, particularly the empire. However, it was precisely the shift toward these universalistic expansionist pretensions of Latin Christianity that allowed both religious and secular western Eurasian authorities to claim unprecedented rights of territorial expansion and power consolidation. As Abulafia (2008, 10) explains,

> It was this sense of the integrity of Latin society, professing one faith or "law," that remained from the aggressive universalism of the late eleventh- and twelfth- century Church, and that still formed a significant core of the teaching of such lawyer popes as Innocent III and Boniface VIII. But by the end of

> the century it was western kings—In France, England, Castile, Naples and so on—who emphatically utilized this awareness of Christian identity in order to enhance their own, and not the pope's, authority. . . . It was secular rulers who most successfully took up the message of submission to higher authority to serve their own ends, and to bring their own subjects securely under their own authority.

Yet these were aspirations. Such aspirations were counterbalanced both by the concrete strength of Islamic kingdoms in the Mediterranean and by the aggressive Mongol expansionism toward the western part of Eurasia. These circumstances forced a greater awareness of peoples and their knowledges in the Asian steppes and the eastern Mediterranean Sea.

THE POLITICS OF LATE SCHOLASTICISM: HETERODOX ARISTOTELIANISM, AVERROISM, ARABISM

Different Christian theological doctrines used to converge toward a certain degree of pluralism, even cosmopolitanism, notwithstanding the fact that, as O'Brien (2013, 8) noted, "the medieval Church had reacted to threats to its power by strengthening its intellectual foundations, in order to resist Muslim infidels, heretics, and secular authorities." Thomas Aquinas (1911) attempted to enlarge and consolidate the claim of Christian superiority by making it more flexible. He condensed these broadly conceived pluralistic views with the hermeneutic circle *credo ut intelligam et intelligo ut credam* (that is, "I believe in order that I may know, and I know in order that I may believe").

During the years of his early period of higher education, Aquinas was a student at the newly born *studium of* Naples, just founded by Frederick II to form the intelligentsia of his empire. As Nardi (1992, 87) points out, "the main difference between Frederick's *studium* and the most important sites of learning in Europe was that the ecclesiastical authorities had no power to recruit teachers, award the *licentia docendi* [teaching license], or exercise jurisdictional powers." Aquinas was a pupil of the greatest Christian Latin translator of Aristotle, Alberto Magno. Aquinas was a Dominican. The Dominicans aimed at fighting heresy and proved less concerned with Eastern influences; Franciscans aimed at reestablishing the pure original essence of Christianity and were hardened against whatever they saw as fatal intrusions of Islamic elements in Christian theology. The two orders had just entered the universities of Paris and other major western European universities after overcoming the fierce, still vehement collective opposition of the majority of secular magisters. Aquinas's research program was located in the wake of the Augustinian problem of managing anthropological differences across a complex geohistorical network of social groups, each with its own knowledges, which made sense of the world by means of their own ethnocentrism and among which Christianity was *prima inter pares*. Aquinas's program reformulated this problem in terms of the possibility of reconciling faith and reason, but the Church in late medieval times was a different institution compared to the times when Augustine elaborated on the same problem. This was not the only difference. Aquinas mobilized new texts, theories, and concepts that the Arabic/Islamic thinkers made available, understandable, and, by means of comments, more relevant for the contemporary world than the original versions. Aquinas extended the sharp Aristotelian distinction between civilization and barbarism; he disclosed the latter into two possible definitions of otherness in order to introduce a third anthropological space. The first definition of barbarism was relative and positional: an "other" is somebody that belongs to another culture (*quod aliquem*); the second definition was still absolute: a barbarian is one who "does not know his own speech," that is, who belongs to a people that does not have a written language. In so doing, he created a potentially worldly hierarchy of peoples and knowledges wherein Christianity was not reconcilable with those who could not write but was put in a dialectical relation with others who could: Arabs, Mongols, or Indians.

The core questions of Aquinas's scholasticism were born at the crossroads of the changing relations between secular and religious powers. Western Eurasian dominant strata lacked a geoculture that could sublimate contradictions into a coherent ideological architecture. Such architecture would have been called on, on the one hand, to offer an acceptable compromise between the papacy and the empire, and, on the other hand, to produce a durable synthesis between the teleological narrative of revealed truth, the epistemological foundation of Christian superiority, and the concomitant hierarchy between human cultures and groups through their position within the late medieval regime of knowledge production. Aquinas's synthesis proved short-lived. Its intellectual endeavor proved anachronistic regardless of its intellectual power to the extent that it did not match the political needs of the ideological project that came to become hegemonic in the political space inhabited by the dominant strata for whom he elaborated his expert knowledge.

Michael Allen Gillespie (2010, 12) uses the word *internecine* to suggest the nature of the crisis in late medieval scholasticism where nominalism became notable in the second half of the thirteenth century. Yet Gillespie himself also has to admit that internal and external conflicts are intimately intertwined, since the separation into distinctive analytical realms is a purely heuristic strategy:

> The immediate dispute that shattered [Aquinas's] synthesis was the growth of Aristotelianism. . . . This phenomenon was seen with deep suspicion by the pious defenders of a more "original" Christendom not merely because of its pagan roots but also and perhaps more importantly because of its connection with Islam. Paganism was a known and tolerable evil; Islam, by contrast, was an ominous theological and political threat. This was especially true after the failure of the Crusades. For almost two hundred years Christendom had seemed to gain ground against Islam, especially in the East, but after the loss of all the Christian colonies in the Levant in the later thirteenth century and the rise of Islamic military power, this optimism dimmed and the suspicion of Islamic influences on Christian thought became more intense.

Gillespie is interested in understanding the way, within premodern structures of knowledge production, new theoretical trends were able to carve out the space for a different epistemology, whose legitimacy subordinated to God who has the absolute power to revoke the laws of nature by a pure act of will. Gillespie (2008, 302) takes to the extreme consequences the epistemological outreach of these new trends associated with late medieval nominalism when he affirms that "it is their particular notion of God that provides the assurance that he is irrelevant for their interpretation of nature." Charles Larmore (1996, 41) grasps the connection between the trends Gillespie focuses on with hegemonic modern thinking when he asserts that "for modern science "the existence of God is not an issue either from an atheist or religious perspective, because while the former does not presuppose the existence of God, the latter assumes that God is so great he is not obliged to exist by any perennial law."

Rather than being only a theological struggle fought both on the battlefield of doctrine and within institutional ecclesiastical hierarchies, the intellectual attack on Aquinas's Scholasticism was part of the confrontation between conflicting powers, whose significance needs to be addressed in geopolitical terms (Küçük 2010). In fact, even though the first condemnation of Aristotle by the Church was in 1210, six years after the Fourth Crusade and in the same year of the institutionalization of the Franciscan order by Innocent III, it was only in the second half of the thirteenth century that it assumed the relevance of a resolute political censorship, and a vehement widespread cultural rejection (Le Goff 1999).

The first episode in the process of the rejection of the circulation of Aristotle's ideas in Latin Christendom occurred in 1210. Soon after that the newly translated texts from Greek to Latin through the Arabic language were adopted by a few secular magisters in theology at the Sorbonne in Paris. In 1210, Amaury de Bène, a prominent philosopher and theologian, was accused of heresy for having affirmed God's immanence in the natural world through the lens of Aristotle's notion of matter. His prosecutors within the faculty of theology maintained that his views attempted to treat God as a philosophical matter—that is, understandable through reason—rather than as a purely theological matter—that is, understandable through faith (Bianchi 1990). When Amaury de Bène appealed to Innocent III, the pope confirmed the condemnation of heresy. In the years that followed, many students decided to enroll in other universities, such as Toulouse or Oxford, where they could study Aristotle. In 1231, a scholarly commission was mandated to remove unorthodox theses and encourage teachers to follow its prescriptions, but the protracted decrease in student enrollment provoked the reintegration of Aristotle's teaching in 1250 (Cobban 1971). This provoked an inversion of tendency in the restrictive policies of the Parisian Christian authority that did not last beyond 1270. From the Seventh Crusade (1249–1250) to the final loss of the remaining possessions in the Holy Land (1289–1291), the relative decline in power of Christian rulers and states in the Mediterranean politically strengthened those groups like the Franciscans, who advocated a rejection of those theological and philosophical trends that could be somehow related to the powerful and advanced Islamic synthesis of Aristotelianism.

The reasons for this fascination, on the one hand, and intolerance, on the other hand, were multiple. The "new" Aristotle talked about philosophical happiness, the state of grace that intellectual activity brings to human mortal experience. The new magister was interested neither in money and political life nor in religion, a virtue that was in sharp contrast with the Christian ideal of faith, prayer, and charity as preamble for the realization of the self occurring in the afterlife of any good believer. More importantly, Christian authorities were suddenly alerted by what they called the *error Averrois*: the notion of the general intellect, into which every single soul would flow after death. It is noteworthy that Guglielmo di Tocco, Aquinas's biographer, wrote that the *error* was so much spread even among the population in France that a soldier convicted in a trial refused to repent because he believed that thanks to the existence of the general intellect, his soul would have been saved. Last but not least, Aristotle's *De Anima* was accused of including obscene sexual references, which legitimized the widespread practice of intercourses *contra natura* (against nature)—that is, homosexual relationships in the community of students at the Sorbonne, which was entirely male (Bianchi 1993, 149–53). More generally, this was because the content of the knowledges coming from the East and rapidly circulating in the vivid environment of the university conflicted with the official doctrine of the Church in crucial respects, and their Arabic imprint provoked fear and suspicion of external pernicious intrusions into the realm of thinking. Fear and suspicion became xenophobia as Islam appeared to grow in power both politically and intellectually throughout the thirteenth century.

For the Church, the most unacceptable theses from Ibn-Rushd's (Averroes) were two: first, the idea that human intelligence is not an attribute of the single individual but a general collective immortal substance and therefore separated by the single individual soul; second, the doctrine of the double truth: truth of faith for the moral conduct of the masses, and the truth of reason for the rational and learned individuals. There logically followed that the single individual soul would be mortal, thus not susceptible to be eternally damned. For this reason, Averroes thought and taught that religion was useful for giving a horizon of sense to ordinary people, while it was useless to whoever embraced philosophy. According to this vision, philosophy is not a discipline or a field of knowledge but an intellectual tension to grasp the cosmos through reason. This is why, even on the Islamic side of the Mediterranean, Averroes and many of his followers were persecuted by Islamic authorities, while his Christian followers, the so-called Latin Averroists, were persecuted by Christian authorities.

The condemnations of 1270 and 1277 mark a racial turn in premodern Western epistemology that exceeds the logic of theopolitical struggle. More specifically, the radicalization of ethnocentric bias in Western premodern thought became more and more evident with the progressive marginalization of both scholars such as Sigieri of Brabante, who was a radical Latin Averroist, and some theses of Aquinas, who was a prominent Christian intellectual. Such a marginalization was motivated by the Church on the basis of the alleged association of Aquinas with theories and doctrines accused of infidelity because "imported" from Arabic thinkers and their ideas that came to be considered dangerous to Christendom. This accusation was not merely a matter of political theology. To be sure, it is only retrospectively that the entire historical process that led to inform premodern epistemology appears confined within the realm of theopolitical struggle, because theopolitics was pivotal in the wider system of alterity construction and ethnocentric self-definition. These alleged accusations, when moved against Latin/Christian/Western thinkers, welded with the suspicion of heresy, and this sufficed for religious authorities to invoke the repressive logic in use against heretics. As Geraldine Heng (2018, 113) puts it:

> Enmity in itself need not be productive of race. In contact zones governed by either Muslim or Christian rulers, day-to-day lived practices often demanded pragmatic accommodations among enemies in order to sustain the survival of all. But where multiple lines of power converged—where, say, febrile propagandist polemics and political theology pushed military responses and fed the needs of war, and vice versa—a crucible could materialize in which racial pronouncements, thinking, and actions could thrive. Holy war—especially the extraterritorial mass military incursions we know today as the Crusades—is a

> matrix conducive to the politics of race, as we will see. Race is a product of instrumentalizations that occur in war, and is also produced by political theology's instrumentalizations in support of war.

From the second half of the twelfth to the last quarter of the thirteenth century, ethnocentrism in political theology no longer worked as the device of hierarchy production and cultural accommodation that it had been since late antiquity. It became a more complex, violent, and rigid system of ideological attack and defense in front of mounting threats coming from multiple sides that the Western ruling elites perceived to be stronger than ever. Difference became racialized: the difference between Latin Western Christian groups, on the one hand, and the others, came to be resignified as under racializing stereotypes. Racialization had been mobilized since late antiquity to define and stigmatize several ethnic groups: Gypsies, Moors, Jews, Mongols, Indians, Chinese. But when the protracted war in the Mediterranean put more challenging organizational and ideological pressures on Christian rulers, the border between the Christian and Islamic sides of the Mediterranean space-time became the anthropological racial boundary between "us" and "them" in every realm where cross-cultural dialogue occurred. Knowledge production was the most relevant of these realms as regards the competing ideologies of cultural supremacy. On the Christian side of this reciprocal denigration, the Saracens became abominable monsters. Heng (2018, 118) continues,

> Racialization of the Saracen is thus a multilayered phenomenon. At its most demonic—one might almost say ludic, or ludicrous—Saracens appear monstrous by being fused with animals, so that in the Chanson de Roland (Song of Roland) they have spiny bristles like a boar, or skin hard as iron, or they bark like dogs. No less damning, however, is to say that Muslims are monstrous in entirely human ways: that their "law" advocates unbridled, insensate lust and polymorphous perversity in this life and in the afterlife, monstrosifying human values. Equally monstrous would be a habitual embrace of lies, so that the relationship of Muslims to deception and falsehood—a relation that is offered as constitutive of their very identity and self-definition—hollows out and denatures their humanity at the core.

Racialization materialized hierarchies of color where Arabic/Muslim perspectives of thought, and the knowledges, theories, and approaches pejoratively labeled as such, became associated with the more general understanding of Saracens, or the Moors, as darker skinned. As per Heng (2018, 42), "Color as a marker of difference answers with precise responsiveness to the demands of the central conceptual paradoxes on which medieval theological Christianity thrives, and on which it is constituted. Color can be deployed conventionally in Christian texts to signal the polar difference between sacred and demonic."

It was not Aristotle as such to be refused, but Aristotle that was informing the debate and inspiring new disclosures within Latin intelligentsia thanks to the commentaries from Islamic, Muslim, non-Christian thinkers and the translations into Latin from Arabic versions of original Greek or Hebrew texts. It was not Aristotle of the pagan ancient Greek philosophers that was circulating since the fifth century in the Christian world, but Aristotle that Latin Christendom had discovered centuries after the Islamic thinkers. It was not Aristotle's *logic* providing Western thinkers with the basic categories, genres, species and deductive reasoning that created doctrinal awkwardness, but Aristotle's *De Anima*, which in Averroes's interpretation undermined the foundations of Christian doctrine of the immorality and personification of the single soul. It was not the white pagan Greek Aristotle that was the problem, but the Moor, Saracen, Muslim, Arabic one. Aristotle had to be epurated from its Eastern, dark, innovative, sophisticated, advanced, and more erudite underside.

It is a matter of fact that, once epurated from the "Eastern" influence, Aquinas's Scholasticism was rehabilitated in 1323 when the condemnations were revoked. Thomism even became official doctrine of the Church, and when Aquinas was canonized in 1561, his anthropology set the terms of the debate about the colonization of the Americas among the newly established Jesuit order. Therefore, it is not a paradox that Aristotelianism became the philosophical pillar of the Catholic Church: its deductive method, its laws of motion, and the finite universe would be the major enemies of the Italian Renaissance thinkers (as we shall see in chapter 2).

This is why Aquinas acted like a tightrope walker. The contradiction between faith and reason, prompted by the epistemological interpretation that the newly circulating Aristotelian texts were disclosing, had become a matter of geopolitical relevance. He tried to provide a solution to the epistemological problem. For him, the most powerful and canonical form to accomplish his task in the intellectual scenario of his times was to place his theses at the highest level of abstraction—that is, to produce a theological axiomatics: a *summa theologiae*. The conventional procedures of intelligibility in high learned elites of Latin Christendom, after the revival of the dialectics that followed the spread of Arabic Aristotelianism, were ruled by the *logica nova*, exposed by the Stagirite in his *Organon* (Biffi 2008). The method of the *logica nova* was syllogism. There followed that Aquinas's epistemological system implied, rather than simply involved, the deduction of epistemological, juridical, ethical, and economic corollaries from the rationalized principles of faith. These corollaries not only had to prove argumentatively coherent, but they also had to comply with formal dialectical reasoning in order to be accepted as legitimate. This looks evident if one considers the way Aquinas's juridical theories were formally inferred by theological truths: the *lex divina* (divine law) and *lex aeterna* (eternal law) emanated from the (however controversial) interpellation of revelation and rationality. This meant that the natural world was ruled by eternal laws that could be grasped through human reason without conflicting with faith. Against this view, within Franciscan circles and among Franciscan thinkers, the radicalization of the doctrinal and cultural fight against heresy led to the idea that God could not be limited by anything, not even by some "eternal laws" of nature he had himself established. This position resonated with the epistemological approach of Al-Farabi in the diatribe against Averroes. For Averroes, God as the principle of knowledge was responsible of the laws of functioning of the universe in all its spheres, including human rationality, yet God's will was not the direct cause of any single event in the universe: for Averroes, the Great Architect of the Cosmos had created the logic and mechanisms of the entire universe, but circumstances depended on efficient causes wherein the concrete processes took place. God will manifest into the code that algorithm of creation, not into the single action, phenomenon, or process.

Franciscans, on the other hand, radicalized the opposite view. But they suspended even Al-Farabi's argumentative logic of philosophical reasoning. For them, God was absolute power: pure will. As such, God's will was everywhere. Being absolute will, God could revoke the laws of nature at any time, and every single action or phenomenon is the particular expression of the same will. For the past could not be in principle cogent to God's own unlimited will. Therefore, reason can also understand the logic of nature, but that very logic submits to God's pure, absolute will. Eventually, reason can understand *how* things are, but not *why* they are the way they are. Only faith can answer the fundamental question *why*.

The fact that the association of Aquinas's Scholasticism with Islamic influences played a role in its marginalization since the last quarter of the thirteenth century is confirmed by rhetorical arguments supporting several *quaestiones* in the course of the doctrinal controversies concerning the ecclesiastic condemnation of the teaching of Aristotle in 1270 and 1277 (Grabmann 1941; Hissete 1977; Piché 1999). It is not a coincidence that the list of condemnations compiled in 1270 contained 13 "errors," while in 1277 the errors were 219. The bitter divergences between Franciscans and Dominicans reverberated into major institutions, including the Sorbonne, where the study of Aristotle was spread both at the faculty of theology and the faculty of arts. Franciscan chairmen such as Bonaventure and William of Baglione launched open attacks on what they called Aristotelian heterodoxy, which included Aquinas. Aquinas returned to chair the University of Paris in 1268–1272, the second time after 1252–1259, in the middle of this climate of aggressive suspicion. The situation was becoming so rapidly polarized that regardless of his role, position and power, in 1270 he felt the urge to write against the Averroists: *Summa contra Gentiles*. Here he took distance from what he described as dangerous misunderstandings in Aristotle's thinking. Nonetheless, seven years later, Aquinas's theses were included in the list of 219 "errors" condemned by Ètienne Tempier, the bishop of Paris, under the general rubric of "heterodox Aristotelianism." From that moment onward, the majority of medieval scholars publicly shifted their intellectual position and declared Aquinas's use of Aristotle as "foreign" to their views. A system of internal academic whistleblowing and anonymous denunciation of unorthodox colleagues, strange behavior, or suspicious heretic teachings was established. Here, there emerged the pejorative term *Arabism* to denigrate such views, concepts, and notions (Bianchi 1990, 21–34). The accusation of Averroism, which corresponded to the expression of the accusation of Arabism and was thus automatically associated with *infidelitas*, consisted in an ideological construction of dualistic opposition between Islam and Christendom that strategically mobilized epistemology as a racialized intellectual weapon within intestine struggles between the two groups of power of the newly established mendicant orders. These groups were competing to acquire dominant positions within the space of power they had jointly obtained within the Church: that is, within the territories of western Eurasian societal formations over which the Church ruled. Powerful processes of circulation of knowledge were ideologically stigmatized as Eastern influences and racialized through the pejorative notion of "Arabism," forging premodern epistemology within an ideological scenario where a racializing cultural turn aimed at responding to geopolitical pressures, political struggles, and internecine reconfiguration of power. To the extent that it was an exteriorization of what were stigmatized as Eastern influences, the crisis of late medieval Scholasticism, the epuration of those influences, and the emergence of nominalism as a radical trend within Christianity that paved the way to the theology of Reformation were thus a regressive response of closure and stigmatization of otherness that reversed previous pluralistic orientations toward cross-cultural dialogue.

The mortification of scholastic pluralistic attitudes was one (prevailing) reaction to a global reconfiguration of power differential between Christianity and Islam from the thirteenth century onward. Matured within the Church, this response transformed a shared and plausible social and political perception of risk and geopolitical scale-down into an adaptive, ethno-centered self-definition of knowledge. The crisis of late medieval Scholasticism favored the emergence of nominalism. In his work on the theological origins of modernity, Gillespie (2008) re-interpellates Hans Blumenberg's thesis of the legitimacy of the modern age. According to both, nominalism represented a reoccupation of the *vacuum* left by the inability of Aquinas's Scholasticism to come to terms with the issue of theodicy (simply put, the debate concerning whether the origin of evil is human or divine). Against Aquinas's Scholasticism, nominalism affirmed God as pure will. Being God's will subtracted to human understanding, reason cannot but succumb to faith when the two are irreconcilable. Ideas are not endowed with real existence, as a long tradition broadly inspired by Platonism had presupposed. Every idea, even the idea of God, is inevitably subordinated to God's freedom to revoke it. Thus, ideas cannot be innate, as they are only particular notions that do not possess the status of reality; they are necessarily contextually meaningful: purely conventional. By questioning the ontological status of ideas, nominalism discredited the notion that Being descends into the world through discrete levels of reality, with the human material body being the lowest. So, the antisomatic attitudes that had prevailed in Christian theology since Augustine were inverted: reincarnation expressed God's might through the redemptive power of materialization by embodiment. This emphasis implied an epistemological turn that redefined the relation between God, man, and nature:

> God is in the world in a new and different sense than what scholasticism and traditional metaphysics imagined. He is not the ultimate whatness or quiddity of all beings but their howness or becoming. To discover the divinely ordered character of the world, it is necessary to investigate becoming, which is to say, it is necessary to discover the laws governing the motions of all beings. (Gillespie 2010, 36)

In establishing this different fault line between reason and faith, nominalism did not merely separate them; rather, it inaugurated the new, post-Scholastic logic of validation for science, and at the same time, it differently normed the limits of the human rational enterprise. As O'Brien (2013, 18) explains, "educated Europeans believed in a God who had created and designed his universe on rational principles, which he could revoke at any time, but rarely did."

A SUBTERRANEAN RIVER TO THE RENAISSANCE

Rather than fully repressing the circulation of nonhegemonic knowledge, the racial turn in premodern epistemology foregrounded future intellectual movements that contributed to vitalizing the complex cultural movement of the Renaissance, two centuries later. Yet even though the historical circumstances for such a reemergence were different in the fifteenth and sixteenth century, the association of heterodoxy and heresy with Eastern influences became a legitimate and efficient weapon of hegemony in the hand of dominant European groups. Hegemonic knowledge, with its armed political and institutional arm, conspired to mortify and annihilate the space of theoretical and conceptual innovation that the Renaissance would inaugurate. Such an ideational space connected not only with nonhegemonic knowledge coming from the south and east, but also with new stimuli from the New World of the Americas. In fact, the dominant master narrative about the historical and epistemological meaning of the Renaissance affirms that it was the premise of Western modern Enlightenment, thereby paving the way for the rule of Western rationality and positivism. Even post-Western, postcolonial, and decolonial approaches align themselves to such a dominant master narrative. This belief is misplaced: a closer look into the ideational rupture provoked by the Renaissance offers new insights, whose relevance creates new possible paths for a different methodology of concept formation in global studies.

NOTES

1. Portions of this chapter have been previously published in *Spectrum Journal of Global Studies Vol.*7, No.2, as "Contrived Civilizations The Western Eurasian Mode of Hierarchies Production and the (Geo)Political Origins of *Scientia*," 2016.

2. To be sure, even the term *gnoseology* (gr. γνῶσις -εως "knowledge" and -λογία "-discourse"), which is often used in modern times to grasp the same field of knowledge in the non-English world, is recent, despite its Latin origin. It was introduced by the German philosopher A. G. Baumgarten (1714–1762) in the eighteenth century and was later deployed in the continental philosophical tradition.

3. Wallerstein (1997) enumerates five dimensions of Eurocentrism: "It has been argued that social science expresses its Eurocentrism in (1) its historiography, (2) the parochiality of its universalism, (3) its assumptions about (Western) civilization, (4) its Orientalism, and (5) its attempts to impose the theory of progress."

4. The Chinese Rites Controversy (c.1582–1742) is a debate among Christian missionaries that involved different Catholic orders in a religious quarrel over whether it was admissible for Chinese converts to Christianity to observe traditional rites and use the terms *tian* and *shangdi* to refer to the Christian God.

BIBLIOGRAPHY

Abu-Lughud, Janet. 1991. *Before European Hegemony: The World System A.D. 1250–1350*. London: Oxford University Press.

Abulafia, David, ed. 2008. *The New Cambridge Medieval History*. Cambridge: Cambridge University Press.

Adas, Michael. 1989. *Machines as the Measure of Man. Science, Technology and ideologies of Western Dominance. Ithaca: Cornell University Press.*

Alatas, Syed Farid. 2014. *Applying Ibn Khaldūn: The Recovery of a Lost Tradition in Sociology*. London: Routledge.

Al-Jabri, Mohammed Abed. 2004. *Formation of Arab Reason: Text, Tradition and the Construction of Modernity in the Arab World.* New York: I. B. Tauris.

Althusser, Luis. 1972. *Politics and History*. London: New Left.

Anievas, A. Manchanda, N. Shilliam, R. (eds.). 2014. *Race and Racism in International Relations: Confronting the Global Colour Line*. Routledge: London.

Anievas, Alexander, and Kerem Nisancioglu. 2013. "What's at Stake in the Transition Debate? Rethinking the Origins of Capitalism and the 'Rise of the West.'" *Millennium—Journal of International Studies* 42, no. 1: 78–102.

Aquinas, Thomas. 1911. *Summa Theologica* (Aquinas's philosophy). Translated by Fathers of the English Dominican Province, Benzinger Brothers Printers to the Holy Apostolic See. New York: Publishers of Benzinger's Magazine.

———. *Liber de Veritate Catholicae Fidei contra errores infidelium*. New York: Hanover House, (1955–57); reprint University of Notre Dame Press, 1975, [1258–1264], 1924.

Arnzen, R., and J. Thielmann, eds. 2004. *Words, Texts and Concepts Cruising the Mediterranean Sea: Studies on the Sources, Contents and Influences of Islamic Civilization and Arabic Philosophy and Science*. Louvain: Peteers.

Arnoux, Mathieux. 2012. *Le temps des laboureurs. Travail, ordre social et croissance en Europe (XIe-XIVe siècle)*. Paris: Albin.

Ascione, Gennaro. 2016. *Science and the Decolonization of Knowledge: Unthinking Modernity*, London: Palgrave.

Bala, Arun. 2006. *The Dialogue of Civilizations in the Birth of Modern Science*. New York: Palgrave Macmillan.

Bethencourt Francisco. 2013. *Racisms. From the Crusades to the Twentieth Century*. Princenton and Oxford: Princeton University Press.

Bianchi, Luca. 1990. *Il vescovo e i filosofi: la condanna parigina del 1277 e l'evoluzione dell'aristotelismo scolastico*. Bergamo: Quodlibet.

———. 1993. "Les aristotélismes de la scolastique." In *Vérités dissonantes: Aristote à la fin du Moyen Âge*, edited by L. Bianchi and E. Randi, 1–37. Fribourg: Editions universitaires.

Biffi, Inos. 2008. *Mirabile Medioevo: La costruzione della teologia medievale*. Milan: Jaca Books.

Blum, R. 1991. *Kallimachos: The Alexandrian Library and the Origins of Bibliography*. Madison: University of Wisconsin Press.

Brams, Jose. 2003. *La riscoperta di Aristotele in occidente*. Milan: Jaca.

Budick, Sanford, and Wolfgang Isen, eds. 1996. *The Translatability of Cultures: Figurations of the Space Between*. Stanford, CA: Stanford University Press.

Cabezón, José Ignacio. 1998. *Scholasticism: Cross-Cultural and Comparative Perspectives*. Albany: State University of New York Press.

Castro-Gómez, Santiago. 2005. *La hybris del punto cero: Biopolíticas imperiales y colonialidad del poder en la Nueva Granada (1750–1810)*. Bogotà: Pontificia Universidad Javeriana.

Cipollone, G. 1992. *Cristianità-Islam. Cattività e liberazione in nome di Dio. Il tempo di Innocenzo III dopo il 1187*. Roma: Pontificia Università.

Cobban, Alan B. 1971. "Medieval Student Power." *Past & Present* 53, no. 1: 28–66.

Coccia, Emanuele. 2005. *La trasparenza delle immagini: Averroè e l'averroismo*, Milano: Mondadori.

Cohen, Floris H. 1994. *The Scientific Revolution. A Historiographical Inquiry*. Chicago: University of Chicago Press.

Couliano, Ioan Petru. 1992. *The Tree of Gnosis: Gnostic Mythology from Early Christianity to Modern Nihilism*. Chicago: University of Chicago Press.

Daibier, Hans. 2012. *Islamic Thought in the Dialogue of Cultures: A Historical and Bibliographical Survey*. Amsterdam: Brill.

Deane, Jennifer Kolpacoff. 2011. *A History of Medieval Heresy and Inquisition*. Lanham, MD: Rowman and Littlefield.

Eisenstadt, Shmuel N. 2000. "Multiple Modernities.." In *Daedalus*, *129*(1), 1–29.

Eliade, Mircea. 1983. *History of Religious Ideas, Volume 2: From Gautama Buddha to the Triumph of Christianity*. Chicago: University of Chicago Press.

Elman, Benjamin. 2005. *On Their Own Terms. Science in China, 1550–1900*. New York: Harvard University Press.

Emery, Kent, and Andreas Speer. 2001. "After the Condemnation of 1277: New Evidence, New Perspectives, and Grounds for New Interpretations." In *Nach der Verurteilung von 1277 / After the Condemnation of 1277: Philosophie und Theologie an der Universität von Paris im letzten Viertel des 13. Jahrhunderts. Studien und Texte/Philosophy and Theology at the University of Paris in the Last Quarter of the Thirteenth Century. Studies and Texts*, edited by Jan A. Aertsen, Kent Emery, and Andreas Speer, 3–20. Berlin: De Gruyter.

Fan, Fa-ti. 2004. *British naturalists in Qing China: Science, empire, and cultural encounter. Cambridge*, MA: Harvard University Press.

Frank, Andre Gunder. 1990. "The Thirteenth-Century World System: A Review Essay." *Journal of World History* 1, no. 2: 249–56.

Frank André Gunter and Barry Gill (eds). 1994. *The World System: 500 years or 5000?*. London: Routledge: 1994.

Frantz, Fanon. 2004. *The Wretched of the Heart*. New York: Grove Press.

Franzen, August. 2009. *Breve storia della Chiesa*, Roma: Editrice Queriniana.

Garrigon-Lagrange, G. 1947. *Essenza e attualità del Tomismo*. Brescia: Fede e Cultura.

Gertz, SunHee Kim. 2009. "Translatio studii et imperii: Sir Gawain as literary critic." *Semiotica* 63, no. 1–2: 185–204.

Gheverghese Joseph, George. 2011. *The Crest of the Peacock: Non-European Roots of Mathematics*. Princeton: Princeton University Press.

Gillespie, Michael Allen. 2010. *The Theological Origins of Modernity*. Chicago: University of Chicago Press.

Ginzburg, Carlo. 1974 *I benandanti: Stregoneria e culti agrari tra Cinquecento e Seicento*. Milano: Adelphi.

Giovannetti-Singh, G. 2022. "Rethinking the Rites Controversy: Kilian Stumpf's Acta Pekinensia and the Historical Dimensions of a Religious Quarrel." *Modern Intellectual History* 19, no. 1: 29–53.

Goonatilake Susantha. 1998. *Toward a Global Science: Mining Civilizational Knowledge*. Indianapolis: Indiana University Press.

Grabmann, Martin. 1941. *I divieti ecclesiastici di Aristotele sotto Innocenzo III e Gregorio IX.* Roma: Saler.

Harding, Sandra. (ed.) 2011. *The Postcolonial Science and Technology Studies Reader*. Duhram: Duke University Press.

Hamilton, Bernard. 2008. "The Albigensian Crusade and Heresy." *The New Cambridge Medieval History*, edited by David Abulafia, 164–81. Cambridge: Cambridge University Press.

Heng, Geraldine. 2018. *The Invention of Race in the European Middle Ages*. Cambridge: Cambridge University Press.

Hissete, Roland. 1977. *Enquête sur les 219 articles condamnés à Paris le 7 mars 1277*. Paris: Publications Universitaires/Vander-Oyez.

Hobson, John M. 2004. *The Eastern Origins of Western Civilization*. Cambridge: Cambridge University Press.

———. 2005. "The Enduring Place of Hierarchy in World Politics: Tracing the Social Logics of Hierarchy and Political Change." *European Journal of International Relations* 11, no. 1: 63–98.

———. 2012. *The Eurocentric Conception of World Politics: Western International Theory, 1760–2010*. Cambridge: Cambridge University Press.

Hodgson, Marshall. 1993. *Rethinking World History: Essays on Europe, Islam, and World History*. Cambridge: Cambridge University Press.

Hui, Wang. 2011. *The End of the Revolution: China and the Limits of Modernity*. London: Verso.

Huntington, Samuel P. 1996. *The Clash of Civilizations and the Other Remaking Of World Order*. New York: The Free Press.

Jaspers, Karl. 1950. *The Origin and Goal of History*. First English edition, translated by Michael Bullock. London: Routledge and Kegan Paul, 1953.

Jordan, Chester. 2002. "'Europe" in the Middle Ages." In *The Idea of Europe from Antiquity to the European Union*, edited by Anthony Pagden, 72–91. Cambridge: Cambridge University Press.

Küçük, B. H. 2010. "Islam, Christianity, and the Conflict Thesis." In *Science and Religion. New Historical Perspectives*, edited by Thomas Dixon, Geoffrey Cantor, and Stephen Pumfrey, 111–30. Cambridge: Cambridge University Press.

Larmore, Charles. 1996. *The Morals of Modernity*. Cambridge: Cambridge University Press.

Le Goff, Jacques. 1999. *Intellectuals in the Middle Ages*. New York: Wiley.

Makdisi Ussama. 2019. *Age of Coexistence: The Ecumenical Frame and the Making of the Modern Arab World.* Oakland: University of California Press.

Makkai, L. 1994. "Transformation into a Western-Type State 1196–301." In *A History of Hungary*, edited by Peter F. Sugar, Péter Hanák, and Tibor Frank. Bloomington: Indiana University Press, 1994.

McMichael, P. (2016). "World-Systems Analysis, Globalization, and Incorporated Comparison." In *Review* (Fernand Braudel Center), 39(1/4), 195–218.

M. R. Menocal. 2002. *The Ornament of the World. How Muslims, Jews, and Cristians created a culture of tolerance in medieval Spain.* Boston-New York-London: Little, Brown and Co.

Mignolo, Walter D. 2000. *Local Histories/Global Designs: Coloniality, Subaltern Knowledges, and Border Thinking.* Princeton: Princeton University Press.

Moore, Robert. 1987. *The Formation of a Persecuting Society.* Oxford: Blackwell.

Nicolle, David. 2011. *The Fourth Crusade 1202–04: The Betrayal of Byzantium.* Oxford: Osprey.

O'Brien, Patrick. 2013. "Historical foundations for a global perspective on the emergence of a western European regime for the discovery, development, and diffusion of useful and reliable knowledge." *Journal of Global History* 8(1):1–24.

Orioli, Raniero. 2008. *Gli eretici "perfetti": i Catari.* Bologna: Arianna.

Pagden, Anthony. 1986. *The Fall of Natural Man: The American Indian and the Origins of Comparative Ethnology.* Cambridge: Cambridge University Press.

Parthasarathi, Prasannan. 2011. *Why Europe Grew Rich and Asia Did Not. Global Economic Divergence, 1600–1850.* Cambridge: Cambridge University Press.

Peck, Marc Gregory. 2008. *A Most Holy War: The Albigensian Crusade and the Battle for Christendom (Pivotal Moments in World History).* Oxford: Oxford University Press.

Pennington, K. 1976. "Pope Innocent III's Views on Church and State: A Gloss to Per Venerabilem," In *Law, Church, and Society. Essays in Honour of Stephen Kuttner,* edited by K. Pennington and R. Somerville, 49–67 Philadelphia: University of Pennsylvania Press.

Perkins, Franklin. 2006. *Leibniz and China: A Commerce of Light.* Cambridge: Cambridge University Press.

Phillips, Jonathan. 2004. *The Fourth Crusade and the Sack of Constantinople.* New York: Viking.

Piché, David. 1999. *La condamnation parisienne de 1277.* Paris: Vrin.

Poovey, Mary. 1998. *A History of Modern Fact: Problems of Knowledge in the Sciences of Wealth and Society.* Chicago: University of Chicago Press.

Popper, Karl. 1994. *The Myth of the Framework. In Defense of Science and Rationality.* New York: Goodreads.

Raj, Kapil. 2007. *Relocating Modern Science: Circulation and the Construction of Knowledge in South Asia and Europe, 1650–1900.* New York: Palgrave Macmillan.

———. 2013. "Beyond Postcolonialism . . . and Postpositivism: Circulation and the Global History of Science." *ISIS* 104(2): 337–347.

Riparelli, Enrico. 2008. *Il volto del Cristo dualista. Da Marcione ai catari.* Bern: Peter Lang.

Ridder-Symoens, Hilde, and Walter Rüegg, eds. 1993. *A History of the University in Europe: Universities in the Middle Ages.* Cambridge: Cambridge University Press.

Saliba, George. 2007. *Islamic Science and the Making of the European Renaissance.* Cambridge, MA: MIT Press.

Sayers, Jane. 1994. *Innocent III: Leader of Europe, 1198–216.* London: Longman.

Sehlikoglu, S., Kurt, M. 2024 “Islam, critique, and the canon: an introduction.” *Contemporary Islam*. https://doi.org/10.1007/s11562-024-00555-y

Sumption, Jonathan. 1978. *The Albigensian Crusade*. London: Faber.

Taylor, Charles. 2007. *A Secular Age*. Cambridge, MA: Belknap Press of Harvard University Press.

Thijssen, J. M. 1998. *Censure and Heresy at the University of Paris 1200–1400*. Philadelphia: University of Pennsylvania Press.

Wallerstein, Immanuel. 1997. “Eurocentrism and Its Avatars: The Dilemmas of Social Science.” Keynote address at ISA East Asian Regional Colloquium, *The Future of Sociology in East Asia*, Seoul, November 22–23, 1996.

———. 1999. “The West, Capitalism and the Modern World-System.” In *China and Historical Capitalism: Genealogies of Sinological Knowledge*, edited by Timothy Brook and Gregory Blue, 10–56. Cambridge: Cambridge University Press, 1999.

———. 2003. “Knowledge, Power and Politics: The Role of an Intellectual in an Age of Transition.” Paper presented at the Unesco Forum on Higher Education, Research and Knowledge, Paris, December 8–9, 2003. https://unesdoc.unesco.org/ark:/48223/pf0000183329 (accessed 07/05/2023).

Watt, James. 2008. “The Papacy.” In *The New Cambridge Medieval History*, edited by David Abulafia, 107–63. Cambridge: Cambridge University Press.

Zamboni, Maria Paola. 2015. *Scioperi e rivolte nel Medioevo: Le città italiane ed europee nei secoli XIII-XV.* Bologna: Jouvense.

Chapter 2

Giordano Bruno and the Decolonial Construction of the Renaissance

THE DECOLONIAL STRATEGIC OVERSIMPLIFICATION

The assumption of the continuity between the Renaissance and the Enlightenment, which postcolonial and decolonial studies share with the Western hegemonic master narrative of modernity, is flawed. Therefore, it is necessary to rethink the Renaissance as an epistemological rupture in space and time. For this reason, a double theoretical disarticulation in space and time is needed. In space, such a disarticulation engages with Walter D. Mignolo's influential interpretation of the "darker side" of the Renaissance and the early modern period, in order to disarticulate the conflation of the Spanish Renaissance with the Renaissance in Italy, where the latter becomes an epistemic space of connection with non-Western knowledges. In time, it questions the historiography that appropriated and deformed the cultural phenomenon of the Renaissance during the late eighteenth and the nineteenth century, from the French encyclopedists to the Romantics. It presents sixteenth-century heretic philosopher and southern Italian migrant Giordano Bruno (1548–1600), his concept of temporality and infinite universe, his pioneering anticolonial critique, and his theory of knowledge as alternative resources for a post-Western theory of concept formation. This restitution of complexity to the Renaissance discloses a different horizon of theorization where non-Western, heretic, Indigenous knowledges ally against Western hegemonic epistemology, functioning as a syntonizer for a variety of forms of knowledge, across the past, present, and future as well as across existing dualisms such as East(s)/West(s), North(s)/South(s). This shared theoretical language for dialogue between multiple epistemologies relies on the generative grammar of teratology. The metaphorical use of monstrosity connects multiplex global epistemics to foster a new sociological imagination for the elaboration of an open-ended methodological approach to concept formation.

Among the many groundbreaking contributions that the broadly conceived decolonization of knowledge research program has produced, at least during the last thirty years, one stands at such a level of generality that its strength has provoked a paradigmatic shift in global studies, cultural and media studies, arts and literary criticism, as well as in the social sciences at large (Cusicanqui 2020). Modernity is not anymore thinkable without taking into account its colonial formation (Quijano and Wallerstein 1992; Quijano 1992; 2000). Modern capitalism and its geoculture is consubstantial with the colonization of the world, since the foundational act of modernity is the colonization of the Americas (Dussel 1993). Therefore, modernity/coloniality is a single conceptual construction that provides a meaningful as well as critical framework for theoretical and narrative elaboration on global historical social change and its cultural productions (Grosfoguel 2006; 2007). The irruption of colonialism into the paradigm of the social sciences has not been pacific: it has involved harsh confrontation with dominant interpretations of modernity in different fields of knowledge production and disciplines (Bhambra 2007).

In order to affirm the colonial matrix of modernity, a multifaceted intellectual move spanning from dependency theories to subaltern, cultural, postcolonial, and decolonial studies has relentlessly attacked the Eurocentric and self-absolutory master narrative of modernity (Dufoix 2023).[1] The Western social sciences had built the master narrative of modernity since the end of the eighteenth century, either to naturalize the rise of the West to world dominance, or to legitimize it by means of historiographical determinism, or to justify its hegemony by systematically neglecting the multiplex worlds that compose the cartography of the modern/colonial world. This arbitrary negligence concretizes in the methodological deformation of the relational construction of the spacetimes, geohistorical entities, subjectivities, histories, and concepts that came to model the dominant archive of Western knowledges, whose unilateral imposition over other structures of knowledge and the social groups that produced them occurred by means of reiteration. Elsewhere I have called this protocol of reiteration "the coloniality of method" (Ascione 2016). Reiteration provoked the hypostatization of epistemological redundancy that ended up creating the Western hegemonic canon of thinkers in both the human and social sciences. Raewyn Connell (1997) denounces the racial and sexist bias of this canon whose iconography crystallized into the intellectual hagiography of the "founding fathers" of modern Western social science: Descartes, Kant, Hegel, Marx, Weber, and Durkheim.

Catherine Walsh and Walter Mignolo have recently clarified the genealogy of their epistemological tension and motivated its politics with the lack of recognition of the asymmetries of power experienced by the colonized subjects they encountered along their early scholarly path during the 1980s: "*against* the colonial tare and *for* something else" (Walsh and Mignolo 2024: 121). This tension epitomizes the core problematique shared since the first half of the 1990s by the Latin American Subaltern Studies Group, who found a more elaborated and extended editorial output through the short-lived, but pivotal, journal *Nepantla: Views from the South* (2000–2003).[2] The oppositional strategy that guides the decolonization of knowledge research program at large deploys three intertwined yet distinctive logics of analysis: dialectical, dialogical, and analectic. It is dialectical to the extent that it brings to the fore what had been neglected and places it in antithetical terms with what is dominant and unilateral. This means that in order to express the relational constitution of the modern world through colonialism, it juxtaposes modernity and coloniality. It creates a more-than-proportional counterbalancing argumentative effect where coloniality is not simply the antithetical pole of a contradiction in Hegelian terms. In other words, coloniality is not the negation of modernity, but rather a newly established conceptual focus in the terminological dyad, which works as a gravitational pole whose force lies in its ability to be modernity's *counterpoint*. Edward Said (1993) introduced counterpoint as a critical methodology, transposing this concept from musical theory. In modern Western classical music, the word *contrapuntal* describes two contradictory themes playing at the same time and creating a harmonious melody. Said was not interested in harmony as a result; rather, he used counterpoint as a process creating constant tensions, resonances, and polyphony, but also irreconcilable dissonances and unsynchronized rhythms able to produce unpredictable outcomes:

> Polyphony, the organization of more than one voice, is what really interests me. I am attracted to the combination of voices, the way one voice becomes subordinated by another. I am interested in the possibilities for the interpreter to bring out voices, which to the author or to the composer may not have been apparent. Bach, for example, had a fantastic capacity for predicting what combinations of sounds could come out of a single phrase. In the interpretation of polyphonic compositions, there is no predictability. (Said, in Bayoumi and Rubin 2000, 425)

When he extended this concept outside the field of music and literary criticism, Said transformed it into an encompassing theoretical device. Said (1993, 52) affirmed that "as we look back at the cultural archive, we begin to reread it not univocally but contrapuntally, with a simultaneous awareness both of the metropolitan history that is narrated and of those other histories against which (and together with which) the dominating discourse acts." In analytical terms, the focus on counterpoint as a patterned relation, rather than its outcomes, shifts the argumentative logic from dialectics conceived as the triad culminating in synthesis to an asymmetric dialogical reasoning. Dialogical logic is asymmetrical because it assumes the existence of hierarchies of power within the dialectical relation but attempts to cope with it (Bala 2006; 2012). Dialogical reason counterbalances the dominant position of the hypothesis (read: "the Western hegemonic conceptual archive") by emphasizing the thesis, the negative, antithetical, side of the dyad (read: "the colonial subaltern conceptual archive"). This means not only that the single concept modernity/coloniality preserves such an intrinsic tension disregarding the problem of the synthesis, but that it also leaves open the theoretical possibility that a part of the negative stance (the more-than-antithetical side of the dyad) could remain exterior to the dialectical couple itself.

Enrique Dussel (1985) has reinterpreted this space of exteriority in his comments on Emmanuel Levinas (Dussel and Mendieta 2003). The philosophy of liberation conceives analectic reason in terms of the rediscovery of the original experience of domination that relationally constructed the dominant and the dominated subjectivity, at multiple intertwined levels:[3] at the global level (modernity/coloniality), in the interstate system (north/south), in civilization (West/East), in the international division of labor (core/periphery), within the nation-state (elites/people), within gender relations (male/female), in history (written/oral). Therefore, what is outside dialectics transgresses the possibility of full reconcilability that dialogical reasoning left, so as to create a space of its own (Dussel 1985). Dussel (2002) has presented this option as the analectic logic of reasoning, where exteriority locates at the margin of modernity/coloniality, but at the same time, it forms the margin itself. This margin would be the privileged locus of enunciation for alternative forms of knowledge production to emerge in what he calls "transmodernity."

Mignolo (1995, 12) moves from this notion of margin, but he admits that his "particular problem with Dussel is the introduction of analectic results in conceiving the margins as fixed and ontological rather than as a movable and relational concept." This is why Mignolo (1995, 1) locates the historical emergence of the margin of modernity/coloniality where the notion of the Renaissance juxtaposes to the notion of early modern times:

> While the concept of Renaissance refers to a rebirth of classical legacies and the constitution of humanistic scholarship for human emancipation and early modern period emphasizes the emergence of a genealogy that announces the modern and the postmodern, the darker side of the Renaissance underlines, instead, the rebirth of the classical tradition as a justification of colonial expansion and the

emergence of a genealogy (the early colonial period) that announces the colonial and the postcolonial.

Mignolo uses the early modern period as counterpoint to the Renaissance, thereby creating a movable and relational imaginative space between two concepts that are nonhomogeneous from a semantic point of view. The two concepts cannot fully overlap: the Renaissance alludes to a cultural movement or intellectual research program and simultaneously to a period in European history (even though its spacetime coordinates appear elusive the more one tries to clearly establish them). The early modern period alludes to the beginning of a world-systemic transition that is global since its origin, thereby involving those geohistorical locations, noncolonized peoples, and non-European knowledges, which the notion of the Renaissance does not include.

Within the coordinates of the debate at the end of the twentieth century when decolonial thinking struggled to affirm the colonial nature of modernity, which had been simply obscured since late-eighteenth-century Western European social thought, the usage of the "European" Renaissance effectively served the purpose of conceiving the margins of modernity as a generative theoretical and political space. And this is true both in Dussel's notion of exteriority and in Mignolo's more flexible understanding of marginality. It also served to predate modernity and let it coincide with the peripherization of the Americas, rather than with industrialization or the French Revolution, in order to give the right place to colonization in the rise of the West to world hegemony. Nevertheless, this same usage had its transitional adequacy limited by the essentialization of the Renaissance as a historical, intellectual, and geopolitical phenomenon. It is not by chance that both Mignolo and Dussel connect the Renaissance with Descartes's introduction of the *ego cogito* ("I think"), which Kant later transformed into the transcendental subject "I," when they affirm that the emergence of modern Western thinking was preceded by the colonial imperative *ego conquero* ("I conquer"). For both Dussel and Mignolo, *ego cogito* is the filiation of the *ego conquero*.

The decolonization of knowledge research program has proved effective in unveiling the underside of the triumphalism of modernity but it has done so by relying on a notion of the Renaissance that oversimplifies important aspects of the phenomenon at stake. Unthinking such an oversimplification discloses silenced and hidden threads within the Renaissance that could appear marginal today but were not so at the time. These visions and threads were intrinsically entrenched within non-Western knowledges, and today they speak a common language of critical thinking. This connection unleashes the epistemological potential of a post-Western theoretical framework wherein an alternative way of concept formation stems from rethinking and rewriting the conceptual archive of global studies, bringing to the fore alternative sources of theorization. These sources annihilate the power of the coloniality of method to render exotic the forms of knowledge coming from other geohistorical locations, which do not conform to dominant knowledges and concepts. Yet in order to engage with such resources, a temptation needs to be resisted. This temptation consists in taking single concepts, notions, theories, and visions from such an alternative conceptual archive and using it as a ready-made tool of problem-solving in the current debate on the globalization of knowledge, presenting them as old, forgotten resolutions of new impasses. This approach would become superficial and less effective when confronted with the analytical method of exploring such alternative conceptual archives with reference to the historical, anthropological, and political routes of their path, trying to mentally enter frameworks and structures of knowledge production that respond to logics or are based upon certitudes different from what is current nowadays. This alternative is anchored in the Gramscian theory of translatability according to which it is not the single word that is relevant but the process of exploration of the territory that words inhabited, since one who writes does not control the space of inquiry to which he or she invites those who read to enter, and one who reads can inhabit that territory autonomously and find other, different, new paths and words. As it will be developed in chapter 5.

MATTERS OF SPACETIME: ANTICOLONIAL EARLY MODERN REASON

The process of unthinking the decolonial oversimplification of the Renaissance takes place in space and time. In space, it disentangles Mignolo's now-classical understanding of the Spanish Renaissance from the Renaissance in Italy. In time, it questions the taken-for-granted narrative of continuity between the Renaissance and the Enlightenment. Mignolo (1995, vii) notes that

> when René Descartes in Amsterdam, toward 1630, merged literacy with numeracy and redirected the notion of scientific rigor and philosophical reasoning in French, the Castilian and Portuguese languages remained attached to the heavy literate and humanistic legacies of the European Renaissance. If we could detect a reorientation of philosophical and scientific discourses toward the beginning of the seventeenth century, it would be worthwhile to note that such reorientation was attached to specific languages (the languages of the modern period: English, German, French) and coincided with the moment in which Amsterdam began to replace Seville as the Western center of economic

transactions at the closure of the Renaissance/early modern/colonial period and the opening up of the Enlightenment/modern/colonial period.

Mignolo inscribes this turn in the transition from Spanish and Portuguese hegemony to the Dutch hegemonic position within the interstate system of the capitalist world economy (Arrighi 1994; Arrighi and Silver 1999). In so doing, he carves out an encompassing epistemic space of knowledge production for the Spanish language. Therefore, he explores this epistemic space in the period of the first decades of the colonization of the Americas and acutely explains the way colonization operated through either the dominant Castilian language, or the technique of alphabetical writing, or a specific object of material culture: namely, the book. The grammars codified Castilian first. Then Spaniards in Mexico and Peru destroyed any form of written and illustrated texts they encountered during the contact with native social groups and cultures, then created Aymara grammars of their own, then started to impose their own culture, language, and system of memories on colonized peoples through their own books and forced teaching in evangelization missions and schools in the colonies, where they educated the native elite (Mignolo 1992).

The characteristic that configures Mignolo's unit of analysis in the Renaissance/early modern period is the Mediterranean/Atlantic space of colonial expansion connecting the Spanish empire with the Americas. Yet this unit of analysis also coincides with the site of enunciation Mignolo thinks from. To be sure, his research concentrates on Mexico, and rhapsodically on Peru. Nonetheless, he projects his totalizing vision over the historical roots and the plurality of meanings of the Renaissance as a worldly significant phenomenon, what he calls the philosophy of language of the colonizers. In contrast with his vision, a different narrative emerged from the perspective of the politically fragmented, pre-unitarian southern Mediterranean peninsula that Italy was during the fifteenth and sixteenth centuries, where the birth of the Renaissance unquestionably occurred before the nation-state building process culminated in 1861 unification. Such an alternative narrative transforms the sociocultural meaning of the Renaissance and the politics of language it entails. The fact that the Renaissance had its roots in Italy is not merely a matter of geography. It is meaningful from an historical-epistemological point of view because the Renaissance is not conceivable without considering the context of crisis that provided the humus for its emergence. Therefore, it is not conceivable outside the intellectual pattern along which it occurs or outside the conjunctural organizational social needs to which it responded. The classical thesis of the *return to the classics* that Mignolo takes for granted conceals the impact that the fall of the Eastern Roman Empire in 1453 produced upon specific intellectual strata located in the Italian peninsula at the time, and the geoepistemic significance of such an impact for the migratory flows of scholars from the East throughout Europe and to the small states of the Italian peninsula (Burke 2017; De la Croix, Doepke, and Mokyr 2018; De la Croix et al. 2022; Setton 1956). The Renaissance in Italy was both an evolutionary phase in the humanist turn that literature and arts were undergoing in the erudite European circles since the first half of the fifteenth century and a rupture provoked by the sudden circulation of scholars, thinkers, intellectuals, ideas, and specific books in the Italian peninsula, coming from the East and moving away from Constantinople before and in the aftermath of the Ottoman conquest (Geanakoplos 1962, 1966, 1976, 1989).

Before addressing this complexity, a preliminary remark is due. It consists in delegitimizing a commonsensical genealogy that connects retrospectively the eighteenth-century Enlightenment with the fifteenth-century Renaissance and the Renaissance with fourteenth-century humanism in terms of successive stage of filiation. From the perspectives of the politics of language, while humanism relates to the erudite glorification of the Greco-Roman cultural canon and the pedantry drifts it produced, the Renaissance constructed a complex dialogue between Greek, Roman, and vernacular languages in the realm of knowledge production and its circulation across multiple social strata as well as geocultural locations. The canonical genealogy that, instead, overlooks such crucial discontinuities and differences is paradoxically reaffirmed even in recent attempts to mobilize the notion of decolonizing knowledge to rethink the Renaissance as a global phenomenon encompassing the colonial world. McManus (2022), on this point deploys the historiographical category of Renaissance humanism to question the Eurocentric narratives of the pristine European character of the Renaissance. He attempts to do so by bringing to the fore the figure of Antonio Valeriano (1521–1605), lamenting that the name of this Nahua humanist from Azcapotzalco in the Valley of Mexico, educated by the Franciscans within their evangelization mission established along with the settler colonization process and very well versed in classical literature, rhetoric, and languages, does not come to mind in the history of culture.

In order to contribute to such a more complex view, I put Mignolo in dialogue with the Italian historian and philosopher Eugenio Garin (1909–2004), whose long-lasting pioneering studies in the Renaissance in Italy revolutionized the field since the 1940s and through the remainder of the twentieth century.[4] In constructing the connection between Mignolo and Garin, I do not adopt a comparative approach as far as "Spain" and "Italy" are concerned. These are not reducible to the geohistorical locations that the advent of the nation-state in the nineteenth century would project backward. Not only because Italy at the time was not a single state, but because they are both coinstantiated by the critical understanding of the Renaissance as the relation that becomes constitutive of both. Therefore, "Italy" and "Spain" here function, as Chakrabarty's (2000) India and Europe do, in terms of hyperreal constructions.[5]

Along this line, Fernand Braudel (1986), too, takes issues with the Western hegemonic thinking that, according to him, uncritically relies on an "unconscious reading" of what it refers to in terms of the Renaissance. Braudel maintains that such an unconscious reading should be unpacked. He thinks of the Renaissance in the *longue durée*. Together with Garin and echoing Armando Sapori, he proposes a chronology of the major transformations in the European and Mediterranean erudite strata culture that runs from the twelfth to the eighteenth century. The master narrative of the modern world usually calls Renaissance the period between the fifteenth and seventeenth centuries. But for Braudel, this period should be called "the Second Renaissance." Nevertheless, beyond the historiographical problem of chronology, what is more relevant here is the way Braudel distinguishes multiple sites of cultural production, which design alternative paths of cultural development and theoretical production. He typifies two major "epicenters" of the Renaissance: Italy and the Arabic-Latin Mediterranean, first, then Europe and the Netherlands, England, and the Baltic area that would include also the coastal area of northern Russia. Within this cartography of the relational construction of the cultural spaces, he accords precedence to the birth and development of the Renaissance to Italian cities. But he also articulates a distinction between maritime cities and interchange cities: the former would be Venice, Genova, and Naples; the latter, those located along crucial commercial routes, both terrestrial or via river ports, like Verona or Padua, but also cities of passage for pilgrimages, such as Bologna, Pisa, and Siena. This complexification of the historical cartography of the Renaissance provides a powerful antidote against both the comparative approach and the totalizing understanding of the Renaissance as a monolithic phenomenon: it unfolds a path into the exploration of the conjunctural situation wherein the Renaissance was born. The Renaissance in Italy spread from Florence, Palermo, Venice, Naples, Palermo, Padua, Rome, and many more among the multiple urban centers belonging to different regions of the scattered and fragmented political landscape of the time. In this landscape, the Aragon kingdom in the fifteenth century and the Spanish Crown of Charles V since 1521 ruled over Southern Italy, which became the southern Mediterranean periphery of the Castilian empire in the same decades of the Atlantic expansion. The narrative that Mignolo reconstructs tells the story of how the Castilian language accompanied the consolidation of Castilian rule in the Iberian Peninsula and the coextensive construction of its overseas Atlantic colonial empire, where native elites were trained by the colonizers both in Castilian and in their own languages by the colonizers themselves. This process produced the instauration of a double border (Mignolo 2000, 29). The inner border came out of the epilogue of the seven-century-long *Reconquista*, that is, the defeat of the Moors and the forced conversion of the Jews to the Christian faith in southern Spain, which dates to January 2, 1492.[6]

The outer border of Europe was delineated from the confrontation with the "New World," which began after Christopher Columbus arrived in San Salvador on October 14 that same year. Therefore, Castilian was the language of the conquerors and the colonizers. It was the linguistic space of a political entity unified under the central authority of an expanding and consolidating power. This is why Mignolo (1993, 13) explains how important the first edition of the Castilian grammar by Nebrija in 1492 was within the process of ethnocentric construction that Spain was undergoing at the turn of the fifteenth century, both inward and outward.

On the contrary, the Italian peninsula was living a period of profound crisis. Depicting this historical condition, Garin (2000, 11) maintains that

> in fact, the world that is reflected in the most notable works and figures of the early Italian Renaissance is a world more often tragic than happy, more often hard and cruel than peaceful, more often enigmatic and unsettling than limpid and harmonious. . . . At the end of the 15th century, a period so rich in documents about the greatness of man, life and history, was really tragic because Italy was cut across by wars, blooded by turmoil, . . . while its major urban centers were witnessing their power crumbling, their trade fading away, their sources of wealth drying.

This political fragmentation and the economic downturn in the second half of the fifteenth century was the heritage of the "Italian" Hundred Years' War of 1350–1454, which remains largely underestimated compared to the contemporary, more famous, Hundred Years' War between France and England (1337–1453). On the one hand, this period saw the flourishing of the financial system led by the Italian bankers from the urban centers of Florence, Siena, and Genoa, who were skilled to create profit by handling the Church's money flows across Europe through pilgrimages and votive offers (Arrighi 1999, 94). Such a central role in the financialization of the premodern European world economy corresponded to a decay in production and trade, with the impoverishment and the social and political unrest that followed (Arrighi 1999, 99–105):

> When at the end of the fifteenth century the European world-economy entered a new phase of expansion under the impact of the so-called Great Discoveries—the opening up of a direct trade link between Europe and the East Indies, and of the conquest and plunder of the Americas—the capitalist classes of Venice, Florence, and Milan played no active role in the promotion and organization of the expansion. By then, their surplus capital had been fully absorbed by the

> process of statemaking and had thereby lost much of its previous flexibility. Worse still, their conspicuous success in the accumulation of wealth and power induced the surrounding territorialist organizations to follow in their path of development but on a much larger scale. As these "modernized" territorialist organizations sought to divert trade from the city-states to their own domains, or to conquer the city-states themselves, the latter were forced to divert an increasing proportion of their resources to protect themselves. (Arrighi 1999, 110–11)

The meaning of the written codification of the Italian language cannot coincide with Mignolo's interpretation of the Castilian. The first grammar of vernacular in Italy—namely, the *Regole grammaticali della volgar lingua*—was produced by Giovanni Francesco Fortunio in 1516, a few years after Nebrija's, in Trieste, near the northeastern corner of the peninsula, which at the time was part of the Austro-Hungarian Empire. This grammar was part and parcel of a more general attempt to emancipate learned elites from the German language that was the official language of the empire, as well as from the omnipresent rule of Latin, which, since it remained the official language of the Church, was also the language of the powerful Papal State in central Italy (Aquilecchia 1993; De Blasi 2008).

Mignolo considers the Renaissance through the lens of the politics of language in the colonies. From this angle the Renaissance in Italy and the Spanish Renaissance are located on two divergent paths. The differences were substantial. Mignolo evidences the role that language, writing, and books had in producing the colonial hierarchy of humans that provided the coordinate of the debate about the possibility to evangelize the Amerindian social groups. The way the diatribe between the Dominican Bartolomé de Las Casas and Juan Ginés de Sepúlveda about the ultimate universal human nature of the colonized peoples in Africa and the Americas (the *pureza de sangre* debate) was framed in the terms that Aquinas had elaborated in the thirteenth century (Pagden 1982). For Mignolo (1995, 129),

> it should come as no surprise that Spanish men of letters appointed themselves to write down the history that Amerindians could not properly write because of their lack of letters. This belief was so long-lived that even Bartolomé de las Casas, who fought all his life against the belief of his compatriots and men of letters that Amerindians lacked intelligence and humanity, had no choice but to admit that they belonged to the class of barbarians identified with the illiterates: "The second class of barbarians are those who lack a literary language [*qui literali semone arent*] which corresponds to their maternal idiomatic language, as is Latin to us, and thus know how to express what they think."

Mignolo thinks that the Renaissance inherited the thirteenth-century doctrinal debate on Aristotelianism within the Christian Church and whose outcome had been the racialization of anthropological difference through the linguistic difference among those who could write and those who could not (see chapter 1). And he is right on this point. What is not analogous, in the early modern period, is that the Spanish empire was not in the fragile position the Christian Church had been in two centuries before. This condition of rising power allowed for a more strategic flexibility in the cultural politics of proselytism. While Mignolo registers this flexibility when he describes the turn to Amerindian languages in the Spanish politics of language, he simultaneously fails to recognize that the same politics was deployed in the southern Mediterranean periphery of the empire. When the Spanish empire grew in the second half of the sixteenth century, the monastic order of the Jesuits, established anew in 1531, changed its linguistic policy for evangelization. The Jesuits decided to replace Latin and Spanish with local languages in order to win the hearts and minds of the "savage" who spoke a great variety of alien idioms. They made efforts to learn the languages of the "primitives." Among the "primitive" cultures and peoples of the expanding empire, since 1561, in their letters and official reports, the Jesuit missionaries moving back from the Antilles and Peru to Southern Italy described those remote regions with the phrase *Las Indias de por acá* (Huamanchumo de la Cuba 2021), that is, "the Indies of this side (of the world)." Within the global network of epistles, letters, and reports that the Jesuit missionaries, clerics, and officers rapidly built across the regions of the Spanish and Portuguese colonial empires, the word *Indipetae* (from the Latin *petere*, to ask for), designed a singular figure (Prosperi 1996). The *Indipetae* was a Jesuit who aimed at obtaining from his superiors the chance to go to evangelize the Indies, which stands as a general linguistic reference for the colonies. The common linguistic and rhetorical structure to apply referred to *las Indias de por acà* or *las Indias interiores* (the "internal Indies"). It assumed a shared formal style that articulated the catechetical vocation in terms of saving the souls of the peoples living in those backward areas of southern Europe, where superstition and ignorance still dominated. From these documents and primary sources, there emerges also that among the *Indipetae* who were selected and then sent around the world where the Jesuits had their outposts, many were disappointed if their destination was Southern Italy. They considered this destination much less prestigious than the Far East, even because it was well known that the selection of candidates obeyed to the criteria according to which only the excellent ones could aspire to be sent in Japan or China, while the less privileged were doomed to the ignorant plebe of *las Indias de por acà* (Prosperi 2016).

At the end of the sixteenth century, the association between the western exterior and the southern interior periphery of the Spanish colonial empire was normalized, and the expression *Indias italianas* (Italian Indies) became synonymous with Southern Italy (Ricci 2012). The Jesuit missionaries returning from the Americas extended the meaning of the concept of *Indios*. As Aníbal Quijano (2000) remarks, the concept of *Indios* was the pillar of the construction of the racial global system of coloniality, which included the social groups that used to inhabit the vast areas outside the few urban centers of the Mediterranean southern periphery of the Spanish empire since the sixteenth century. By thinking from fifteenth- and sixteenth-century Italy, the emphasis moves away from the darker side of the Renaissance in terms of the racialization of difference, toward the relevance of the Renaissance as a mainly cultural phenomenon whose epistemological outreaches beg to be addressed.

The most clamorous of these outreaches consisted in the life and thought of Giordano Bruno. Bruno was born in the countryside around Naples, but he left Naples and then Italy when he was in his twenties. He radically challenged the durable synthesis between anthropocentrism, ethnocentrism, and cosmocentrism that Western hegemonic thought had produced during its long-term confrontation with non-Christian and non-European social groups and their epistemics since the thirteenth century. This was possible, in the first place, because of the fact that in the context of knowledge production where he was educated, the organizational need of managing anthropological difference was not an issue for learned strata in the political entities that formed the mosaic of the Italian scenario at the time. In fact, the Italian language, which coexisted with Latin and gained relevance throughout the fifteenth and sixteenth centuries in expert knowledge production, was not the colonizers' language. Yes, it would become the colonizers' language in Libya and northeastern Africa, to be sure. Yet this happened only at the turn of the nineteenth century with the unification of the state and the process of nation building where the colonial construction of Southern Italy and its inhabitants played a central role before and after the fascist regime (Lombardi-Diop and Romeo 2012).

A consistent part of Renaissance thinkers worked for their lords in Italian city-states like Tuscany, while others were under the rule of the Spanish or Austro-Hungarian empires and others still under the papal secular power. Others, like the Greek intellectuals, were migrants coming to Italy following the fall of Constantinople (Binzel, Link, and Ramachandran, 2023). Yet others were displaced itinerants for political, economic, or religious reasons. Elisabeth Blum (2005: 171) paints this itinerant social group in her vibrant fresco:

> They are anti-Petrarchist, anti-Aristotelian, anti-theologians. They are Pythagoreans, academics, epicureans, skeptics, magicians, or else philosophers of nature, atomists and materialists; they are moralists, or else libertines or pornographers, *polygraphi* [who lived by publishing any sort of marketable

> gender], plagiarians, religious and political dissidents; they are pacifists and preachers of tolerance, and yet intolerant know-it-alls, satirists, slanderers, and troublemakers; they are tongue-in-cheek hypocrites, clandestine Luterans or Erasmian Nicodemites, possibly even antitrinitarians or neo-pagans, animists or atheists, but seldom openly self-declared heretics, so they seem to be under-cover-men with a hidden agenda. But then they are loquacious braggarts, graphomaniac publicists, self-advertising ego-maniacs who make excessive use of modern mass-communications (i.e., they will take roots at a printer's press if they are not printers themselves); they are freethinking independent intellectuals instead of conformist university-teachers, and therefore try to survive on their own wits; or, rather, unscrupulous or intellectual prostitutes, always on the lookout for some Maecenatic noblemen to sell themselves to, body and soul. They stick together in teams, they form a network, maybe a secret society. No, the opposite is true, they are rivals, deadly and unrestrained foes, slandering and denouncing each other in the strongest of terms. They tend to get in difficulties with ecclesiastical authorities, be it Catholic or Protestant ones, and there is more than one runaway monk among them.

The young Giordano Bruno was one of these apostate monks. Like many talented kids who did not belong to aristocratic families, he entered the Dominican order when he was sixteen to have the opportunity for an education. In Naples, he accessed the same monastery where Aquinas had been educated. When he was twenty-four, he moved away from Naples, then from Italy, to Genève, Lyon, and then Toulouse. Everywhere he engaged in public debates, a habit thanks to which he still stands out in the history of ideas because he proved able to earn excommunications from all of the three Christian confessions of the time: Catholic, Lutheran, and Calvinist. Due to the climate of religious war, he was appointed as special (read: "precarious") lecturer in philosophy at the Sorbonne upon reaching Paris in 1582. He refused to become an ordinary lecturer since this would have obliged him to attend Mass. He accordingly settled for a single course of thirty lessons on Aristotle (Spampanato 1921). He took the occasion to teach Aristotle's doctrine of God's attributes, rethinking the topics that had fallen under Tempiér's condemnation in 1277. Thereafter, in 1584 he was in London, where he decided to write in *volgare*, not in Latin. At the Elizabethan court and in the intellectual circles in England, Italian was currently spoken and read, and this could have been a further motivation to adopt vulgar language instead of Latin (Aquilecchia 1993a [1953]), although the main declared reason was to experiment with a major linguistic freedom that could fit his rampant desire to elaborate a new form of knowledge against the limitations that the dominant paradigm imposed (Blum 2005).

Once in contact with the intellectual circles in London and Oxford, he published five works, in the typical dramatized forms that Renaissance intellectuals preferred for argumentation: dialogues (Canone and Spruit 2007). In these dialogues the colonization of the Americas finds its distinctive place. Bruno harshly condemned the violence and brutalities that Spanish colonizers were perpetrating in the *West Indies*. Shocking news was arriving to Europe through the tales of travelers (Binotti 1992; Cro 1992). After fifteen years in the Americas, an Italian adventurer and explorer from Milan, Gerolamo Benzoni, had published in three volumes the *Historia del Mondo Nuovo*, in which he violently attacked the methods of the conquistadores and the slave trade from Africa. The 1572 second edition of his book rapidly circulated in Italy, its success being also due to mounting anti-Spanish sentiment against the historiographers of the empire who claimed Columbus was Spanish (Aquilecchia 1993b [1955]). This sentiment existed even within political and intellectual Elizabethan circles, but for totally different reasons: the mounting imperialist competition with Spain that England was launching to become the hegemonic power in the Atlantic Sea (Arrighi 1994).

While Bruno was in Paris, Montaigne's chapter *Les cannibales* in his *Essays* stimulated great debates in France. A few years later, the manuscript containing the polemic attack against colonialism that Montaigne entrusted to the English translation of John Florio ended up in Bruno's hands even before it was published, thanks to their friendship. Differently from Montaigne, though, Bruno did not stick to the myth of the good savage (Ciliberto 1999). He did not project the mythical Golden Age into the savage colonial space. Fulvio Papi (2006 [1968]), Jordi Bayod (2004) and Rachel Ashcroft (2017) agree on this point. In *Spaccio della Bestia trionfante*, Bruno directly engages with Montaigne's essay. For Bruno the savages are not better than other social groups because they are so pure and primitive that they have no vices as the colonizers, since the absence of vice does not automatically imply the presence of virtues. For him they are not pure because they have their own history, as the colonizers have theirs. They are not happy because naturally idle as if they lived in Eden; rather, they are ingenious in accordance with the environment they inhabit (MacPhail 2014). What is specifically human is the tension to find ways to cope with natural needs. In this respect, humans are not different from any other animal, plant, or spirit. To the extent that this tension does not negate the principle of *philautia*—that is, the tension toward the preservation of one's own life in accordance with a knowledge of its natural origin inscribed in the differentiated multiplicity that the generative process of matter-life accords the manifold instantiations of the unity of the cosmos—any human form of social organization is *civile* (Papi 2006 [1968], 315). Bruno's anthropology is inextricably a matter of knowledge production and natural philosophy. He sees the world as a polycentric mosaic of geohistorical locations where different peoples produce knowledge according to their own needs thanks to their own *genius loci,* within their own linguistic structures.

In one of the opening passages of *The Ash Wednesday Supper* (retranslated by Ilary Gatti), Bruno (2018, 33) overlaps Columbus with Tiphys, the first helmsman of the Argonauts. And he accuses,

> Tiphys and his like discovered how to disturb the peace of others, how to violate the local genius of a place, how to confuse those things which nature had kept apart, how to duplicate one's faults through commerce, how to add new vices to old and propagate new follies by means of violence, how to introduce unheard-of forms of madness where before they were unknown. Finally they demonstrated that wisdom lay in strength, and introduced the arts of tyranny and murder, for which they developed ever more refined instruments and techniques. The time will come when the natives of those places, having learnt their lesson only too well, will discover in the inevitable course of events how to repay us in the same coin, perhaps even improving on the wickedness they were taught.

The content of this frontal attack conveys a critique against the universalistic pretentions of the Spanish colonizers and against their theological framework according to which colonization would draw legitimacy from a specific biblical trope: the instauration of the City of God on Earth (Granada 1990). Bruno (2018, 35) does not distinguish the violence of the system of knowledge that legitimates colonization from the materiality of colonization and its anthropological concreteness: "These, with impostures of all kinds, have filled the whole world with countless follies and bestial vices disguised as virtue, piety, and discipline, dimming that light which made the souls of our ancient fathers heroic and divine, while welcoming and preferring the obscure shadows of sophists and fools." Elisabetta Tarantino (2002, 220) remarks on the biographical dimension of this critique: Bruno's intent is to attack colonizers, who, "for obvious historical reasons, not least linked to Bruno's own Neapolitan provenance, would be readily identified with Spain."[7]

For Bruno, the anthropology of separation between continents is a matter of knowledge production, since it implies that different geohistorical locations are equally legitimate to produce systems of knowledge responding to their needs, articulated in their logic, expressed in their own language (Aquilecchia 1993a [1955]; Ciliberto 2005; Ricci 1990). The naturalization of man corresponds to the end of the identification between either humanity and its eternity in God as a transcendent being or humanity and its mortality in matter. Since *anima mundi* is coextensively both the possibility of knowledge and knowledge itself, the relation between the object and the subject of knowledge is not articulated along a hierarchy of being, but rather in resonance with the infinite possibilities that the unity of *anima mundi* is instantiated in the multiplicity of the forms in the universe. Difference exists between the human and nonhuman as an instantiation of the multiplicity among the infinite multiplicity of all the other forms in the cosmos. The same generative principle produces difference among human groups that are intrinsically created by the forms of knowledge human societies elaborate, since what defines the specific quality of living instantiations in the form of anthropological multiplicity is the ability to appropriate the object of knowledge that each of these specific instantiations defines as adequate in their own terms (Papi 2006 [1968], 157). Therefore, the problem of the "New World" transforms into the worldly vitalization of the possibility to produce knowledge both about the multiplicity and about the unity, where multiplicity is finite, unity is infinite, and the possibility of knowledge is articulated in anthropological, linguistic, and ecological terms.

Colonization, on the contrary, does not simply merge these locations but allows the knowledges of the colonizers to dominate over all the others through violence (Granada 1990).[8] This does not mean that Bruno would be an adherent to the decolonization of knowledge research program *ante litteram* or that his view on the different lineages of humans would not resonate with nineteenth-century theories of scientific racism. Such a presumption would be anachronistic. Yet his view belongs in a different horizon of sense, both anthropologically and geographically, as well as in his philosophy of nature. In a later work written in Latin during the same period while he was in London, published in 1591 in Frankfurt with the title *De immenso et innumerabilibus, seu de universo et mundis*, Bruno (1980 [1591], 783) exposes his geoanthropological cartography of the world:

> Human species are multicolored: the black progeny of Ethiopians, the one which generates the red America, the one that use to leave underwater, hidden in the caves of Neptune, the pygmies who pass their lives closed beneath the surface, citizens of the veins of Earth as guardians of the mines, and the Giants, portents of the Austral, they all do not come from common origins and do not descend from the generative forces of a unique ancestor of all the humans.

This anthropological vision belonged in a wider critique against the Judaic-Christian-Protestant creationist theology according to which all of humanity descended from Adam. Since late antiquity, there existed a so-called pre-Adamite gnoseological current. The pre-Adamites belonged to heterodox rabbinic currents. For them, Ennoc and Leviathan preexisted Adam. This heterodoxy, which had resurfaced in the thirteenth century, was a common trait of Sabei, Nabatei, and pre-Islamic Arabic doctrines (Papi 2006 [1968], 120–23). And it was present in early Islam and in several Sufist doctrines, too (El-Zein 2009). Pre-Adamite anthropogenesis was antihegemonic to the extent that it negated the monogenesis of humanity, which, when the Americas erupted in the geographical and anthropological imagination of the European Renaissance thinkers, led many of them to imagine that the *Indios* descended from groups that had reached the Americas from Eurasia in very ancient times (Papi 2006 [1968],178–81). As a logical consequence, for Giordano Bruno the very notion of a "New World" was non-sensical from a onto-historical point of view.

More importantly, this view was irreconcilable with the biblical dogma because it endorsed an alternative naturalistic logic of historical causation. On the one hand, there were those who believed both in the moral dogmas and the philosophy of nature of the Scriptures. On the other hand, there were those like Bruno, who separated the moral value of the Scriptures from the irrationalities and nonsense that they contained when they tried to explain natural phenomena. Bruno adhered to the second view: the doctrine of the double truth. This makes Bruno a direct interpreter of Averroes and his legacy in the Renaissance, reading Averroes within the coordinates of the Arabic Scholasticism of premodern times with much greater awareness than the partial and misplaced interpretations of that debate by Latin Christian interpreters since the period of the condemnations of Aristotle. Accurate philological inquiries have demonstrated that Bruno read Averroes directly rather than the "northern Italy Latin averroists" (Papi 2006 [1968], 264–176), and his knowledge of Averroes was therefore necessarily limited to the only two of his numerous works that were available in Latin since the thirteenth century: namely, the *Comments on Aristotle's De Anima* and the *Destructio destructionum* (Campanini 2006):

> In order to find a real advocate of the averroistic doctrine . . . we need to leave Christian averroism behind us, as it was then overwhelmed by orthodox aristotelianism, and reach Giordano Bruno. Among all the doctrines, this one (*the doctrine of the relation between faith and reason)* should have appeared to his tormented soul really worth surviving the dissolution of averroist aristotelianism [heterodox aristotelianism]. (Nardi [1965] in Papi 2006 [1968], 273; my translation)

The doctrine of the double truth, according to which religion served the purpose of mass manipulation while true knowledge could be accessible by any human as such endowed with the potential of learning, remained particularly undigested to Christian authority. It remained as a hidden track that barely resurfaced in official documents under the name of Averroism, even though it was clearly and diffusely present in the content of the accusations. This is because even to name Averroism was immediately problematic. As seen in chapter 1, after Aquinas's refutation of the part of his own work that had been censored, his doctrine, now purged of Eastern influences, had become the official doctrine of the Church: namely, Thomism. The method of Thomism was deduction, and this method was in use also in Inquisition trials. When applied to ideas, it worked by demonstrating step by step that given some premise that raised doubts about their orthodoxy, the inquisitors were able to logically deduce from them that the ideas under severe scrutiny were heretical, even though not declared as such. Easily imaginable, the formal rigor accorded to deductive logic offered a large space of maneuver in the realm of argumentative justifications for political decisions. In fact, this logic was the only operational logic that the Inquisition used against individuals and against books that were included in the *Index Librorum Prohibitorium*. This explains why the simple suspicion of Averroism could be easily transmuted into an accusation of heresy. And the fact that even the word Averroism or the name Averroes had been taboo since the thirteenth century condemnation explains the extreme attention Bruno and his Inquisition counterpart adopted when handling such dangerous arguments (Baldini and Spruit, 2009).

Bruno stands on the naturalist side of the diatribe. He endorses an animist and immanentist vision of the cosmos. The generative principle of the cosmos does not correspond to what in modern Western thought would be Nature, but is rather *matter-life*. Matter-life is a concept that brings together matter as inert substratum and life as the vital energy of the universe. But these two principles are one and the same, and its generative power is infinite. The eternal and interrupted transformation of matter-life generates infinite instances. Man is an instantiation of matter-life on par with all other beings, vegetables, minerals, animals, demons, winds, or spirits. In a dialogue Bruno published while in London in 1585, *The Cabal of Pegasus* (Bruno [1585] 2002, 56), the character Onorio maintains,

> That of the human is the same in specific and generic essence as that of flies, sea oysters, and plants, and of anything whatsoever that one finds animated or having a soul, as no body lacks a more or less lively communication of spirit within itself. Now such spirit, according to fate or providence, decree or fortune, links up now with one species of body, now with another; and by reason of the diversity of constitutions and limbs, it comes to have diverse degrees and capabilities of mind and functions. Therefore, that spirit or soul that was in the spider—and there has its industry and the claws and limbs in like number, quantity, and form—the same connected to human generation acquires other intelligence, other implements, attitudes and skills.

If, analogously to animals, plants, or minerals, humans are produced by matter-life, then different material configurations of the instantiation called *man*, in different parts of the world, produce equally human but ethnically different lineages. If man is a by-product of matter-life that extends throughout the entire cosmos and functions according to natural forces in different parts of the world, the biblical narrative of creation collapses together with the presumed historical relevance of biblical chronology. What is common to all men is *anima*, which in English would translate as *soul*, while in Italian it preserves the same etymological root of *animal*. For Bruno everything is an animal because it is endowed with living energy: plants, planets, stones, demons, the entire universe is an animal. They all belong to a single *anima mundi* (soul of the universe). In order to remark the positive connotation of his usage of the attributive form *animal*, he opposes it to *bestial*, *beast*, *or beastlike* as pejorative semantic forms for colonial, religious, or single-individual brutality. Therefore, the infinite generative power of matter-life renders inconceivable the centrality and superiority of man, thereby rendering inconceivable both anthropocentrism and its modern philosophical foundation: that is, the metaphysical unity of the transcendental subject, be it the Kantian 'I,' Descartes's *ego cogito*, or what Dussel sees as its corrolary, *ego conquero*.

For Bruno, the colonization of the Americas assumes a general relevance. In *De Immenso*, he explicitly accuses even the British of suffering from the same colonizers' illness as the Spaniards (Bruno, cited in Ciliberto 2005, 272). Spanish colonialism is a synecdoche for colonialism as such, since all the European colonizers belong to the same continent, living the same decadence and forgetting the relevance of matter-life. Granada (1990) notes how Bruno appears irritated by the fact that the overall historical and moral judgment about the positive and progressive aspects of colonization is possible exclusively because of the inversion of the system of values that presides over knowledge production. It is a matter of the dominant paradigms of knowledge in use. The topic of the world turned upside down thus brings together Bruno with Erasmus from Rotterdam (D'Ascia 2002).[9] Yet, while Erasmus imputes the inversions of value to a reaction against the effects of prolonged war in Europe, Bruno explicitly blames colonialism and religious war as two historical sides of the same coin. He "signals that the concrete characteristics of colonization are 'by-products' of a specific moral, political and religious configuration of European society; 'by-products' whose negativities are hidden beneath the ideological cover that orthodox Aristotelianism and Christianity provide" (Granada 1990, 14). This negative configuration lies in the Europeans' inability to come to terms with multiplex knowledges that do not conform to the dominant ideology.

This is why Bruno concludes the aforementioned passage of his Italian dialogue prefiguring the social logic of anticolonial struggles. For someone who had prefigured the infinite universe with innumerable worlds inhabited by unknown forms of life, it would not have been absolutely impossible to trust the histories of the violent domination the humans of his own ethnic group could have been responsible for once overseas. He aligns with the social logic of anticolonial reaction by opposing this subverted, violent, oppressive, universalizing colonial system of knowledge from his own situated locus of enunciation: a migrant philosopher from the periphery of the expanding Spanish colonial empire. In the vast polemical space of his thought, anticolonial reaction is the only reference to social struggle, given his absolute disinterest in any rural or urban unrest, which were quiescent in the period between the peasant revolts in central Europe (1524–1525) and those in Southern Italy (1599). Bruno arrives at blaming the globalization of markets because the intensification of commerce between continents, he maintains, doubles preexisting vices. Yet, as Ricci (1990, 276–78) observes, he affirms that the discovery of previously unknown lands inhabited by other humans would not be negative *in se*, if Europe would be ready to conceive such an encounter outside the logic of depredation, exploitation, domination, and destruction because it lacks a different, new, and more adequate system of knowledge. When such a system of knowledge would be accepted and deployed, cross-cultural exchange and ethnic relations across the global space that the new cartography of the continents designs would respond to a different ethics. This is why, a few lines after the attack against the Tiphys, Bruno announces his research program of cosmological, epistemological, anthropological, and political liberation. Such a program conveys a diachronic and a synchronic sense of crisis that had invested Europe and, through colonialism, brutally interfered with the historical development of the rest of the world. Diachronically, it consists in the maturation of the unprecedented synthesis between ancient, pagan, hermetic, Eastern, Arabic, and Indian cosmologies and epistemologies of the Renaissance in Italy, combined with the new and still unaccepted horizons disclosed by Copernicanism, as I shall argue. Synchronically, it consists in the sudden, unexpected increase in acuteness of the sense of decadence due to the presence of colonialism, the Reformation and the Counter-Reformation in his intellectual *problematique*.

MATTERS OF TIMESPACE: THE SEMANTIC INVERSION OF THE "MODERN"

Bruno represents the apical expression of the inquietudes agitating Renaissance Italy, both for those who focus on the relevance of hermetism and magic (Couliano 1987; Bassi, Scapparone, and Tirinnanzi 2000; Yates 1964) or those who focus on natural philosophy and science (Aquilecchia 1993b; Ciliberto 2022; Gatti 2002; Spruit 1988). He is also relevant to those who, like the Russian Christian philosopher Lev Karsavin (2014), see Bruno as epitomizing what they consider the hubris of the entire Renaissance that conflated the empirical naturalistic infiniteness of the universe with the divine transcendental infiniteness of God. Yet Bruno's thought on colonization was mostly unknown to his contemporaries, and even today it remains largely excluded from scholarship on the relation between the Renaissance in Italy and the changing horizon resulting from what, in the European perspective, was the "discovery" of the Americas (Romeo 1953).

Michele Ciliberto (2005) explains the blanket of silence that fell on this part of Bruno's thinking after his stake with his radicalism and uniqueness about the issue of the slaughter of the *Indios*. Mignolo (1992) reconstructs how the Spaniards, in Mesoamerica since the early decades of the sixteenth century, burned the *amoxtlii* and *vuh*, which were illustrated texts on water plant paper in Maya and Nahuatl languages, because these texts were so different from the book as a material object since they were "written by the devil." In *De Immenso*, Bruno hypothesizes that the written codes in native languages that the *Indios* had were even more ancient than the ones Mediterranean civilizations had produced during antiquity. It is evident that his position on colonization was unique among his contemporaries and irreconcilable with the dominant ideology. Nonetheless, Bruno was a prominent figure in Europe. His writings were widely diffused, read, and commented on by his contemporaries, at least in intellectual circles among philosophers, astronomers, and theologians. His prominence increased even more after his death, however hidden in secret collections or concealed under modified titles (Ciliberto 1997).

After eight years of trial, prison, and torture, Bruno's public execution at the stake in Campo de' Fiori, in the center of Rome, was the first public event in the early Jubilee of 1600, exactly three hundred years after the first jubilee (Firpo 1949). This might at first look paradoxical, since in Christianity the jubilee is the year of universal pardon. It is not, in fact, because Bruno's execution is exemplary of the historical relevance of the challenge his program and writings had launched against authority in many respects. His public execution connects with a variety of antihegemonic knowledges under the perspective of the relation they entail with the repressive power of the existing epistemological authority: the Holy Inquisition. Seen from this perspective, Bruno sits on the metaphorical inquisition dock of history in the company of witches, heretics, shamans, slaves, rebels, servants, medicine men, infidels, Moors, vagabonds, idolaters, displaced workers, psychiatric patients, atheists, scientists, crypto-Jews, Gypsies, and many other individuals, from Lima to Goa (Bethencourt 2009). In the globalizing space of the Spanish and Portuguese colonialism, they formed, in one way or another, a heterogeneous and scattered epistemic community. This commonality emerges as a subaltern space facing the dominant discursive ideology (Guha 1997). This epistemic community existed as a common space only against dominant discourse, which repressed and persecuted those knowledge producers that, because of what they thought, professed, taught, or simply because of the way they lived, were killed either because of their biographical path or because they represented uncanny sites of enunciation. These sites of enunciation were located too far beyond the necropolitical border traced by the dominant ideology. This ideology consisted in the anthropological-theological-epistemological synthesis that aspired to become the geoculture of the ascending ruling strata in the period of world history when the fragile Latin Christian identity of the thirteenth century had transmuted into the European colonial program of global expansion that Portugal and Spain launched from the periphery of a world-system whose global center was China (Frank and Gills 1990; Hobson 2012; Pomeranz 2000; Wong 2011).

The construction of this scattered epistemic space of critical human knowledge in early modern times is at odds with several mental images and historiographic mantras that the social sciences uncritically reproduce, even in those regions of their analytical spectrum that the anti-Western-centric critique to modern hegemonic knowledge inhabits. The decolonization of knowledge research program reaffirms in a more sophisticated way the continuist thesis that the Enlightenment thinkers elaborated to create a direct connection between modern Western rationality, the experimental method of modern science, the Renaissance as the revolt against the dark Middle Ages, and the Greek origins of Europe. Martin Bernal (1987) and Cecil Blake (2009) described this invention with the metaphor of the *temporal tunnel* connecting the self-biography of the West and its invented white classical origins. In his *Discours préliminaire* to the *Encyclopédie*, published in 1751, Jean le Rond d'Alambert crystallized this view and gave it a worldly significance. His genealogy of modern rationality is a linear sequence of epistemological shifts that oriented humanity toward unprecedented possibilities of progress. Against d'Alambert, Jean-Jacques Rousseau denounced that the Renaissance had been fatal to morality and ethics: it had corrupted the purity of human society and inserted the decadence of virtue into the living tissue of European culture. Yet, even if Rousseau condemned what d'Alambert exalted, they agreed on the same narrative. In his 1753 *Discourse on the Sciences and Arts*, in the wake of *La querelle des Anciens et des Modernes* even though half a century later, Rousseau admitted that

> Europe had fallen back into the barbarity of the first ages. People from this part of world, so enlightened today, lived a few centuries ago in a state worse than ignorance. Some sort of learned jargon much more despicable than ignorance had usurped the name of nowledge and set up an almost invincible obstacle in the way of its return. A revolution was necessary to bring men back to common sense, and it finally came from a quarter where one would least

> expect it. It was the stupid Muslim, the eternal blight on learning, who brought about its rebirth among us. (Rousseau 1992 [1753], 57)

Eventually, in 1773, from his anti-Enlightenment and pre-Romantic perspective, Johann Gottfried von Herder conceded that the Renaissance performed the revolutionary role that the two French thinkers recalled, yet condemned the progressive value of the transformations it generated and wished for the return to the superstition, devotion, ignorance, and obscurity of the Middle Ages. In his glosses to David Hume, William Robertson, and other thinkers of the Scottish Enlightenment, Herder blamed those who championed this novel rationality. Nonetheless, he agreed on the same genealogy, which the late-eighteenth- and nineteenth-century positivists would inscribe in the genetic code of the western social sciences.

Mignolo (2012, vii) reaffirms this view that remains unchallenged along his intellectual path:

> The "Western code" serves not all humanity, but only a small portion of it that benefits from the belief that in terms of epistemology there is only one game in town. The "code" has been preserved in the security box since the Renaissance. Diverse knowledge has been generated from that secret code in six European modern or imperial languages: Italian, Spanish, Portuguese, French, German, and English. One may discern a hierarchy within modern European languages when it comes to epistemology. Certainly, theology was grounded in Latin and translated to vernaculars, while romance languages enjoyed a certain respectability in terms of knowledge making. However, after the Enlightenment, French was the romance language that led the second modernity, while German, and more recently English, have come to be the language that preserves and hides the code.

Mignolo oversimplifies what he names the code, while the "box" he depicts as severed and locked is actually a Pandora's box whose seal is the totalizing understanding of modernity that the decolonial construction of the Renaissance corroborates. During the last fifty years, the inadequacy of this master-narrative emerged from specialistic historiographical inquiry in the wake of Garin's perspective. Paraphrasing Garin (2000), there obviously exist lines of continuity between the Renaissance and the "modern world" but, in the last instance, they are profoundly different intuitions about life, nature, and reality. From this vantage point, to continue presenting the Renaissance in terms of the genesis of the modern world is not useful to research, nor is it useful to think of "modernity" as if it were entirely resolved by the great thinkers of the "Scientific Revolution." The thinkers of the Renaissance should be freed from the existing hegemonic and Eurocentric philosophy of history that forces their ideas within the frame of modernity (Ciliberto 2021,

11). In this sense, modernity is an epistemological ritual that the social sciences constantly reinterpret in order to constrain the horizons of global studies within the very boundaries that should undergo the process of unthinking in order to prevent post-Western approaches from revoking the status of unquestionability that modernity as a frame preserves, even in its "modernity/coloniality" version (Ascione 2016).

Unthinking modernity/coloniality thus leads to a new critical journey into what historiographical reason had for a long time considered the essence of the Renaissance: the social consciousness of rebirth. Yet, Garin (2000) remarks, this was not actually a self-consciousness of what was ongoing. Rather, in the beginning, the Renaissance was a research and cultural program. The core of this research program was the return to ancient knowledge, true—a rediscovery. Yet this ancient wisdom that Western historiography calls classic Greek or Latin was mainly pagan and Eastern, where—as we have seen—"pagan" was a metacategory that gathered complex systems of knowledge whose construction was in itself a hybrid form connecting different parts of the world system in late antiquity and premodern times. The core idea of rebirth endorsed a notion of temporality that becomes counterintuitive even in relation to the temporality endorsed by the framework of modernity/coloniality. This is so in three respects: first, the construction of the "Middle Ages"; second, the definition of "modern"; and third, the specific sense of cyclical time.

Anti-Eurocentric critics converge with their Eurocentric foes when they assert that the Renaissance claimed anew its prerogatives as a way out of the dark age of medieval times (Blaut 2000; Subrahmanyam 1997, 2005, 2022). This claim would mark the onset of the modern/colonial era by establishing coextensively the legitimacy of the modern age and the Middle Ages (Blumenberg 1983; Cole and Smith 2012). From a more specialistic position, in the early aftermath of World War II, the historian Herbert Weisinger lamented how it had become commonsensical that the Renaissance as a new era in world history originated after centuries of medieval darkness (Weisinger 1945). Garin explains in detail how critique of their own time, which they accused of being obscurantist and barbarian, was already a central topic during the fourteenth century among those thinkers who contested the dominant cultural climate of intellectual repression and geocultural regressive fear of cross-cultural exchange. They denounced the closures, the reactionary tendencies, and the violence of intellectual censorship that the reaction to the circulation of non-Western knowledges had produced since the last quarter of the thirteenth century, in a period when the Plague had become epidemic, decimating European populations since its first appearance in 1347–1348 and during its following cyclical recrudescence (Aberth 2020).

According to Garin (2000, 15), this sense of rejection for the contemporary dominant culture and political situation matured throughout the fifteenth century. It diffused and became the leitmotif of critical thinking. This sense of rejection became stronger and stronger through discursive polemical redundancy until it detached itself from the conjunctural context of its own emergence and became a quest in time for the roots of the decadence and, consequently, the source of potential regeneration. In a few decades, the time span for this rejection of contemporaneity extended from one century in Domenico Bandini (1335–1418), who wrote in 1367 the encyclopedia in Latin named the *Fons memorabilium universi* (*Source of Notable Information about the Universe*), to one millennium spanning from 412 to 1412, according to Flavio Biondo (1392–1463), the historian, archeologist, and apostolic secretary in Rome who devoted his studies to exalt ancient Rome against barbarians. To stress his apologetic vision of Rome against the entire ten-centuries-long period of time that separated him from the fall of Rome, Biondo coined the word *medioevo*: the middle age. Biondo's work started to spread in the first half of the fifteenth century, but the meaning of the word he coined underwent an important resignification during the following two centuries before acquiring the meaning that modern Western hegemonic Eurocentric thinking inherited from the Enlightenment.

It was only in 1688 that Christoph Cellarius's *Historia Medii Aevi* made accessible, first to his students of history at the University of Halle and later to learned Western European elites, the chrononym "Middle Ages." By this locution, Cellarius conceptualized a sense of historical change that, for a relevant part of the learned elite in Western Europe, had acquired prominence within various intellectual contested spaces of knowledge production and collective identity formation. Contested had become, after the Renaissance, the reliability of alchemy, hermetic tradition, natural philosophy; contested, too, had become, in the wake of the Reformation, the legitimacy of the position of the Catholic Church, both as a temporal and spiritual power, and the role of trade after mercantilism because of the expectations it raised among statesmen as a reliable knowledge in orienting political decisions toward the production of wealth. The millennium the term "Middle Ages" referred to came to be associated with a dark age, and these contestations were transformed into the reciprocally interpellating assumptions the Enlightenment coordinated into a coherent *Weltanschauung* (Davis 2006).

If the welding between the denigration of the dark middle age and the production of anthropological hierarchy of colonized peoples occurred in the context of the Spanish empire across the sixteenth and seventeenth centuries, it would be anachronistic to apply this interpretation to the fourteenth and fifteenth centuries. Not because a premodern racial system of managing anthropological difference did not exist at that time; it did exist, was current in premodern times, and was in operation during the intercultural encounter with non-European or extra-Mediterranean peoples in the early modern period (Bethencourt 2013; Heng 2019). The anachronism rather stems from the fact that the connection between the Portuguese explorations of the African shores that preceded Columbus's arrival in the Caribbean and the construction of the idea of the Middle Ages during the Renaissance in Italy does not make sense historically. They are separate. What will become the denial of coevalness of the modern/colonial hegemonic thinking that associated the time of the Middle Age with the space of colonization was extraneous to the research program of the Renaissance in Italy. The construction of the Middle Age and its negative connotation was a critical reaction to the sense of self-alienation from contemporaneity, when dominant thinking belonged to the most conservative and anticosmopolitan approaches. The contemporary times, rather than the distant past, were obscurantist. This is why the Renaissance was a program rather than a consciousness. From Lorenzo Ghiberti's *Commentarii* in 1447 to Giorgio Vasari's *Vite de'più eccellenti pittori scultori e architettori* (*Lives of the Artists*) in 1550, a line of reasoning consolidated among intellectuals, philosophers, and artists (skills and talents that most of the times coexisted within the same individual). Consolidation and diffusion imply the diversification and pluralization of ideas and perspectives to the point that, taken together, an entire cultural movement becomes self-contradictory when considered as an integrated whole. Nonetheless, a general agreement resisted in all the critical trends of the Renaissance around the idea that Christendom was responsible for the pernicious decline of ancient arts, knowledges, and civil spirit. This was because Christianity had destroyed temples and images of pagan gods, as well as prohibiting or burning precious books by all the thinkers labeled as pagans or infidels as a reaction to the diffusion of non-Christian knowledge (Nixey 2017). This consequently led to cultural decadence in the fourteenth century (Garin 2000, 17). Modern historiography has widely documented and proved this systematic politics of cultural persecution and material destruction in late antiquity, premodern, and modern times (Berkowitz 2021; Blum 1991; Murray 1999; Rohmann 2016). The Spaniards, Mignolo (1992) confirms, were coherent with this politics of knowledge in Mesoamerica, as illustrated by their stance against *amoxtlii* and *vuh*.

Dissatisfaction oriented itself toward polemical targets that were located within Christianity, not outside of it. Such dissatisfaction found expression in architecture, for instance, in terms of aesthetic and functional critique against the gothic and byzantine styles. Yet the terms of the accusation are terminologically destabilizing for the conceptual archive of the West. To the modern/colonial lens looking backward, this story would suggest that the thinkers of the Renaissance in Italy called themselves "modern." This is not the case. As it results evident at first glance in any philological analysis of major figures, such as Vasari, the "modern" was the style produced by the "barbarian" destruction of the pagan heritage. "Old" was the attribute of the byzantine style in architecture and literacy, which, however, had assured the survival of pagan knowledge but had not been able to avoid Christian orthodox doctrinal dogma mortifying its potential vitality. The distance of either the "modern" or the "old" from Nature and Truth was a measure of the decadence against which the rebirth of the "ancient" could provoke the radical shift in the production of knowledge that the Renaissance as a research program hoped for (Garin 2000, 18–20).

Thus, the "ancient," on the one hand, stands as the opposite of the "modern" and the "old," on the other hand. Both the old and the modern are associated with "barbarian," by means of a semantic inversion that shows the programmatic nature of the Renaissance as an epistemological rupture whose terms are irreducible to those of modern Western thought. The modern/traditional binary to which the historical social sciences have adhered since the nineteenth century is unable to mirror such a semantic inversion because the terms of the coordinates of the debate in the Renaissance formed a triad. The dyad tradition/modernity remains within the orthodox Scholastic-Thomistic-Englightenment-positivist logic of binarism, whose roots originate in Artistotle's logical principle found in his *De Interpretatione* (that was part of the *Organon*: namely, *Tertium non datur*, also known as "the excluded middle"). Aristotle also affirmed the principle of noncontradiction in his *Methaphysica*. According to this principle, if two propositions are reciprocally contradictory, one of the two must be false. *Methaphysica* and *De Interpretatione* were two among the few books in the *Corpus Aristotelicum* that circulated in the Latin Christian world since late antiquity, independently from the Arabic translations of the eleventh, twelfth, and thirteenth centuries. Therefore, the epistemological program of the Renaissance is intrinsically different from the image that the modern/colonial framework projects retrospectively. To the extent that the two frameworks forcedly overlap, a space of incommensurability emerges. What Bruno set as coeval geoepistemic incommensurability between continents, Garin articulates retrospectively in time between the Renaissance and modernity.

For Bruno, the historical and theoretical references of the ancient-old-modern triad offered a logical framework to configure the problem of knowledge in historical terms. For him, orthodox Aristotelianism was "old" because it was sterile and inadequate to the new image of the world after Copernicus. The Reformation, as the culmination of the Judaic-Christian-Protestant system of knowledge production, was "modern" because of its pedantic attachment to the strict literal meaning of the Scriptures, mortifying the generative power of life-matter as immanent presence of the supernatural in an animistic vision of the cosmos. What he called *renovatio mundi* (world renovation) instead was the form of knowledge that could lead to a more adequate understanding of reality according to the new vision of the world, a vision that was transformed by the discovery of both a new continent on Earth and the infinite universe. This new science would have been able to bring back nature and the nonhuman at the center of the relation between humanity and the supernatural. Here the term *science* indicates something neither reducible to the modern Western understanding of what science is—or prescriptively, should be—nor describable in terms of the notion of epistemology that from Kant onward designs the contour of the so-called demarcation problem, that is, the possibility to draw the boundaries between science and nonscience.

Given the reliance upon ancient, non-Western, non-Christian knowledges and nonanthropocentric philosophies of nature, Bruno's notion of "new" science calls for a clarification. It depends intimately on a particular sense of cyclical time, which is at the core of the Renaissance research program since its beginning. The idea of rebirth relies strictly on the life cycle, but it resembles metempsychosis more than resurrection. Resurrection is an exceptional event. Its occurrence marks the apocalypse and the end of history, therefore presupposes an ultimate teleology aiming at the end of times. Metempsychosis suggests the palingenesis of entities in different times and spaces, under multiple possible forms. Bruno defended this position even against the inquisitors when he maintained that given the immortality of the soul and its natural disembodiment after death, it was not impossible for it to take new material forms in nonhuman living beings (Firpo 1949, 80). Yet he was not interested in the soteriological outcomes of this notion of time. The problem was not salvation but the implications for knowledge that the possibility for the soul to exist perpetually entailed. Reincarnation was interesting because it was possible on a rational basis. It was equally possible on a rational basis, as per Averroes, that after leaving the body, every single soul would return to the *anima mundi*, thereby transforming into a collective intelligence. The theological implications of this Averroistic position were problematic: negating the individuality of the soul entailed that the full individual responsibility of human actions would collapse, whether for religious authority or its secularized political version. On the contrary, the eternal connection of everything with everything substantiated the animistic and naturalistic vision of the cosmos.

The difference between the Renaissance notion of cyclical time and the Christian one is not strictly hermeneutical, as it derives from the particular genealogy of the idea of cyclical time that informed Bruno's thinking through the writings of Origen of Alexandria (185–253). Origen was an early Christian theologian of the Hellenistic period, largely influenced by Hinduist and Buddhist ideas that traveled to the Mediterranean via the terrestrial route opened up by Alexander the Macedonian's expansionism to the Caucasus and

Southern Asia. Origen's heterodox views were out of the official doctrines of the Christian Church in premodern times. Yet, because patristic literature was a consistent part of the education of literates, Origen was compulsory reading. This was particularly true among those ecclesiastical orders, such as the Dominicans, who were devoted to fighting heresy and unorthodox theories and were therefore committed to studying them in order to recognize both (Tirinnanzi 2013).

In this sense, the cyclical time of the Renaissance is distinct from Friedrich Nietzsche's myth of the "eternal return," which Auguste Blanqui had anticipated while imprisoned in the fortress of Mont-Saint-Michel after the repression of the Commune in Paris in 1871. Yet it is also different from Gianbattista Vico's notion of course and recourse in history, according to which human history always undergoes the same threefold pattern of repetition. The cyclical sense of time of the Renaissance is more a morphodynamic process that brings together knowledge and society, where the resurgence of views, theories, images, and ideas informs the relevance of contents in relation to the existing configuration in the structures of power. Cycles do not design the circular repetition of different ages in a supposedly eternal wheel of time, since history does not repeat itself identically after each single cycle. Therefore, knowledge is not valid or true *in se* and *per se*, that is, outside any connection with the time of its appearance. Knowledge appears more or less valid according to the general historical conditions that provide the social and political context wherein it is received, understood, debated, contested, accepted, refused, diffused, blamed, or exalted. In order to grasp this specific sense of the relation between time, knowledge, and power, an effort is due to recode it into the ideational paradigms of the Renaissance, where words such as "society" or "politics" were not in use but the concepts they referred to fell under the notion of "public life" (Ciliberto 2005). The language of the social sciences did not exist, and even public life was coded into the more general ideational time and space coordinates that natural philosophy provided. This is why Bruno (2018, 45) entrusts his explanation of the relation between time and knowledge to Theophilus, the main character in the dramatized dialogical style that Renaissance thinkers in Italy largely preferred to the form of the essay, or *tractatus*:

> THEOPHILUS. Your Aristotle himself, as I was saying, observed that opinions in their various forms have their vicissitudes just like other things; so that to judge philosophies by their antiquity is like trying to decide which comes first, day or night. The question we should really be asking ourselves is whether it is daytime with us, and if the light of truth is above our horizon or that of the adversaries at our antipodes. Are we in the dark, or are they? And finally are we, who are beginning to revive the ancient philosophy, in the dawn or in the dusk

of a closing day? And this is really not a difficult question to answer, even if we judge only approximately the fruits of one and the other schools of thought.

Leen Spruit reads this passage against the grain of Bruno's writing in Italian and Latin, as well as against the background of the notion of cyclical time that was current among Renaissance scholars and intellectuals. He evidences how this conception does not impede the possibility of an increase in knowledge along the successions of historical cycles, since their overall property is not immutability. Cycles are coordinated by a pattern that runs across the "days" (Spruit 2006, 20–21). In fact, here the day/night cycle should be understood not as a metaphor, but rather in terms of a structuring analogy where the cycle provides a formal structure of repetition, yet the accidental forms that such repetition produces is never the same as the previous one. Humanity, plants, planets, stars, demons, spirits, ideas, theories, and concepts, as everything else in the cosmos, undergo the same structuration of time, since they are all accidents of the same generative principle. As such, they are configured, transformed, undone, and re-created by the generative force of matter-life.

It is noteworthy that Bruno aligns with a consistent tradition of pagan and hermetic thought that pictures whoever brings the light of understanding not as an author but as a messenger: either a Mercury (in the Greek pantheon), who brings knowledge from elsewhere to disclose new horizons, thereby exiting the time of obscurantism or, equivalently, a rooster, whose voice crowing at dawn is heard as soon as the night is still dark yet coming to its end. Bruno himself names this stratified understanding of the relation between knowledge and time *vicissitudine* (vicissitude). Its literal meaning conveys a sense of tragedy that makes the absolute time of the cosmos one and the same with the limited lifetime of embodied beings.

Wondering to what extent would this conception be "Western" is a theoretical pitfall, both philologically and hermeneutically: philologically, because the genealogy that connects Bruno with Origen has nothing to do with any essentializing vision of "Western" knowledge, since it is hybrid from its origin (Terracciano 2013); hermeneutically, because even recent literature in anthropology has proven this dichotomization of time between Western and non-Western conceptions to be flawed in many respects. To be sure, the state of the art on this subject tends toward rejecting this Western/non-Western dichotomization since linear and cyclical time, together with other representations of time, coexist and are not made invalid through this coexistence in both Western and non-Western systems of knowledge production (Mughal 2023).

The rejection of the essentialist dichotomization between Western and non-Western conceptions of time and the disarticulation of the continuity between the Enlightenment and the Renaissance exposes this approach to critical knowledge production in its antihegemonic potential. It resonates in many dimensions with those that contemporary post-Western approaches to global studies claim as a possible way out of the cul-de-sac of dominant, Western, hegemonic, colonial knowledge (Layug and Hobson 2022; Shahi 2021)—*inter alia*: nondualism, animism, antianthropocentrism, postsecularism, anthropological egalitarianism, the reconfiguration of the border between human and nonhuman agency, antispeciesism.

The legitimacy of the cyclical yet not immutable time of the Renaissance was based upon the general acceptance of astrological models from Arabic astronomy and mathematics. The Arabic astrological doctrine of the great conjunctions belonged to Abū Maʿshar (787–886) and his pupil Ibn al-Bāzyār. It was circulating in the Mediterranean since the twelfth century and was still dominant when Copernican heliocentrism began to circulate among the European ruling strata (Yamamoto and Burnett 2000). This doctrine of cyclical time, together with the presence of comets whose timing was puzzling because it perturbed any notion of the eternal return of the identical, provided the metatheoretical framework both for knowledge production and for forecasting the future of individuals and political organizations (Garin 1996). When the Renaissance in Italy went from being a research program during the fifteenth century to being a historiographical myth of self-representation for the learned elites in Europe at the turn of the sixteenth century, these astrological frameworks contributed to transforming the idea of cyclical time from the myth of rebirth into a field of tension for delimiting what knowledge was new and acceptable and what remained attached to the Middle Ages. This branch of astrology was called *judicial astrology*. It was very powerful for its political implications. Bruno's "new" science stood against its hegemony.

THE "INFINITE" AS THE INTRINSIC LIMIT OF CONCEPT FORMATION

What made Bruno's science "new" and marked a departure even from the most radical Renaissance thinkers was his engagement with Copernicanism. Such an engagement was both operational and theoretical. In *De Immenso*, published at Frankfurt in 1591, Bruno included an enthusiastic eulogy of Copernicus in the rhetorical form of direct invocation, half a century after Copernicus's death: "It is wonderful, Oh Copernicus, that you were able to emerge from the immense darkness of our age, when the entire light of philosophy lies extinguished, as well as the light of the other subjects which depend on it" (Bruno 1980 [1591], 563). Historians of science agree that Copernicus was so aware of the disruptive power of his findings against the dominant Ptolemaic astronomy that he had precirculated his heliocentric theory only among a very restricted number of individuals to whom he had sent redux versions of his calculations (Koyré 1957). In fact, he waited until he clearly understood his agony was coming to an end to allow his typographer in Nuremberg to print the manuscript to distribute it.[10] The first edition, in 1543, was incomplete, and so was the second, in 1566. Only in 1616 did the full version of the *De Revolutionibus Orbium Coelestium* become available (Koyré 1957). By that time, Bruno had been dead for sixteen years already. Nonetheless, he had fully grasped the importance of his work from the very first edition he had in his hands, and he became the most convinced of the Copernican revolution, in the context of European learned elites who refused, denigrated, or misunderstood that heliocentrism was going to substitute the Aristotelian-Ptolemaic astronomy, which wanted the Earth at the center of a closed universe.

The rejection of Copernicanism from the puritan scholars in Oxford who ridiculed him was a major reason for Bruno to leave London (Aquilecchia 1993c). Bruno did not limit himself to relentlessly explaining to whatever audience he had in front of him that Copernicus's calculations of the planetary orbits were correct and the conclusions that anyone could draw from them were more coherent with a rational understanding of the mechanics of the entire universe. Even though some astronomers agreed with those calculations, they simply used them as new and more accurate ephemerid tables to keep doing astrological previsions (Bucciantini and Torrini 1997). Bruno pushed Copernicanism toward new frontiers and used the demonstrations of heliocentrism to prove on a rational basis the revolutionary idea that the universe was infinite. The implications of this idea are crucial in two respects for the protocols of knowledge production and the problem of conceptualization: first, the delegitimation of spacetime ethnocentrism, and second, the interiorization of the notion of limit in the process of concept formation.

If planet Earth is not the center of the universe, if the sun is the center of our system and what appears as the sky of the fixed stars is nothing but the image of very distant lightning suns in the sidereal space, then there is no valid conception of the center as far as the infinite space in concerned. This idea of infinity is the attribute of the supreme entity of the universe. God, being coextensively will and reason, cannot produce himself in the form of a finite and spherical universe because this would imply that there exists something exterior to the universe—that is, exterior to God himself—and this exteriority might function as what presupposes God, thereby limiting his infiniteness. Moreover, infinity is not only a quality of extension; it also implies innumerability. This means that there exist countless astronomical systems analogous to ours where a star like the sun is the relative center of each of those systems, as Leucippus and Democritus thought in antiquity, or in the Hindu cosmology of Advaita, where Being and Knowledge, Atman and Brahman, coincide (Shahi and Ascione 2016). There follows that the sun is a star among innumerable others; there exist innumerable worlds in the universe with their innumerable forms of life (an object of inquiry nowadays called exobiology).

Consequently, anthropocentrism does not make sense, either in the sublunary world of planet Earth or in the universe at large. This delegitimation of the idea of the center is together spatial and temporal. The universe being infinite, it is uncreated because it is eternal. There follows that if a center in space does not exist, then a center in time does not exist. Thus, no epoch is legitimate in calling itself the center of history and becoming the measure in human history that establishes what is meaningfully before and afterward in terms of anthropological distance. The concept of an infinite universe dethroned astrology from the position of dominant framework. Constellations were only optical illusions, since the stars that formed them from the perspective of an observer on Earth are not placed on the same spherical surface in the last sky of the fixed stars, and there is therefore no possible influence of constellations and stars on psychology, or health, or politics, or fortunes.

More importantly, though, the irruption of the notion of the infinite universe posed a conceptual problem: "the infinite" is itself a concept. As a concept, the infinite is a linguistic, theoretical, and semantic construction aimed at grasping something that is out of reach compared to the human possibility of definition. But unlike "God," which immediately alludes to the metaphysical dimension of what is supernatural, "the infinite" refers to a property of spacetime in a scientific endeavor to qualify and quantify the universe as the object of astronomical knowledge. The infinite posed a metaconceptual problem of definition for conceptualization. Definition itself means delimiting something that needs to be conceived, but in this case, the reference of such a linguistic construction exceeds any possibility of limitation and transgresses any boundaries. Moreover, as we have seen, the infinite is not only extension but also innumerability. This complicates the problem, making it possible to understand the relation between the linguistic construction of the infinite and the reality it aspires to refer to exclusively in terms of incommensurability or in terms of irreconcilable disproportion between the concept, the human mind that thinks it, and what it refers to.

This problem gives a special position to the concept of infinite in concept formation. The infinite works as a concept limit itself that deforms the conceptual apparatus, since it inscribes into the genetic code of the operation of conceptualization the impossibility of normalizing something whose uncanny presence is, nonetheless, as noneliminable as it is nonnormalizable. The obtrusive presence of such deformation in the living tissue of concept formation has linguistic implications. If concept formation has to accept its limited condition of operability to the extent that it is a dimension of knowledge production that cannot aspire to fully domesticate what it aspires to grasp, then the full adherence of such reference to any semantic field or even multiple semantic fields associated with it moves asymptotically toward a shifting horizon of sense whose end draws its legitimacy only from an act of decision. Otherwise the process of conceptualization of that reference would move infinitely: *regressio ad infinitum*.

This means, first, that in the diatribe between idealism and nominalism, the latter is misplaced because there is no inextricable correspondence between words and their object. And this explains why Bruno, together with radical Renaissance thinkers, stood against the literal interpretation of the Scriptures, in the Judaic-Christian-Muslim tradition as in any world religion. Second, any strictly philological approach to knowledge production that claims to retrieve ancient wisdom in the exact translation of sapiential text prevents adequate knowledge from emerging. At the juncture between the infinite and language, the anticolonial position of Bruno connects with the politics of translation. He affirms that many grammarians superbly claim to be superior to those they call savage on the basis of their pedantry in analyzing ancient texts, while he himself esteems much more the culture and the *genius loci* expressing relevant meaning and knowledge than any rigorous devotion to erudite words (Bruno, cited in Ciliberto 2022, 251). The historical fact that the greatest interpreter of Aristotle was Averroes, who did not know the Greek language, is not to be underestimated.

To be sure, Bruno was not the only post-Copernican thinker to fall under the axe of the Holy Inquisition. The other celebrity was Galileo Galilei. But while Galileo's life was saved, Bruno's was not. The notion of the infinite universe that Bruno had been insinuating to learned European minds was somehow shocking. It frightened even some of those scientists whom the master narrative of Western modernity consecrated as the founding fathers of modern science. In 1610, ten years after Bruno's execution at the stake, Johannes Kepler, who was a young student at the University of Tübingen while Bruno was teaching, wrote to Galileo, as he regularly had since 1597. He wanted to discuss Galileo's fresh discovery of the satellites orbiting Jupiter, which Galileo had made thanks to the rudimental *perspicullum*, the first prototype of instrument for telescopic observations. In that letter, Kepler congratulated Galileo and confessed that he felt a sense of relief because the fact that these satellites orbit Jupiter proved Bruno's thesis of the infinite universe false:

> In the first place, I rejoice that I am to some extent restored to life by your work. If you had discovered any planets revolving around one of the fixed stars, there would now be waiting for me chains and a prison amid Bruno's innumerabilities, I should rather say, exile to his infinite space. Therefore, by reporting that these four planets revolve, not around one of the fixed stars, but around

> the planet Jupiter, you have for the present freed me from the great fear which gripped me as soon as I had heard about your book from my opponent's triumphal shout. (quoted in Rosen 1965, 37)[11]

This shared sense of the uncanny notion of the infinite universe also provoked violent reactions of condemnations. The Catholic polemist Kaspar Schoppe wrote to the German humanist Konrad Ritterhude:

> Today (17 February 1600) eventually Bruno has been brought to the stake. . . . So he miserably died, burned, I believe to announce in the other worlds that this is what the Romans use to treat the wicked and the blasphemous. Here it is, my dearest Rotterhausen, the way we proceed with those men, or better, against this kind of *monsters* (Schoppe, cited in Ciliberto 1997).

Since 1612, Galileo was himself accused of heresy by Cardinal Roberto Bellarminio, who was the same inquisitor who judged Bruno. Yet Galileo could abjure in 1616 and have his life saved, while Bruno had been executed, regardless of his late abjuration in 1599 (Firpo 1949). This historical bifurcation is exemplary of the Renaissance path that terminates with Bruno, while modern sciences, with Galileo, take the controversial but not impossible path of coexistence with the dominant ideology in an enduring configuration (Cohen 1994). Bruno was a Pythagoric mathematician learned in cabalism, whose mathematical toolkit reached him through the mediation of Plato and Aristotle as reinterpreted through Arabic astronomical geometry, Indian numerology, or Egyptian mathesis, in which numbers either express enumerable quantities or coextensively embody symbolic properties (Matteoli 2016). Galileo was a mathematical physicist who did not consider numbers as endowed with inner qualities so relevant as to become useful in the scientific process of unveiling the dynamics of the planetary motions. In other words, Galileo accepted the mathematization of the universe within the epistemological horizon of the quantification of observables through numbers deprived of their linguistic, and hence their philosophical and cosmological, significance. Biographies tell the story of this bifurcation. Bruno returned to Venice in 1591, after about eighteen years of roaming throughout Europe, because he desired to see if there was any concrete chance for him to obtain the prestigious cathedra of mathematics at the University of Padua that had been vacant for three years since the passing of Giuseppe Moleti in 1588. Unfortunately, after a few months, Bruno was arrested by the Inquisition based on the delation that his Venetian aristocratic host orchestrated as a personal revenge (Firpo 1949). Galileo Galilei took that position during the same year and held it for about eighteen years.

The acceptance of the concept of the infinite outside the realm of mathematical reasoning in terms of the inner limit to concept formation nonetheless delineates the nature of possible knowledge. If the threshold between the finiteness of human knowledge and the infiniteness of the universe is linguistic, this does not exclude the possibility of coping with this limitation using imagination as a theoretical tool to push human understanding into those regions that are not accessible to words. Here imagination is literally the ability to create and mobilize mental images. The connection between words and images in the process of thinking is crucial to Bruno's entire philosophical experience as well as to his rhetorical style (Saiber 2005). What is relevant specifically for the process of concept formation is that image is a powerful thinking tool, able to overcome the linguistic impasse that the process of concept formation is intrinsically programmed to face. This does not mean that language is rational and image is irrational. The dichotomy between rational and irrational is precisely the extremization of the nominalist theological separation between being and knowledge that the modern Western epistemology rearticulated into science and metaphysics, and Kant crystallized in terms of what can be understood from what cannot be understood, but at best experienced as intuition. Thinking through images, in the Renaissance's gnoseological horizon, instead remains a rational approach to the threshold of the infinite, where the meaning of rationality is not conformal with Kantian reason.

The disproportion between the finite and the infinite, and hence between the limits of human knowledge and the limitless of the ultimate object of knowledge, is the generative tension that fosters the method of using images as a way of thinking that supports conceptualization within the border set by the impossibility of addressing the ultimate "truth" by means of words. Therefore, writing through images is to be conceived as a linguistic rather than a pictoric procedure: the use of mental images that are not fixed icons or given simulacra discloses the operational language of theorization to the creative space of concept formation. Unfortunately, Giordano Bruno never had the chance to encounter the writings and thoughts of Felipe Guamán Poma de Ayala (1534–1615). Guamán Poma wrote detailed chronicles of the Spanish colonization in Peru, and he arrived at analogous epistemological conclusions, though from a radically different point of departure. As Silvia Rivera Cusicanqui (2018) explains, the indigenous pre-Columbian lens he developed along the many years he spent documenting and understanding Aymara culture exposed his reasoning to the fact that the linguistic construction of written knowledge about the way of living and thinking of the colonized could not grasp its own object of study, because the epistemological architecture wherein it was inscribed belonged in the cultural ethnocentrism of the colonizers. Therefore, the history of the conquest and colonization of Latin

America, as well as the epistemic genocide critical theory refers to nowadays, should be produced by means of a different methodology that is situated at the border between words and images: written texts need to be read against the grain of the iconographic material that the colonized produced about their own views of the world. These images exceed the visual archive of Western thinking. Therefore, to the extent that this vision is meaningful as a general methodological assumption, the elaboration of a new protocol of concept formation for global studies does not limit itself to a set of linguistic operations. Rather, it engages with the imaginative power of monstrosity.

THE RENAISSANCE OF MONSTROSITY

The Renaissance mushroomed in Italy, but it was not a pristine Western, Latin, Christian, or European phenomenon, nor was it a path whose manifest destiny was designed by single European geniuses (Bala 2006). In fact, "The inventions of that time were in part from their brain, in part from the antique fragments they have seen from here and there" (Garin 2000, 17). The transformations of the historical and geopolitical context of theoretical elaboration had made non-Western knowledges available, and these knowledges created novel perspectives for knowledge production. This acknowledgment provides the debate about the classical meaning of the Renaissance between Garin and Paul Oskar Kristeller with a new, decolonizing and post-Western nuance. The critique of the decolonial oversimplification creates a new outreach that shifts the significance of the Renaissance outside the restricted Western-centric views from a nonhegemonic position. The terms of the debate, which never entered global studies from the perspective of knowledge production, opposed two complementary visions:

> Kristeller saw humanism as essentially a literary movement concerned with the *studia humanitatis*, which he defined (following the subject divisions of the famous library canon of Tommaso Parentucelli) as grammar, rhetoric, poetry, history and moral philosophy. Humanists were defined by their professional roles as schoolmasters and professional rhetoricians, and as such were the heirs of the medieval grammarians and *dictatores*. They represented, in other words, a classicizing period in the history of Western rhetoric. They were men of letters and not philosophers. . . . Garin, on the other hand, saw humanism as a period in the history of Western and especially Italian philosophy, and the humanists as philosophers in the broadest sense of the term. He laid great emphasis on their originality and their break with the traditions of medieval philosophy. Unlike some earlier historians of Renaissance philosophy, Garin knew a great deal about and published important research on medieval philosophy. He was well aware of the difficulty in pointing to particular doctrines held by humanists

> that were not anticipated by medieval thinkers of the twelfth and thirteenth centuries. For him, the originality of the humanists lay not in content but in their approach: their animo, sguardo, coscienza, in the forma of their philosophical reflections. (Hankins 2011, 489)

The Western-centric framework of the debate had forced the interpretation within the problem of establishing whether the Renaissance in Italy was a prosecution of late medieval Scholasticism (as per Kristeller) or the turning point to modernity. It becomes clear that if spatialized from a global epistemic perspective, Kristeller was right when he saw a difference with the Enlightenment, even though this difference was limited to those knowledges that did not fit the project of expansion of European colonial empires. In a specular way, Garin was right to affirm what was a rupture with premodern epistemology, even though this rupture was selective of those knowledges that did not fit the project of expansion of European colonial empires.

This is why rather than assuming the continuity between the Renaissance and the Enlightenment, the former can be rethought against the grain of the recessive dimension it endorsed. While some of the theoretical innovations that the Renaissance brought about disclosed the path of hegemonic Western rationality, the overall cultural meaning of the Renaissance as it originated in Italy marks a distinctive program from the Enlightenment. This means something different from the idea that the Renaissance was the infantile age in the development of modern Western thought. The analogous strategy of hierarchy production, in fact, is the same idea of the infantilization of non-Western knowledges that European anthropology has deployed in the construction of epistemic alterity about the social groups Europeans encountered during the colonization of the planet, together with their knowledge systems. Rather, it means engaging with the possibility of the relative irreconcilability of the epistemological and imaginative framework of the Renaissance with Western hegemonic thinking of the modern/colonial world. At the same time, this relative irreconcilability creates an imaginary space for an epistemic alliance between this underside of the Renaissance and non-Western, marginalized, indigenous, silenced knowledges that survived the epistemic genocides of modernity/coloniality.

During the last two decades, from different sites of enunciation, the calls for native, Indigenous, Taoist, Hindu, animistic, Aymara, and even psychedelic renaissance have provocatively affirmed their relevance in the social sciences at large. Sometimes these claims have attempted a reciprocal connection; more often they have spoken in soliloquies. The obstacles to the reciprocal understanding gain strength to the extent that the ethnocentric vision of each of these different sites of enunciation speaks for its own on the basis of what Joseph Leigh and Christopher Murray (2022) refer to in terms of epistemic mapping. One way to pursue the objective of creating global epistemic spaces gives priority to the geoethnic dimension of mapping. Another way consists in the effort to translate this view into something different. Here mapping is not limited to the geoepistemic spatial hierarchies of modernity. It engages with power relations that are geohistorical, intertwined, heterarchical, translating non-Western into nonhegemonic knowledges. What is non-Western and nonhegemonic today might be hegemonic tomorrow. Therefore, post-Western is the proper adjectival form to express the transitional adequacy of non-Western knowledges in expressing their nonhegemonic condition against the present moment within the temporality of the movement of hegemonic cycles. The exploration at the bifurcation that separates modern Western hegemonic thinking from the interrupted and hence never-taken path toward cross-cultural dialogue and the possibility of a different form of knowledge production in the realm of global epistemics is coextensively an exploration at the spacetime borders of modernity/coloniality.

This historiographical, geoeconomic, ideational disarticulation would remain confined within the space of analytical argument without a coherent effort in visualizing the possibilities that a different gnoseological imagination can unleash in that segment of theory production that is concept formation. This is why disarticulation benefits from an aesthetic dimension exhorting us to practice imagination as a metalinguistic process. The Renaissance was a global space of confrontation between different cultural and artistic forms as well as aesthetic visions from different and distant parts of the world (Burke 2017). Recent critical scholarship in art history provides new insights into this topic from a global studies perspective (Savoy 2017). Among the issues at stake, the relative disentanglement of Renaissance art and neoclassicism in figurative art stands out. Neoclassicism was a by-product of the European Enlightenment. It considered ancient Greek and imperial Roman aesthetics as the model of perfection that artists should rigorously replicate. Perfect bodies responded to the logic of adopting the given proportions in the different parts of bodies, drawn from the findings that the tremendous impulse toward the construction of a coherent European self-biography was giving to archeology (de Beaune, Sophie A.; Tarantini, Massimo; Moro Abadía, Oscar; Guidi, Alessandro 2021). The unilaterally established model of perfect human shape together with the white surface of the human body sculptures that formed the neoclassical canon deeply contributed to the racialization of beauty that is a pillar of the colonial hierarchy among humans and social groups in the modern/colonial/capitalist world economy.

Renaissance art in Italy, instead, was full of monsters (Ghadessi 2018; Niccoli 1990). The genealogy of this passion with monstrosity dates back to the second half of the thirteenth century. In his now-classic study of monstrosity in medieval art, Jurgis Baltrušaitis (1999) remarks that monstrosity was intimately related to the nonhuman and supernatural dimension of human life that became visible, concrete, and experienced through the materialization of what could not be normalized. The phantastic unrealism in visual and figurative arts connects ordinary experience with both the supernatural and the geographically and anthropologically distant, in time as in space. Premodern and early modern arts and crafts prove that Greek-Roman monuments; Arabic objects, decorations, or geometrical paintings; or figures and styles from Asia were all gathered under the word *saraceno* (Saracen) to define whatever influence was *non-Christian* (Baltrušaitis 1999). The passion for anatomic monstrosity was a cultural trait of the Italian Renaissance since the fifteenth century. Some of the most significant illustrations of the extent to which the aesthetic of monstrosity marks a sharp difference from neoclassicism in the eighteenth century are the sculptures of gods and goddesses that inhabited Renaissance gardens in Italy. The most significant example of these gardens of monstrosity is the Sacred Wood of Bomarzo in Viterbo, Italy. Here the figures of Neptune, Cerere, Pegasus, and Venus, as well as a gigantic tortoise and elephant, are disproportionate, grotesque bodies, whose shape show specific motifs from Etruscan elements, alchemical, astrological, cross-cultural, Epicurean, and even Aztec themes (Bredekamp 1989). These statues of pagan deities were stylistically coherent with a series of other monsters disseminated along the intricate paths of these very strange landscapes that the learned elite often frequented as a mundane space of exchange.

The garden was also the first public space of body dissection. In his study devoted to this specific topic, Luke Morgan (2016, 1) notes that

> in 1536, two female conjoined twins were dissected in the Orti Oricellari (Rucellai Gardens) in Florence. The humanist Benedetto Varchi, who was in attendance, gave a detailed account of the twins' anatomy in his lectures on the generation of monsters (1548), before concluding that owing to "these & many other similar Monsters & different ones, like those that you see in the loggia of the Scala Hospital, we philosophically believe that there have been, & can be monsters."

Morgan notes that the theme of the garden as a public space for the learned strata, both in terms of the imagery and the uses of historical landscape design, problematizes the traditional view that Renaissance aesthetics was motivated by a coherent desire to reinstate the classical *locus amoenus*. Rather, he explains, the relevance of monstrosity originated in the revived interest in the ideational and generative power of the concept of metamorphosis. Whether this interest was strictly dependent on the editorial fortunes of the revival of the circulation of Ovid's *Metamorphoses* or not, monstrosity became a generative locus of theory production. It soon came to transgress the boundaries of signification that had circumscribed it to the corporal or dimensional unproportioned monstrosity. Transgressions included sexual examples of impossible normalization, such as hermaphroditism or intersexuality, which in several ancient or pagan cultures were accommodated among other bodily attributes of cosmic, superhuman divinities, or creatures beyond the normal border between animals, plants, humans, and nonhumans. Morgan (2016, 5) recalls the myth of Hermaphroditus in Ovid's *Metamorphoses*:

> Hermaphroditus's metamorphosis takes place in a peaceful, sylvan landscape, the main feature of which is a pool of water "like crystal," its edges "ringed with fresh turf and grass that was always green." There were "no marshy reeds around it, no barren sedge or sharp-spiked rushes." This idyllic place is the setting for Salamacis's violent, sexually motivated attack: "she twined around him, like a serpent when it is being carried off into the air by the king of birds: for as it hangs from the eagle's beak, the snake coils round his head and talons and with its tail hampers his beating wings." Despite the desperate attempts of Hermaphroditus to break free, Salamacis "was like the ivy encircling tall tree trunks, or the squid which holds fast the prey it has caught in the depths of the sea, by wrapping its tentacles round on every side."

Asa Simon Mittman and Peter J. Dendle (2013, 7) give monstrosity an abstract, transcultural, and global dimension when they maintain that

> a monster is not really known through observation; how could it be? How could the viewer distinguish between "normally" terrifying phenomena and abnormally terrifying monstrosity? Rather, I submit, the monster is known through its *effect*, its impact. Therefore, from this perspective, all the monsters are real. The monsters in all of the traditions discussed here had palpable, tangible effects on the cultures that spawned them, as well as on neighboring and later cultures. . . . We live with the *vagina dentata*, the cyborg, the hostile alien living beyond our reach (though we live within its). As we cannibalize the Others of others, as we tear them apart and stitch them back together, we continually redefine the parameters of the monstrous. . . . Above all, the monstrous is that which creates this sense of vertigo, that which calls into question our (their, anyone's) epistemological worldview, highlights its fragmentary and inadequate nature, and thereby asks us (often with fangs at our throats, with its fire upon our skin, even as we and our stand-ins and body doubles descend the gullet) to acknowledge the failures of our systems of categorization.

In what follows, the operational approach to concept formation therefore translates the generative power of monstrosity into a site of theory production, where monstrosity is not specific to a particular culture or any determined geohistorical location, because the impossibility of normalization of monstrosity stands as the limit of ethnocentrism *in se* and *per se*. Whereas an affirmative universalist understanding of the human is at the foundation of anthropological reason, monstrosity performs the oppositional, negative, specular image of indefiniteness of the nonhuman as an antianthropocentric active principle to generate new linguistic cross-cultural devices of understanding. What constantly keeps concepts in tension is the irreducibility of monstrosity whose obtrusive yet ineliminable presence resists linguistical normalization.

NOTES

1. For the genealogy of such an intellectual move, see chapter 4.
2. The period of thirty years here is symbolic and refers to the foundation of the Latin American Subaltern Studies Group in 1993 (LASSG 1993). Contribution to the wider decolonization of knowledge research program can be extended back in time and space.
3. It is analectic since *analessi* is the rhetorical figure of facts that take place in a time that precedes the narration.
4. Garin's studies never entered the social sciences, neither in global studies nor in the vast territory of the critique to Eurocentric and Western-centric knowledge. The reason for the social sciences being deaf to these thick historiographies might be the reciprocal unawareness of the respective relevance or because of the structural impediments to move across disciplinary boundaries that global studies are questioning in the current debate, but more probably because questioning the myth of the origins of modernity such as the Renaissance means to undermine the pillars of the self-understanding of the social sciences (Ascione 2014).
5. With "hyperreal" I refer to Chakrabarty's reformulation of Baudrillard's concept: "'Europe' and 'India' are treated here as hyperreal terms in that they refer to certain figures of imagination whose geographical referents remain somewhat indeterminate" (Chakrabarty 2000, 27).
6. Mignolo's notion of the construction of the double border as a way to define what stands inside or outside the hyperreal geocultural location named "Europe" is conceptually effective, yet it is terminologically misplaced. What the concept of *Reconquista* (to reconquer) refers to was actually *Conquista* (to conquer). Mignolo uncritically uses *Reconquista* to define the process of territorial expansion that the Castilian power conducted against the Muslim/Arabic rulers of Al-Andalus, who were ruling over that land since the eleventh century CD, thereby reproducing a Eurocentric, Christian master narrative that is fundamentally wrong, as it has been extensively demonstrated by means of thick historiographical inquiry by Alejandro García Sanjuán (2013). The idea that the "Spanish" conquered back lands that were theirs in the past has been radically confuted. The concept of *Reconquista* was constructed as such much later (around the nineteenth century) in nationalistic narratives of historical revisionism (i.e., that "Spain" existed before Muslim rule and was hence "reconquered" rather than actually "conquered" from the Muslims). Regardless of

this flawed historiographical narrative, the sociological implications of Mignolo's theory of a "double border" are relevant in epistemological terms.

7. To be sure, after that the puritan scholars in Oxford belittled his heterodox thinking in public discussion, dressing their disagreement with derision about his stature and Italian accent; he had a spark of ethnic pride that exemplified the problematic relation with Italy: "A Neapolitan born and bred under a more benign sky."

8. Bruno's idea of separated continents articulates in geoepistemic perspective the recent ontological turn in anthropology, therefore connecting with the relative untranslatability among systems of knowledge from a geoepistemic point of view that both Thomas Kuhn and Paul K. Feyerabend conceived in terms of the problem of incommensurability in the restricted realm of competing scientific theories formulated in alternative languages with alternative conceptual apparatuses (Feyerabend 1978).

9. Erasmus had been a juvenile reading for Bruno. When he was a student in the Dominican monastery of Naples, he got in trouble because of a delation against him from another novice to their superiors, because Giordano Bruno secretly held a copy of a forbidden Erasmus book.

10. This version includes a famous introduction by the publisher himself, Osiander, who shared Copernicus's preoccupations and attempted at framing Copernicus's calculations within simple astronomical calculations with no general theological implications.

11. Elsewhere Kepler also added,

> Wackher, on the other hand, maintained that these new planets undoubtedly circulate around some of the fixed stars (he had for a considerable time been making some such suggestion to me on the basis of the speculations of the Cardinal of Cusa and of Giordano Bruno). If four planets have hitherto been concealed up there, what stops us from believing that countless others will be hereafter discovered in the same region, now that this start has been made? Therefore, either this world is itself infinite, as Melissus thought and also the Englishman William Gilbert, the founder of the science of magnetism; or, as Democritus and Leucippus taught, and among the moderns, Bruno and Bruce, who is your friend, Galileo, as well as mine, there is an infinite number of other worlds (or earths, as Bruno puts it) similar to ours.

BIBLIOGRAPHY

Aberth, John . 2020. *The Black Death. A New History of the Great Mortality in Europe, 1347–1500*. Oxford: Oxford University Press.

Amitav, Acharya, and Barry Buzan, eds. 2016. *Non-Western International Relations Theory Perspectives on and beyond Asia*. London: Routledge.

Aquilecchia, Giovanni. 1993a. "L'adozione del volgare nei dialoghi londinesi di Giordano Bruno (1953)." In Aquilecchia, Giovanni. *Schede Bruniane (1950–1991)*, pp. 41–64. Manziana: Vecchiarelli.

———. 1993b. "Bruno e il 'Nuovo Mondo (1955)'." In Aquilecchia, Giovanni. *Schede Bruniane (1950–1991)*, pp. 97–100. Manziana: Vecchiarelli.

———. 1993c. "Ancora su Giordano Bruno a Oxford 1963[1964]." In Aquilecchia, Giovanni. *Schede Bruniane (1950–1991)*, pp. 243–252 Manziana: Vecchiarelli Arrighi, Giovanni. 1994. *The Long Twentieth Century: Money, Power, and the Origins of Our Times*. London: Verso.

Arrighi, Giovanni, and Beverly Silver. 1999. *Chaos and World Governance in the Modern World System*. Minneapolis: University of Minnesota Press.

Ascione, Gennaro. 2014. "Unthinking Modernity: Historical-Sociological, Epistemological and Logical Pathways." *Journal of Historical Sociology* 27, no. 4: 463–89.

———. 2016. *Science and the Decolonization of Social Theory: Unthinking Modernity*. London: Palgrave.

Ashcroft, Rachel. 2017. "(Re)thinking Time: Giordano Bruno and Michel de Montaigne." *Journal of Early Modern Studies* 6: 157–81.

Bala, Arun. 2006. *The Dialogue of Civilizations in the Birth of Modern Science*. New York: Palgrave Macmillan.

———, ed. 2012. *Europe, Asia and the Emergence of Modern Science: Knowledge Crossing Boundaries*. New York: Palgrave Macmillan.

Baldini, Ugo, and Leen Spruit, eds. 2009. *Catholic Church and Modern Science: Documents from the Archives of the Roman Congregations of the Holy Office and the Index*. (Fontes Archivi Sancti Officii Romani, Series Documentorum Archivi Congregationis Pro Doctrina Fides, 5) xxiv. Rome: Libreria Editrice Vaticana

Baltrušaitis, Jurgis. 1999. *Fantastic in the Middle Ages: Classical and Exotic Influences on Gothic Art*. Martelsham: Boydell and Brewer.

Bassi, Simonetta, Elisabetta Scapparone, and Nicoletta Tirinnanzi, eds. 2000. *Giordano Bruno: Opere Magiche*. Milan: Adelphi.

Bayod, Jordi. 2004. "Bruno Lector de Montaigne." *Bruniana & Campanelliana* 10, no. 1: 11–26.

Bayoumim, Mustafa, and Andrew Rubin. 2000. *The Edward Said Reader*. New York: Vintage.

Bernal, Martin. 1987. *Black Athena: The Afroasiatic Roots of Classical Civilization*. New Brunswick, NJ: Rutgers University Press.

Berkowitz, E. 2021. *Dangerous Ideas: A Brief History of Censorship, from the Ancients to Fake News*. Boston: Beacon Press.

Bethencourt, Francisco. 2009. *The Inquisition: A Global History*. Cambridge: Cambridge University Press.

———. 2013. *Racism from the Crusades to the Twentieth Century*. Princeton, NJ: Princeton University Press.

Beyer, Marshal J. 2005. *International Relations in Uncommon Places: Indigeneity, Cosmology, and the Limits of International Theory*. London: Routledge.

Bhambra, Gurminder. 2007. *Rethinking Modernity: Postcolonialism and the Sociological Imagination*. Basingstoke, UK: Palgrave.

Binotti, Lucia. 1992. "Liburnio e Ramusio Lettori Delle 'Crónicas' Delle Conquiste Spagnole." *Annali d'Italianistica* 10: 80–95.

Binzel, Christine, Andreas Link, and Rajesh Ramachandran. 2023. "Language, Knowledge, and Growth: Evidence from Early Modern Europe." CEPR Discussion Paper 15454. https://dx.doi.org/10.2139/ssrn.4381287.

Blake, Cecil. 2009. *The African Origins of Rhetoric*. London: Routledge.

Blaut, James M. 2000. *Eight Eurocentric Historians*. New York: Guilford.

Blum, Elisabeth. 2005. "Qua Giordano parla per 'volgare': Bruno's Choice of Vernacular Language, as a Clue to a Heterodox Cultural Background." *Bruniana & Campanelliana* 11, no. 1: 167–90.

Blum, Rudolf. 1991. *Kallimachos: The Alexandrian Library and the Origins of Bibliography*. Madison: University of Wisconsin Press.

Blumenberg, Hans. 1983. *The Legitimacy of the Modern Age*. Cambridge, MA: MIT Press.

Braudel, Fernand. 1986. *Il secondo Rinascimento: Due Secoli e tre Italie*. Torino: Einaudi.

Bredekamp, Horst. 1989. *Vicino Orsini e il Bosco Sacro di Bomarzo: Un principe artista ed anarchico*. Translated by Franco Pignetti. Rome: Edizioni dell'Elefante.

Bucciantini, Massimo, and Maurizio Torrini, eds. 1997. *La diffusione del copernicanesimo in Italia, 1543–1610*. Florence: Olschki.

Bruno, Giordano. 2018. *The Ash Wednesday Supper*. Translated by Ilary Gatti. Toronto: University of Toronto Press.

———. 2002 [1585]. *La cabala del cavallo pegaseo*. Translated by Sidney L. Sondergard and Madison U. Sowell, *The Cabala of Pegasus by Giordano Bruno*. New Heaven: Yale University Press.

———. 1980 [1591]. *L'immenso e gli innumerevoli*. In *Opere latine*, Carlo Monti (ed.). Torino: Unione Tipgrafico-Editrice Torinese.

Burke, Peter. 2017. *Exiles and Expatriates in the History of Knowledge 1500–2000*. Waltham, MA: Brandeis University Press.

Campanini, Massimo. 2006. *Il trattato decisivo sull'accordo della religione con la filosofia / Averroè*. Milano.: Rizzoli (2006)Canone, Eugenio, and Leen Spruit. 2007. "Rhetoric and Philosophical Discourse in Giordano Bruno's Italian Dialogues." *Poetics Today* 28, no. 3: 363–91.

Cellarius, Christoph. 1727. *Historia medii aevi a temporibus Constantini Magni ad Constantinopolam a Turcis captam deducta, cum notis perpetuis ac tabulis synopticis*, Ieanae, sumtu Io. Fel. Bielkii.

Chakrabarty, Dipesh. 2000. *Provincializing Europe: Postcolonial Thought and Historical Difference*. Princeton, NJ: Princeton University Press.

Ciliberto, Michele. 1997. "Giordano Bruno Tra Mito e Storia." *I Tatti Studies in the Italian Renaissance* 7: 175–90.

———. 1999. *Umbra profunda: studi su Giordano Bruno*. Roma: Edizioni di Storia e Letteratura.

———. 2005. *Pensare per contrari: Disincanto e utopia nel Rinascimento*. Roma: Edizioni di Storia e letteratura.

———. 2021. *Giordano Bruno e la ruota del tempo*. Rome: Editori Riuniti.

Cohen, Floris. 1994. *The Scientific Revolution: A Historiographical Inquiry*. Chicago: Chicago University Press.
Cole, Andrew, and D. Vance Smith, eds. 2010. *The Legitimacy of the Middle Ages: On the Unwritten History of Theory*. Durham, NC: Duke University Press.
Connell, Raewyn. 1997. "Why Is Classical Theory Classical?" *American Journal of Sociology* 102, no. 6: 1511–57.
Cro, Stelio. 1992. "Italian Humanism and the Myth of the Noble Savage." *Annali d'Italianistica* 10: 48–68.
Culianu, Ioan Petru. 1987. *Eros and Magic in the Renaissance*. Chicago: Chicago University Press.
Cusicanqui, Silvia Rivera. 2020. *Ch'ixinakax utxiwa: On Decolonising Practices and Discourses*. New York: Polity.
Davis, Kathleen. 2006. *Periodization and Sovereignty: How Ideas of Feudalism and Secularization Govern the Politics of Time*. Philadelphia: University of Pennsylvania Press.
D'Ascia, Luca. 2002. *Antibarbari, Erasmus*. Roma: Aragno.
De Blasi, Nicola. 2008. *Piccola storia della lingua italiana*. Naples: Liguori.
De Beaune, Sophie A.; Tarantini, Massimo; Moro Abadía, Oscar; Guidi, Alessandro (eds.). 2021. *New Advances in the History of Archaeology: Proceedings of the XVIII UISPP World Congress (4–9 June 2018, Paris, France)*. Oxford: Archaeopress.
De la Croix, D., F. Docquier, A. Fabre, and R. Stelter. 2022. "The Academic Market and the Rise of Universities in Medieval and Early Modern Europe (1000–1800)." CEPR Discussion Paper 14509. https://ssrn.com/abstract=3560317.
De la Croix, D., M. Doepke, and J. Mokyr. 2018. "Clans, Guilds, and Markets: Apprenticeship Institutions and Growth in the Preindustrial Economy." *Quarterly Journal of Economics* 133, no. 1: 1–70.
Dufoix, Stéphane. 2023. *Décolonial*. Paris: Anamosa.
Dussel, Enrique. 1985. *Philosophy of Liberation*. New York: Orbis.
———. 1993. "Eurocentrism and Modernity (Introduction to the Frankfurt Lectures)." *Boundary 2* 20, no. 3: 65–76.
———. 2000. "Europe, Modernity, and Eurocentrism: The Semantic Slippage of the Concept of 'Europe.'" *Nepantla: Views from South* 1, no. 3:465–68.
Dussel, Enrique, and Eduardo Mendieta. 2003. *Beyond Philosophy: Ethics, History, Marxism, and Liberation Theology*. Lanham, MD: Rowman and Littlefield.
El-Zein, Amira. 2009. *Islam, Arabs, and Intelligent World of the Jinn*. Syracuse, NY: Syracuse University Press.
Firpo, Luigi. 1949. *Il processo di Giordano Bruno*. Naples: Edizioni Scientifiche Italiane.
Frank, Andre Gunder, and Barry K. Gills. 1990. "The Cumulation of Accumulation: Theses and Research Agenda for 5000 World System History." *Dialectical Anthropology* 15, no. 1: 19–42.
Garcia Sanjuàn, Alejandro. 2013. *La conquista islámica de la península ibérica y la tergiversación del pasado*. Madrid: Marcial Pons.
Ghadessi, Touba. 2018. *Portraits of Human Monsters in the Renaissance*. Kalamazoo: Western Michigan University.

Garin, Eugenio. 1996. *Lo zodiaco della vita*. Bari: Laterza.
———. 2000. *La cultura del Rinascimento*. Milan: Il Saggiatore.
Gatti, Ilary, ed. 2002. *Giordano Bruno: Philosopher of the Renaissance*. London: Routledge.
Geanakoplos, D. J. 1962. *Greek Scholars in Venice: Studies in the Dissemination of Greek Learning from Byzantium to Western Europe*. Cambridge, MA: Harvard University Press.
———. 1966. *Byzantine East and Latin West: Two Worlds of Christendom in Middle Ages and Renaissance*. New York: Harper Torchbooks.
———. 1976. *Interaction of the "Sibling" Byzantine and Western Cultures in the Middle Ages and Italian Renaissance (330–1600)*. New Haven, CT: Yale University Press.
———. 1989. *Constantinople and the West*. Madison: University of Wisconsin Press.
Granada, Miguel Angel. 1990. *Giordano Bruno y América: de la crítica de la colonización a la crítica del cristianismo*. Barcelona: Universitat de Barcelona.
Grosfoguel, Ramón. 2006. "World-Systems Analysis in the Context of Transmodernity, Border Thinking, and Global Coloniality." *Review (Fernand Braudel Center)* 29, no. 2: 167–87.
———. 2007. "The Epistemic Decolonial Turn." *Cultural Studies* 21: 211–23.
Guha, Ranajit. 1997. *Dominance without Hegemony: History and Power in Colonial India*. Cambridge, MA: Harvard University Press.
Hankins, James. 2011. "Garin and Paul Oskar Kristeller: Existentialism, Neo-Kantianism, and the Post-War Interpretation of Renaissance Humanism." In *Eugenio Garin: Dal Rinascimento all'Illuminismo*, edited by Michele Ciliberto, 481–505. Rome: Edizioni di Storia e Letteratura.
Heng, Geraldine. 2019. *The Invention of Race in the European Middle Ages*. Cambridge: Cambridge University Press.
Hobson, John M. 2012. *The Eurocentric Conception of World Politics: Western International Theory, 1760–2010*. Cambridge: Cambridge University Press.
Huamanchumo de la Cuba, Ofelia. 2021. "Las 'Indias de por acá' en el discurso italiano de la época de la Contrarreforma." In *Rutas Atlánticas. Redes narrativas entre América Latina y Europa*, edited by Simone Ferrari and Emanuele Leonardi. Milan: Milan University Press.
Karsavin, Lev Platonovič.2014. *Giordano Bruno*. Parma: E-theca OnLineOpenAccess Edizioni.
Koyré, Alexandre. 1957. *From the Closed World to the Infinite Universe*. Baltimore: Johns Hopkins University Press.
———. 1975. "La costituzione generale dell'universo." Copernico, Nicolò. *De revolutionibus orbium coelestium*. Torrino: Einaudi.
Latin American Subaltern Studies Group. 1993. "Founding Statement." *Boundary 2* 20, no. 3: 110–21.
Layug, A., and John M. Hobson, eds. 2022. *Globalizing International Theory: The Problem with Western IR Theory and How to Overcome It*. London: Routledge.
Leigh, Joseph, and Christopher Murray. 2022. "Ethno-Culturalism in World History: Race, Identity and 'the Global.'" In *Globalizing International*

Theory: The Problem with Western IR Theory and How to Overcome It, edited by A. Layug and John M. Hobson, 139–65. London: Routledge.

Link, Andreas. 2023. "The Fall of Constantinople and the Rise of the West." BGPE Discussion Paper No. 223. https://dx.doi.org/10.2139/ssrn.4372477.

MacPhail, Eric. 2014. "Anthropology and Anthropocentrism in Giordano Bruno and Michel de Montaigne." *Bruniana & Campanelliana* 20, no. 2: 531–46.

Matteoli, Marco. 2016. "Giordano Bruno, Pitagora e i pitagorici: distanze e debiti." *Clìope. Presença Clássica* 31.

McManus Stuart Michael. 2022. "Decolonizing Renaissance Humanism," In *The American Historical Review*, 127, No. 3: 1131–1161

Mignolo, Walter D. 1992. "On the Colonization of Amerindian Languages and Memories: Renaissance Theories of Writing and the Discontinuity of the Classical Tradition." *Comparative Studies in Society and History* 34, no. 2: 301–30.

———. 1995. *The Darker Side of the Renaissance: Literacy, Territoriality, and Colonization*. Ann Arbor: University of Michigan Press.

———. 2000. *Local Histories, Global Designs: Coloniality, Subaltern Knowledges and Border Thinking*. Princeton, NJ: Princeton University Press.

———. 2012. *The Darker Side of Western Modernity: Global Futures, Decolonial Options*. Durham, NC: Duke University Press.

Mittman, Asa Simon, and Peter J. Dendle, eds. 2013. *The Ashgate Research Companion to Monsters and the Monstrous*. Dublin: Ashgate.

Morgan, Luke. 2016. *The Monster in the Garden: The Grotesque and the Gigantic in Renaissance Landscape Design*. Philadelphia: University of Pennsylvania Press.

Mughal, M. A. Z. 2023. "The Western and Non-Western Dichotomization of Time in Anthropology." *International Journal of Anthropology and Ethnology* 7, no. 7. https://doi.org/10.1186/s41257–023–00086-z.

Murray, S. A. P. 1999. *The Library: An Illustrated History*. New York: Skyhorse Publishing.

Nardi, Bruno. 1965. *Studi su Pietro Pomponazzi*. Firenze: Olschki.

Niccoli, Ottavia. 1990. *Prophecy and People in Renaissance Italy*. Princeton, NJ: Princeton University Press.

Nixey, C. 2017. *The Darkening Age: The Christian Destruction of the Classical World*. London: Palgrave Macmillan.

Pagden, Anthony. 1982. *The Fall of Natural Man: The American Indian and the Origins of Comparative Ethnology*. Cambridge: Cambridge University Press.

Papi, Fulvio. 2006 [1968]. *Antropologia e civiltà nel pensiero di Giordano Bruno*. Napoli: Liguori editore.

Pomeranz, Kenneth. 2000. *The Great Divergence: China, Europe, and the Making of the Modern Economy*. Princeton, NJ: Princeton University Press.

Prosperi, A. 1996. *Tribunali della coscienza. Inquisitori, confessori, missionari*. Torino: Giulo Einaudi editore.

———. 2016. *La vocazione: storie di gesuiti tra Cinquecento e Seicento*. Torino, Giulo Einaudi editore.

Quijano, Aníbal. 1992. "'Raza,' 'etnia,' 'nación' en Mariátegui: cuestiones abiertas.'" In *Mariátegui y Europa: La otra cara del descubrimiento*, edited by R. Forgues and José Carlos. Lima: Amauta.

———. 2000. *Colonialidad del poder, eurocentrismo y América Latina, Perspectivas latinoamericanas*. Buenos Aires: CLASCO.

Quijano, Aníbal, and Immanuel Wallerstein. 1992. "Americanity as a Concept, or the Americas in the Modern World." *International Social Science Journal* 44, no. 4: 549–57.

Rousseau, Jean-Jacques. 1992 [1753]. *Discourse on the Sciences and Arts: (first Discourse) and Polemics*. Lebanon (New Hampshire): University Press of New England.

Rohmann, D. 2016. *Christianity, Book-Burning and Censorship in Late Antiquity*. Boston: De Gruyter.

Romeo, Rosario. 1953. *Le scoperte americane nella coscienza italiana del Cinquecento*. Naples: Edizioni Scientifiche Italiane.

Lombardi-Diop, Cristina and Romeo, Caterina (eds.). 2012. *Postcolonial Italy: Challenging National Homogeneity*. London: Palgrave Macmillan.

Ricci, Antonio. 2012. "I suoni delle Indias de por acá." In *La musica dei semplici: l'altra Controriforma*, S. Nanni (ed.), 371–80. Roma: Viella libreria editrice.

Ricci, Saverio. 1990. "Infiniti mondi e mondo nuovo: Conquista dell'America e critica della civiltà europea in Giordano Bruno." *Giornale Critico Della Filosofia Italiana* 10, no. 2: 204–21.

Rosen, Edward. 1965. *Kepler's Conversation with Galileo' s Sidereal Messenger*. New York and London: Johnson Reprint Corporation.

Saiber Arielle. 2005. *Giordano Bruno and the Geometry of Language*. New Haven, CT: Yale University Press.

Said, Edward. 1993. *Culture and Imperialism*. New York: Knopf.

Savoy, Daniel, ed. 2017. *The Globalization of Renaissance Art. A Critical Review*. Leiden: Brill.

Setton, Kenneth Meyer. 1956. *The Byzantine Background to the Italian Renaissance*. Philadelphia: American Philosophical Society.

Shahi, Deppeshikha, ed. 2021. *Sufism: A Theoretical Intervention in Global International Relations*. Lanham, MD: Rowman and Littlefield.

Shahi, Deppeshikha, and Gennaro Ascione. 2016. "Rethinking the Absence of Post-Western International Relations Theory in India: 'Advaitic Monism' as an Alternative Epistemological Resource." *European Journal of International Relations* 22, no. 2: 313–34.

Spampanato, Vincenzo. 1921. *Vita di Giordano Bruno con documenti editi e inediti*. Messina: Principato editore.

Spruit, Leen. 2006. *Il problema della conoscenza in Giordano Bruno*. Naples: Bibliopolis.

Subrahmanyam, Sanjay. 1997. "Connected Histories: Notes Towards a Reconfiguration of Early Modern Eurasia." *Modern Asian Studies* 30, no. 3: 735–62.

———. 2005. *Explorations in Connected History*. New Delhi: Oxford University Press.

———. 2022. *Connected History: Essays and Arguments*. London: Verso.

Tarantino, Elisabetta. 2002. "Ultima Thule: Contrasting Empires in Bruno's Ash Wednesday Supper and Shakespeare's Tempest." In Gatti, Hilary (ed.) *Giordano Bruno. Philosopher of the Renaissance*, 201–226. London and New York: Routledge.

Terracciano, Pasquale. 2013. *Omnia in figura: l'impronta di Origene tra '400 e '500*. Roma: Edizioni di Storia e Letteratura.

Tirinnanzi, Nicoletta. 2013. *L'antro del filosofo*. Roma: Edizioni di Storia e Letteratura.

Walsh, Catherine and Mignolo, Walter. 2024. "Foundational Concepts and Struggles for Dignity and Life." In Makoni Sinfree, Kaiper-Marquez Anna and Madany-Saá Magda (eds.) *Foundational Concepts of Decolonial and Southern Epistemologies*. Bristol: Multilingual Matters, 121–158.

Weisinger, Herbert. 1945. "The Renaissance Theory of the Reaction against the Middle Ages as a Cause of the Renaissance." *Speculum* 20, no. 4: 461–67.

Wong, Bin. 2011. *Before and Beyond Divergence: The Terms of Trade in Theory and Practice the Politics of Economic Change in China and Europe*. Cambridge: Cambridge University Press.

Yamamoto, K., and C. Burnett, eds. 2000. *Abū Ma'šar on Historical Astrology: The Book of Religions and Dynasties (On the Great Conjunctions)*. Leiden: Brill.

Yates, Frances. 1964. *Giordano Bruno and the Hermetic Tradition*. Chicago: University of Chicago Press.

Chapter 3

Teratologic Concept Formation

A SPECIFIC THEORETICAL TASK

Concept formation is an essential part of social science. It is an activity intrinsic to any attempt to produce knowledge about history and society, but it often remains implicit in research, investigation, and inquiry. This allows for the reproduction of existing structures of power whose methodological guardians patrol the borders of the holy temple of Eurocentric, capitalist, masculine, heterosexual, monotheistic, speciesist, and anthropocentric hegemony—in a word: theory. Such an implicitness confines nonhegemonic expert knowledges to the realm of gnoseological apartheid, where the coloniality of method mortifies any new theoretical language that threatens the status quo. Coloniality sterilizes the possibility of questioning the lexicon of the dominant conceptual archive erected by Western social science upon the ruins left everywhere on the planet by the epistemic genocides of modernity (Grosfoguel 2013). True, concepts constantly either undergo resignification or experience alternative demarcations of their semantic fields or enjoy extensions and limitations of the argumentative and empirical realms they are devoted to circumscribe as well as of the normative-explanatory task they are devoted to fulfill. Nevertheless, the analysis of the way this crucial activity takes place, the rules it follows (or should follow), and the theoretical potential it holds often remain relegated to a derivative stance of the terminological results of specific research or theoretical constructions. Therefore, the panoply of the concepts we currently use in global studies remains mainly Western: born within the Western self-biography of the modern world, regardless of other voices from other spacetimes of the planet.

Ongoing transformations in expert knowledge production for global studies change the context for theory in two dimensions: geopolitics and social relevance. First, the geopolitics of knowledge is radically transforming in this age of hegemonic transition, and multiplex geohistorical locations put pressures on the existing conceptual archive to make their own voices heard. Yet this wide space of theoretical production is not homogeneous. It is hierarchical, organized according to differences in geopolitical power. On the one hand, rising economic and political powers such as India, China, and Russia and their structures of knowledge production enjoy increasing relevance. For their voice is stronger within the interstate system; therefore, the field of international relations theory becomes the space wherein new concepts and words connected to the geohistorical tradition they put forward or rediscover take momentum. On the other hand, subaltern, Indigenous, or marginalized social groups remain largely unheard, even though the conceptual shifts their intervention could potentially produce are as much relevant as that of the rising global powers (Layug and Hobson 2022). In this sense, the ancient separation between pagans and barbarians, and between civilized and primitive cultures, is still at work (Shiliam 2012).

Second, the structures of knowledge production everywhere face the challenge of integrating existing disciplinary approaches and methodologies while interrogating the impact of the social sciences in world politics and in national contexts. Debates about whether and how social science matters show that the realms of politics and theory production are not reciprocally extraneous (Fuller 2006; Rehg 2009). The fact that social theory appears reluctant to look at the domain of the public sphere and that politics is not interested in engaging with the implicit assumptions it relies upon haunts social science (Dewey and Rogers 2012; Flyvbjerg 2001; Steinmetz 2015). Michie and Cooper (2015) reaffirm the relevance of social science in policymaking. Yet the broad frame they adopt is problem oriented: social science, they argue, produces expert knowledge; this knowledge is a valuable resource for making or communicating decisions that are hardly restricted to an exclusively technical endeavor. The relevance of the field of social science, as per Bourdieu (Bourdieu, Chamboredon, and Passeron 1968; Bourdieu 2001), intersects with politics since the protodisciplinary configuration of *Polizeiwissenschaft* (Wakefield 2009). And it extends to the broad sphere of social action as an arena where discussions influence, legitimize, or contest the processes of decision-making. Problem-oriented approaches are advantageous because they directly respond to the demand to demonstrate "impact" that social science in general, and social theory in particular, engage with nowadays (Abbot 2005; Holmwood 2011), even though well-known controversies exist about the efficacy of this presumed impact (Jennings and Callahan 1983; Miller, Fredericks, and Perino 2008). While the appeal to the problem-solving approach in European social science is extremely relevant to the content of policymaking, it underrates the difficulties that derive from the ways actors frame, describe, and explain problems themselves (Gilbert 2008; Lindblom and Cohen 1978).

When the analytical focus shifts from the Weberian approach to concept formation surrounding the functions of concepts according to social action, the problematique of concept formation enlarges its horizon to engage with polysemy, de-contextualization, and the re-contextualiuzation of notions and lemmas (Edgerly, Toft and Veden 2011; Rakova 200; Said 1983). In the context of the contemporary globalizing knowledge, problem-oriented approaches are unable to offer responses to the geocultural problematiques emanating in the global space. Lexicon is inevitably informed by concepts, which explicitly or implicitly convey, reproduce, or exclude meanings, stories, and perspectives (King, Keohane, and Verba 1994). Meanings, stories, and perspectives differently and selectively reflect social groups, individuals, and stakeholders, as well as political and cultural sensibilities and heritages (Abbott 2004). As William Outhwaite (1983, 1) remarks, "social scientists are inevitably pushed to take serious notice of semantic aspects of their own practice, they are also compelled to adopt positions in the philosophy of meaning and science."

It is symptomatic, in fact, that Outhwaite's seminal book *Concept Formation in Social Science* remains the only systematic work that directly addresses the problem of the protocols of conceptualization. In the last forty years, this problem has undergone a reconfiguration: it is now obvious that Outhwaite's work remains entirely confined within the Western tradition of social thought. The problem of concept formation outside the Western conceptual archive was external to his own epistemological horizon. Today, instead, the global dimension of the social sciences is inevitably entrenched with non-Western worlds and therefore with post-Western approaches to knowledge production.

A classical cleavage defines the complex relation between the epistemologies of social science and the methodologies of concept formation that draw their legitimacy from these epistemologies. This is related to the divide that Bevir and Kedar (2008, 2) recall between naturalist and nonnaturalist approaches: "Whereas naturalism assumes that the study of human life is not essentially different from the study of natural phenomena, anti-naturalism highlights the meaningful and contingent nature of social life, the situatedness of the scholar, and so the dialogical nature of social science." Recent debates in the methodology of international relations have questioned the strict determination between ontology, epistemology, and methods (Lacatus, Schade, and Yao 2015). On the one hand, Patrick Jackson (2015) restates the position that Bevir and Kadar share in the field of political science. For Jackson, the ontological positioning of theory logically precedes the construction of theory and thus restricts the realm of consistent epistemologies, which, in turn, allows for a limited number of methodological options. On the other hand, Bennett (2015) makes the methodological case for mixed methods of inquiry. For him, it is not just a matter of being methodologically eclectic; rather, mixed methods are what complex and ambitious inquiries always force the researcher to embrace. Bennett subverts Jackson's hierarchy of abstraction that descends from ontology to method. He assumes the pragmatic relevance of mixable methods of inquiry and research design as the logic of his methodological theorization and makes a strong methodological case for mixing methods when the materials to work with are mainly textual data. In this case, he argues, the potential of mixing methods overcomes epistemological divides established a priori. Barkin (2015) enhances the argument made by Bennett and suggests that, rather than being ascribed to inner properties, epistemological frameworks are conceivable as relationally constructed and selectively interpellated by multiple methods pragmatically mobilized. By looking at this articulation from a global perspective, the coherence of each framework looks grounded in the axiomatization of a restricted number of assumptions that are geohistorically determined and thus potentially questionable, even though plausible and consuetudinary (Ascione 2014; Shahi and Ascione 2016). From an antipodal position connecting Aristotle, Augustine, Aquinas, the Scottish Enlightenment, and Hume's empiricism, Alasdair MacIntyre registers the same impasse. His suggestion of a plausible way out of this epistemological impasse resonates with the current issues facing the globalization of European knowledge in its attempt to confront the possibility of post-Western approaches to global studies. The solution, for him, "requires the invention or discovery of new concepts and the framing of some new type or types of theory" (MacIntyre 1988, 362). Thus, the question arises: where can one locate the effort to produce a post-Western approach to concept formation, given the ongoing reconfiguration of knowledge in a worldly context, where other non-Western research traditions intervene in the conceptual and terminological landscape of social theory?

To the extent we assume this condition as a critical platform from which to move forward and elsewhere in order to produce nonhegemonic knowledge about long-term and large-scale processes of historical and social change, a theoretical problem arises: how could, or should, concepts be elaborated in order to cope with the asymmetrical power relations that materialize colonial history through heterarchies of class, gender, race, ethnicity, culture, knowledge, cosmology, and ecology?

To answer this question, the heuristic strategy to concept formation illustrated herewith is articulated in four stances. The first locates teratologic concept formation within the context defined by the most systematic approaches to the globalization of social science and the methodologies of concept formation associated with them: namely, John Gerring's criterial framework for concept formation in social science, Boaventura de Sousa Santos's strategy for intercultural dialogue through "diatopic hermeneutics," Gurminder Bhambra's historical-sociological research program of "connected sociologies," and Xiaoying Qi's "globalized knowledge flows" argument. The second unravels the meaning of "teratologic" toward post-Eurocentric concept formation, reelaborating the theoretical relevance of the notion of monstrosity through Imre Lakatos's seminal *method of monster-barring*. The third section outlines teratologic concept formation as procedural method. The fourth section formalizes a protocol of teratologic concept formation.

DATA AND CLASSIFICATION

Concept formation is inextricably related to the notion of data. Data is itself a concept. Yet in global studies and in social science at large, the word "data" refers to the sources and the material that concepts are called to linguistically organize. What are the primary sources that provide the concrete material for abstraction? In other words, what is the material for concept formation in global studies? Data are not only quantitative. Data are both quantitative and qualitative. Quantitative data are ordered sequences of instances of the same phenomena, organized in numeric sets. Qualitative data are narrative discourses about the same phenomena, articulated as stories. Quantitative data form indicators. Qualitative data form histories. Their epistemological status—that is, the degree of reliability they enjoy in terms of building blocks for concept formation—is closer to each other than it may seem. They are both socially constructed; therefore, their degree of truth depends not simply on the methodological accuracy deployed in their elaboration, but also on the cultural, linguistic, and political coordinates within which elaboration takes place. In the case of both measurement and narration, the social sciences attempt to discover the possible causes, the current configuration, and the probable developments of the phenomena under study. In the social sciences, data serve the purpose of establishing a nexus between past, present, and future. In so doing, they never start from a neutral position. The words at our disposal when it has to be decided what to measure and what to narrate themselves belong to a specific cultural context wherein existing social hierarchies give priority to certain worldviews over others. These hierarchies are structured by race, gender, class, sexual orientation, age, geographical location, cosmology, idiom, and religion. Altogether, these intersectional hierarchies compose the colonial matrix of power that informs the entire process of concept formation from socially constructed data.

For example, in order to study global inequalities, a set of indicators can be built to address poverty. Such indicators would measure the income of an individual. Yet it is rare that an individual is totally isolated and self-sufficient. More often, the individual is a component of a household. Therefore, the distribution of wealth and resources is better measured by taking into consideration the household the individual belongs to and their position within the household according to gender, disability, or age. Moreover, the single household is located in a particular region that can be more or less economically affluent or depressed; therefore, significant correlations can exist between the ethnic group the household is associated with and the class structure of that region in the global economy. Two words at our disposal to study the global phenomenon of inequality in a given geographical area are significant from a concept formation perspective: "household" and "poverty." Usually, household refers to a family. A family is automatically associated with what is considered the normal nuclear family, made up of a mother, a father, and their children. Yet concept formation in global studies is not commonsensical, and it often serves to reverse what common sense might suggest to social analysis. In fact, a household can be formed by individuals who are not necessarily connected via blood ties, nor are they relatives more generally. For analytical purposes, a household can be constructed as a group of people who share income and expenses (Martin and Wallerstein 1982). As such, a household can be a larger group than a family, including also members who partake in income and expenses for a limited time (like a student who cohabits with other peers in a city different from her or his hometown), or across different geographical spaces (as in the case of a seasonal migrant sending money back home). Furthermore, it is important to note that according to convention, the income that the household gathers is monetary, like a salary. Nonetheless, there exist other forms of income that are nonmonetary yet are a fundamental part of wealth and resources for a household. Housekeeping is an example. If a member of the household is responsible for housekeeping, they are producing a nonmonetary income that corresponds to the amount of money that the household would need if it had to pay for the same service. This different conceptualization has both methodological and political implications. Usually these works pertain to those located at lower levels in the hierarchy within the household as well as in society: women or elder people, for instance, who concretely contribute to the wealth of the household, yet the activities they do are relegated to less important functions that typically disempower those in charge of them. Therefore, being aware of the words used implies both rethinking what to measure and simultaneously shedding a different light over the original focus of investigation: in this case, inequalities.

Measuring, however, is only the quantitative side of the problem of data. The so-called normal family draws legitimacy from a particular way of narrating social change supported by modernization theories. According to their 1950s original formulation, modernization theories affirmed that the world had entered into a process of social homogenization. For this reason, all the countries around the world were expected to follow the path of social change that was unfolding in the more industrialized countries, located mainly in the West. According to this view, which became hegemonic under the period of US world dominance, the so-called traditional large family formed by many relatives across multiple generations would be progressively replaced by the so-called mononuclear family: father, mother, children. In the wider context of society, the form of income of the household would become more and more dependent on the salary and less and less on other forms of income, both monetary and not. This presumably unique historical path of social change justified a particular way of conceptualizing poverty, that is, the quantitative measurement of the aggregate wellness of every single nation-state: the gross domestic product (GDP).

However, in the last five decades, strong criticisms have been raised against this whole way of conceptualizing inequalities and explaining them, as well as the social construction of data that has supported it. It has been shown, for example, that more than half of the world population lives in complex, multilayered, spatially scattered households. Accordingly, the predictions of modernization theories proved to be wrong prophecies. Moreover, the quantitative evaluation of inequalities ignores a variety of indicators that combine to define wellness, access to resources, political empowerment or disempowerment, and other factors of well-being (Walter and Andersen 2013). Even the geographical significance of data collected at the scale of the nation-state has resulted in a reduction of the complexity of social reality (Boatça 2015). Finally, the very meaning of poverty is socially constructed according to systems of value that can modify the social perception of the conditions of life across the globe, referring to alternative systems of value, from ecology to *buen vivir* (García-Quero and Guardiola 2017).

Walter and Andersen (2013) have proposed to look at the production of data from an Indigenous perspective. They focus on *Indigenous statistics* as a different way to use quantification of qualitative data in order to endow Indigenous communities with new tools of empowerment. They conceptualize such a methodological proposal in terms of *nayri kati*, which, in the Tasmanian Aboriginal language, means literally "good numbers":

> The relationship and power interactions of the Australian nation-state towards its Indigenous peoples are also theoretically central. This conceptual grid can be figuratively and theoretically mapped as the domain of Aboriginality. Within this context, the term Aboriginality does not denote identity. Rather, the term encapsulates the lived experience of being Indigenous in Australia in relation to the settler population and the broader impact of these power relations on

> individual and group life chances and life options. The domain is multifaceted, with intersecting layers, but components can be identified within thematic clusters. (Walter and Andersen 2013, 91)

These clusters are: (1) material poverty, pointing to colonial dispossession; (2) absences and omissions, pointing to the systematic erasure of Indigenous communities' issues in the public agenda; (3) burden of disregard, pointing to the normalization of disrespect toward Indigenous peoples; (4) ongoing dispossession, pointing to all-encompassing dispossession, including material and immaterial dimensions of the coloniality of power. Indigenous statistics expose the way data, whether in the form of indicators or histories, can be selected according to different agendas. Thinking globally, today, means the ability to disclose the process of concept formation to histories and facts to which the Eurocentric social sciences have remained blind and deaf. New narratives of social change and the relative data sets can emerge when Europe or the West at large ceases to be thought of in terms of the unique and more advanced historical path of social change. There exist different ways to address this problem. These ways designate a theoretical landscape that limits the possible responses because they oscillate between the reinstantiation of the presumed universal Western-centric approaches, on the one hand, and the assertion of a particularistic or exoticized non-Western conceptual and historical archive, on the other. The teratologic method, as in what follows, aims at transgressing these limits.

The path that a teratologic approach to concept formation suggests moves from and beyond four landmarks in present knowledge on the topic of concept formation: Gerring's criterial framework for concept formation in social science, Santos's strategy for intercultural dialogue through "diatopic hermeneutics"; Bhambra's historical-sociological research program of "connected sociologies"; and Qi's "globalized knowledge flows" argument.

Gerring (1999, 2011) locates his approach in an intermediate position between those who think that concepts derive their meaning from the theoretical framework wherein they are employed (Hempel 1965; Faeges 1999), and those who counterargue that in most cases the relation is inverse, and concepts drive theories (Jones 1974; Kaplan 1964). Gerring's criterial framework (2001) is based on the assumption that between concepts and theoretical frameworks there exists a circular relation of codetermination. What is more relevant to Gerring is that concept formation needs to tackle the compelling challenge of being "classificatory." Drawing critically on Giovanni Sartori (1984), John Gerring (1999, 2001) argues that a classificatory approach endorses a naturalist epistemology and infers a method of concept formation according to which a concept has to meet three requirements: "First, when constructing definitions, aim for a one-to-one correspondence between words and things. Second, employ only those attributes that are necessary and sufficient to bound the concept extensionally—i.e., only those attributes that are found always-and-only among a concept's referents. Third, organize concepts along a pyramid of terms, from those that are most specific to those that are most general." But Gerring raises one major issue related to this "classic" approach: classification of this sort overlooks the linguistic element in concept formation. This neglected aspect of concept formation conveys two dimensions: the first is polysemy, that is, the multiple possible meanings of the same term; the other is the reversal, synonymy, that is, the conceptual convergence, but noncoincidence, of different terms into overlapping semantic fields.

Santos (1997, 2007a, 2007b) tackles this overall fallacy and limit in European social science. Santos transposes this issue on the global scenario of cross-cultural dialogue, over long-term/large-scale historical processes of ideational exchange. He affirms that rather than looking at the possibility of full translation across cultures, the semantic spaces that are not overlapping should be taken into account: no culture can presume to fully express meaning for all other cultures (Santos 1997). Thus, each concept has to be pluralized in order to make room for non-European experiences and understandings. In so doing, each of the culture-bound concepts considered will shed light on territories of meaning that the other excludes. Polysemy, in this sense, is not a limit. It becomes an opportunity to seize, in order to enrich concepts with meanings deriving their value from other cultures and contexts. Both Gerring and Santos appear reluctant to use neologisms as a way out of the impasse generated by the inability of certain concepts to give form to reality and understanding. But while this is true for the activity of classification and cross-cultural dialogue they respectively aspire to contribute to, Santos proves keen to adopt neologisms to define his own methodology. The term Santos uses to name his strategy of concept formation through concept-to-concept cross-cultural translation is *diatopic hermeneutics*. Diatopic hermeneutics was introduced by the theologian Raimon Panikkar (1979), who affirmed that this strategy is able to bridge the distance between cultures that is not merely temporal, but spatial: a distance separating two human *topoi*, "places" of understanding and self-understanding, between two—or more—cultures that have not developed their reciprocal patterns of intelligibility.[1]

Bhambra (2014, 2015) offers a more advanced option in terms of methodological formalization compared to Santos, but at the same time, she is not interested in putting in conversation concepts belonging to different cultures. Here the strategy is simultaneously sociological and historical. Bhambra disjoins the simplistic association in social science between concepts and ideal types. She chooses Weberian ideal-typization as a polemical target and hits the intersection between history-as-eventuation and sociology-as-structuration, as the space for reconstructing social science (Abbott 1991; Abrams 1980). Bhambra thus opts to intervene in concept formation by changing the historical records upon which concepts in social science are grounded and ideal types are formed. She relocates the global connected histories that European knowledge has typically forgotten at the center of the process of the elaboration of categories and frameworks to understand social change. Thanks to connections (historiographically) and relations (methodologically), Bhambra's (2014, 147) connected sociologies approach denounces the irresolvable contradictions of ideal types:

> Since ideal types are necessarily selective, those other circumstances can be represented within another, different ideal type, which merely sits alongside other ideal types as part of the conceptual armory of interpretations that are dependent on the purpose at hand. . . . The failure to reconstruct ideal types in the light of new evidence suggests not only a commitment to the theoretical construct separate from its relation to the empirical, but also a commitment to the evaluative schema associated with it.

Connections between the spacetimes of the modern world are thus a suitable alternative to comparisons between presumed essential traits of European history with non-European histories.

Qi (2014) suggests an interesting alternative to investigate the issues that Santos constructs in terms of cultural frameworks, that Bhambra translates methodologically in terms of alternative schemas, and that Gerring unproblematically takes for granted within a pristine European horizon. Qi brings in a Chinese perspective on cross-cultural dialogue that moves along two directions: the way European knowledge transforms the lexicon of Chinese social science and the way Chinese notions inspire, enter, or are incorporated into European social science. Qi (2014, 8) pinpoints that while some concepts are "engineered neologisms that serve specific analytic functions," others are shared with ordinary language and become "transformed by virtue of the specialized role they are given in exposition and explanation." A further group of concepts, Qi continues, derives from "the vocabulary of non-English-writing theorists." In this last case, concepts such as *verstehen*, *anomie*, or *habitus* have entered the vocabulary of social science as neologisms thanks to the overall theoretical relevance of the framework and the thinker that "sponsored" them. What Qi (2014, 26) suggests is that "the potential contribution to social science of concepts drawn from the Chinese language may be sufficiently significant" without any sponsorship, simply thanks to the theoretical adequacy and power they convey, even outside the Chinese context. Chinese concepts in social science would thus be inherently significant and relevant enough to influence the vocabulary of social science without the assessment of any procedural intervention in concept formation.

The lacuna existing in the theoretical space that the relational construction of these four strategies of concept formation delineate is that methodological formalization (MF), on the one hand, and the globalization of knowledge (GK), on the other hand, remain substantially disjoined. My hypothesis is that this lacuna derives from the circumstance that the convergence between MF and GK is not considered a valuable object of inquiry, or it is looked upon with suspicion because of the risk of theoretical reification. For this reason, it becomes my specific research objective to address this lacuna.

Gerring's criterial framework (CF) adopts eight broad criteria to form and test a concept: familiarity, resonance, parsimony, coherence, differentiation, depth, theoretical utility, and field utility. These eight criteria are conceived entirely within the horizon of the universal applicability of European concepts and do not consider the problem of how to scale geoculturally to grasp and represent other non-Western experiences. The criterion of familiarity, for example, operates a cultural/civilizational control over the boundaries that define whether a concept is adequate or not. Santos's diatopic hermeneutics (DH) is open to non-Western concepts, but it does not aspire to the level of formalization proposed by Gerring. DH does not go beyond the boundary that separates the discourse over method from the elaboration of a method. In contrast with Santos, the methodological option Bhambra brings to the fore does not present indications of method, but it also does not foresee any protocol of control and testing for the concepts that would eventually arise from its application, as Gerring does. Moreover, the connected sociologies (CS) approach overlooks the issue of cross-cultural concept formation that Santos raises with the strategy of DH and Qi raises with argument of the global knowledge flows (GF). CS adopts a vertical process of abstraction from histories to concepts and disregards the horizontal relation between concept and concept across cultural boundaries. So while the approaches of Qi and Gerring put emphasis respectively on GK over MF, and vice versa, the approaches of Bhambra and Santos mark the thresholds where present theories line up. Qi radicalizes the possibility of translations and interpellation among concepts across cultures, but nonetheless reduces the process of concept formation to the logic of ideational influence. In the context of methodology, influence is far too elusive: it limits the inquiry between philological research, on the one hand, and thematic analogies, on the other. On the whole, GF does not infer a valuable method to understand, and learn from, the way Chinese and European concepts might reciprocally interact to co-form what Christian Ersche (2014) refers to as the shared language of social science.

In order to map the theoretical space these four options delineate in terms of their commitment to concept formation, one can imagine a single

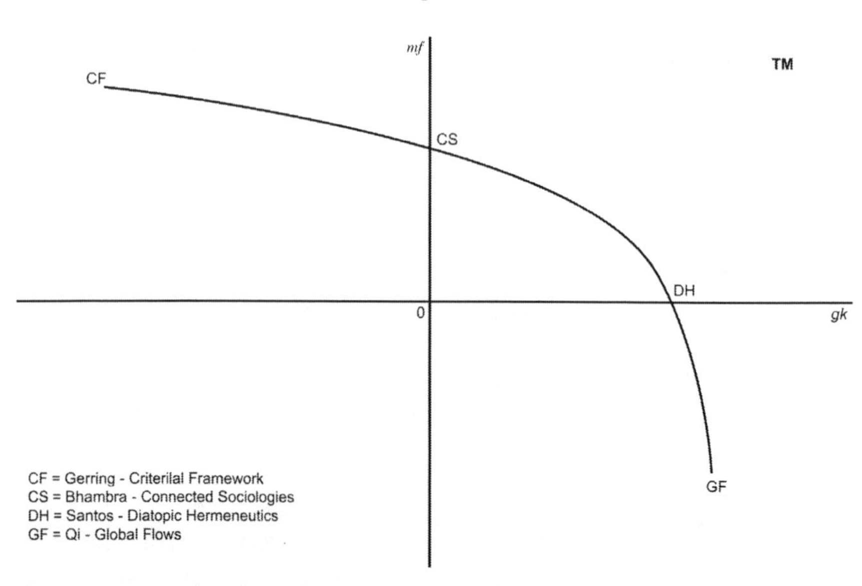

Figure 3.1. Mapping alternative conceptualizations

Cartesian diagram where *x* expresses the degree of MF and *y* expresses the degree of acquaintance with non-European experiences in terms of the GK. The threshold-value *0* here indicates respectively the passage from methodology to method on the ordinate axis (as in Gerring's framework), and the passage from vertical ideal-typization (histories-to-concept, as in Bhambra's approach) to horizontal conceptual translation (concept-to-concept confrontation, as in Qi's approach) on the abscissa axis.

The graph illustrates, with reasonable approximation, the way the teratologic methodology (TM) aspires to locate itself at the top right corner of the diagram, outside the frontier of the region delimited by the elliptic curve obtained by conjoining the positions the existing four strategies occupy. This overall objective would thus be a substantial step forward in the attempt to respond simultaneously to the call for formalization and the call for globalization. The advantage of this diagrammatic description is that its logic remains open to further elaboration and discussion. Another advantage it offers is the possibility of a concurrent validation of the two aspects of MF and GK. Non-Western knowledges are perturbative of the imaginary geometrical space such an illustrative diagram designs. They add further unexpected and nonrepresentable dimensions to the twofold axes of the Western Cartesian imagination. Here, the TM stands as a perforation of this two-dimensional space. It rips its surface and lets the non-Western conceptual archive irrupt into the lexicon of global studies.

THINKING WITH THE NON-WESTERN: CALIBAN AS A *MAÎTRE* À PENSER

Thinking with the non-Western is one among other possible ways to engage with the multiplicity of valuable forms of knowledge stemming out of cultural, social, and historical differences on a planetary scale. It presupposes that the construction of what is Western is not separable from the construction of what is other than Western. Therefore, the non-Western itself is a relational theoretical construction modeled on the definition of what is dominant, on the one hand, and what is subaltern to such a dominance—and therefore nonscientific, marginal, or exotic—on the other. The non-Western, in fact, results from a derivative definition of a series of characteristics that appear visible against the grain of what is Western, even though such an oppositional logic becomes very ambiguous every time one among the many concrete alternatives to Western thinking comes closely under scrutiny. It is undeniable that several features of what should be inherently specific to Western knowledge are not extraneous to other non-Western forms of knowledge; vice versa, even Western knowledge is not a singular monolithic block reducible to a limited set of features composing the panoply of modern social sciences.

The relational nature of the non-Western is a precondition to avoid essentialism in concept formation. Non-Western sources of knowledge production are a by-product of concrete political power configurations in global politics, which, in turn, depend on historically determined conditions in the *longue durée* and not on the inner properties of concepts, categories, or entire philosophical traditions. This is true at every level of analysis. Even when anti-Eurocentric and post-Western critiques accuse dualism to be the source of all the evils in dominant Western ontology, epistemology, and methodology, from Descartes to Kant to Hegel, they forget that dualism is not a prerogative of Western thinking. Dualism is a theoretical worldview that exists in many other civilizational sources of knowledge, from Zoroastrian wisdom, Gnosticism, Taoism, and Aymara sciences to Indian philosophy. Nonetheless, dualism, as an intellectual pillar of Western modernity historically overrides the hierarchical organization of human groups in global politics. It shapes the dominant theoretical approach in global studies, while nondualism is not allowed to shed light upon not only the conventional issues that Western theories claim to explore, but also numerous new issues that could potentially be included in the agenda of global studies. The dominance of dualism marks the significance of nondualism or monism as a generative epistemological locus for knowledge production (Shahi and Ascione 2016), even though this contemporary historical condition may change in time and also reverse the current configuration of what is dominant and what is marginal.

Once the transformative role of what appears as non-Western is at least accepted in principle against the epistemological supremacy of the West, this supremacy can more readily be seen as a historical and social construction articulated in either time or space. In time, it establishes the intellectual superiority of the modern age over its past. In space, it establishes the centrality of the West as the place from which new and more advanced forms of knowledge emerged for the others to follow, imitate, and learn from (Bhambra 2014). Space and time connect through the delegitimation and marginalization of alterity, by means of what the German anthropologist Johannes Fabian (1990) called the "denial of coevalness": non-Western human forms of knowledge and the social groups who produced them are displaced in an antecedent historical epoch. This means that there exists a link between those forms of European knowledge that were disdained during modernity and those erased in the non-Western world through colonialism. Colonialism as such created a postcolonial world where the mortification of ideational alternatives to dominance shaped both sides of the colonial relation. For this reason, an implicit alliance is at work between non-Western knowledges and other critical perspectives born within the Western tradition. This link provides new generative grammars, insights, and horizons.

A systematic description of the adjectival form "non-Western," referring to knowledges, cultures, and social groups, relies on the definition of a specific theoretical space. Such a space is where the so-called non-Western diverges from the dominant, modern, Western that the social sciences refer to when they are in search of their own legitimation. The non-Western questions a specific feature of the self-biography of Western modernity: the idea that modern Western civilization is progressive because it is the historical outpost of the process of secularization. From the perspective on non-Western knowledges, this presumption is misplaced for two intertwined reasons: first, because if secularization is the historical tendency to replace religious with secular authority, then the modern West is neither the only nor the first geohistorical entity that experienced this process; second, because, at a closer analytical gaze, secularization in the West did not provoke such a displacement of religion but rather configured a different reciprocal legitimation between politics and religion, between science and theology, between faith and reason, that guaranteed a durable synthesis by negotiating what the spheres of competence were, in order to preserve the dominant geoculture from the challenge to European world hegemony (Ascione 2016). Nonetheless, beyond the problem of the geopolitics of knowledge, to the extent that secularization refers to the historical process that tends to overthrow religion or spirituality as a primary source of explanation of the cosmos in favor of more scientific (that is, rationalized) reasoning, this reconfiguration conveys an epistemological meaning. The separation serves the purpose of setting what basic questions about the cosmos can be asked and who is authorized to ask them (Chambers 2017). This architecture encapsulated a historically determined tie between Christian theology and Western philosophy, between modern science and Christian theology, and between modern science and Western philosophy. Scientists affirmed the essential difference of their own object of study from philosophers' on the basis that their objectivation of nature allowed them to attain a higher degree of certitude (Daston and Galison 2007). There follows that scientific knowledge came to be understood as a neutral matter of fact: independent from the possible usages and scope it could serve, transparent as to the interests of the different and often conflicting social groups experiencing unequal distribution of power and resources, moved by its own inner logic separated from the different interests behind it. At the same time, the exclusion of philosophical reasoning from the realm of scientific knowledge production tended to silence those voices that called for the responsibility of science toward society, or alternatively, vis-à-vis the discriminatory value science can assume against the grain of existing social hierarchies as well as the damages it can produce to the very object of its own inquiry: nature itself.

For this reason, non-Western knowledges reassert the theoretical relevance of those systems of knowledge production that refuse the neat separation between religious and spiritual beliefs, as well as between metaphysical reasoning and science. They reaffirm the inextricability of all these dimensions in the production of knowledge. From the vantage point of non-Western knowledges, this condition appears already given in the form of a holistic view of the cosmos according to which the prominence of causal explanation does not belong exclusively in a rationalist horizon of understanding. While modern Western thinking sets the borders between what human knowledge can achieve and moves fundamental questions about nature and existence outside the realm of science, non-Western knowledges assume the limited horizon of human rationalist knowledge as internal to knowledge production itself (Harding 1987). This posture enables a different understanding of what rationality is, and for whom. Here the concept of non-Western knowledges exposes the original conflation it emerges from when disentangled from the oppositional logic against dominant western hegemonic knowledge. Within the "non-Western" heterogeneous space of theory production there exist two major paths: one conceives its own site of enunciation located in the multiple locations of the Global South and draws inspiration from the living history of anticolonial struggle (see Santos and Meneses 2020; Connell 2007); the other adopts a long-term temporal perspective that extends much further backward and draws inspiration from ancient wisdom and more sedimented systems of knowledge in Asia (Acharya and Buzan 2019). These paths are not disjunct, yet they entail a nonhomogeneous relation with hegemony and with national identity. The former is more focused on the social sciences at large, while the latter finds international relations theory as its own space of gnoseological effervescence. Non-Western knowledges from the Global South are relatively more inspired by antihegemonic claims (Ramose 2002; Mamdani 2018): they seem uninterested in creating an institutionalized form of hegemonic power of their own within the existing structures of domination, which would remain unchanged. They conceive knowledge formation as a process in the making of the struggle for recognition, liberation, and social justice (Medrano Valdez 2020; Tiong'o 2009). Non-Western knowledges, particularly from Asia, are relatively more counterhegemonic (Chu 2022; Mallavarapu 2014): they look to the multipolar configuration of the global world order as a way to reshape the hierarchy of world hegemony (Watanabe and Rösch 2018; Zhao 2021). The geohistorical reference of the former are the Indigenous subaltern groups (Escobar 2008; Lipsham 2020; Subramani 2003). The geohistorical reference of the latter mostly coincides with existing global powers where identity gets stronger approximating to the level of the nation-state, such as India, Japan, or China (Alejandro 2018; Shimizu 2022).

An underlying logical structure of thinking is common to all the antidualist position that connotes the heterogeneous space of non-Western epistemologies in their attempt to question the validity of the presumed reliability of modern Western knowledge grounded upon the scientific method: the separation between rational human agents and nonhuman agents loses its overwhelming validity and appeal (Kohn 2013). In fact, in modern Western hegemonic thinking, the separation between the realm of the human and the realm of the nonhuman represents the last degree, the bottom line, of the production of alterity that lies at the foundation of the process of concept formation (Pagden 1984). The dehumanization of anthropological alterity is the quintessence of colonial modernity. Historically, it connects the genocide of pre-Columbian native communities in the Americas with the slave trade in the Atlantic and Indian oceans, with the twentieth-century totalitarian extermination of racialized ethnic groups, with migrants' onslaught in the Mediterranean Sea or at the border between the United States and Mexico. The border between human and nonhuman, under the rule of the nation-state in colonial capitalist modernity, is always a necropolitical border. Achille Mbembe has grasped the social construction of such a border through the reconceptualization of necropolitics. Necropolitics is the technology of social control that colonial capitalist modernity implements to unilaterally establish which people are human and have the right to live and which people are less than human and therefore can die. According to Giorgio Agamben (1998), necropolitics consists in the power to suspend ordinary law and unilaterally declare an exception, resonantly with the notion of the absolute power of the state that Michel Foucault envisioned as the quintessence of modern governmentality (Foucault 2010). Mbembe clarifies that from a postcolonial vantage point, necropolitics operates asymmetrically across what W. E. B. Du Bois called the color line: necropolitics is the global technology of social control that assures Western hegemonic power with the legitimacy to contextually define which bodies are authorized to live and which are not authorized to live because they are not human enough (Mbembe 2003). Yet, to the extent that the necropolitical relation produces the boundary between the human and the nonhuman, it also enables such a boundary to be a border of existence, that is, to become a spacetime of resistance (Mezzadra and Neilsen 2013). In the borderscapes across nonhuman spacetimes of resistance, mysterious things happen. Borderscapes are disseminated on the planet even though they seldom appear on the map of the world that composes the Western cartography of global capitalist colonial modernity.

The Cuban writer Roberto Fernàndez Retamar traced a route to one of these borderscapes at the turn of the 1960s. He got on William Shakespeare's trail, following the footprints Shakespeare had left before he died in 1616, when he wrote his last play, *The Tempest* (1610). More than his footprints, in fact, Retamar sailed through the sea waves guided by the imaginary map that the English playwright had suggested, in search of an island hidden in the Mediterranean Sea. Nothing is known of the exact coordinates of this hidden island, only that it is located between the coastal city of Naples on the northern shore and the coastal city of Cartagena on the southern shore of the Mediterranean. Twelve years before the facts that *The Tempest* narrates, a powerful magician and former Duke of Milan named Prospero and his young daughter Miranda had their lives saved when they approached the mysterious island. They were castaways. Prospero's rival brother Antonio, together with the king of Naples, Alonso, plotted a maneuver against him and his successor daughter who was the legitimate heir to the throne. The conspirer committed father and daughter to exile and left them on a fragile boat in the sea, dooming them to death while ascending undisturbed to power. When Prospero and Miranda reached the island, a creature was already inhabiting it: Caliban. Shakespeare presents Caliban as an almost-human deformed being. Through the other characters' voices, Shakespeare describes Caliban's physical appearance as "freckled, a misshapen knave, not honoured with a human shape, thou tortoise, a strange fish. . . . Legged like a man." Caliban has the semblance of a monster. His dead mother, Sycorax, was a powerful witch who had been a castaway herself when, while pregnant, she had reached the island escaping from Algiers. Sycorax taught Caliban natural magic and witchcraft. Together with the perfect handling of the natural environment of the island, its territory, waters, flora, fauna, winds, and seasons, Caliban thus possessed a precious knowledge that the civilized urban Prospero and Miranda absolutely needed to survive as castaways. The story goes that Prospero enslaved Caliban with his powerful influence but then became dependent on his slave's workforce for all the material condition of his and his daughter's existence. This is the backstory to the narrative that unfolds in the play. *The Tempest* begins with Prospero using his magic powers to take advantage of the news that Ariel, a spirit of the air that serves him, brings him: namely, that the usurpers are navigating next to the hidden island. Unaware of Prospero's presence there, they fall victim to his revenge as Prospero generates a tempest that forces their shipwreck on the island and makes Ferdinand, heir to the king of Naples, fall in love with Miranda to restore his position in Milan and simultaneously assure his lineage on another throne. In the end, then, everyone lives happily ever after.

Yet, in his analysis Retamar disregards this revenge story side of the plot and focuses on Caliban. In his interpretation, Caliban becomes the real protagonist of the counterhistory of *The Tempest*. Who is Caliban, then? Why is he relevant? Retamar answers by starting from taxonomy. The Elizabethan theater inherited the narrative strategy of naming characters with words that personify their essential traits. *Nomen omen* is the ancient Latin motto for the literal correspondence of taxonomy with characteristics. *Prospero* means prosperous and *Miranda* is the Italian passive form of the verb *mirare,* "to look," to look at with admiration; therefore, it means "to be seen," which, personified, becomes "who deserves to be looked at." Miranda, eventually, is a circumlocution for aesthetic beauty. Retamar unveils that *Caliban* is the phonetic anagram Shakespeare invented from the word "cannibal." *Canìbal,* as it originally appeared, is the phonetic deformation of Caribe, which is the name under whose taxonomic umbrella multiple indigenous pre-Columbian Amerindian ethnic groups inhabiting central and southern America were called by the other inhabitants of the same archipelago, such as the Taìnos, who were the principal local informants of Columbus and early Spanish conquistadores in the Antilles. The Caribe were sea travelers, which is why the Caribbean Sea took their endo-ethnonym. They had their own language. They were militarily organized, and they fiercely opposed colonization in the early stage of the European arrival. The Caribe represented the opposite side of the Taìnos who, instead, were peaceful and welcoming to the conquistadores, therefore domesticable.

From the diary of navigation that Columbus wrote between autumn 1492 and summer 1493, this opposition emerges clearly. The Caribe people provided the first anthropological material to nourish the colonizer's imagination of the evil savage. Columbus describes them as one-eyed, dog-snouted, anthropophagus men. The phonetic deformation of Caribe, Carib, Caribas, Caribàles, in the Italianized Spanish idiom of Columbus, became Canibales, the plural form of Canìbal, and thus *cannibal*, i.e., anthropophagus. This is only one of the oddities that historians discovered in Columbus's diaries. These were pages written by sailors who were starved, victims of collective mirages or individual hallucinations. To be sure, on the other side of the colonial encounter, the leadership of the peaceful Taìnos used to interpret the unknown and foresee the future by means of the ritual usage of the visionary hallucinogen source ayahuasca. The Caribe, instead, were feared and respected also by the other ethnic groups in the region. These voices fed the information that the first colonizers received about them. On these bases, in a successive page of the same diary, Columbus provided the etymology of Canibal. According to him, Canibal is the name of the people populating the Gran Can Island (Retamar [1971] 2000). While in English the word *can* is a modal verb, in Italian it function as a prefix in Canibal and this word means only and simply "dog." It is not a coincidence that the same etymology transpires in the name given to the equatorial archipelagos of the Canary Islands, located opposite Morocco off the western Atlantic coast of Africa, two centuries before Columbus wrote his diaries. Europeans named those African islands "Canary" after the very first expeditions in the area led by Genoese, Spanish, Portuguese, and Florentine sailors in the late thirteenth century. Why did they thus name those islands, after naming Gran Canaria, the major island in the archipelagos? Because the conceptual archive they possessed to define the unknown ethnic groups they met there for the first time had been modeled upon a weird ethnographic work that had been circulating since 1249: the *Istoria Mongalorum quos nos Tartaros appellamus* (*The History of the Mongols We Call Tartars*), written by Giovanni da Pian del Carpine. Giovanni was one of the first Franciscans, a close friend of Saint Francis of Assisi. During the period of the Crusades, the newly elected pope, Innocent IV, appointed Giovanni to run a very delicate diplomatic mission: to ask the Gran Khan to retire the Mongol troops that had conquered the entire Eurasia from China, penetrating as far as less than a hundred kilometers from the northeastern Italian region of Friuli. The ethnography Giovanni wrote along his journey was published immediately after he returned to Rome in 1247. Along with notes about the history, culture, and customs of the several ethnic groups he encountered in the obscure Eastern lands, it is also full of oddities. He probably heard these legends and unverifiable narratives about imaginary inhabitants of the territories he crossed during his adventurous journey toward Karakorum, the city in Northern China, which the Gran Khan had chosen as the site for the capital of the Mongol empire. The word *Khan* in ancient Mongol (and Turkish) means "prince, sovereign." In the process of Latinization through transmission with its phonetic transcription, oral circulation, and orthographic errors, Khan became Can (in the Venetian dialect that was the language of the chronicles from travelers to the East as they all departed from and returned to Venice); *cane* (in Italian): dog (Pesce 2020, 14–16). In fact, among the most important ethnic groups Giovanni wrote about in his notes are those of the land of Cynocephali: dog-head men.

The Cynocephali were not exactly savage. They had their own civilization, their own religion with its clergy, their own institutions and customs. The Cynocephali would have lived in the region around Lake Baikal, in Siberia. To be sure, Giovanni's ethnographical notes were not astonishingly novel to his Christian European audience. The *Istoria Mongolarum* confirmed the customary European late medieval cartography according to which different species of monstrous creatures inhabited those regions that had remained inaccessible to Western terrestrial travelers. A peculiar example was the periodical revival (in the aftermath of failure in the crusades) of the legend of the existence of a mysterious Christian kingdom that Prester John would have founded in the East, where he would guard the Holy Grail. Such a strategy of managing diversity was parallel to the one Chinese cartographers of the Celestial Empire would use when they had to describe the western regions beyond India and the Caucasus (Smith 2013). As Marshall Sahlins (1993, 16) ironically put it, Western people are not playing with amateurs in the game of constructing the other.

By analogy, the same logic that served the geographical imagination and its ethnographic rationale served to map maritime regions in the space surrounding the territories of Christendom until the cartographic revolution that Dutch explorers achieved during their hegemony in the seventeenth-century world-system (Cook 2007). Thus, when Columbus associated Cynocephali with cannibalism, he created an anthropological monster coherent with the system of production of alterity that was part of the conceptual archive Christian European knowledge of non-Western worlds had managed for at least two centuries: the conceptual archive that they brought with them to codify the anthropological unknown since the early stages of the Age of Explorations in the fifteenth century (Adas 1990).

Caliban was just one among many other creatures of a Eurocentric bestiary by which the Europeans filtered and materialized their worldviews in the premodern and modern globalizing world-system of colonial interethnic relations. Ladies and gentlemen, Caliban:

> *Act I, Scene* II
>
> PROSPERO [*to Caliban*]
> Thou poisonous slave, got by the devil himself
> Upon thy wicked dam, come forth!
> *Enter Caliban.*
>
> CALIBAN
> As wicked dew as e'er my mother brushed
> With raven's feather from unwholesome fen

Drop on you both. A southwest blow on you
And blister you all o'er.

PROSPERO
For this, be sure, tonight thou shalt have cramps,
Side-stitches that shall pen thy breath up. Urchins
Shall [forth at] vast of night that they may work
All exercise on thee. Thou shalt be pinched
As thick as honeycomb, each pinch more stinging
Than bees that made 'em.

CALIBAN
I must eat my dinner.
This island's mine by Sycorax, my mother,
Which thou tak'st from me. When thou cam'st first,
Thou strok'st me and made much of me, wouldst give me
Water with berries in 't, and teach me how
To name the bigger light and how the less,
That burn by day and night. And then I loved thee,
And showed thee all the qualities o' th' isle,
The fresh springs, brine pits, barren place and fertile.
Cursed be I that did so! All the charms
Of Sycorax, toads, beetles, bats, light on you,
For I am all the subjects that you have,
Which first was mine own king; and here you sty me
In this hard rock, whiles you do keep from me
The rest o' th' island.

PROSPERO
Thou most lying slave,
Whom stripes may move, not kindness, I have used thee,
Filth as thou art, with humane care, and lodged thee
In mine own cell, till thou didst seek to violate
The honor of my child.

CALIBAN
O ho, O ho! Would 't had been done!
Thou didst prevent me. I had peopled else
This isle with Calibans.

MIRANDA
Abhorrèd slave,
Which any print of goodness wilt not take,
Being capable of all ill! I pitied thee,
Took pains to make thee speak, taught thee each hour
One thing or other. When thou didst not, savage,
Know thine own meaning, but wouldst gabble like
A thing most brutish, I endowed thy purposes
With words that made them known. But thy vile race,
Though thou didst learn, had that in 't which good natures
Could not abide to be with. Therefore wast thou
Deservedly confined into this rock,
Who hadst deserved more than a prison.

CALIBAN
You taught me language, and my profit on 't
Is I know how to curse. The red plague rid you
For learning me your language!

PROSPERO
Hagseed, hence!
Fetch us in fuel; and be quick, thou 'rt best,
To answer other business. Shrugg'st thou, malice?
If thou neglect'st or dost unwillingly
What I command, I'll rack thee with old cramps,
Fill all thy bones with aches, make thee roar
That beasts shall tremble at thy din.

CALIBAN
No, pray thee.
[*Aside.*] I must obey. His art is of such power
It would control my dam's god, Setebos,
And make a vassal of him.

PROSPERO
So, slave, hence.
[*Caliban exits.*]

This scene is clearly exemplificative of the colonial relation, but also of the reciprocal interpellation that produces the semantic space between Western, non-Western and post-Western knowledge. Caliban has learned the language of the colonizer. He is able to curse his usurper by speaking the words of domination. In Retamar's view, Caliban occupies the subaltern position in the oversimplified social hierarchy of the island, but he is not annihilated. Caliban is the center of Retamar's interpretation. True, the enslaved monster works hard for his master. He feels betrayed like an ingenuous savage, but while Prospero has appropriated the material knowledge of what he desires to satisfy his and his daughter's basic needs by exploiting the natural resources of the island, Caliban has appropriated the grammatical and phonetic structure that codifies Prospero's magic powers. Caliban knows more about Prospero than Prospero knows about Caliban, since Prospero, for twelve years, was never interested in the prelinguistic dimension of the form of knowledge that Caliban handled to make sense of the world before they met. Caliban preserves a generative space of knowledge formation hidden from Prospero. Such a subtraction disables the possibility of Prospero's appropriation and full control. The Martiniquan writer Édouard Glissant (1990) conceptualized the possibility for the colonial subject to escape the colonizer's ability to make the non-Western worlds transparent, and hence exposed to grabbing, through the concept of opacity. Caliban does not make his world fully transparent to Prospero. In so doing, Caliban inhabits a border that Prospero ignores. The prelinguistic space that Prospero ignores does not fully overlap with the colonial border between Caliban and his own civilized, erudite, urban, aristocratic Renaissance world. Caliban inhabits the border between the opacity he preserves on his own side of the colonial relation and the realm of the nonhuman. Such a border is not thinkable in terms of a geometric line, a boundary: it is a wide and extended space, an abyss of understanding that Caliban is able to experience while Prospero cannot.

Eduardo Kohn (2013) conceives of this borderscape by means of a conceptual difference between language and representation. For him, the nonhuman produces knowledge that is irreducible to the conventional linguistic or symbolic understanding of what a concept is (Kohn 2013, 51). Nonhuman entities think through processes of concept formation whose semiosis functions in ways that share only a limited number of commonalities with how language functions for human agents (Kohn 2013, 8–9):

> We conflate representation with language in the sense that we tend to think of how representation works in terms of our assumptions about how human language works. Because linguistic representation is based on signs that are conventional, systemically related to one another, and "arbitrarily" related to their objects of reference, we tend to assume that all representational processes have these properties. But symbols, those kinds of signs that are based on convention (like the English word *dog*), which are distinctively human representational forms, and whose properties make human language possible, actually emerge from and relate to other modalities of representation. . . . These non-symbolic

> representational modalities pervade the living world—human and nonhuman—and have underexplored properties that are quite distinct from those that make human language special. Although there are anthropological approaches that do move beyond the symbolic . . . these approaches fail to recognize that signs also exist well beyond the human (a fact that changes how we should think about human semiosis as well). Life is constitutively semiotic. That is, life is, through and through, the product of sign processes. What we share with nonhuman living creatures, then, is not our embodiment, as certain strains of phenomenological approaches would hold, but the fact that we all live with and through signs.

Here, the notion of nonhuman includes what conventionally would be distinctively animated or nonanimated. This dualism is based upon an individualist understanding of consciousness where every living being is an entity whose existence is an instantiation of singularity. From such a vantage point, forms of nonhuman agency like a river, a lagoon, a mountain, or a forest would be the sum of single animated consciousnesses embedded in a system of relations that entail nonanimated objects such as stones or minerals. Instead, a forest, a river, and a lagoon are nonhuman agents that involve a complex system of relations of beings where the nonanimated does not exist, since they are able literally *to think*. The separation between human and nonhuman assumes a specific analytical value: it serves to focus on the specificity of human language in order to provincialize it and to unveil to what extent anthropocentrism is a tool to colonize our entire view about the ways everything that does not instantiates in the form of human beings functions by means of language, yet differently conceived, and responds to other-than-human logics of concept formation. This implies a novel and wider understanding of *concept*: a form, rather than a specific content:

> For example, the associational logic of symbolic reference, which is so central to human thought and language, results in the creation of general concepts, such as, say, the word bird. Such a general concept is more constrained than the various actual utterances of the word *bird* through which it is instantiated. Utterances, then, are more variable, less constrained, and "messier" than the concept they express. That is, there will be great variation in how any particular utterance of a word such as bird actually sounds. And yet the general concept, to which all of these particular utterances refer, allows these many variable utterances to be interpreted as meaningful instantiations of the concept "bird." This general concept (sometimes termed a "type") is more regular, more redundant, simpler, more abstract, and, ultimately, more patterned than the utterances (referred to as "tokens" in their relation to such types) that instantiate it. Thinking of such concepts in terms of form gets at this characteristic generality that a type exhibits.

> Because language, with its symbolic properties, is distinctively human, it is all too easy to relegate such formal phenomena to human minds. And this encourages us to take a nominalist position. . . . But taking such a position would be tantamount to allowing human language to colonize our thinking. Given that, human language is nested within a broader representational field made up of semiotic processes that emerge in and circulate in the nonhuman living world, projecting language onto this nonhuman world blinds us to these other representational modalities and their characteristics. (Kohn 2013, 158)

The possibility of translation across the human/nonhuman border of thinking transposes the question of the relation between language and representation onto unconventional levels of understanding wherein new ways of concept formation become possible. Language, human language, is not authorized to fully represent nonhuman understanding, but this condition of impossibility is immanent in language itself. This condition is critical, in a specific meaning, as far as the problem of human knowledge is concerned.

According to nineteenth-century German philosopher and literary critic Friedrich Schlegel, *critique* is the interminable human activity concerning the redefinition of the limits of what can be known: it is the art of designating the borders of what is not knowable. Agamben (1993, xv) writes,

> It is common to expect results of a work of criticism, or at least arguable positions and, as they say, working hypotheses. Yet when the "criticism" appears in the vocabulary of Western philosophy, it signifies rather inquiry at the limits of knowledge about precisely that which can be neither posed nor grasped. If limits, insofar as it traces the limits of truth, offers a glance of truths homeland like "an island nature has enclosed within immutable boundaries, it must also remain open to the fascination of the wide and storm-tossed sea that draws the sailor incessantly toward adventure he knows not how to refuse yet may never bring to an end.

In this sense, Caliban is a *maître à penser* for critical human knowledge. Caliban, the monster, epitomizes the process of concept formation whereas thinking takes place from the epistemological borderscape where the non-Western, the nonhegemonic, and the nonhuman cohabit. The space of critical human knowledge is thus inherently transient. Caliban's island in Shakespeare's imagination was located in the Mediterranean, but he painted it with the colors of the palette that the fascinating traveler's diaries of missionaries and explorers returning from the New World suggested to his artistic mind. Shakespeare drew the immediate inspiration for his plot from the 1609 shipwreck in the Bermuda Island of a Vauxhall of the Virginia Company, operating in the context of the nascent British colonial expansion. Yet before this episode, he had read Montaigne's essay on cannibals.

He was a close friend of John Florio, the English translator of Montaigne's essays who had also been one of the few friends of Giordano Bruno, the figure who inspired the character of the erudite magician Prospero, during his stay in London between 1585 and 1587 (Go 2012). The hidden island with Caribbean features could be one of the small ones off the northern African shores of Libya or Tunisia. It could be Pantelleria, Lampedusa, or Lesbos, where migrants in the Mediterranean Sea who survive the contemporary trade of humans challenge the linguistic and epistemological order of modernity (Chambers 2008). The instauration of the nation-state as the overarching system to create the spatial boundaries between human groups in the modern world presumes a homolinguistic regime (Sakai 1991, 1997, 2000). Until the early modern period, learned Europeans proudly flaunted that they were polyglot, and all the other groups in the social stratification managed to use a variety of languages and vernacular that responded to the fragmented status of political and juridical authority that the concentration of power into the nation-state tendentially transformed and simplified (Sakai and Mezzadra 2014). Migrants, because of their mobility, their postcolonial plurilingualism, and the antihegemonic body politics they enact, challenge the homolinguistic regime that associates a single language with a dominant ethnocentric group within the border of a single nation-state; therefore, the migrant as a concept is the form of an epistemological alterity.

Also migrants are castaways, as Sycorex and her Caliban were, or the thousands of African mothers who were forced through the Middle Passage of the Atlantic to the Americas. In the 1990s, the Du Bois–inspired Detroit Afrofuturist electronic music ensemble Drexciya invented an imaginary civilization that would thrive in the abysses of the Atlantic, a dystopic version of the myth of Atlantis. Drexciya is the name of the underwater colony populated by the hypertechnological amphibious humanoid civilization made of the progeny that descended from the first generation of children of enslaved black women who died in the Middle Passage to the Americas. Fetuses matured in the ocean, first learning to breathe in deep water by surviving encapsulated in the bloody wombs of their agonized mothers. This dystopia empowers the figure of monstrosity with a hypertechnological dimension that projects the migrant, enslaved, dehumanized, non-Western, nonhuman, and more-than-human into a futuristic dimension of possibility. In so doing, it expands what C. Wright Mills (1959) called the sociological imagination beyond the suffocating boundaries of the hegemonic modern Western thinking. Historically, language has been a major colonial tool to dehumanize anthropological difference. Social groups that were unable to write their own language were considered less human than the others, and to the extent they proved unable or unwilling to learn the ways the colonizers imposed their own language or even the way the colonized had to think to their own language after the colonizer had coded it in grammars or books, they were considered less than human: beast-like beings with the bodily semblances of humans, closer to animals than citizens. The mobility of this threshold between human and nonhuman exposes the logic of dehumanization beyond the space of anthropological reason: it establishes not only who is more human than others but also that human language is the only language properly conceived. In so doing dehumanization conceals that nonhuman languages deploy different modalities of functioning. These different modalities are either "iconic" (involving signs that share likenesses with the things they represent) or "indexical" (involving signs that are in some way affected by or otherwise correlated with those things they represent; Kohn 2013, 9). Iconic and indexical modalities belong both to human and nonhuman process of thinking through single linguistic forms of instantiations, namely concepts. Therefore, if dehumanization is the limit of conceptualization, then monstrosity becomes the methodological principle of a teratologic approach to concept formation that acts as the antonym of dehumanization.

To be sure, whatever aspiration to elaborate a "method," "a way to think through," or "a way to form concepts and operationalize them" implies the conformation of differences and terminological normalization over historical particularities and social specificities. To the extent concepts are assumed in their heuristic and transitional adequacy, they can be constructed as networks of meanings historically determined and constantly in tension: always unstable. As such, every concept is the by-product of generalization. Generalization implies a reduction of complexity. Reduction of complexity consists in silencing the multiplicity of instances. Silencing nonhegemonic voices in global studies means excluding the non-Western histories, words, and visions from the global conceptual archive of the social sciences. Therefore, every concept can be constantly rethought against the grain of what it had previously excluded and reexamined by exploring the relation between its historical formation and the process of transformation of alterity into deformity that is the foundational act of concept formation in dominant, Western social sciences. Thus dehumanization means producing contextually what is nonhuman, what is irreconcilable with humanity: that is, monstrosity. For this reason, questioning the border between human and nonhuman translates into the alternative strategy of concept formation whose generative grammar is monstrosity. As far as monstrosity is a process rather than a given condition of essence, it is located at the core of such a method. Here, monstrosity becomes the operational logic of a teratologic approach to concept formation.

Teratology implies a further and more sophisticated operationalization of the notion of monstrosity. Teratology is the science of the abnormal development of living beings, the study of physiological monstrosity and deformation that have their origin in embryonic life. During antiquity, at all latitudes, teratology was a form of knowledge that served anthropological, scientific, theological, and geographical purposes (Taruffi [1881] 2006). Teratology is not, however, strictly confined to pathological anatomy. It has served to explain human difference, to locate unknown peoples in space and time, and to construct alterity against presumed antipodal difference. Human groups used teratology to produce their own understanding of the nonhuman and locate the causes of such monstrosity at the level of the generative process of life (Mittman and Dendle 2013). As Lorraine Daston and Katharine Park (2001) have eloquently shown, the transformation of teratology into a more rational enterprise during the fifteenth and sixteenth centuries marked the shift toward a rationalist imagery: from the acceptance of monstrosity as something that was located at the limits of rational understanding to the refusal of monstrosity based on the process of rationalization of the contingent causes for the genesis of monstrosity. In other words, monstrosity lost its etymological sense of epiphanic marvel and passed to signify and delimit the ultimate frontier of the pathological. Teratology, thus, is exemplificative of the way the social sciences established the boundary between the human and the nonhuman, the East and the West. By marking the separation from what was normal and acceptable, rational and human, on the one hand, and what was deviant, abnormal, residual, on the other hand, modernity dropped an intimate colonial line within humanity. This fault line is epitomized by the so-called Siamese twins: at the same time monstrous and exotic. To be sure, this evocative strategy of tracing the border, which is either cultural, geohistorical, or anthropological, is not exclusive of European modern hegemonic thinking. Premodern Chinese culture worked in a similar way as regards the construction of alterity along the fault line that separates civilizations from barbarism (Yue 2010). Thus, teratologic methodology tries to move in the opposite direction than the process of production of otherness, that is, to include what European thinking had excluded to elaborate its conceptual apparatus, into the heart of the linguistic and ideational process of concept formation.

Teratology places a particular emphasis on the generative strategy this method suggests. Teratologic concept formation consists in the methodical effort to think, unthink and rethink notions, by bringing the "global" and the "non-Western" into the morphogenesis—the genesis of the form—of concepts. This aspect can be imagined through a genetic metaphor: the ability to intervene in the genetic code of the conceptual generative grammar considered by changing the basic coordinates of definition, enunciation, and application of a concept. In other words, a controllable, testable, and thus confutable path to de-form existing notions and to form concepts and understandings differently, in order to tackle the instantiations of alterity that the concepts social sciences is used to otherwise are not able to grasp and re-present.

In his doctoral dissertation, *Proofs and Refutations*, Imre Lakatos (1976), unleashed the analytical potential of theoretical monstrosity from within the discipline of philosophy of science. He pioneered the possibility of a rigorous formalization of the role of monstrosity in definitional protocols as well as in concept formation at large. In his imaginary dialogue with his students, Alpha, Delta, and Gamma, in a geometry class, he constructed the difference between counterexamples, aimed at confuting hypotheses about the plausibility of geometrical objects, and a *monstrous polyhedron* whose geometrical deformity challenged taken-for-granted assumptions. Monstrosity thereby installs the "pathological" within the theoretical imagination (Lakatos 1976, 15). The theatrical scene the young Lakatos imagined in a classroom has a teacher as protagonist and facilitator for the students to elaborate their ideas about monstrosity. In the class of teratologic concept formation herewith, beneath the semblance of Lakatos's teacher, appears Caliban:

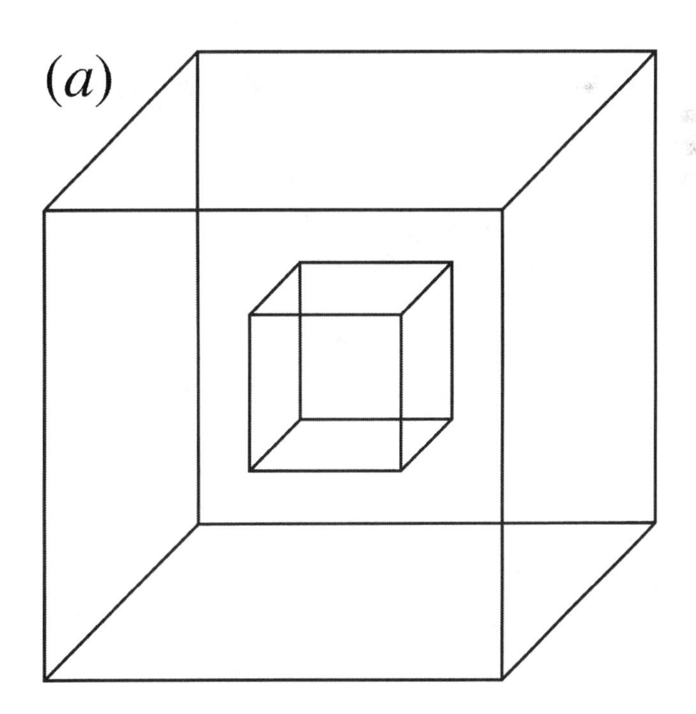

DELTA: I admit that [our theorem] clashes with this so-called "counterexample." One of them has to go away. But why should the theorem give away, when it has been proved? It is the "criticism" that should retreat. It is fake criticism. This pair of nested cubes is not a polyhedron at all. It is a *monster*, a pathological case, not a counterexample.

GAMMA: Why not? *A polyhedron is a solid whose surface consists of polygonal faces*. And my counterexample is a solid bounded by polygonal faces.

CALIBAN: Let's call this *Def.1*.

DELTA: Your definition is incorrect. A polyhedron must be a *surface*: it has faces, edges, vertices, it can be deformed, stretched out on a blackboard, and has nothing to do with the concept of "solid." *A polyhedron is a surface consisting of a system of polygons*.

CALIBAN: Call this *Def.2*.

DELTA: So really you showed us two polyhedra—two surfaces, one completely inside the other. A woman with a child in her womb is not a counterexample to the thesis that all the humans have one head. . . .

ALPHA: Take two tetrahedra which have an edge in common. Or, take two tetrahedra which have a vertex in common. Both these twins are connected, both constitute a single surface.

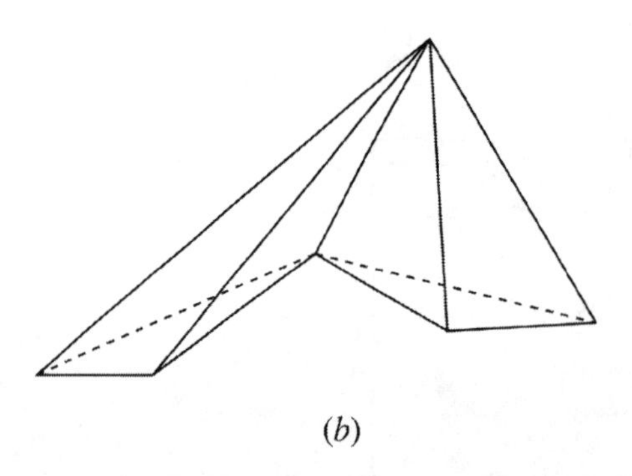

(*b*)

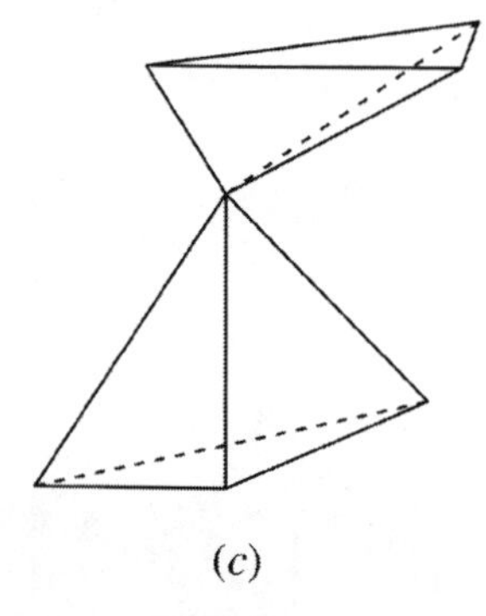

(*c*)

CALIBAN: I am sorry to interrupt you. . . . We *may* achieve such an agreement by defining the term where communication broke down. I, for one, didn't define "polyhedron." I assumed *familiarity* with the concept, i.e., the ability to distinguish a thing which is a polyhedron from a thing which is not a polyhedron—what some logicians call knowing the extension of the concept of polyhedron. It turned

> out that the extension of the concept wasn't at all obvious: *definitions are frequently proposed and argued about when counterexamples emerge*. I suggest that we now consider the rival definitions together.

Before moving to an operational definition of teratologic methodology, let me outline three aspects that emerge from this intertwined reading of monstrosity at the crossroads of the social sciences and the philosophy of science. At a higher level of abstraction, teratology forms a shared space where it becomes possible to conceive the possibility of deforming, informing, and transforming existing concepts toward a global social science: first comes the figurative power of the embryo metaphor between the "pathologic" generation of the new form and the maternal womb of the existing form; second, the heuristic power of the Siamese twins analogy to shift concept formation to the borders of colonial definitions based on the normalization of heterogeneity; and third, the viable strategy of questioning assumptions by destabilizing the familiarity with existing notions and concepts that are taken-for-granted postulates.

PROCEDURAL PROTOCOL

The overall aim of teratologic concept formation is to introduce an adequate methodology bridging methodological formalization and the globalization of knowledge, and to infer a testable method of concept formation out of this methodology. It points to a higher level of formalization. The pathway so conceived aims at informing, deforming, and transforming a concept by disclosing its significance to counterhegemonic, antihegemonic, or nonhegemonic narratives and notions that solicit the elaboration of more adequate conceptual and terminological landmarks, whose cross-cultural semantics exceeds the theoretical archive of the Western social sciences. This aim can be split into objectives that work as interlocked modules. Being a method, the objective consists in connecting successive steps in the flow of reasoning. These steps are modules, each of them working as a set of processes connected to the previous module and the following one for analytic purposes, even though the boundaries between one module and another are arbitrary by-products of the specific methodological premises of teratologic concept formation and are therefore heuristic devices rather than distinct epistemological functions. Modules are connected by means of articulation, as per Stuart Hall's notion. For Hall,

> Articulation is the form of the connection that can make a unity of two different elements, under certain conditions. It is a linkage which is not necessary,

> determined, absolute and essential for all time. You have to ask, under what circumstances can a connection be forged or made? The so-called "unity" of a discourse is really the articulation of different, distinct elements which can be rearticulated in different ways because they have no necessary "belongingness." (Grossberg 1986, 53)

The objectives/modules are three: *definitional*, *procedural*, and *applicative*. A rationale for controlling inference across modules is outlined below.

Definition: Thinking with the Unfamiliar

The first operation, then, consists in removing the epistemological and terminological barriers that oppose to the elaboration of a post-Western globalization of the conceptual language for global studies: the reproduction of Eurocentric paradigms by the criterion of familiarity. Familiarity alludes to an intuitive dimension of language, a dimension hidden beneath what Noam Chomsky's now-classic paradigm of transformational grammar (1978) named "deep structure."[2] Two interlocutors communicate at the superficial level, but the meaning their communication conveys is deeply stratified. Communication at deep strata is possible thanks to an implicit agreement on certain unexpressed rules of interpretation that privilege some intentions over others.

Familiarity operates a double control over the possibility of transgressing the borders of Eurocentrism or, vice versa, rendering those borders more porous in order to allow exchange coming from epistemological otherness. Familiarity establishes a temporal boundary and a spatial one, which together operate an *a priori* control over whether a concept is adequate or not. The temporal boundary consists in a conservative bias, according to which there exists a hierarchy between the old and the new: the already accepted sounds familiar, the never heard sounds unfamiliar. This gives to Western concepts an automatic comparative advantage. This advantage is not simply a historical by-product of academic colonialism and epistemological imperialism (Lander 2001). It is a by-product of Popperian, falsificationist epistemology that, as Lakatos (1976) and Feyerabend (1975) demonstrated in the realm of the philosophy of science, resists change even when adequacy appears largely compromised. The spatial boundary pertains to the civilizational divide that safeguards the ascribed superiority of the concepts elaborated within the Western tradition and its languages over the concepts that belong to other locations and practices. Any attempt at using concepts from other languages, traditions, and geohistorical locations produces perturbations. The former, temporal boundary reasserts the ontology of nineteenth-century positivism.

The latter, spatial boundary relegates non-Western notions to the exotic territory of cultural particularism.

This implies methodically exploring the tension between known concepts and the concurrencies of European and non-Western notions regarding analogous social and historical spaces that the concept under scrutiny is devoted to grasp. Unthinking familiarity means providing room for including the possibility of evaluating the geocultural adequacy and the global/non-Western historical relevance of each concept. The aim is to explore, interrogate, validate, or question formed and forming concepts. The heuristic strategy that teratologic methodology introduces consists in systematically making concepts and notions unfamiliar, rather than judging their relevance on the basis of how familiar they are. Questioning familiarity is intended to show the historically determined relations of power and self-ascribed authority underlying given concepts.

According to Antonio Gramsci, when freed from evolutionism and positivism, the core theoretical problematics of sociology share the same epistemological issues with political science. For both, however, noncoincident forms of knowledge, the elaboration of concepts, and the use of categories relate to a wider Weltanschauung (Gramsci 1975, 80), which points to overlapping methodological questions. From the perspective of the profound critique of Western thinking that Linda Tuhiwai Smith (1999, 172) elaborated in her research program of decolonizing methodologies from the so-called Māori Renaissance, *mātauranga* (knowledge and wisdom), its constant production, reproduction, and transmission implies a nongeneralist yet technical dimension:

> When Cook arrived here in the eighteenth century, he found a thriving and complex society. Later voyagers and travelers, including Christian missionaries, were fascinated and heartened that Māori concepts relating to cosmology and spirituality were so sophisticated. Missionaries, for example, were reported to have had little difficulty in talking about spiritual concepts with Māori people. Although later settlers saw little that was civilizing in Māori beliefs or practice, earlier visitors, including many missionaries, were appreciative of the breadth and sophistication of Māori epistemology. Because of the way Māori society was structured, because of its unique world view, and because of its strong oral tradition, knowledge itself was never held to be universally available. Māori society valued knowledge highly, to such an extent that certain types of knowledge were entrusted to only a few members of the whanau. Some knowledge was considered to be *tapu* and there were sanctions that ensured that it was protected, used appropriately, and transmitted with accuracy.

The reproduction of the hegemony of the colonial conceptual archive works also thanks to the presumption that the production of knowledge in non-Western epistemologies is something either spontaneous, therefore casual, or atavic, therefore immutable. This presumption automatically downshifts non-Western epistemologies to a lower level of possible formalization that allows Western social sciences to not taking into consideration the inadequacy of the Western hegemonic conceptual archive to perform complex, abstract, specific linguistic and conceptual tasks when related to non-Western contexts of knowledge production, where the same tasks are performed by other, different, adequate concepts elaborated in others terms, on other social needs, in other languages. Karen Fisher (2022, 22) explains, "Mātauranga is enacted through a range of means including *whakapapa*, the perspective *kanga* (customs and protocols), *kaitiakitanga* (guardianship), *karakia* (prayer and incantations), *mō teatea* (chants), *pūr ākau* (stories and narratives), *pepeha* (tribal sayings) and *whakatauk ī* (proverbs)."

From the perspective of the reciprocal co-formation of concepts across Western and non-Western epistemologies in the methodological space of global studies, it becomes clear how Gerring's eight criteria of classification remain entirely within the horizon of the universal applicability of Western notions, in two respects. First, these criteria are elaborated without taking into consideration the problem of scaling up geoculturally, in order to create the possibility of a dialogue between Western and Non-western experiences and ideas, oriented toward the process of concept formation. Second, they do not allow for the possibility that the newly forming conceptual archive of global studies is open to include concepts that are not translatable into the existing Western notions, as they are able to emerge from the dialogue within the nonhegemonic across non-Western knowledges and sites of enunciation. By transforming the criterion of familiarity into *unfamiliarity*—that is, a dynamic entry point for rethinking and unthinking existing concepts—concept formation becomes open to incorporate the generative nexus between methodological formalization and globalization of knowledge, and remains open to what cannot be conceived from within its restricted Eurocentric intellectual horizon.

Procedure

The objective is to establish a protocol of concept formation that enables active engagement with the process of deforming, informing, and transforming existing notions, currently challenged by the globalization of European knowledge and the destabilization produced by non-Western epistemologies, notions, and experiences. This objective is achieved by means of three intertwined strategies. The first is genealogical/geocultural. The second is epistemological. The third is logical/semantical.

The *first procedural step* pertains to the possibility of extending in space and time the genealogy of the concept considered. In other words, it sets out to produce a cross-genealogy oriented toward other civilizational and cultural traditions and epistemologies. The aim is to find out whether and how analogous conceptions exist and in what way they differ from those elaborated within Western knowledge. This concept-to-concept analysis puts particular emphasis on the processes of construction of conceptual and historical otherness that lie at the foundation of Eurocentric notions. The result expected from this first step is to create a porous semantic field wherein the reciprocal interpellation of concepts across cultures allows alternative narratives—narratives that are potentially able to inform the process of concept formation by questioning some of the Eurocentric assumptions that ground existing concepts—to find a place.

The *second procedural step* to be formalized follows from the former. It consists in assuming that the alternative histories and experiences under consideration provide plausible epistemological foundations for the concept under scrutiny. A concept elaborated and used in accordance with the dominant Western epistemology is a linguistic form that may overlap with a conceptual set of references conceived within an alternative epistemology grounded in a set of basic foundations different from the one derived from the European experience. The process of putting into dialogue a single concept with the histories and data that exceed it because they are produced by different nondominant and non-Western social groups may deform it. This deformation enables non-Western experiences and approaches to find representation within the enlarged semantic space of the concept itself. But this attempt can also show the inadequacy of the concept under scrutiny to refer to this excluded otherness. This means that dialogue is a possible strategy that consists in the collective creation of a space of concept formation, where this space is transformed by the copresence of different stories, data, experiences (and their voices), and networks of words insisting upon a shared semantic territory of definition. The "global" itself is the space of tension where multiple voices speak for themselves on the basis of multiple worlds, histories, and visions they entail, and create either shared but complexified meanings, partially common understanding, or mutually exclusive understandings that expose the existing power relations or evidence the impossibility of a concept to function as linguistic form for non-Western, nonhegemonic references, thereby redefining this space of tension and disclosing it to unexpected horizons due to uncanny presences.

The questions to be answered could be put as follows:

1. In a conservative articulation: "what would the assumptions that provide the concept in question with different epistemological foundations

be in order for the same concept to be as inclusive as possible of the non-Western experiences it dialogues with?"
2. Or, in a more disruptive articulation: "what are the non-Western epistemological and historical differences that the western concept at stake is unable to refer to?"
3. Or, in an other-than-Western articulation: "what do the non-Western experiences share with other non-Western, or even Western yet non-hegemonic experiences that the concept at stake misrepresents or silences?"
4. Or, in a generative articulation: "what new concept would be more adequate to linguistically represent what the original Western concept called into question unilaterally subsumed under the hegemonic pretension to establish, in Linda Smith's (1999,44) words, 'what counts for real'?"

Four approaches to concept formation exemplify each of these possible outreaches, even though they do not express isolable strategies, since they are intimately entrenched to one another. They work as illustrative tools: they are not ideal types.

1. *River* by Karen Fisher. Drawing on Lisa Smith's *Decolonizing Methodology*, Fisher (2022, 20) focuses on the concept of the river as a privileged site of difference that from Māori knowledge production perspective is able to question Western hegemonic assumptions about "rivers." River is an epistemological locus of confrontation that does not exclude *a priori* the contribution of modern Western science to decolonize its meaning and contribute to the defense of Indigenous communities and postcolonial repair of capitalist destruction. Therefore, "research about rivers reveals a range of perspectives and epistemologies that emphasize relationality, complexity and connectivity," including fluvial geomorphological studies concerned about the physical degradation of rivers, pollution, and possible restoration and rehabilitation of previous conditions, making rivers seen as coproduced systems co-constituted by social, natural, and cultural processes. The problem of rethinking the river here stems from ecological concerns. It acknowledges intercultural communication, particularly with regard to Indigenous peoples and Indigenous knowledges, and allows to look at rivers in holistic terms allowing to accommodate epistemological differences, including Māori ways of knowing, doing, and being. River preserves its linguistic presence, yet its epistemological and semantic foundation is enlarged to include *Ki uta ki tai*, a Māori concept that means literally "from the mountains to the sea." *Ki uta ki tai* emphasizes

the interconnectedness and complexity of natural and social systems grounded upon the assumptions according to which the environment is as an indivisible and holistic system that connects humans to other humans and nonhumans across time and space (Fisher 2022, 21–22). In Māori epistemology, rivers are a lively assemblage of physical, social, and metaphysical properties, knowledge, and relations that connect people, places, waters, and beings (including the supernatural) across time and space. It is relational and inseparable from identity, ways of knowing and being, history, and the indivisibility of rivers as a physical and metaphysical entity.

2. *Abstract labor* by Dipesh Chakrabarty. In his path-breaking study of the history of class consciousness among the jute workers in Bengal since the turn of the nineteenth century, Chakrabarty (1988) takes issue with Marx's central category of abstract labor. For Chakrabarty, the history of class consciousness was Eurocentric to the extent it was based on the assumption "that workers all over the world, irrespective of their specific cultural pasts, experience 'capitalist production; in the same way. Since there cannot be any 'experience' without a 'subject' defining it as such, the propositions end up conferring on working classes in all historical situations a (potentially) uniform, homogenized, extrahistorical subjectivity" (Chakrabarty 1988, 223). In his *Provincializing Europe*, Chakrabarty (2000, 52) further exposed how abstract labor endorses a categorical structure "predicated on the Enlightenment ideas of juridical equality and the abstract political rights of citizenship. Labor that is juridically and politically free—and yet socially unfree—is a concept embedded in Marx's category of 'abstract labor.' The idea of abstract labor thus combines the Enlightenment themes of juridical freedom (rights, citizenship) and the concept of the universal and abstract human who bears this freedom." Marx explained the dynamics of subsumption of historical differences under the monolithic law of capitalist accumulation through the constant dialectics between two kinds of histories: histories "posited by capital" and histories that do not belong to capital's "life process." From a postcolonial perspective on class consciousness history, Chakrabarty entered this distinction and renamed these two terms History 1 and History 2. He emphasizes the way Marx accorded universal meaning to History 1 and particularistic meaning to History 2, gathering the multiplicity of historically determined forms of concrete configuration of the capital-labor relation in every single spacetime context of colonial world capitalism. Chakrabarty shows that History 1 is universal only to the extent the history of class consciousness in Europe is transformed by Marx into the Eurocentric reference for all the other histories of class consciousness to be understood.

History 1 does not exist in itself. Every single History 2 could undergo an analogous process of abstraction. Therefore, abstract labor is the conceptual by-product of a particular process of concept formation from a specific history that places itself as the paradigmatic experience thanks to the power relation it draws legitimacy from. In so doing, Chakrabarty delegitimizes the colonial and Eurocentric meaning of the concept of abstract labor and discloses its relative inadequacy, thereby calling for its rethinking in the perspective of the possibility of global history of class consciousness open to non-Western experiences, articulated into post-Western categories of inquiry.

3. *Tianxia* by Zhao Tingyang. In the debate about the existence of alternative conceptual resources in International Relations Theory during the last twenty years, contributions from China have been terminologically relevant. Zhao (2002) entered the debate proposing the *Tianxia* as an alternative conceptualization one of the pillars of Western political lexicon: cosmopolitanism. He maintains that "[t]o [re]order the world we need to first create new world concepts which will lead to new world structures." Zhao juxtaposes *Tianxia* and cosmopolitanism in order to show the ability of the former to include normative and analytical dimensions that the latter is unable to fulfill: "The [concept of] All-under-Heaven (Tianxia) means firstly the earth, or the whole world under heaven. Its second meaning is the 'hearts of all peoples,' or the 'general will of the people.'" Zhao returns to the notion of *Tianxia* as it emerged in the Chinese tradition during the Zhou dynasty (c.1100–256 BCE), and not on the unified Chinese empire after 221 BCE, because, according to him, the practice of imperial China deviated from the best practices of the Zhou dynasty, thus distorting the *Tianxia* ideal: "An emperor does not really enjoy his empire of All-under-Heaven, even if he conquers an extraordinary vastness of land, unless he receives the sincere and true support from the people on the land. Its third meaning, the ethical and/or political meaning, is a world institution, or a universal system for the world, a utopia of the world-as-one-family" (Zhao 2006, 30). *Tianxia* would then imply a structuralist dimension to the extent it sees the world in terms of underlying unity between its physical, psychological, and political components. These structural dimensions of *Tianxia* are intrinsically entrenched with functional dimensions as well. *Tianxia*, as Zhao proposes it, aspires at synchronizing the physical, psychological, and institutional aspects of worldly existence, by coordinating the different parts of the all-under-heaven, each of them implementing a dedicated function whose underlying logic is that of universal harmony under a single and superior logic of functioning. For this reason, *Tianxia* parallels structural functionalism, its holistic pretentiousness, and the

systemic logic it introduced in Western social sciences since the late 1960s, which reoriented theory and methodology toward the global as a unified space of inquiry (see chapter 5). Yet *Tianxia* adds its own particularistic ethical projection onto the issue of cosmopolitanism, which Western structural functionalism excluded since its presumed objectivity and a-valutativity. From a traditionalist Chinese vision of the connection between the world as global society and traditional Chinese family, *Tianxia* promotes its own ideal of the good society promoted in terms of the greatest worldly family. The family ship grants political and ethical consistency, as well as transitivity, to the good society. It is presumed that the family ship that ethically underpins the structural and functional claims of *Tianxia* theory essentially reflects the general will of all people (Shahi and Ascione 2016).

4. *Ubuntu* by Mogobe Ramose. Since the early emergence of Pan-Africanism during the decolonization struggle in the second half of the twentieth century, *ubuntu* served as a crucial gravitational pole to conceptualize the sense of communalism and reciprocal care, which propelled transnational solidarity among African social movements (Samkange and Samkange1980). In the language Nguni Bantu, the concept of *ubuntu* designs the fundamental relational constitution of humanity, meaning "I exist because you exist." For this reason, Ramose (2022) begins his critique of the Western notion of human rights through *ubuntu*, by posing the question whether the singular "I" is the appropriate pronoun to speak from, since he belongs to that human social group that Frantz Fanon called the wretched of the Earth. Ramose (2022, 59–60) takes issues with the separation between reliable knowledge, on the one hand, and passion, on the other hand, as it would presume the impossible fragmentation of being into *be-ing*: "Often the fragment is presented dogmatically as the truth as it is the case with the unilaterally defined concept of 'science.' On this basis, the present essay does not have a 'scientific' method. . . . My method is not disorderly just because it is not in search of order from the perspective of 'science'. . . . Rather it is the movement of critical reason encountering a complexity of contrasting and contending experiences speaking to the insight that motion is the principle of be-ing. My method may be described as chaorder, chaos and order together on the understanding that the connective 'and' is unacceptable to the extent that it establishes a divide between chaos and order." Ramose's method consists in transformational dialogue, which presupposes that "the recognition that one's ways of thinking and doing are on the same level as those of the other and may therefore be compared," in order to promote what he refers to in terms of "horizontal reasoning." Dialogue cannot be unilateral. This is why Ramose

laments the "cremation" of the wretched of the Earth and the displacement of *ubuntu* into the cinerarium, outside the lexicon of the social sciences. Ramose claims the legitimacy of *ubuntu* that creates a wide south-to-south dialogue among subaltern social groups across the globe, whose voice is never heard. *Ubuntu* itself has never been considered endowed with potential universal value in the lexicon of the social sciences. *Ubuntu* exceeds the dominant Western notion of human rights because it establishes, terminologically and conceptually, that wherever a human being suffers from discrimination or assault, it is the entire humanity that is undergoing that discrimination. Whereas "human rights" is the semantic umbrella under which difference exists in form of alterity and separated existence, *ubuntu* establishes the inner condition of coexistence of human beings as relational constructions that can be fragmented only artificially, negating the reality of connectedness that makes society a human by-product: "Ubuntu as the ethics of 'promote life and avoid killing' shall not die even if all the Bantu peoples shall, by a mysterious human act, be totally and completely obliterated from planet Earth. At that mysterious moment there shall be no one trying to find the cinerarium for uncremated ubuntu" (Ramose 2022, 75).

The *third procedural step* consists in actively generating the new or renewed concept by logically inferring the alternative semantic paths disclosed by changing epistemological assumptions. The global debate in the relevant historical, sociological, and political literature over the notion of the nation-state exemplifies the procedural realm of conceptualization involved. For instance, to the extent the concept of the nation-state is not limited to reflecting the geohistorical space delimited by its political boundaries, as nineteenth-century European science crystallized, but is rethought in the wider context of the colonial history it was part of, the space between the metropolis and the colony would be transformed into an integrated, relational, coextensive one. In this space, borders would work as filters for flows occurring within it rather than separating the two previously imagined spaces. And this would force us to rethink, for instance, the way migratory flows are framed, narrated, communicated, and discussed. Instead, new and alternative conceptions of the state deriving their legitimacy from non-Western historical experiences and conceptual vocabularies are now at odds with the European notion of sovereignty and the way it is entrenched in territorial control. Here, the point would be to bring into consideration the borders of the semantic field of the notion of state, with different possible outcomes, as I shall argue in chapter 5.

Application

The scope is to test the extent to which the newly formed or reformed concepts effectively extend their adequacy: namely, to practice the strategies previously outlined and explore to what the extent they are able to acquire and systematize new non-Western historical evidence, experiences, and standpoints that were not part of the alternative non-Western experiences selected in the previous definitional step, engaging with assertions that become plausible new assumptions to ground alternative conceptualizations into different data or histories. Application invokes the collective critical investigation into the current usage of the concept, which is customary in the social sciences yet derives its legitimacy from the unquestioned reliance on the Eurocentric foundations of the epistemology that global studies has inherited from the social sciences. Two outcomes are discernible in this regard, provided that the entire method is designed to respond to an initial condition of dissatisfaction with the available conceptual vocabulary. The first possible outcome is the extension of the semantic field of the concept considered, together with the enhancement of its descriptive and explanatory power. The second possible outcome is the inconsistency of the concept, which legitimates the argument for abandoning it, because of a manifest inadequacy or inconsistency with the project of a post-Western, non-Eurocentric, global knowledge. The applicative step here introduced, it should be noted, does not necessarily end up following an incremental path. In fact, it is not always possible to reformulate a concept and make it more globally oriented and inclusive. Existing concepts could end up being ineffective from a global perspective. Whereas conceptual redefinition is possible, the objective of extending and improving the vocabulary of the social sciences would be achievable. In this scenario, the usage of the concept reformulated and the reiteration of this new and enlarged meaning would stabilize the semantic field of the newly conceived concept. Whenever, instead, conceptual redefinition is not possible, the concept in question would be forced to become increasingly obsolete. Such obsolescence should be justified and explained. Abandoning a dominant and hegemonic concept should not be driven by pure dismissal, but rather follow from a process of thoughtful rationalization, albeit a rationalization that does not strictly correspond to the dominant mode of Western rationality and is open to other rationalities. Nonhegemonic and non-Western rationalities are called to explain the inadequacy of the concept to abandon and express the alternative rationales they invoke. Through this approach, non-Western epistemologies would not affirm their relevance simply in terms of an act of presence: their relevance to their superior adequacy rather than to their mere declaration of existence. This strategy would serve the purpose of overcoming the particularism to which Western hegemonic knowledge had relegated them and affirm their global projection. This is why the thought process of concept dismissal needs a controllable mode of adequacy evaluation. This second scenario opens the theoretical space of concept formation to acknowledge the limitedness of translation in cross-cultural dialogue toward the possibility of shared narratives not in terms of apodictic statements, but rather in procedural terms.

Inferential Control

The simple rule that regulates the thought flow from one module to another derives from the definition of "method" that drives the so-called Port-Royal Logic. In 1662, Antoine Arnauld and Pierre Nicole synthetized this approach with a single directive: *Ars bene disponendi seriem plurimarum cogitationum*, method is the "art of correctly disposing a series of multiple thinkings." The passage from one module to the following one is constructed along a sequence, being the outcome of the preceding module and the premise of the following one. Rather than being a rigid inferential thought flow, however, this logic is designed to introduce an open-ended metatheoretical control of logical consistency between the first module (definitional) and the second module (procedural). This permits a recursive path of validation of the transitional results across the steps that precede the reformulation, resignification, or generation of a concept (that is, the last and third step of the second, procedural module/objective). The intention is to reach the last, third step of the procedural module (concept generation) with a set of newly established assumptions that will meet the requirement of responding to the globalization of knowledge and at the same time will have sufficient consistency to serve as axioms, and thus meet the requirement of formalization. Inasmuch as this part of the protocol of concept formation is adequately operationalized, the new axioms will be able to operate as newly established foundations for the creative potential of conceptual generative grammar in the last, third step of the procedural module/objective.

Formalization

Introducing and sketching out teratologic concept formation is a way forward from existing impasses in the debate about the possibility of making the conceptual vocabulary in global studies more adequate to the challenges posited to Western thought by the globalization of knowledge and the rising relevance of other, non-Western intellectual and theoretical approaches. The main limit in existing approaches to the problem is the low level of formalization of the endeavor to question or extend the adequacy of existing concepts, thus tying this endeavor to two horses pulling in opposite directions. On the one hand, strong criteria of conceptual adequacy prevent social science from seriously engaging with non-Western concepts, at the same time safeguarding the primacy of the West in the realm of concept formation but simultaneously fostering the rigidities that make these same concepts unable to cope with the globalization of knowledge. On the other hand, the attempt to take into consideration non-Western concepts remains largely on the terrain of cross-cultural translation, ultimately fostering a cultural relativism that prevents social science from producing new, adequate, and scalable concepts whose validity can aspire to draw from local and regional geohistorical and cultural locations to actively respond to the challenges of the globalization of knowledge. Teratologic concept formation mobilizes the "monster analogy" from the social sciences and from philosophy of science in order to rethink the conceptual vocabulary of social science by taking into account the destabilizing effects of reintroducing those narratives and understandings of history and societies from non-Western perspectives, whose *a priori* exclusion from the realm of concept formation was the foundational act of the elaboration of the Western conceptual vocabulary of the social sciences.

NOTES

1. Panikkar explains:

> I call it *diatopical* hermeneutics because the distance to be overcome is not merely temporal, within one broad tradition, but the gap existing between two human *topoi*, "places" of understanding and self-understanding, between two—or more—cultures that have not developed their patterns of intelligibility. . . . Diatopical hermeneutics stands for the thematic consideration of understanding the other *without assuming that the other has the same basic self-understanding*. The ultimate human horizon, and not only differing contexts, is at stake here. (Santos 2007, 92)

2. In extreme synthesis, transformational grammar is a part of the research program in generative grammar that aims at uncovering the hidden rules of communication and meaning in natural languages.

BIBLIOGRAPHY

Adas, Michael. 1990. *Machines as the Measure of Man: Science, Technology, and Ideologies of Western Dominance*. Ithaca, NY: Cornell University Press.

Abbott, Andrew. 2005. "The Idea of Outcome in U.S. Sociology." George Steinmetz (ed.) *The Politics of Method in the Human Sciences: Positivism and Its Epistemological Others*, pp. 393–427 Duhram: Duke University Press.

Abbott, Andrew. 2004. *Methods of Discovery: Heuristics for the Social Sciences*. New York: Norton.Abrams, Philip. "History, sociology, historical sociology." In *Past and Present*, 87: 3–16.

Agamben, Giorgio. 1993. *Stanzas: Word and Phantasm in Western Culture*. Minneapolis: University of Minnesota Press.

———. 1998. *Homo Sacer: Sovereign Power and Bare Life*. Stanford, CA: Stanford University Press.

Akiwowo, Akinsola. 1999. "Indigenous Sociologies. Extending the Scope of the Argument." *International Sociology* 14, no. 2: 115–38.

Alatas, Farid. 2006. *Alternative Discourses in Asian Social Science: Responses to Eurocentrism*. New York: SAGE.

Alatas, Syed Hussein. 2006. "The Autonomous, the Universal and the Future of Sociology." *Current Sociology* 54, no. 1: 7–23.

Alejandro, Audrey. 2018. *Western Dominance in International Relations? The Internationalisation of IR in Brazil and India*. London: Routledge.

Andreopoulos, George J., ed. 1994. *Conceptual and Historical Dimensions of Genocide*. Philadelphia: University of Pennsylvania Press.

Acharya, Amitav, and Barry Buzan, Barry. 2019. *The Making of Global International Relations*. Cambridge: Cambridge University Press.

Ascione, Gennaro. 2014. "Unthinking Modernity: Historical-Sociological, Epistemological and Logical Pathways." *Journal of Historical Sociology* 4, no. 27: 463–89.

———. 2015. "Dissonant Notes on the Post-Secular: Unthinking Secularization in Global Historical Sociology." *Journal of Historical Sociology* 30, no. 2: 403–34.

———. 2016. *Science and the Decolonization of Social Theory: Unthinking Modernity*. London: Palgrave.

———. 2017. "Unthinking Capital: Conceptual and Terminological Landmarks." *Sociology* 51, no. 1: 162–80.

Ascione, Gennaro, and Iain Chambers. 2016. "Global Historical Sociology: Theoretical and Methodological Issues—An Introduction." *Cultural Sociology* 10, no. 3: 301–16.

Bar-Ilan, Meir. 1995. "Prester John: Fiction and History." *History of European Ideas* 20: 291–98.

Barkin, J. Samuel. 2015. "Translatable? On Mixed Methods and Methodology." In *Millennium-Journal of International Studies*, 43.3: 1003–1006.

Bennettt, Andrew. 2015. "Found in Translation: Combining Discourse Analysis with Computer Assisted Content Analysis." In *Millennium-Journal of International Studies* 43.3: 984–997.

Bevir, Mark, and Kedar, Asaf. 2008. "Concept formation in political science: An anti-naturalist critique of qualitative methodology." In *Perspectives on Politics*, 6.03: 503–517.

Bhambra, Gurminder K. 2014. *Connected Sociologies*. New York: Bloomsbury.

———. 2015. "Citizens and Others: The Constitution of Citizenship through Exclusion." *Alternatives: Global, Local, Political* 40, no. 2: 102–14.

Boatcă, Manuela. 2015. *Global Inequalities Beyond Occidentalism.* New York: Routledge.

Bourdieu, Pierre. 2001. *Science de la science et Réflexivité*, Paris: Raisons d'agir, coll. Cours et travaux.

Bourdieu, Pierre, Chamboredon, Jean-Claude, and Passeron, Jean-Claude. 1969. *Le métier de sociologue: Préalables épistémologiques*, Berlin: de Gruyter.

Burawoy, Michael. 2005. "Provincializing the Social Sciences." In *The Politics of Method in the Human Sciences: Positivism and Its Epistemological Others*, edited by George Steinmetz, 508–25. Durham, NC: Duke University Press.

———. 2008. "Open the Social Sciences: To Whom and for What?" *Portuguese Journal of Social Science* 6, no. 3: 137–46.

Chakrabarty, Dipesh. 1988. *Rethinking Working-Class History. Bengal 1890–1940.* Princeton: Princeton University Press.

———. 2000. *Provincializing Europe: Postcolonial Thought and Historical Difference.* New York: Princeton University Press.

Chakraborty, Titas, and Matthias van Rossum. 2020. "Slave Trade and Slavery in Asia: New Perspectives." *Journal of Social History* 54, no. 1: 1–14.

Chambers, Iain. 2008. *Mediterranean Crossings: The Politics of an Interrupted Modernity*. Durham, NC: Duke University Press.

———. 2017. *Postcolonial Interruptions, Unauthorized Modernities*. Lanham, MD Rowman and Littlefield International.

Chomsky, Noam. 1978. *Topics in the Theory of Generative Grammar*. Berlin: de Gruyter.

Chu, Sinan. 2022. "Fantastic Theories and Where to Find Them: Rethinking Interlocutors in Global IR." In *Millennium: Journal of International Studies*. https://journals.sagepub.com/doi/full/10.1177/03058298221110923

Collier, David, Henry E. Brady, and Jason Seawright. 2004. "Critiques, Responses, and Trade-Offs: Drawing Together the Debate." In *Rethinking Social Inquiry: Diverse Tools, Shared Standards*, edited by Henry E. Brady and David Collier, 195–228. Lanham, MD: Rowman and Littlefield.

Connell, Raewyn. 2007. *Southern Theory: Social Science and the Global Dynamics of Knowledge*. New York: Polity.

Cook, Harold J. 2007. *Matters of Exchange: Commerce, Medicine, and Science in the Dutch Golden Age*. New Haven, CT: Yale University Press.

Daston, Lorraine, and Peter Galison. 2007. *Objectivity*. Princeton, NJ: Princeton University Press.

Daston, Lorraine, and Katharine Park. 2001. *Wonders and the Order of Nature, 1150–750*. Princeton, NJ: Princeton University Press.

Dewey, John, and Melvin L. Rogers. 2012. *The public and its problems: An essay in political inquiry*. Philadelphia: Pennsylvania State University Press.Edgerly, Louisa, Amoshaun Toft, and Mary Lynn Veden. "Social movements, political goals, and the May 1 marches: Communicating protest in polysemous media environments." In *The International Journal of Press/Politics*. 16.3 (2011): 314–334.

Ersche, Christian, et al., eds. 2014. *Global knowledge production in the social sciences: made in circulation*. Dublin: Ashgate Publishing.
Escobar, Arturo. 2008. *Territories of Difference. Place, Movements, Life, Redes*. Duhram: Duke University Press.
Fabian, Johannes. 1990. "Presence and Representation: The Other and Anthropological Writing." In *Critical Inquiry*, 16(4), 753–772.
Faeges, Russell S. 1999. "Theory-Driven Concept Definition: The Challenge of Perverse Classifications." In *Annual meeting of the American Political Science Association*, Atlanta, Georgia.
Feyerabend, Paul, K. 1975. *Against Method: Outline of an Anarchistic Theory of Knowledge*. London: Verso.
Fisher, Karen. 2022. "Decolonizing Rivers in Aotearoa New Zealand." In *Indigenous Women's Voices:: 20 Years on from Linda Tuhiwai Smith's Decolonizing Methodologies*, edited by Emma Lee and Jennifer Evans, 17–31. London: Zed.
Flyvbjerg, Bent. 201. *Making social science matter: Why social inquiry fails and how it can succeed again*. Cambridge: Cambridge University Press.
Foucault, Michel. 2010. *The Birth of Biopolitics: Lectures at the Collège de France, 1978–1979. (Michel Foucault Lectures at the Collège de France, Vol. 7)*. London: Palgrave McMillan.
Fox-Keller, Evelyn. 2014. *Secrets of Life, Secrets of Death: Essays on Science and Culture*. New York: Routledge.
Fuller, Steve. 2006. *The new sociological imagination*. New York: Sage.
García-Quero, Fernando, and Jorge Guardiola. 2017. "Economic Poverty and Happiness in Rural Ecuador: The Importance of Buen Vivir (Living Well)." *Applied Research in Quality of Life* 13: 202–26.
Gerring, John. 1999. "What Makes a Concept Good? A Criterial Framework for Understanding Concept Formation in the Social Sciences." *Polity* 31, no. 3: 357–93.
———. 2001. *Social Science Methodology: A Criterial Framework*. Cambridge: Cambridge University Press.
———. 2011. *Social Science Methodology: A Unified Framework*. Cambridge: Cambridge University Press.
Gilbert, Nigel, (ed.). 2008. *Researching social life*. New York: Sage.
Glissant Édouard. 1990. *Poetique de la relation*. Paris: Gallimar.
Go, Kenji. 2012. "Montaigne's 'Cannibals' and 'The Tempest' Revisited." *Studies in Philology* 109, no. 4: 455–73.
Gramsci, Antonio. 1975. *Quaderni del carcere, Vol. 1. Il Materialismo storic e la filosofia di Benedetto Croce*. Turin: Giulio Einaudi Editore.Grosfoguel, Ramon. 2013. "The Structure of Knowledge in Westernized Universities: Epistemic Racism/Sexism and the Four Genocides/Epistemicides of the Long 16th Century." *Human Architecture: Journal of the Sociology of Self-Knowledge* 11, no. 1: 73–90.
Grossberg, Lawrence. 1986. "On Postmodernism and Articulation: An Interview with Stuart Hall." *Journal of Communication Inquiry* 10, no. 2: 45–60.
Haraway, Donna. 2000. "A Cyborg Manifesto: Science, Technology and Socialist-Feminism in the Late Twentieth Century." In *The Cybercultures Reader*, edited by David Bell and Barbara M. Kennedy, 291. London: Routledge.

Harding, Sandra G. 1987. *Feminism and Methodology: Social Science Issues.* Bloomington: Indiana University Press.

Hempel, Carl G. 1965. *Aspects of Scientific Explanation.* New York: Free Press.

Holmwood, John. 2010. "Sociology's misfortune: disciplines, interdisciplinarity and the impact of audit culture." In *The British journal of sociology,* 61.4: 639–658.

Holmwood, John. 2011. "Viewpoint: The impact of 'Impact' on UK social science." In *Methodological Innovations Online*, 6.1: 13–17.

Kaplan, Abraham. 1964. *The Conduct of Inquiry: Methodology for Behavioral Science.* San Francisco: Chandler Publishing.

Karatani, Kōjin. 2014. *The Structure of World History: From Modes of Production to Modes of Exchange.* Translated by Michael K. Bourdaghs. Durham, NC: Duke University Press.

King, Gary, Robert O. Keohane, and Sidney Verba. 1994. *Designing social inquiry: Scientific inference in qualitative research.* Princeton: Princeton University Press.

Kohn, Eduardo. 2013. *How Forests Think: Toward an Anthropology beyond the Human.* Berkeley: University of California Press.

Kontopoulos, Kyriakos M. 2006. *The Logics of Social Structure.* Vol. 6. Cambridge: Cambridge University Press.

Jackson, Patrick Thaddeus. 2010. *The Conduct of Inquiry in International Relations: Philosophy of Science and Its Implications for the Study of World Politics.* London: Routledge.

Jennings, Bruce, and Daniel Callahan. 1983. "Social science and the policy-making process." *Hastings Center Report*: 3–8. Jones, Charles O, 1974. "Doing Before Knowing: Concept Development in Political Research." In *American Journal of Political Science,* 18 (1974): 215–28.

Lacatus, Cora, Daniel Schade, and Yuan Joanne Yao. 2015. "Quo vadis IR: method, methodology and innovation." In *Millennium-Journal of International Studies* 43.3: 767–778.

Lakatos, Imre. 1976. *Proofs and Reutations.* Cambridge: Cambridge University Press.

———. 1999. "Lectures on Scientific Method." In *For and Against Method: Including Lakatos's Lectures of Scientific Method and the Lakatos-Feyerabend Correspondence*, 19–109. Chicago: University of Chicago Press.

Lakatos, Imre, Paul Feyerabend, and Matteo Motterlini. 1999. *For and Against Method: Including Lakatos's Lectures on Scientific Method and the Lakatos-Feyerabend Correspondence.* Chicago: University of Chicago Press.

Lander, Edgardo. 2001. "Pensamiento crítico latinoamericano: La impugnación del eurocentrismo." In *Revista de Sociología,* (15):13–25.

Layug, A., and John Hobson, eds. 2022. *Globalizing International Theory: The Problem with Western IR Theory and How to Overcome It.* London: Routledge.

Lipsham, Marjorie. 2020. "Mātauranga-ā-Whānau: Constructing a methodological approach centred on whānau pūrākau." In *New Zealand Social Work* 32(3):17–29.MacIntyre, Alasdair C. 1988. *Whose Justice? Which Rationality?* London: Duckworth.

Mallavarapu, Siddhartha. 2014. *Theory Talks*. https://www.files.ethz.ch/isn/176692/Theory%20Talk63_%20Mallavarapu.pdf

Mamdani, Mahmood. 2018. *Citizen and Subject: Contemporary Africa and the Legacy of Late Colonialism*. New York: Princeton University Press. Mbembe, J. Achille. 2003. "Necropolitics." *Public Culture* 15, no. 1: 11–40.

Medrano Valdez, Yanett. 2020. "*Chacha-warmi*: Another Form of Gender Equality, from the Perspective of Aymara Culture." In Santos, Boaventura de Sousa, and Maria Paula Meneses, eds. 2020. *Knowledges Born in the Struggle: Constructing the Epistemologies of the Global South*, 96–113. London: Routledge.

Mezzadra, Sandro and Neilson, Brett. 2013. *Border as Method, or, the Multiplication of Labor*. Durham: Duke University Press,

Miller, Steven I., Marcel Fredericks, and Frank J. Perino. 2008. "Social science research and policymaking: Meta-analysis and paradox." In *Protosociology* 25: 186–205.Mills, C. Wright. 1959. *The Sociological Imagination*. New York: Oxford University Press

Michie, Jonathan, and Cary Cooper, eds. 2015. *Why the social sciences matter*. London: Palgrave Macmillan.

Mittman, Asa Simon, and Peter J. Dendle, eds. 2013. *The Ashgate Research Companion to Monsters and the Monstrous*. Dublin: Ashgate.

Outhwaite, William. 1983. *Concept Formation in Social Science*. London: Routledge.

———. 2010. *Concept Formation in Social Science (Routledge Revivals)*. London: Routledge.

Pagden, Anthony. 1984. *The Fall of Natural Man: The American Indian and the Origins of Comparative Ethnology*. Cambridge: Cambridge University Press.

Patel, Sujata, ed. 2009. *The ISA Handbook of Diverse Sociological Traditions*. Los Angeles: SAGE.

Panikkar, Raymond. 1979. *Myth, Faith and Hermeneutics*, New York: Paulist Press.

Pesce, Roberto. 2020. "'Figlio d'un cane!' La figura di Attila nel folklore medievale tra tradizione epico-cavalleresca e zooerastia." In *Journal of California Italian Studies*, 10(1). https://escholarship.org/uc/item/1sk130b0.

Qi, Xiaoying. 2014. *Globalized Knowledge Flows and Chinese Social Science*. Vol. 83. New York: Routledge.

Raj, Kapil. 2007. *Relocating Modern Science: Circulation and the Construction of Knowledge in South Asia and Europe, 1650–1900*. Basingstoke, UK: Palgrave Macmillan.

———. 2013. "Beyond Postcolonialism . . . and Postpositivism: Circulation and the Global History of Science." *Isis* 104, no. 2: 337–47.

Rakova, Marina. 2003. *The Extent of the Literal. Metaphor, Polysemy and Theories of Concepts*. London: Palgrave.

Ramose, M. B. 2002. "The philosophy of ubuntu and ubuntu as a philosophy." In P. H. Coetzee, & A. P. J. Roux (Eds.), *Philosophy from Africa: A text with readings*, pp. 230–238. Cape Town: Oxford University Press.

Rehg, William. 2009. *Cogent science in context: The science wars, argumentation theory, and Habermas*. Cambridge, MA: MIT Press.

Retamar, Roberto Fernàndez. 2000 [1971]. "Calibano." In *Obras Vol.1*. Havana: Letras Cubanas.
Said, Edward W. 1983. *The World, the Text, and the Critic*. Cambridge, MA: Harvard University Press.
Santos, Boaventura de Souza. 1997. "For a Multicultural Conception of Human Rights." *Lua Nova: Revista de Cultura e Política* 39: 105–24.
———. 2007a. "Beyond Abyssal Thinking: From Global Lines to Ecologies of Knowledges." *Review* 30, no. 1: 45–89.
———, ed. 2007b. *Another Knowledge Is Possible: Beyond Northern Epistemologies*. London: Verso.
Santos, Boaventura de Sousa, and Maria Paula Meneses, eds. 2020. *Knowledges Born in the Struggle: Constructing the Epistemologies of the Global South*. London: Routledge.
Sartori, Giovanni, ed. 1984. *Social Science Concepts: A Systematic Analysis*. Los Angeles: SAGE.
Sahlins, Marshall. 1993. "Goodbye to Tristes Tropes: Ethnography in the Context of Modern World History." *Journal of Modern History* 65, no. 1: 1–25.
Sakai, Naoki. 1991. *Voices of the Past: The Status of Language in Eighteenth Century Japanese Discourse*. Ithaca, NY: Cornell University Press.
———. 1997. *Translation and Subjectivity. On "Japan" and Cultural Nationalism*. Minneapolis: University of Minnesota Press.
———. 2000. "'You Asians': On the Historical Role of the West and Asia Binary." *South Atlantic Quarterly* 99, no. 4: 789–817.
Sakai, Naoki, and Jon Solomon. 2006. "Introduction: Addressing the Multitude of Foreigners, Echoing Foucault." In *Biopolitics, Colonial Difference*, edited by Naoki Sakai and Jon Solomon, 1–35. Hong Kong: Hong Kong University Press.
Samkange, S., and T. M. Samkange. 1980. *Hunhuism or Ubuntuism: A Zimbabwe Indigenous Political Philosophy*. Salisbury: Graham Publishing.
Shahi, Deppeshikha, and Gennaro Ascione. 2016. "Rethinking the Absence of Post-Western International Relations Theory in India: 'Advaitic Monism' as an Alternative Epistemological Resource." *European Journal of International Relations* 22, no. 2: 313–34.
Shapin, Steven. 1994. *A Social History of Truth: Civility and Science in Seventeenth-Century England*. Chicago: University of Chicago Press.
Shiliam Robert. 2012. "Civilization and the Poetics of Slavery." *Thesis Eleven* 108, no. 1: 99–117.
Shimizu, Kosuke. 2022. *The Kyoto School and International Relations: Non-Western Attempts for a New World Order*. New York: Routledge.
Smith, Linda Tuhiwai. 1999. *Decolonizing Methodologies: Research and Indigenous Peoples*. Dunedin, NZ: University of Otago Press.
———. 2021. *Decolonizing Methodologies: Research and Indigenous People*. London: Bloomsbury.
Smith, Richard J. 2013. *Mapping China and Managing the World: Culture, Cartography and Cosmology in Late Imperial Times*. Vol. 9. London: Routledge.

Subrahmanyam, Sanjay. 2011. *Three Ways to Be Alien: Travails and Encounters in the Early Modern World*. Hanover, NH: University Press of New England.

Subramani. 2001. "The Oceanic Imaginary." In *The Contemporary Pacific*, 13(1): 149–162.

Sugihara, Kaoru. 2004. "The State and the Industrious Revolution in Tokugawa Japan." Economic History Working Papers 22490, London School of Economics and Political Science, Department of Economic History.

Steinmetz, George. 2015. "Historical Sociology, Ethics, Policy and Politics‖. In Trajectories: Newsletter of the ASA Comparative and Historical Sociology Section (December 2015) in symposium on the question "Can Comparative Historical Sociology Save the World?."

Swedberg, Richard. 2014. *The Art of Social Science*. Princeton, NJ: Princeton University Press.

Taruffi, Cesare. 1881. *Storia della teratologia*. Vol. 1.Bologna: Regia tipografia.

Thiong'o, Ngugi wa. 2012. *Globalectics: Theory and the Politics of Knowing Hardcover*. New York: Columbia University Press.

Wakefield, Andre. 2009. *The disordered police state: German cameralism as science and practice*. Chicago: University of Chicago Press.Wallerstein, Immanuel, et al. 1997. *Open the Social Sciences: Report of the Gulbenkian Commission on the Restructuring of the Social Sciences*. Stanford, CA: Stanford University Press.

Wallerstein, I., Martin, W. G., & Dickinson, T. (1982). Household Structures and Production Processes: Preliminary Theses and Findings. *Review (Fernand Braudel Center)*, *5*(3), 437–458.

Walter, Aggie and Andersen, Chris. 2013. *Indigenous Statistics: A Quantitative Research Methodology*. New York: Routledge.Ward, Sylvia A. 2012. "The Hierarchical Terminology Technique: A Method to Address Terminology Inconsistency." *Quality & Quantity* 46, no. 1: 71–87.

Watanabe, Atsuko and Felix Rösch. 2018. *Modern Japanese Political Thought and International Relations*. London: Rowman and Littlefield.

Woodside, Alexander. 2009. *Lost Modernities: China, Vietnam, Korea, and the Hazards of World History*. Cambridge, MA: Harvard University Press.

Yue, Isaac. 2010. "Barbarians and Monstrosity: A Thematic Study of the Representation of Foreignness in Early Chinese Vernacular Stories." *Études chinoises: bulletin de l'Association française d'études chinoises* 29: 221–41.

Zhao, Tingyang. 2006. "Rethinking Empire from a Chinese Concept of 'All-Under-Heaven' (Tian-xia)." In *Social Identities* 12(1): 29–41.

———. 2021. *All Under Heaven: The Tianxia System for a Possible World Order*. Translated by Joseph E. Harroff. Oakland: University of California Press.

Chapter 4

The Global as the Unit of Analysis[1]

THINKING THE WORLD IN NINETEENTH-CENTURY PARADIGMS

In the conceptual archive of global studies, the "global" is obviously crucial. Yet it remains problematic because often uncritically used. It is commonly deployed in globalization theories and critical globalization studies (Robertson 2001). Yet the idea to reach a general agreement around its meaning risks to remain a chimerical aspiration unless the analysis of its historical construction is left outside the horizon of conceptual and terminological inquiry. The "global" today is the methodological field of battle wherein new rising powers exert pressures on the existing structures of knowledge as rewrite the lexicon of the social sciences that express their own alternative visions. In a long-term historical perspective, this condition corresponds to the current hegemonic transition following the crisis of United States political and economic world hegemony. This hegemonic crisis began after the end of World War II in1945, announcing the end of the planetary cultural hegemony of the West that had followed the defeat of imperial China in the First Opium War of 1842 (Wallerstein 1991). The uncertain configuration of the international system has forced the debate to disclose the bastions of Eurocentrism to other perspectives, philosophical traditions, sociological analyses, and conceptual archives, whose non-Western promoters share the conceptual space of the "global" as the unit of analysis wherein the struggle for recognition should take place. This theoretical attitude exposes the fact that even previous dominant Eurocentric views about the world were global in their stance, even though their worldly projection took the analytical form of methodological nationalism having the nation-state as a relevant unit of analysis.

Yet assuming the global as an explicit unit of analysis is a by-product of the conflictual historical dialectics in the long-term and large-scale environment in the wake of the current hegemonic transition (Arrighi and Silver 1999).

Tony Bennet, Lawrence Grossberg, and Meaghan Morris (2005) note that

> the concepts of the globe as a spherical object and, metonymically, as the planet earth appeared together in the XVI century. The adjectival form (global) appeared in the XVII century referring only to the former. In the late XIX century "global" appeared in its more common contemporary sense, combining a geographical ("the whole world; world-wide; universal") and a mathematical or logical meaning ("the totality of a number of items, categories, etc.; comprehensive, all-inclusive, unified, total"). In the XX century, the more active and historical form—globalization—appears, parallel to other comparable historical markers such as "modernization" and "industrialization" and related to the notions of postmodernity.

The global is both a methodological issue and a cultural product. Such an assertion does not imply either the narrative construction of influence or the supposed logic of impact-response between culture and methodology in a given historical-social context. "Influence" is an unmanageable theoretical instrument in conceptual history, as it is almost impossible to define despite its immediate allusive power (Said 1975). Impact-response logic works only retrospectively as a justificative argument rather than providing a useful tool in conceptual and terminological analysis (Toulmin 1958). Therefore, the ways the "global" is connoted are articulated into an integrated lexicological unity. As previously stated in chapter 3, Stuart Hall (Grossberg 1966, 53) defined articulation as "the form of connection that can make a unity of two different elements, under certain conditions. . . . The 'unity' which matters is a linkage between the articulated discourse and the social forces with which it can, under certain historical conditions, but need not necessarily, be connected."

The condition of possibility for the articulation of the cultural and the methodological global in post–War World II Western thinking is diffusionism. James Blaut (1993, 1) defined Eurocentric diffusionism as

> the theory about the way cultural processes tend to move over the surface of the world as a whole. They tend to flow out of the European sector and toward the non-European sector. This is the natural, normal, logical, an ethical flow of culture, of innovation, of human causality. Europe, eternally, is Inside. Non-Europe is Outside. Europe is the source of most diffusions; non-Europe is the recipient.

This means that the path beyond the ethnocentric construction of the global as a relevant unit of analysis implies questioning the colonial foundations of the notion of the global as it emerged coextensively with the institutionalization of the social sciences in the nineteenth century and evolved with the aspiration of sociology to become worldly relevant in the second half of the twentieth century. Therefore, the preliminary question one should ask: is it possible to reconstruct the "global" beyond its Eurocentric foundations? A plausible path resides in our ability to investigate the limits that these Eurocentric foundations keep imposing on the aspiration to take a global turn that posits the centrality of the colonial question, in order to reconstruct a more adequate historical and sociological context for contemporary global studies. Yet, the effort to affirm the global dimension of social change as an assumption risks transmuting the operational notion of the global into a purely logical premise, thus subtracted from the critical understanding of its historical constitution: a metaphysical, ahistorical, apodictic spacetime dimension.

The path proposed here consists in sociologically conceptualizing the ways in which global studies unintentionally or intentionally reproduces the Eurocentric paradigms of modernization and globalization theories, even when the construction of the global aspires to overcome the limits of state-centrism and methodological nationalism. One such way that the logic of paradigmatic reproduction operates is by means of erasing, eclipsing, or mystifying the constitutive nexus between the colonial difference and the construction of the "global" as a theoretical issue, rather than simply as an allusive dimension to "thinking globally." To be sure, thinking globally was not extraneous to the institutionalization of disciplinary sociology in Europe during the nineteenth century either. As Marcel Merle (1987) recalls, Henri de Saint-Simon and his followers promulgated the quintessential views related to *Le Nouveau Christianisme* through their newspaper, eloquently named *Le Globe*. David Harvey (1982, 1985, 2002) points out that Marx's historical materialism was entirely developed within the historical awareness of the globalizing forces of capitalism. Raewyn Connell (1997) has argued that Weber's generalizations about world civilizations contained, in a nutshell, many of the connotations that global studies should avoid in order not to replicate the fallacies that the hegemony of modernization theories and structural-functionalist sociology have systematically reproduced. David Inglis and Roland Robertson (2012) have traced the origins of global sociology back to Émile Durkheim's analysis of supranational phenomena, but they have shown the limitations of Durkheim's views about the worldly significance of social change outside the realm of the nation-state and the Eurocentric tradition-modernity dichotomy. There existed only one significant and destabilizing exception to this narrative and epistemological architecture. This exception was W. E. B. Du Bois. For two reasons: first, because he questioned the assumption according to which Georg Wilhelm Friedrich Hegel's *Phenomenology of the Spirit* was the highest form of universal history of civilization at a planetary scale. Whereas

Hegel used the metaphor of the torch of progress to maintain that the modern West in general and the German nation-state in particular were the outpost of human progress, Du Bois designed the Negro civilization as a distinctive and more advanced historical-social formation, whose cultural emergence was displaced in space and hence not integral to the geohistorical imaginary of Western modernity; and second, because his subversive reading of Hegelian dialectics was based on a radical understanding of the relational nature of historical change, and therefore, instead of looking at American society as a self-contained unit of analysis, he took the historically determined condition of Black Atlantic diaspora as the privileged epistemological standpoint from where he produced an *ante litteram* intersectional understanding of the morphogenesis of the global world. In so doing, he anticipated Fernand Braudel construction of the Mediterranean as a transnational unit of analysis beyond the nation-state. From this perspective, it was possible to understand the worldly configuration of capitalist colonial modernity through the lens of mobility rather than through the lens of fixed geohistorical locations (Boy 2015). Yet the problem of addressing the global as the meaningful unit of analysis, rather than a derivative by-product of the development of the inner social forces of colonial modernity, was outside Du Bois's theoretical horizon.

Despite these early predecessors, thinking of the global as a unit of analysis implies the more specific idea that it is plausible, and theoretically advantageous, to understand the world as a single integrated timespace. Historically, the reorientation of sociological analysis toward the global marks a shift in emphasis that is characteristic of the post–World War II period, when the problem of decolonization erupted in theory production. This irruption involved many different and divergent political attitudes toward the colonial when thinking globally.

THE COLONIALITY OF METHOD AND BEYOND

Because the legitimacy of the Eurocentric construction of the global is often established in implicit ways and buried under the categories that are constantly but uncritically used and reproduced, the different political and theoretical attitudes toward the "colonial" that are conflated under fundamental categories of thought such as "relation" and "asymmetry" need to be unveiled, made visible, and questioned. In order to make this possible, a decolonizing perspective on the historical construction and reciprocal interpellation of these notions in historical sociology has to be adopted. Specifically, it is possible to reinterrogate the genealogy of the global turn through the introduction of the *coloniality of method* as a strategy to place the colonial at the center of social theory. Through this lens, the move toward the decolonization of the genealogy of the global turn has to address the politics of method behind the call for a global sociology in American sociology in the late 1960s. This conceptual history is often untold, as the global turn has remained associated with world-systems analysis and globalization theories since the second half of the 1970s. To be sure, it was the effort of the American Sociological Associatio to turn sociology into a global discipline that provided the institutional and intellectual context for the emergence of world-systems analysis and later globalization theories, and some of the expectations, orientations, and normative assumptions that constitute the premises of the current claim for sociology to take a global turn, as expressed during Michael Burawoy's presidency of the International Sociological Association in the early 2000s. Given this alternative genealogy, some of the most radical upshots of the critique of Eurocentrism in historical and social sciences during the last four decades can be selectively mobilized as a possible antidote to the palingenesis of ethnocentrism, whether Eurocentric, Sinocentric or "globocentric."

In a polemical vein against Immanuel Wallerstein, his predecessor as chairman of the International Sociological Association, Burawoy (2005) called for a global sociology that would be able, in theory, to address global inequalities. This call suggests a double move. A first move consists in what Robertson (1998) called the "globalization of sociology," that is, the institutional and demographic transformation of sociology into a discipline whose space of theorization needs to be shaped by non-Western research traditions, even if defined on a national basis. The second consists in the collective critical effort to decolonize sociology from its Eurocentric constraints. Gurminder Bhambra correctly argues that the second issue is more compelling and uncertain, and hence necessary (Bhambra, 2014, 104–12), not only because, more often than not, Eurocentrism is reproduced through national structures of knowledge, but also because it is precisely the reproduction, aware or unintended, of Eurocentric premises in the non-Western academy that works as a mean of selection, cooptation, and international legitimation of non-Western national traditions and scholars into the worldly academia.

In order to transform the global from an adjectival form into a substantivated lemma able to constitute a plausible unit of analysis, the neologism "coloniality" is needed. Coloniality was introduced by Peruvian anthropologist Aníbal Quijano (1992). It conceptualizes the alleged totalizing colonial nature of power within modernity. The coloniality of power takes the form of a complex dynamic matrix that operates regardless of the end of formal colonialism. Quijano elaborated coloniality in the context of International Relations Theory, aiming to unveil the persistence of colonial hierarchies in the international system after the completion of decolonization in the second half of the twentieth century. Ramon Grosfoguel (2004) expanded its meaning and theorized coloniality in terms of intertwined hierarchies of culture, class, race, ethnicity, gender, and cosmologies by which the colonial difference is translated into naturalized hierarchies of power whose original, yet mobile, configuration is White capitalist masculine heterosexual Christian dominance. It is my contention that the global as a post-Western category for the analysis of long-term/large-scale processes of historical and social change is limited by the presence of a set of epistemological mechanisms that I call the "coloniality of method." The notion of coloniality of method I describe here conceptualizes these mechanisms in order to expose and disarticulate them. The coloniality of method is to be thought of as the ability to sterilize the transformative potential of the colonial difference, both historically and epistemologically, by incorporating asymmetries of power into categories of analysis whose colonial construction is made invisible by an apparent conceptual and terminological transparency. The coloniality of method operates through three devices: *negation*, that is, the assertion of the irrelevance of colonial relations in causal explanations and historical narratives; *neutralization*, that is, the acknowledgment of colonialism as a global relation of asymmetric power distribution with the simultaneous presumption of the irrelevance of nondominant agencies within the colonial relation; and *sterilization*, that is, the exoticization of nondominant epistemologies and their displacement from the realm of theoretical production to that of particularistic cultures, standpoints, and spacetimes, as such unable to express transformative universalisms. The coloniality of method materializes in shifting combinations of these three devices.

Thus, decolonizing genealogy exploits its own semantic ambiguity. It means both that the genealogy of the global turn needs to be decolonized from its Eurocentric assumptions and that the different genealogy that emerges enacts an alternative elaboration of the notion of the global. Too often the acceptance of the global as a meaningful condition for the study of long-term and large-scale processes of historical-social change is reduced to the formal overcoming of state-centrism in a chronological succession of paradigms that goes from modernization theories to dependency theories to world-systems analysis, up to the proliferation of divergent strains of historical sociologies, and globalization theories (Go 2014). Rather, the emergence of the global as a methodological issue derived its cogency from the irruption of the colonial difference in the realm of theoretical production that followed the reconfiguration of global powers, due to the worldly process of decolonization and the multiplex ways it took in different parts of the globe. In the sociological imagination of the global turn, World War II splits the 1940s irrevocably. Yet, as is clear to any historian of the Cold War, the debates and concerns that emerged after the end of the armed conflict pursued and reformulated political and theoretical issues that had been raised before, when the problem of the hegemonic transition from Great Britain to the United States of America, and from colonies to independent states, came to be understood as a process to be managed: in other words, a matter of global governance. The construction of the global, then, is not the formal succession of paradigms from methodological nationalism and state-centrism to the world as unit of analysis; it is, rather, rooted in the politics of the global governance of post–World War II decolonization.

From a critical geographical perspective, Neil Brenner (1999, 59) correctly notes that

> The emphasis on global space does not necessarily lead to an overcoming of state-centric epistemologies. Global territorialist approaches represent global space in a state-centric manner, as a pregiven territorial container within which globalization unfolds, rather than analyzing the historical production, reconfiguration, and transformation of this space.

In a similar vein, but from a critical international relations theory perspective, David Chandler (2009, 535) registers a risk of oversimplification about the label "global" attached to social theory:

> In understanding the globalisation of politics as a response to processes of social and economic change the shift towards the global has been essentialised or reified. Rather than the shift from national to global conceptions of politics, power and resistance being a question for investigation, it has been understood as natural or inevitable: as a process driven by forces external to us and out of our control.

Nonetheless, this spatial (and temporal) critique as well as this political-ideological critique are insufficient in the context of my argument, because they both fail at addressing the colonial genealogy of the global. Eurocentrism pervades the genealogy of the global to such an extent that the colonial question is often erased from the construction of the methodological problem of the elaboration of a meaningful unit of analysis. Such a pervasiveness relegates coloniality outside the realm of the theoretical practice of concept formation in thinking the global through a post-Western approach.

Decolonizing genealogy, conversely, is based on the assumption that methods themselves are articulations of the historically determined relations between power and culture, and that therefore a different, non-formalist, substantial criterion of relevance is needed: one that consists in the assertion that thinking the global is coterminous with the political and theoretical problem of how to think the colonial. In this sense, if the formal shift from state-centrism to the global does not suffice *in se* to overcome Eurocentrism and resist the coloniality of method, conversely, not all forms of state-centrism imply an equivalent attitude toward the colonial.

For this reason, the entire genealogy of the global turn has to be rethought, specified, and partially reversed. This posture is supported by a revisionist historiographical gesture of rewriting the intellectual history of post–World War II attempts to think the global, to eventually operate a theoretical displacement of the Western theoretical archive that showcases the latter's inability to autonomously overcome the limits of its own premises.

MODERNIZATION THEORIES AS EPISTEMOLOGICAL COUNTERINSURGENCY AGAINST THE DECOLONIZATION OF KNOWLEDGE

In order to dismantle the taken-for-granted genealogy of the global, the supposed beginning of such a genealogy has to be questioned: modernization theories. In what follows, the chronology of the relation between modernization theories and the early attempts to think globally from a decolonization of knowledge perspective must be reversed. As a matter of fact, the post–World War II terms-of-trade controversy around the role of international commerce in the worldly distribution of wealth was the first attempt to think the global by decolonizing theory. And it historically and logically predates the early formulations of modernization theories. There follows that, rather than 1960s Latin American dependency theories being a newly born reaction to the spread of modernization theories since the late 1950s, it was the latter that came out as an early theoretical counterinsurgency movement to repress the first formulations of the core-periphery theory, in the context of critical inquiry into the conditions of poverty and marginalization of Latin America countries. In this regard, John Toye and Richard Toye (2004) have convincingly reconstructed the genesis of the terms-of-trade controversy from a global perspective on political economy. They document how in 1948, one year before the famous "point four" outlined in Harry S. Truman's presidential address that according to the now-classical Arturo Escobar (1994) and Gilbert Rist (1997) discursive analyses (1997) announced the era of developmentalism, German economist Hans Singer was working on a paper for the newly born Economic Development Commission of the United Nations. Singer's research pertained to some quantitative analyses of serial data on international trade from the nineteenth century onward, which Folke Hilgerdt, the UN Statistical Office director at the time, had compiled since 1943. Singer embarked on studying a very specific problem in economic history that puzzled economists in the interwar period. The problem was formulated as follows: a number of former colonies (particularly India toward Great Britain) had run export surpluses that they subsequently wished to use to import capital goods for their national economic plans, but during the same interval, the prices of capital goods had risen, so the export surpluses were worth less in terms of imports than they had been when they were earned (Toye and Toye 2004, 110–36). Singer's finding posed a problem to political economy since it contradicted what economic theory was used to predict according to the epistemology of the self-regulating market and its presumed power to reciprocally counter-balance the import-export ratio between two trading countries in the global market. Such a problem came to be interpreted in a more radical and political manner by Raul Prebisch, who took the president chair of the Economic Commission for Latin America and the Caribbean of the United Nations in the 1950s. Prebish affirmed that while poor countries were helping to maintain a rising standard of living in industrialized countries, they themselves were not receiving any compensation; rather, they were getting poorer and poorer. Prebisch enriched Singer's thesis with a methodological coherence that Singer's analysis had lacked by introducing the fortunate meta-geographical interpretative model of core and periphery. This view rapidly created a vast consensus among scholars from former colonies within the United Nations. But Prebisch polemically argued also against the presumed universalism of economic theory, analogously to what Friedrich List had advocated against Smith and Ricardo's theory of free trade in the first quarter of the nineteenth century: "One of the most conspicuous deficiency of general economic theory, from the point of view of the periphery, is its false sense of universality . . . an intelligent knowledge of the ideas of others must not be confused with the mental subjection to them from which we are slowly learning to free ourselves" (Toye and Toye 2004, 131).

The project of decolonizing knowledge was thus entering the worldly theoretical scenario of political and scholarly controversies in a manner that immediately created two irreconcilable sides: Western industrialized countries on the one hand, and former colonies, mainly agricultural and raw materials exporters, on the other hand. Toye and Toye have defined the firm reaction that followed the exposure of the Prebisch-Singer thesis as the "North American critical onslaught." North American economists attempted to delegitimize the Prebisch-Singer thesis by affirming the inaccuracy of its statistical base or the inconsistency of its explanatory multifactorial model. More broadly, the whole embryonic perspective that was emerging within the United Nations was soon dismissed as "speculative" by the leading figure of the opposite camp, Walt Whitman Rostow.

What was the methodological and epistemological context wherein the dialectics between Rostow and Prebish took place? As all economists of their generation, Rostow and Prebisch shared an analogous intellectual horizon that was also significantly similar to Singer's: they all went from studying economic cycles of depression during the 1930s, inspired by Pitirim Sorokin's theories of cyclical temporalities, to include secular trends and linear patterns of growth in the analysis of economic development by the end of World War II. Nonetheless, their heuristic questions were radically different since their analytical tensions were determined by opposite political attitudes toward the colonial question. Simply put, Rostow focused on the preservation of colonial privileges of the West. Prebish focused on the possibility to redistribute global wealth. In a crucial paper, split into two articles successively published in 1950 and 1951 in the *Economic History Review*, Rostow (1950, 1951) proved aware of the political pressures on world trade coming from the changing configuration of powers within the international system. Rostow (1950, 1–2) declared that his intention was

> to indicate the schismatic state of economic theory and analysis with respect to the terms of trade, [since] movements in the terms of trade hold a central position in the analysis of current international (and inter-sectorial) economic problems and in the formation of policy designed to solve them. The issues involved in the structural adjustment of world trade, which has been proceeding over recent years, are not likely to be transitory in nature, although their form and impact on different portions of the world economy will certainly change.

Among his major sources was the same statistical body undersigned by Hilgerdt and his colleagues at the United Nations, which Singer had used too. But Rostow's core question was designed entirely within the logic of hegemonic transition, from an economic point of view. As Nils Gilman (2003) points out, Rostow's intent consisted in the use of economic history to suggest international trade policies that could effectively enhance the newly established US power at the world level, as a reoccupation of the spaces disclosed by the relative collapse of the European colonial empires. Rostow's theoretical problem was provoked by the rise of the United States (and its structures of knowledge) to world hegemony that followed the decline of the British economy after the demise of Great Britain's colonial empire: how, in the interwar period, had Great Britain dissipated the advantages accruing from highly favorable terms of trade? Rostow (1950, 20) brought in a vast "array of variables" and called for a closer interaction between economists and historians in order to construct an interpretative model that could grasp the "continuous interplay of short-term and long-period forces." But the history and the economics he relied upon did not envisage the colonial question at all.

Modernization theories were effective in crystallizing into method the North American critical onslaught against the first elaboration of the decolonization of theory, by means of a radical state-centrism that negated the colonial question. In the context of the mounting Cold War and the rising US hegemony, methodological state-centrism was not a neutral, however limited, analytical option: it was an important pillar of an entire epistemological architecture where developmentalism was the recipe offered to newly independent countries. To be sure, the notion that each nation-state corresponds to an autonomous political entity whose space is defined by the geohistorical borders within which a distinctive society evolves through time was familiar to Western thinking. Yet the formalization of the nation-state as a unit of analysis in 1950s American social sciences marked the construction of a distinctive normative epistemological strategy to the extent that it involved the underlying cogent notion of replicability.[2] Replicability has informed the entire debate over the methodology of the social sciences, both for qualitative and quantitative methods (Marradi 2016). The notion according to which the measure of the validity of a method of inquiry resides in the possibility for it to be applied in different circumstances, presenting an analogous research question is a way to affirm the aspiration to universality where the imprint of positivism onto the genetic code of the social sciences proves long-lasting (Steimnetz 2006).

More specifically, though, within the politics of method that the frame of modernization theories endorsed, replicability is something different from the simple aspiration of mimicry toward a path or a competitor, because of the promise that the historical experience of the more advanced nation-state could have been replicated elsewhere in space and time, that is, *ad libitum* and *urbis et orbis*. The bulk of modernization theorists, both in sociology and in IRT, were well aware of the global dimension of world politics.[3] State-centrism and methodological nationalism within the horizon of modernization did not mean naively ignoring the single worldly context within which political entities exist. It rather meant that the worldly context for the historical development of a distinctive society within a single nation-state had to be thought in a way that could not interfere with the presumed replicability of the path to modernity. It had to be thinkable, before even being feasible through policies, that the capacity of each state to break through to modernity could depend exclusively on the correct implementation of the packaged model of modernization and not be disturbed by whatever possible external interference.

The replicability of modernization theories involved a pragmatist credo in social engineering whose underlying foundation consisted in an extremely determinist notion of *program* as historical, economic, cultural, and social ontogenesis. This established irrelevance of global connections actually meant the domestication, in both a performative and an etymological sense, of colonialism in sociological explanation: the negative effects of the colonial relations of power were transmuted into the domestic incapacity of the locals or the structural obstacles inherent in that particular society to move from tradition to modernity: nothing but the hallucinatory and enduring mantra of developmentalism.[4]

SYSTEM THEORY AS THE HEGEMONIC VERSION OF HOLISM UNDER US HEGEMONY

As previously noted, the canonical literature about the history of sociology as an academic discipline as well as the existing genealogies of the global turn in the wider field of historical-social sciences is mostly oblivious to the circumstance surrounding the first explicit call for the methodological formalization of the global as a single space of theorization. This first directive dates to 1966, as formulated by Wilbert E. Moore, just a few months before he was elected as 56th president of the American Sociological Association. The move toward the global inaugurated a distinctive trend in United States sociology, which, however, remained largely anchored to its own tradition of methodological nationalism, quantitative methods, and individualist behavioralism. As George Steinmetz has argued, the knowledge transfer of social scientists from Nazi refugee scholars to the United States did not affect the ahistorical orientation of American sociology, and historical sociology remained a niche from the 1930s to the 1970s.[5]

Nonetheless, Moore's article "Global Sociology: The World as a Singular System" put a straightforward emphasis on two theoretical and methodological innovations: the global and social systems. Moore maintained that social systems were "sovereign systems" and that the system was a meaningful unit of analysis, whose implementation suggested a new direction toward the global that, he argued, American sociology should have taken. In a polemical vein against his predecessor, Pitirim Sorokin, Moore (1966, 479) affirmed that

> it is only in social systems that one makes explicit the emergent qualities that derive from the interaction of the human actors in any social context, and thus avoids the kind of classical exemplification of the reductionist fallacy embodied in George Homans' presidential address to the American Sociological Association in 1964.

In his excursus over the history of the discipline, Moore described the interwar period as the beginning of the process of the Americanization of sociology, which corresponded both to the crisis of European national schools of sociology and to the narrowing of the sociological imagination to a certain parochialism. For Moore, the global turn in sociology coincided with the Americanization of the discipline worldwide. In fact, as a reaction against the parochialism of existing sociological thinking, the Americanization of sociology was expected to take the opposite direction: instead of looking inward to domestic issues, it had to reinforce a trend that was marginal from the 1930s to the 1950s and focus on looking outward to the world. This also implied a partial rejection of Sorokin grand-theory of civilizational cycles. Rather than looking at the world through historical civilizations, as the former European sociological tradition had done, American sociology would have marked a new stage in the history of the discipline by turning its attention to the ethnography and anthropology of "primitive cultures" in order to understand, comparatively, the process of modernization on a global scale that the United States was presumably leading. To parochialism, Moore remarked, relativism offered an alter ego. But it was precisely this binarism between the two far distant poles of modernization—namely, the sociological universal and the anthropological particular—that had to be overcome. To be sure, sociology and anthropology across the Atlantic were very close to each other from a methodological point of view: Ludwig von Bertalanffy (1950, 1951), with his general systems theory (GST) offered an innovative path of analysis for both. GST merged history, ecology, engineering, and communication studies into a common metatheory. Talcott Parsons's (1951) application of this approach to social systems was largely hegemonic in sociology (Steinmetz 2005). The hegemony of structural functionalism resulted in statements such as the following from Moore (1966, 59): "Social systems are real, they are earnest, and they may be both smaller and larger than societies, however defined."

The notion of system was, in fact, a reification of a particular sort: it accorded ontological presence to an interpretative tool—the system—and provided social theory with a strong version of neopositivist realism, which coextensively overcame the weak version of ontological realism that liberalism ideology had impressed over the emergence of the social sciences in the nineteenth century. Whereas ontology was the strictly philosophical eighteenth-century problem about what being is, liberalism had transfigured the separation of the three powers within the state theory of sovereignty into the assertion of the existence of three separated realms of human collective existence of economy, politics, and society. When applied to sociology, System Theory reaffirmed the original early nineteenth-century positivist view of the existence of a single underlying structure of being encompassing natural and human world, establishing as real the existence of an integrated global supersystem of relations called "the world." It implied holism, that is, the epistemological irrelevance of the single part outside the integrated understanding of the whole. It buttressed relationalism, that is, the prevalence of forming relations over formed entities. There followed that social wholes were thought as integrated systems whose dimensions and activities were defined in space and time by the extension and duration of their constitutive relations. In his introduction to *Social Anthropology*, Edward Evans-Pritchard (1951, 11) echoed this understanding of holism as he stated that "the social anthropologist studies societies as wholes—he studies their ecologies, their economics, their legal and political institutions, their family and kinship organizations, their religions, their technologies, their arts etc. as parts of general social systems." Against functionalism in social science, Talal Asad (1973) proposed a seminal critique of anthropological reason. Edward Said recognized such a critique as one of the premises of his Orientalism (1975). Asad explained that the functionalist aspiration to study "primitive" social systems soon collapsed into microanalysis under the pressures imposed by the emergence of nationalist structures of knowledge production in the newly decolonized countries. This collapse depended on the fact that functionalist anthropology's authority was a direct expression of colonial rule, therefore it came to be immediately associated with the pervasiveness of former colonial knowledges about non-western societies that the newly established national structures of knowledge considered the first one to delegitimize in order to produce knowledge about their societies on their own terms. In the Third World, Asad (1973, 13) continued, scholars began to "recover indigenous history and denounced the colonial connections of anthropology." They were moved by aspirations that were different from the Western anthropologists' ones, even though both the groups focused on analogous object of social inquiries. This means that sociology and anthropology were both affected by decolonization, but their respective institutional backgrounds and social legitimation produced divergent methodological responses. American sociology responded to the changed political conditions of knowledge production by constructing a frame that was able to literally *englobe* the worlds of historical and social change.

The sociological conceptualization of the global was not limited to such a level of formalization. Moore was also concerned, from an institutional point of view, with the problem of the globalization of sociology and the demographic shift it was expected to produce in the structures of knowledge production worldwide. Nation building and state building initiated relevant demographic changes in the constitution of sociology as an international academic field and as a community of scholars, thanks to the construction of national sociological schools—that soon came to think in terms of traditions—either in former colonies and other non-Western countries in the Soviet bloc: a change that, for intrinsic reasons, could not be paralleled by anthropologists, whose geographical horizon of possibility was dramatically going to change in few years. The horizon Moore took for granted was the modernization of the colonial worlds as a selective implementation of Western structures of thinking and meaning. And the globalization of sociology should have followed an analogous path. For Moore (1966, 483), ethnography and anthropology did not suffice anymore:

> For dealing with the modernization of traditional societies . . . two-party transactional models as contained in the older theory of "acculturation" simply will not fit most of the evidence. . . . We may "take a giant step" toward global sociology

> by returning once more to the *exotic* places, dearly beloved of ethnographers. . . . The main, overwhelming fact about them is that they are losing their pristine character at an extremely rapid rate.

Nonetheless, System Theory endorsed a first version of epistemological holism to the extent the analytical prevalence was accorded to a totality rather than some parts of it. Even though what a totality is was a matter of methodological concern. Holism, as an option, did not survive the collapse of functionalist anthropology in the decolonizing countries. Yet, conversely, it enjoyed a more favorable institutional space of intellectual citizenship within the context of American sociology. Holism seemed to offer the theoretical advantage of dismantling the limits of the nation-state as a unit of analysis and the legitimacy it took from an overall state-centrist frame of analysis for political economy and international relations. As Moore (1966, 480) proposed,

> In practice, society has come to be defined "operationally" either as units identified by anthropologists as "cultures," not always with explicit criteria, but duly recorded as separate entities in the Human Relations Area Files, or as coterminous with national states, which, though they may not be truly self-subsistent, do mostly get represented in the United Nations, and do form the principal takers of national censuses and assemblers of other aggregative and distributive social quantities.

Even though it may retrospectively appear as a critical drive within the context of the mounting intellectual hegemony of the American structures of knowledge production in the context of the US rise to world power, the call for a global sociology was both compatible with modernization theories and coherent with a wider effort of American social science to think globally the post-colonial world. This convergence was epitomized by the transformation in the way American social sciences transformed classical European orientalism, anthropology, and ethnology, into the newly born field of area studies. Ravi Palat (1997) defines area studies as the new imaginative geographies of US hegemony. For him the creation of the multidisciplinary field of study of Third World countries from an integrated perspective that included, but was remarkably more extended and multifaceted than, anthropology.

Within the newly-born and interdisciplinary field of area studies, the embryo of what would become world-systems analysis during the 1970s locates. By the turn of the 1950s, Immanuel Wallerstein, Terence Kilbourne Hopkins, Giovanni Arrighi, and other scholars who were in the field of development studies had been studying Africa before experiencing the political uprising that, from 1968 social movements to the oil crises of 1972, impressed a new course to world politics and the forms of production and distribution of wealth. In an interview for the American Sociological Association, Wallerstein remembers:

> I was a product of Columbia sociology, but I was also a heretic. Columbia sociology in the 1950s was the center of the world. It thought of itself, and was thought of, as the center of the sociological world. And it had a very strong point of view. But within that framework, they were somewhat tolerant. . . . But a number of years later, Paul Lazarsfeld said of me and Terry Hopkins that we were "His Majesty's loyal opposition." (quoted in Williams 2013, 207)

The experience of 1968 as a "world revolution," its interaction with Third-Worldism and feminism, as well as the radical critique that the organizations of the New Left posed both to imperialism and to institutional parties of the "Old" Left, played a crucial role in the theoretical commitment to rethink politics as well as historical and social change (Bhambra and Demir 2009). It gave different and often divergent imprints to the generation of scholars whom Zine Magubane (2005) refers to as the second wave of historical sociologists.

Coincidentally with the temporal boundaries of the lustrum 1968–1972, a crucial transformation occurred in the way the world was constructed in its singularity. A. C. T. Geppert (2007, 594) does not make a particularly problematic statement when he declares that the significance of the Christmas 1968 Apollo 8 space expedition

> was not at all the continued exploration of outer space, its scientific results, or the proof of the actual technical possibility for so doing. It was, rather, a radical change in self-perception on a genuinely global level, literally resulting in a new Weltanschauung, i.e., ways of viewing the world. For the first time ever, it was felt that the entire earth could be seen—and see itself—from without and as a whole.

The visual imagery has been radically transformed since the late twentieth century by the famous *Earthrise* photograph that the Apollo 8 spacecraft sent back to Cape Canaveral as the first image of the planet seen from the outer space. *Earthrise* was a partial view of the planet, but it was the first eyewitness picture taken from a sufficient distance to capture the whole globe. The accuracy and spectacularity of *Earthrise* were largely overtaken by the photograph popularized with the name of *Blue Marble* and distributed worldwide by global media, which the successive Apollo 17 mission took in 1972. Derek Cosgrove (1994, 270) has paid particular attention to these events

> with the intention of placing them in the cultural and historical context of Western global images and imaginings. [These] representations of the globe and

> the whole Earth in the twentieth century have drawn upon and reconstituted a repertoire of sacred and secular, colonial and imperial meanings, and these representations have played an especially significant role in the self-representation of the post-war United States and its geo-cultural mission.

For Cosgrove (1994, 290), the intertextuality of these two iconic images combines two overlapping discourses about the global: *one-world* and *whole-Earth*: "One-world is a geopolitical conception coeval with the European and Christian sense of *imperium*. It signifies the expansion of a specific socio-economic order across space. . . . Whole-Earth is an environmentalist conception that appeals to the organic and spiritual unity of terrestrial life. Humans are incorporated through visceral bonds between land and life (individual, family, community)." The characterization of these two discourses with their reciprocal interpellation and the non-coincidental nature of the semantic spaces they dwell upon, loudly resonates with non-Western yet dominant holistic notions of the global such as the contemporary revival of the Chinese concept of *Tianxia* (Tingyang 2005; Shahi and Ascione 2016). Such a reciprocal interpellation also recalls the totalizing integrated understanding of historical, ecological, and societal processes that systemic thinking such as General System Theory aspires to achieve. The visual imagery of planet Earth seen from the outer space from the Nasa missions provided a synthetic and powerful representation of the US geopolitical and geocultural projection of its role in history. Also more evident is how it served the geopolitical purpose of controlling the world imagination about the global, given the symbolic relevance that emerging global powers such as India, China, Russia, or Saudi Arabia accord to space missions.

It is important to remark, however, that this reciprocal interpellation between the world as a single entity and the world as a living whole was asymmetrical. The discourse of one-world subsumed the planetary imagination of whole-Earth and its ecological attitude. Linda Billings (2007, 484) clarifies that this asymmetrical conflation is a projection of an ideological structure "that draws deeply on a durable American cultural narrative of frontier pioneering and continual progress."

Cosgrove can hardly be confuted when he locates the production of the global as a cultural artifact into an ideological architecture of Western dominance that emerged coextensively with the European colonization of the Americas and prosecuted from the age of explorations throughout the creation of empires during the nineteenth century until the rise of the United States to world hegemony. This ideological architecture is thus a reconfiguration of the coherent, long-term, transforming system of beliefs, which Blaut (1993) named "the colonizer's model of the world." Blaut provides a general principle of interaction between theories, beliefs, and values that accounts for the conformality, rather than the simple intuitive conformity, between the social needs of dominant groups and the array of scholarly ideas and concepts deployed to make sense of the world. For Blaut (1993, 38),

The judgment of conformality is a complex binding process: "the notion that beliefs are culture-bound is of course a familiar one, but the idea that this proposition applies fully to the belief systems of scholars is not really accepted. . . . All new ideas in social science are vetted for their conformality to values, and more precisely to the value system of the elite of the society, which is not necessarily the value system of the scholars themselves.

The global emerged as a construction that is—in Blaut terminology—conformal with Eurocentric diffusionism. Conformality provided Western social theory with a self-legitimating radicalization of its theoretical power of representation. If, as Steinmetz (2005, 1, 5) maintains, the critique of methodologies implies "making the epistemological stakes and disputes explicit," and if even "the philosophy of science is more than a meta-reflection on the sciences, [but] it is shaped by those sciences and by the broader sociopolitical environment," then even the global as a methodological issue is situated within complex interactions of culture and power as well as systems of beliefs. As Derek Gregory (1994, 204) points out, "the global is not the 'universal,' but is itself a situated construction." And this construction consists in a historically determined colonial configuration of power, vision, representation, logic, and narrative.

DIFFUSIONISM AS THE LOGIC OF WORLD-CAPITALIST EXPANSION OR UNTHINKING INCORPORATION

World-systems analysis elaboration of the world-system as a unit of analysis was not much "an exception that confirms the rule," as Go (2012) concedes: it was culturally conformal and intellectually loyal to the global as a holistic and relational construction that emerged in the intellectual climate of American sociology effort to turn global. No doubt, in the realm of social theory, it offered an important antidote to Parson's ahistorical understanding of the social system. For Wallerstein (1976), in fact, the modern world was a historical living system with its multiple temporalities, its spatial organization, its onset, development, and possible end. Jason Moore's notion of Anthropocene and the transformation of the concept of world economy into world ecology has given voice to the adjective "living" that Wallerstein had used but never took seriously as a determinant aspect in conceiving the historical threshold beyond which the existence of capitalism as a mode of production would imply a shift in its foundational mechanisms of functioning, what Moore (2017) conceptualizes in terms of the metabolic rift. To be sure, the debates around the ecological base of modern capitalism involved, as the so-called regulationist approaches maintained, the study of global social change (Brenner and Glick 1991). Through a wider world-ecological view about world-systems, it was possible to look back at premodern and ancient times as the geohistorical space of coexistence of connected multiple socio-political entities. Yet, as John Hobson (2013) has argued, the unproblematic association of holism and relationalism was profoundly Eurocentric too. Such an association implied that the world became global only when the West managed to incorporate the rest of the world within a single capitalist world-system. Modernity, as a self-expanding capitalist system, was imagined as a historical force that radiated from a center and enlarged its space by violent processes of inclusion that implied the simultaneous peripherization of new areas, peoples, and resources. In this narrative of expansion and diffusion, the incorporating and self-expanding "whole" (the West) is active, transformative, modern; the outside (the Rest) is passive, stagnant, traditional. In a sense, the former is the subject of history; the latter, the object of history. This narrative structure persists in histories of globalization, even though the causes of this expansion vary and the spacetime coordinates of diffusion dramatically change between those who think of globalization as an original phenomenon of modernity and those who see it as a characteristic of post-1972 world configuration. Wallerstein (1999, 21) himself restates this overwhelming diffusionist and Eurocentric logic of historical thinking when he affirms that the geography of the globalizing forces of capitalism corresponds to the geometry of the global commodity chains:

> The historical geography of our present structure can be seen to have three principal moments. The first was the period of original creation between 1450 and 1650, during which time the modern world-system came to include primarily most of Europe (but neither the Russian Empire nor the Ottoman Empire) plus certain parts of the Americas. The second moment was the great expansion from 1750 to 1850, when primarily the Russian Empire, the Ottoman Empire, southern and parts of Southeast Asia, large parts of West Africa, and the rest of the Americas were incorporated. The third and last expansion occurred in the period between 1850 and 1900, when primarily East Asia, but also various other zones in Africa, the rest of Southeast Asia, and Oceania were brought inside the division of labor. At that point, the capitalist world-economy had become truly global for the first time.

The geometry of global commodity chains derives from relationalism as a methodological option to think the global. As Terence K. Hopkins (1982, 149) clearly put it,

> Our acting units or agencies can only be thought of as *formed*, and continually re-formed by the relations between them. Perversely, we often think of the relations as only going between the end point, the units or the acting agencies, as if the latters made the relations instead of the relations making the units. Relations, generally, are our figures and acting agencies are our backgrounds. At certain points, in conducting the analyses, it is of course it is indispensable to shift about and focus on acting agencies; but I think we too often forget what we have done and fail to shift back again."

It is true that relationalism within the holistic frame of historical analysis that world-systems approach endorsed reduces the fallacies of replicability as a mechanism of social change, because makes social change unconceivable at the level of the single state. Social change is conceivable only at the level of the system. Nonetheless, as Brenner (1999, 57–58) remarks, "the primary geographical units of global space are defined by the territorial boundaries of states, which in turn constitute a single, encompassing macro-territoriality, the world interstate system. The national scale is thereby blended into the global scale while the global scale is flattened into its national components . . . the global and the national scales are viewed as structural analogs of a single spatial form: territoriality." Wallerstein's approach to world-systems analysis entails the replication of a territorialist model of space not only on the national scale of the territorial state but on the global scale of the world-system.

From the perspective of the coloniality of method, the notion of incorporation conceals the colonial gaze and neutralizes the colonial difference by obscuring non-Western, non-capitalist agency. Incorporation expresses a function performed by the system to adapt its structures to the pressures generated by its own inner historical contradictions. The critique to the dynamics of the fall of the rates of profit that Marx had seen as a long-term secular trend is resolved by rearticulating in space the possibility of reestablishing highly profitable conditions for accumulation through the inclusion of cheap colonial labor and natural resources into the enlarged cycle of accumulation. Yet incorporation, which accounts for colonialism as large-scale/long-term relation, works as a reductionist hyponym of the colonial. Incorporation overrides colonialism by reducing it to its function within capitalism. It simultaneously gives prominence to exploitation, domination, and hierarchies formation, but it also neglects and mortifies the historical possibility of non-Western, postcolonial, and post-Western agency, and the way these agencies coproduce social change in heterogeneous metageographies other than the core periphery structure. Nominally, agency, as per Hopkins's claim, is subdued to the relations that produced it. But this assertion conceals the fact that the same relation, as object of analysis, is presumed analytically neutral and operationalized as such, whereas it is not neutral at all. The historical agency described as the dynamics of the colonial relation is implicitly coincidental with the dominant subjects, class, and groups that are located in the higher power position in the hierarchies that relations inevitably design. Only the West, or the Western nation-states, or the dominant group within these states operating at a transnational level, becomes agents of history in the dialectics with social structures.

To be sure, it could not be otherwise, since for any theory whose narrative logic is constructed upon the axiom of the endless accumulation of capital, the spatial rearticulation of the Marxian logic of accumulation is based upon the assumption that capitalists' contradictory agency is an embodiment of the logic of capital, whereas capital, as Marx constantly repeats, is the overarching social relation. In David Harvey's (2010, 40) words, "Capital is not a thing but a process in which money is perpetually sent in search of more money. Capitalists—those who set this process in motion—take on many different personae." When this postulate is translated into methodology, the historically determined asymmetry of power, intrinsic in the colonial relation but not exhaustive of its properties, capabilities, and limits, becomes a totalizing qualifier of its correspondent simplified function, which is expressed through the concept of incorporation as a conceptual articulation of Eurocentric diffusionism.

RETHINKING THE "ABSTRACT" AND THE "CONCRETE"

This condition, once acknowledged, is not easy to overcome. It mortifies conceptualization as far as a narrow theoretical imagination is concerned. This *problematique* implies a direct confrontation with a single methodological issue raised by Hopkins in chapter 7 of *World-Systems Analysis: Theory and Methodology*. Hopkins introduces the problem by exhorting the reader to an intellectual counterintuitive detour: "Forcing ourselves to think in ways we are not used to" (Hopkins and Wallerstein 1982, 146). In his dense phrases under scrutiny here, Hopkins first resumes the usual way sociology thinks to concept formation: the relation between abstract and concrete. Usually, he explains, we move from the level of concept (what is considered "the abstract") downward toward the level of indicator (what is considered "the concrete"). Through such a descending movement, we include layers of attributes that, one by one, visualize the concrete presence of the object we want to study in the real world; finally, we materialize what the abstract concept captures in theory. The opposite yet complementary movement returns inductively from the indicator back to the concept by dropping these attributes and sublimating the concrete into the abstract. According to the classical sociological view, which Hopkins epitomizes with Paul Lazarsfeld, such a vertical double movement comes together with a horizontal one. This horizontal movement takes place at the level where concepts lie. On such an abstract layer, there would exist the network of concepts that forms the lexicon of the social sciences in general, or the one of a specific theory in particular. Hopkins invokes Carl Gustav Hempel's analytical philosophy to figure it: "The imagery of a theory as a network of substantive concepts (nodes) and logical relations between them (threads), floating, as it were, above a world of reality to which the theory is linked by 'rules of interpretation'" (Hopkins and Wallerstein 1982, 146). How does Hopkins rethink the *concrete-abstract* from here, then?

It is important to remember that according to Hopkins and Wallerstein, the significant unit of analysis for long-term and large-space processes of social change at the global level is the world-system. In extreme synthesis, a world-system is a spatiotemporal entity whose extension defines the geography of the commodity chains that interconnect the multiple places into a single integrating whole, ruled by a single overwhelming principle of social action. In the modern world-system, this principle is the endless accumulation of capital. The world-system is a whole that enjoys a higher degree of reality than its constitutive parts, which, conversely, lose their own significance if taken in isolation from the constitutive whole. Different world-systems have existed in history, yet the capitalist mode of production would be the only one that has reached the entire world to the point that the global world and the modern world-system came to coincide when exploration and colonization where geographically completed.[6]

Now, Hopkins questions the significance of the concept indicator interpretation of the abstract-concrete movement: that is, "the inclusion-relations in terms of the part-whole relations" (Hopkins and Wallerstein 1982, 147). The usage of the word "relation" is ambiguous, here. We need to go deep into it and make it explicit. The word "relation" in the previous textual citation assumes two distinctive meanings within the same short utterance, which has the form of an equational sentence.[7] When coupled with "inclusion," relation designs the abstract level where Lazarsfeld's classical sociological view locates the interaction among different concepts in a Hempel-like ontology. Differently from this view, the second part of the same equational sentence involves an alternative understanding of the word "relation": relation is what makes possible the existence of the part-whole as a single conceptual unit. Hopkins extrapolates relation from "inclusion-relations" in order to stress the autonomy of relation in this particular context of conceptualization for sociological thinking. Relation possesses a stronger ontological status than the two entities that relation produces in the act of connecting them two.

Hopkins clarifies the proper location of relation in social thinking: not a concept among other concepts, but a category of thought, something that makes possible concept formation.

The part and the whole are ontologically distinct. First, because even though they are inextricably intertwined, the whole is prominent over the part. Second, the part is not something given, nor an essence, nor something fixed, nor existing out there as such: the part is a theoretical process to be conceived, defined, named, and analyzed. As such, the part, which is a process, is not concrete: it is the abstract; while the whole, which consists in the totality, is the concrete. Yet the concrete (the totality, the whole, the world as a unit of analysis) does not refer to the "real world": the concrete is a form of abstraction itself. The concrete is abstract too:

> The part-whole directive gives an utterly different set of directions. It says to keep moving out by successive determinations, bringing in successive parts—themselves abstract processes—in continuous juxtaposition and in this way form the whole, which you need for interpreting and explaining the historical changes or conditions under examination. (Hopkins and Wallerstein 1982, 147)

Operationally, relation is the category that provides the condition of possibility for thinking the part-whole; semantically, relation qualifies the hyphen symbol with the theoretical ability to allow for further specifying what the particular connection is made of. The hyphen in the attribute "non-Western" does not express a relation. The hyphen in the attribute "geo-cultural" does not qualify a relation between geography and culture. Instead, the hyphen in "part-whole" as well as in "core-periphery" is a matter of method that involves a procedure of conceptualization and defines a way to conduct research.[8]

This appropriation has major implications for our ability to look inside how notions work and how to form concepts, particularly when they are formed by two words that become a single unity, for three reasons: first, because they couple in multiple, different ways, and each way orients research in direction of the full awareness of the theoretical tools available and their proper usage;[9] second, because the juxtaposition of words to form concepts is a viable path to cope with cultural, civilizational, and linguistic differences in order to maintain an acceptable degree of pluralism, whereas a synthetic option would irremediably sacrifice meanings;[10] and third, because another viable path is to move further from juxtaposition and pass from a concept formed by two or more words to a single-word synthetic concept expressed with still another word. In any case, the words we chose to combine in a concept always become other than the words previously expressed through each of the two single terms used. So, for instance, in "world-system," the world connotes the whole as historical formation; the system connotes the whole as theoretical construct based on relation. In core-periphery, the core is a socioeconomic part where the international division of labor locates specific activities and the periphery is another socioeconomic part where the international division of labor locates the activities other than the one associated with the core. The world-system is a concept that designs the whole, a totality, the unit of analysis. It is more concrete than core-periphery. Core-periphery designs a set of processes not entirely reducible to a spatial matrix, where the international division of labor designs one among the relations between different parts.

The part of the whole is a process, not an entity existing *in se* and *per se*. It is a process that we are called to study through an adequately formed concept or set of concepts, whose formulation does not exclude taxonomical creativity, linguistic contamination, and cross-cultural dialogue, rather than necessarily sticking our sociological imagination to a region in world economy named India, Latin America, southern Europe, or even Italy, or to a notion such as class, gender, or status group.

Hopkins's methodological directive enables us to step into an epistemological territory where, paradoxically, elaborating concepts for thinking the world forces us out of either strict geographical locations or any usual spatialized coordinate to which our *forma mentis* would automatically refer. The vertical-horizontal architecture of the movement from concept to indicators proves inadequate to represent the historical processes of social change that need to be conceived within the world as a single unit of analysis, where concepts allow a different sociological imagination to thrive via the constitutive relation between the parts and the whole. This suspension creates an intellectual space of its own. Thrown into this alien methodological landscape, the sociological imagination experiences an uncanny, fluctuating condition of disorientation.

Hopkins rescues the reader by invoking Marx. He asserts that the methodological choice he is proposing "is the one that Marx discusses in his very brief and elliptical remarks on 'The Method of Political Economy'" (Hopkins and Wallerstein 1982, 147). To be sure, Marx made explicit that the concrete is the synthesis of multiple determination the relations in which they are seized, in which they participate.

The reader will notice how Hopkins resonates with Marx, but also how Hopkins transforms Marx's notion of society (that is, the whole of the relations between men) into the notion of system (that is, the whole of the relations between parts). On his turn, Marx inherited from Hegel the notion of integrated totality. For the idealist philosopher Hegel, totality is a metaphysical whole endowed with ontological presence. For the materialist social scientist Marx, this whole is society as a conceptual construction. For the historical sociologist Hopkins, society is meaningless unless we think the world in terms of an integrated spacetime coproduced by long-term and large-scale processes of social change. Hopkins and Wallerstein (1982, 111) affirm that

> the arena where social action takes place and social change occurs is not "society" in the abstract, but a definite "world," a spatiotemporal whole, whose spatial scope is coextensive with the elementary division of labor among its constituent regions or parts, and whose temporal scope extends for as long as the elementary division of labor continually reproduces the "world" as a social whole.

All of them assume totality as an intrinsic limit of abstraction whose taken-for-granted ontological presence informs the presumed adequacy of the concepts formed to study the parts of the whole. Yet the meaningfulness of totality comes at a cost: a theoretical "escamotage." They affirm that the concrete is itself abstract, but they keep on deploying the concept of abstract-concrete as terminological invariant: *as if* the abstract would be *less concrete* than the concrete, even though, in fact, the concrete is abstract too. There follows that the movement toward the concrete, the totality, the whole, the world, cannot but be purely asymptotical: it is a constant tension toward an unknown reality: the abstract-concrete describes a permanent condition of incompleteness. In so doing, the methodological problem of concept formation shifts from ontology to heuristics.

This shift is crucial to allow Western thinking to dialogue with other forms of knowledge that are not structured in terms of hierarchy between ontology, epistemology, and methodology without delegitimizing the theoretical tools of the social sciences. Confronted with this transformed self-understanding, Western social science matures the awareness that the world is not only the geohistorical space that the capitalist world-system came to englobe by waves of successive incorporations until it covered the entire surface of the planet. The world is also the vast spacetime of multiple epistemologies that Eurocentrism had marginalized and silenced, which coinhabited a global space that preexisted the full colonization of the world by Europeans at the turn of nineteenth century and kept existing in recessive forms regardless the hegemonic knowledges. The world of the capitalist world-system is one among other parts of the whole, and these parts are either regions or processes, but also knowledges that a global social science is called to register and understand.

ASYMMETRIES OF POWER, POSTCOLONIAL AGENCIES: THE PREDICAMENT OF RELATIONALISM

The adequacy of the Eurocentric understanding of the global and its related concept formation protocols has been effectively confuted by the vast field of anti-Eurocentrism, in many interrelated respects. The increasing legitimacy of these intellectual transformations, and the wide range of options by which it is possible to categorize the proliferation of such perspectives, cannot be disjoined by the profound reconfiguration of the distribution of world power, resources, and wealth at the global scale that accompanies the decline of US hegemony and, more generally speaking, the partial, ongoing, contradictory displacement of Europe and the West from their dominant cultural and ideological position.[11] Dissimulating it would be, at best, an intellectual ingenuity, equivalent to the illusion that a direct factual correlation explaining this conjunction is empirically discernible.

From a methodological point of view, the overall effect of the critique of diffusionism has been the rupture of its core presumption, the breaking of the covalent bond holism-and-relationalism, the disentanglement of relations from the whole. Relations do produce entities, which thus do not possess any essentialist innate trait as such, and it is thus relations, rather than inner properties, that determined the emergence of capitalism and modernity as worldly significant long-term/large-scale processes of historical and social change. Nonetheless, the global as a holistic construct does not provide a strong overdetermining unit of analysis which comprehension has to be constantly referred to as a prevailing horizon of sense.

This disentanglement has disclosed divergent ways of adopting relationalism in sociological thinking. Bhambra has convincingly argued that this disentanglement is simultaneously both a departure from the previous articulation of the global in the context of modernization and globalization theories as well as a surreptitious reaffirmation of some of the most enduring tenets of Eurocentrism in social theory. This is particularly so where historical sociology ends up endorsing the assumption that the transition to modernity remains predominantly a European phenomenon, an assumption buttressed by the sociological paradigms of multiple or alternative modernities (Bhambra 2007). In order to explore the ambiguities inherent in the attempt to reformulate the methodological and theoretical approach to the conceptualization of the global as a by-product of constitutive long-term/large-scale relations, Sanjay Seth (2007, 335) provides a fruitful entry point:

> One way contests the privileging of Europe by questioning, and in some cases providing an alternative to, the conventional historical narrative according to

> which modernity begins in Europe and then radiates outward. Since the focus is on the story to be told, this is an enterprise that conducts its battles largely on the terrain of the empirical, counterposing some facts against other facts, and making "hard" claims to accuracy and truth. . . . Postcolonial works are "thicker" histories, often based upon archival research and, partly as a result of this, usually confined to one place (Egypt, India, Latin America). Unsurprisingly, since their aim is to mobilize a non-Western history or slice thereof in order to show that the categories through which we think are not fully adequate to their task, what they lack in terms of empirical range, compared to the first group, they make up for with a wider range of theoretical referents.

Western social sciences aim at explaining the rise of the West, or the transition to capitalism, or the breakthrough to modernity. Here the global is understood as the result of either a dialogical exchange between the East and the West, with the West acting as a borrower of Eastern resources portfolios, both material and ideational (Bala 2004). Alternatively, it is understood as the result of the interconnection of geohistorical paths between more "advanced" regions of world economy, due to diverse responses to cultural, institutional, and socioeconomic civilizational needs and pressures contextually defined but worldly interconnected.[12] In these accounts, relations include non-Western agency, yet the heuristic problem of explaining societal divergence in terms of fluctuating power differentials, between advanced zones of the derivative global space, limits the relevance of this agency to those dominant social groups located outside Europe. In this sense, the coloniality of method allows for the exclusive relevance of those non-Western agencies that could compete with the West on the terrain of modernization and that concurred to form modernity by means of the conscious or unintended outcomes of the responses they provided to the interaction between global connections and local needs and pressures. Consequently, the relevance of nondominant agencies is relegated to the effects they produce in terms of pressures that exist locally and considered only in their vertical dialectics with modernizing power, rather than historically existing in a multiplicity of other ignored relations of social coextensiveness.

Moreover, while these explanatory/narrative approaches share the tendency to neutralize all the other forms of nondominant agency, at the same time they also sterilize the transforming potential of existing epistemologies of otherness by never questioning the heuristic apparatus derived from the threefold conundrum of the breakthrough to modernity, the rise of the West, and the transition to capitalism. As Bhambra (2014) remarks, this strategy limits its scope to providing new data to confute or support existing narrative structures yet precluding the theoretical possibility of engaging with the elaboration of not-yet-existing structures of meaning and narratives, wherein qualitatively new data can be produced, elaborated, and placed.

Differently from this view, postcolonial theory sees modernity in terms of a discursive formation through which the rest of the world was simultaneously subjugated and relegated to the role of Europe's binary opposed Other(s). Against this Eurocentric bias that Du Bois and Frantz Fanon first explored, both postcolonial theory and the paradigm of decoloniality affirm the reciprocal historical, social, cultural, and identitarian coformation and codetermination of binary hyperreal constructs, such as colonizer/colonized, in order to dismantle the diffusionist logic that is implicit in whatever conceptualization of the global in terms of centers and peripheries. This epistemological critique is double: on the one hand, Seth explains, it is affirmed that not just the dominant accounts offered by the social sciences, but the very concepts through which such accounts are fashioned, have genealogies that, as Chakrabarty (2000, 4) underlines, "go deep into the intellectual and even theological traditions of Europe." On the other hand, "colonial subjects, even subaltern, or marginal and silenced, are able both 'to actively appropriate, re-elaborate and transform institutions, practices and knowledges received' and to interpellate alternative, indigenous, knowledges and epistemologies." As Kapil Raj further argues, this shift in emphasis means rethinking the colonial relation by postulating that "being colonized and having agency are not antithetical." Achille Mbembe (2014, 36) makes this point when he states that the threshold from asymmetry to annihilation is necropolitical:

> An unequal relationship is established along with the inequality of the power over life. . . . Because the slave's life is like a "thing," possessed by another person, the slave existence appears as a perfect figure of a shadow. In spite of the terror and the symbolic sealing off of the slave, he or she maintains alternative perspectives toward time, work, and self. . . . Treated as if he or she no longer existed except as a mere tool and instrument of production, the slave nevertheless is able to draw almost any object, instrument, language, or gesture into a performance and then stylize it. Breaking with uprootedness and the pure world of things of which he or she is but a fragment, the slave is able to demonstrate the protean capabilities of the human bond through music and the very body that was supposedly possessed by another.

Postcolonial counterhistories mistrust the hegemonic construction of any master narrative as well as those universalizing understandings of the world that attempt to conceal their site of enunciation. From a gender perspective on science, Donna Haraway (1988) has unleashed the potential of the critique of the situatedness of whatever form of knowledge.[13] Santiago Castro-Gómez (2004) has conceptualized the geocultural nature of the geopolitics of knowledge to denounce the self-concealing epistemological strategy that western social and historical sciences have adopted in their attempt to construct a *science of society.* Castro-Gómez makes explicit the "hubris of the *point zero,*" that is, "the illusion that science can create valid knowledge about the world only if the observer situates himself on a neutral and objective platform of observation that, at the same time, cannot be observed by any other observer." According to Fernando Coronil (2000), this ability to hide the partiality of universalism is the hallmark of the underlying transformation and resurgence of Eurocentrism under the semblance of "globocentrism." The disarticulation of the image of Europe as a geohistorical construction integral to a spacetime location does not imply the automatic demise of the hegemony of the discursive frame that legitimated its superiority, since the deterritorialization of Europe or the West has been followed by their less visible reterritorialization within an elusive image of the world that hides transnational financial and political networks, socially concentrated but geographically diffused.

BORDERS VIS-À-VIS ASSEMBLAGES

If relations of domination are never able to completely transform asymmetries of power into absolute inanity on the colonial side of exploitation and cultural domestication, then there exist *loci* of reemergence to be explored. For Walter Mignolo (2007), these spaces are *borders*: multiple generative epistemic territories from which European universalism can be questioned. Whereas Western thinking presumes its own universality, decolonizing knowledge multiplies the sites of enunciation toward pluriversality, that is, the coexistence of interactive universalisms relationally constructed and historically enacted by the multiple articulation of the colonial difference, whose horizons, as Iain Chambers and Lidia Curti (1996) have registered, differ yet coexist under a common sky. Sandro Mezzadra and Brett Neilson (2013) expand the notion of border. Borders are conceived in terms of epistemological devices of connections and disconnections produced by social and historical relations. Yet the very definition of this device is itself a limit, according to Étienne Balibar (2002, 76):

> The idea of a simple definition of what constitutes a border is, by definition, absurd: to mark out a border is precisely to define a territory, to delimit it, and so to register the identity of that territory, or confer one upon it. Conversely, however, to define and identify in general is nothing other than to trace a border, to assign boundaries or borders (in Greek, *horos*; in Latin, *finis* or *terminus*; in German, *Grenze*, in French, *borne*). The theorist who attempts to define what

> border is is in danger of going round in circles, as the very representation of the border is the precondition of any definition.

Mezzadra and Neilson (2013, 16) specify that "[i]nsofar as it serves at once to make divisions and establish connections, the border is an epistemological device, which is at work whenever a distinction between subject and object is established." As they suggest, the determination of border relies on the dualism of subject/object, as an expression of historically determined power relations.

The fact that the signification of border pertains to a more abstract level of concept formation is inferred from Balibar's passage itself and the circularity of its formulation. The problem is not only that the term "border" seems to preclude any possible definition *in se*. It is rather that the trope of the border works as a nonquestionable semantic axiom to conceptualize identity and difference within the epistemological frame of modernity. This definition of the epistemological foundation of border as a device is overdetermined by the theoretical frame of modernity and the significance that "relation" acquires within this frame. For Balibar (2013), in fact, the conceptual reelaboration of René Descartes's dualism by John Locke is quintessential to the self-understanding of modernity. The transition from the ontological distinction between *res extensa* and *res cogitans* to the self-reflexive individual political and moral responsibility of individual consciousness set the terms of the question of the relation between subject and object that would be later developed in diverging positions by Hume and Kant, *inter alia*, who nonetheless shared Locke's premises. Yet the importance of Locke's conceptualization of consciousness lies not so much in its efficacy and influence but rather in the logical inconsistency of its own premises. Balibar's accurate exegesis of Locke's "invention of consciousness" shows that the theoretical attempt to build modern subjectivity upon the schismatic relation between interiority and exteriority results in irresolvable aporias that haunted Locke himself: "The limit regresses indefinitely towards a unity of contraries enigmatically indicated by Locke with the term 'power.' But it may also be said that the ever-renewed question of this unity is nothing more than the shadow cast by the initial theoretical distinction." (Balibar 2013, 68) The power Locke is exerting upon the creation of the cognitive border that defines the modern subject is nothing but the power to postulate, that is, to establish the nonquestionable nonlogical axiom of a self-legitimating axiomatic. Thus, one option to think the aporetic definitional status of the border consists in rethinking the border by questioning this very postulate, through a single-step logical regression: if the border subverts whatever essentialist discourse of historical presence by opposing to it the dynamic process of its formation, then it cannot consider itself in terms of essential definitional traits, but exclusively in terms of *relation*. The condition of possibility to think the border is given by the notion of relation. So it is relation at the borders of modernity that needs to be addressed.

Manuel De Landa (2006, 3) attempts to rethink the epistemological foundations of modernity by reelaborating the notion of relation through Deleuze's concept of assemblage: "the realist social ontology to be defended here is all about objective processes of assembly: a wide range of social entities, from persons to nation-states, will be treated as assemblages constructed through very specific historical processes, processes in which language plays an important but not a constitutive role." De Landa separates relations from totalities by distinguishing between properties and the capacity to interact. While relations are usually thought of as occurring between entities, and these entities formed by relations themselves have certain properties, assemblage theory replaces *properties*, as transient *loci* of essentialization, endowed with the ability of these entities to produce new relations through interaction. Here a distinction is made between relations of interiority (associated with the classical notion of *properties*) and relations of exteriority (transformed by the introduction of the notion of *capabilities*): "These capacities do depend on a component's properties but cannot be reduced to them since they involve reference to the properties of other interacting entities. Relations of exteriority guarantee that assemblages may be taken apart while at the same time allowing that the interactions between parts may result in a true synthesis" (De Landa 2006, 100). Relations of exteriority would thus be generative of a variety of social entities, such as the individual, the state, the market, the international system, and borders as well, "whose historical appearance is to be understood in terms of the interactions between members of a collectivity may lead to the formation of more or less permanent articulations between them yielding a macro-assemblage with properties and capacities of its own. Since the processes behind the formation of these enduring articulations are themselves recurrent" (De Landa 2005, 13). Saskia Sassen (2004, 10) has extended this logic to conceptualize the emergence of the global as the multiscalar structuring pattern of change that connects the Middle Ages to contemporary globalization in a complex matrix of interaction with the nation-state. She speaks of

> the centrifugal scalings of the Late Middle Ages held together by several encompassing normative orders, the centripetal scaling of the modem nation-state marked by one master normativity, and the centrifugal scalings of the global that disaggregate that master normativity into multiple partial normative orders, thereby leaving open the questions as to its sustainability if we take history as a guide. In this regard then, the global is novel—different from earlier

> centrifugal scalings in that it also disaggregates normativity into specialized subassemblages.

In this sense, the global as well as colonialism would be assemblages themselves, produced and coproduced by scattered conflictive logics of structuration whose operation takes place over time, being thus inevitably path dependent. Assemblage theories, then, provide both an ontological foundation for social heterogeneity and a historical narrative of nonlinear development that, nonetheless, constructs an inner continuum from the Middle Ages to the contemporary "global era." Yet it is not only the endogenous logic of cumulative causation informing such historical narrative of the emergence of the global that needs to be closely scrutinized. Methodologically, assemblage theories open up the notion of relation to include the possibility that the degree of freedom of capabilities to give birth to new relations is a measure of the potential transformative historical power involved in relation itself. Yet this move is possible if, and only if, the problem of postulating the distinction between exteriority and interiority is simply transposed from the ontological level of the border to the ontological level of relation. The definitional conundrum that Balibar set as unresolvable is thus merely eluded but remains still unresolved. Why?

One of the possible answers lies in reframing the question and wondering: is the Western conceptual archive alone able to question its own premises? It might not be accidental that the entire construction of assemblage theory reaffirms the genealogy of what Connell has called the Western canon of sociology: Smith, Comte, Marx, Durkheim, Weber, Tonnies, Parsons, and the sociological concepts of *division of labor*, *state*, *market*, and *social cohesion*. It climbs upon the shoulders of the shamble giants and, from the ethno-story it prosecutes, it draws legitimation without engaging with the creative role of existing epistemologies of otherness. Assemblage theories remain entangled within the limits of the postmodern presumption that the West, in the guise of advanced societies or late capitalist societies, is simultaneously the historical outpost of the crisis as well as the autonomous authoritative locus of emergence of the theory to cope with the crisis itself. Within this horizon, assemblage theory works as a metatheory that implicitly oversubsumes under the notion of social heterogeneity either colonialism as a global hegemonic project, or coloniality as matrix of power, or alternative epistemological resources. Heterogeneity, in the context of assemblage theory, neutralizes the pervasiveness of the colonial difference, which, instead, does exist already and inevitably as a by-product of global geocultural hierarchies of classification of human groups and their knowledges, produced by colonialism as a process and by coloniality as matrix of power. Coloniality thus cannot be constructed as a recurrent expressive pattern of social heterogeneity for analytical purposes, not only because, in so doing, the colonial relation is neutralized, but also because it is made equivalent and homologous to other assemblages. For the search for an ahistorical definition of relations outside the colonial translates into a chimerical quest for an epistemological foundation that proves unable to provide new premises to rethink the global outside those Eurocentric presumptions of modernity that were recognized as the limits to be overcome by assemblage theory itself. Rather than either colonialism, or coloniality, or epistemologies of otherness being assemblages among assemblages, the social heterogeneity that the notion of assemblage conceptualizes is nothing but a transient, historically determined expression of the coloniality of method.

Assemblages and borders share the geohistorical imagery of global modernity. In fact, this imagery is not one of connections, but rather one of divisiveness: an imagery of geohistorical locations to which specific cultures were integral. And while concepts such as *border* or *assemblage* strategically oppose divisiveness, they end up opposing something that perhaps has never been opposed. As Doreen Massey (2005) notes, being a reaction against the fixities of state-centrism, they take seriously a representation of the global that has never been actual outside the ideologies produced in the making of European colonial expansion. The spacetime imagination both borders and assemblages pertain to is one that, having once been used to legitimate the territorialization of society/space, now is deployed in the legitimation of a response to their undoing.

EXPLORING CONNECTIONS, REFRAMING THE NOTION OF CIRCULATION

The problem of reconstructing the global after the critique to Eurocentrism directly affects the way the relation between how sociology is able to explore new territories and histories previously ignored and the way these territories and histories are allowed to transform the structures of meaning and concepts sociology uses. Bhambra (2014, 150) maintains that "it is this process of reshaping shared narratives in light of what is presented as new data and accounting for why it is understood as new that opens up the space for further insights about historical and social processes." A relevant part of these "new data" are being produced by connected histories of science. When the histories of scientific modernity are seen through the connections that made the world an integrated space, then the globalization of ideas and practices does not appear anymore as the diffusion of knowledge radiating from the European center to its peripheries. This shift interpolates the terms of the relation between Europe and the colonial worlds that the global history of the transition to modern science takes for granted. A metaphor may catch the reader's imagination: figure to play with a bifocal lens. Usually, global history of science focuses on a Scientific Revolution that happened in Europe, against the background of the world as a scenario. The global scenario is that of colonial expansion. From outside Europe ideas and discoveries were spread to the world, according to the diffusionist narratives of modern science; ideas and discoveries converged in Europe and here they were used to produce the breakthrough to modernity, according to the global dialogical history of science. Connected histories of science instead displace the European colonial expansion to the background and move to the fore other locations, experiences, and spacetimes where exchanges, transmissions, negotiations, and translations of scientific knowledges historically existed. These relations were nonetheless asymmetrical in power, because colonialism and imperialism partly overdetermined the day-to-day practices and lived experiences that gave birth to brand new hybrid knowledges.

Bhambra (2014, 151) is right in underlining that "the different 'facts' and 'consequences' of interest to social scientists in different social and cultural contexts are mutually implicated and the selections made from the perspective of different cultural contexts cannot be so easily insulated from their explanatory consequences." In the process of tackling new *explanantes*, in fact, connected histories of science elaborate new sets of heuristic *explanans*: circulation, go-betweens, and trading zones.

Raj (2013) explains that circulation means

> not the "dissemination," "transmission," or "communication" of ideas, but the processes of encounter, power and resistance, negotiation, and reconfiguration that occur in cross-cultural interaction. Rather, the circulation of knowledge implies a double movement of going forth and coming back, which can be repeated indefinitely. In circulating, things, men and notions often transform themselves. Circulation . . . therefore . . . implies an incremental aspect and not the simple reproduction across space of already formed structures and notions.

Circulation designs spacetimes that overlap neither with the map of modernity that has Europe at its center nor with a polycentric cartography of civilizational dialogue. The spacetime processes of circulation coagulate into cross-cultural *loci* of "contact" where exchange and negotiation occur, such as trading zones, where a multiplicity of actors, previously separated by geographic and historic disjunctures intervenes in the making of knowledge. Relations inevitably involve "conditions of coercion, radical inequality, and intractable conflict." As Mary Louise Pratt (1992, 6–7) suggests, the notion of *contact* emphasizes

> the interactive, improvisational dimensions of colonial encounters so easily ignored or suppressed by diffusionist accounts of conquest and domination. A "contact" perspective emphasizes how subjects are constituted in and by their relations to each other. It treats the relations among colonizers and colonized, or travelers and "travelees," not in terms of separateness or apartheid, but in terms of copresence, interaction, interlocking understandings and practices, often within radically asymmetrical relations of power.

Actors such as travelers, local informants, or naturalists thus actively participated in these cross-cultural encounters; their translations between cultures caused new scientific knowledge to emerge. Within the contact zones, go-betweens moved across colonial and cognitive borders; these borders were both physically and territorially articulated into either jurisdictional, formal, and informal boundaries, or subjectively perceived and experienced as cultural difference and power differentials in the realm of personal interaction with other actors from different geographical and historical backgrounds.

Notwithstanding the heuristic potential of the methodological approach of connected histories, issues regard the limits of reconstructing the global as a unit of analysis from these theoretical tools. They are able to provide new data, previously ignored by sociology, in the context of new narratives, previously dismissed by historiography; at the same time, they reiterate the irreducible dichotomy that lays at the foundation of the geohistorical imagery of colonial modernity and its Western and Eurocentric categories of thought. What spacetime configuration does emerge when one attempts to think circulation by conjugating the territorial definition of trading zones with the relational geographies designed by the intersubjective relation between social actors?

THE PLANETARY GLOBAL

Massey has explored this dilemma and conceptualized this dichotomy by opposing two irreducible conceptions of spacetime that we can refer to as representational and nonrepresentational. She argues that based on the fundamental dichotomy between subject and object, which is the epistemological foundation of modernity, spacetime is often conceived as a container (representational), while it actually is constantly formed and reformed by relations (nonrepresentational). So where is our understanding of the global located against the grain of this dichotomy that keeps on articulating our sociological imagination when it comes to terms with the elaboration of the global as a category of thought?

Bhambra's *Connected Sociologies* proposes an understanding of the global that opposes the diffusionism inherent in the Eurocentric master narrative of modernity and its partial reformulation in terms of globalization theories. Rather than a condition of possibility to conceptualize large-scale/long-term processes, a global sociology has thus to be reoriented toward "the histories of interconnection that have enabled the world to emerge as a global space" (Bhambra 2014, 155). Rather than a by-product of modernization or globalization, Bhambra thinks of the global as an "always/already there." Rather than a condition of possibility for the expansion of modernity, or a condition of impossibility for the elaboration of postcolonial modernities, the "global" can be thus reconstructed as the methodological tenet that establishes the global character of historical change as an assumption, and not as a consequence.

Yet, to the extent the global as a condition is postulated, a different set of questions arise regarding the theoretical nexus between modernity and the global. Are modernity and the global coextensive or codetermined? Was the world global before the colonization of the Americas? And if some of the planetary connections of the world were already/always global, do we need to reconfigure the spacetime coordinates of world histories according to a different cartography? Would it then make sense to speak of modernity, if those connections render inconsistent whatever narrative of "transition to modernity"? Or are we satisfied with conceptualizing the global as an immanent and perennial *ab origine* condition for conceptualizing history and social change? And if such a condition of thought is presumed in order to rethink modernity, aren't we running the implicit risk of translating a methodological premise into a metaphysical foundation? Therefore, finally, should we not tackle the limits that the ubiquity of modernity imposes on the sociological conceptualization of the global?

It is my contention that the global becomes stretched between the irreconcilable poles of the dichotomy Massey has defined. This condition reflects a predicament of the sociological imagination when it comes to addressing the issue of how to imagine the global outside or beyond the configuration of knowledge production that is inherent in the acceptance of modernity as a frame. The omnipresence of modernity, both as a historical-sociological and as an epistemological frame, translates the polarization between representational and nonrepresentational spacetimes and results in the polarization between two irreconcilable positions: either history becomes global exclusively when modernity emerges (coextensively and simultaneously, or as a consequence of European colonial expansion) or the global has to be thought of as a transhistorical "always/already there," even projected into the perennial spacetime of universal history. The global, in effect, seems to oscillate between two discrete statuses: a by-product of social relations or a property of what lies outside human activity. This polarization is due to the persistence of modernity, which constrains historical-sociological *explananda* within the gamut of possible configurations of space, time, and relation of modernity itself. The challenge for a global social theory thus becomes how to reconstruct the global as a category of analysis that goes beyond the coloniality of method inherent in the frame of modernity but at the same time proves able to reimagine long-term/large-scale process as by-product of social relations existing through and within human history and not outside of it: in other words, in the borderland that separates (and connects) theoretical adequacy with contested spacetime coordinates.

This position conveys an aporia: it simultaneously holds the static logic of the "always/already there" with the dynamic process-like logic of the historical emergence of the world as global. This aporia, I contend, is not the fallout from an intrinsic problem of concept formation. Rather it derives from the historical condition of transitional (in)adequacy that the global expresses in the context of the inability of the Western conceptual archive to attune itself to the need to decolonize social theory and expose its architecture to non-Western and post-Western histories and concepts. The predicament of the global is a privileged locus of terminological analysis for rethinking the possible post-Western grammar of global studies. Its ambiguity calls for an exploration of the limits of the sociological imagination that gird world historical analysis. Gayatri Chakravorty Spivak captured this discrepancy between the vocabulary of social sciences and the reconfiguration of the postcolonial world. She wrote that the global is inevitably associated with the idea of making the world a controllable spacetime. The global suggests the ability of the subject to figure the world she/he inhabits: a figure endowed with plastic, visual, and geohistorical determinants that provide the subject with the coordinates to encode a presumably intelligible nonsubjective and objective alterity. Against this she proposes that the planet is in the species of alterity, belonging to another system, and yet we inhabit it, on loan. It is not really amenable to a neat contrast with the globe. I cannot say "the planet, on the other hand." When I invoke the planet, I think of the effort required to figure the (im)possibility of this underived intuition (Spivak 2003, 72).

The planet is thus the epistemological transfiguration of the methodological figure of the global. It interrupts the continuity between the situated Western thinking-subject that presumes to be the unique model of rationality, historically the bearer of the sociological imagination, on the one hand, and the world as the reified spacetime wherein such a subject locates long-term and large-scale historical processes of social change, on the other. Planetary imagination exceeds the established colonial social fabric of spacetime and makes the coordinates that define the specific, colonial situatedness unfamiliar, uncomfortable, and uncertain. This destabilized condition renders the global a space contested by other, non-Western understandings of the world as a singular spacetime from alternative standpoints. The latter are diversely situated in the present hierarchy of the geopolitics of knowledge but are nevertheless endowed with their own alternative narratives, distinctive conceptualizations, and alien theoretical grammars. It follows that the global as a significant unit of analysis is irreducible to an emergent spatiotemporal envelope produced and reproduced by processes; nor is it the ultimate and overall geohistorical entity that generates processes. The "global" here stands as a negative limit: a horizon to theorization. As such, it traces the transient threshold from where the impossibility of unambiguous definitions imperceptibly slides into the possibility for transgressing and unthinking the Eurocentric boundaries of historical sociology. The global as methodological limit translates into the heuristics of the methodological attitude toward the global: that is, the endeavor to move beyond sociology's parochialism in disguise toward what remains outside the borders of the colonial conceptual archive of the West and resists conceptual and terminological homogenization. This implies enlarging and democratizing the foundations of global historical sociology.

But such an objective also necessitates a movement in the opposite direction, evoking a predisposition to make the conceptual grammar of sociology more permeable to multiple outside(s) and planetary other(s). Planet-thought opens up to embrace an inexhaustible taxonomy of such names, including but not identical with the whole range of human universals: aboriginal animism as well as the spectral white mythology of postrational science. If we imagine ourselves as planetary subjects rather than global agents, planetary creatures rather than global entities, alterity remains underived from us: it is not our dialectical negation; it contains us as much as it flings us away (Spivak 2003, 73).

Far from being definitive or necessarily "progressive," the predicament of the global mirrors the territory of uncertainty where the social sciences find themselves awoken from a nineteenth-century positivist dream turned into a nightmare of failed attempts to make the world fully transparent through the colonial gaze. It figures the specific condition of contemporary social theory, its transitionally adequate epistemological status of intelligibility, which is nevertheless able to expose current sociology to post-Eurocentric, decentered, unexpected, and uncanny interventions that the coloniality of method makes otherwise invisible, irrelevant, and exotic. Thus the unit of analysis migrates toward the disunity of planetary understandings. This is a route that links the impossibility of fully thinking the worlds of historical and social planetary connections and disconnections in terms of an exhaustive spacetime singularity, with the awareness that this disunity is the premise for new regimes of theoretical and empirical validation. The latter are grounded in geocultural pluralization as well as in the possibility for reciprocal interpellations and frictions between overlapping, but irreducible, histories, explanations, and conceptualizations.

NOTES

1. A previous version of this argument appears in Ascione G. 2016. "Science and the Decolonization of Social Theory," London: Palgrave.

2. On this point, see Bach (1982, 159–80) and Agnew (1993, 251–71).

3. See Galtung (1966), Etzioni (1965), Nettl and Robertson (1968), and Lagos (1963).

4. Among the vast literature of critique of the concept of development, see the fundamental Arrighi and Drangel (1988), Escobar (1995), Mitchell (2002), Rahnema and Bawtree (1997), and Sachs (1992).

5. On the so-called *Methodenstreit*, see Di Meglio (2004).

6. The year 1902, with the "conquest" of the South Pole, marked the beginning of the extinction of the terrestrial frontier to conquest from the colonizer's imagery (see Blaut 1993). Yet the Congress of Berlin and the political division of Africa among the imperial European states had de facto materialized this process already in 1885.

7. A nonverbal phrase that expresses meaning without a predicate.

8. This methodological stance has been rarely further developed, except by McMichael (2000).

9. For example, there exists a crucial difference between thinking in terms of world-system rather than assuming the world-system as a unit of analysis, or talking of center and periphery rather than analyzing processes through core-periphery as a singular, intrinsically relational spacetime. See Wallerstein (1991). Analogously, for the notion of core-periphery, see Wallerstein (1979).

10. Grosfoguel's elaboration on Anibal Quijano's concept of coloniality is exemplificative of this strategy. For Quijano (1991), coloniality originally expressed a complex matrix of power in the interstate system, across race and class. For Grosfoguel (2005, 85) the colonial matrix is "the entanglement of multiple and heterogeneous hierarchies of sexual, political, epistemic, economic spiritual and racial forms of domination and exploitation."

11. This aspect of the transformations of knowledge, with particular reference to the spread of postcolonial studies has been critically analyzed by Arif Dirlik. Dirlik (1998) explains the relevance of postcolonialism with the demise of the tripartite global order of the Cold War and the reconfiguration of what was the divide between the First, the Second, and the Third World into the split between the Global North and the Global South. On this point see also Arrighi (2001). More recently, Mignolo (2014) has argued for a radical reconsideration of the global cartographic imagery of modernity based on the reconfiguration of hemispherical view of the world.

12. See the different position expressed in the debate over global economic history by Pomeranz (2000), Rosenthal and Bin Wong (2011), and Parthasarathi (2011).

13. The problem of the situatedness of knowledge owes much of its genesis to the feminist critique of science. Evelyn Fox-Keller, as a prominent physicist, was among the first scientists to radically attack modern science from a gender perspective. Among her works, see Evelyn Fox-Keller (1985, 1992). Donna Haraway (1988, 1990, 1991a, 1991b) shares analogous premises, but her research has moved toward the theorization of hybridity. Her groundbreaking work on hybridity between male and female, animal and human, human and machine has been fundamental even outside academia.

BIBLIOGRAPHY

Agnew, John. 1993. "Representing Space: Space, Scale and Culture in Social Science." In *Place/Culture/Representation*, edited by James Duncan and David Ley, 251–71. London: Routledge.

Arrighi, Giovanni, and Beverly Silver. 1999. *Chaos and Governance in the Modern World System*. Minneapolis: University of Minnesota Press.

Arrighi, Giovanni. 2001. "Global Capitalism and the Persistence of the North-South Divide." *Science & Society* 65, no. 4: 469–76.

Asad, Talal. 1973. "Introduction." In *Anthropology and the colonial encounter*, edited by Talal Asad. Atlantic Highlands, NJ: Humanities Press, 1973.

Bach, Robert L. 1982. "On the Holism of a World-Systems Perspective." In *World-Systems Analysis: Theory and Methodology*, edited by Terence K. Hopkins and Immanuel Wallerstein, 159–80. Beverly Hills: SAGE.

Bala, Arun. 2006. *The Dialogue of Civilizations in the Birth of Modern Science*. New York: Palgrave Macmillan.

Balibar, Étienne. 2002. *Politics and the Other Scene*. London: Verso.

———. 2013. *Identity and Difference: John Locke and the Invention of Consciousness*. London: Verso.

Bennet, Tony, Lawrence Grossberg, and Meaghan Morris, eds. 2005. *New Keywords: A Revised Vocabulary of Culture and Society*. Oxford: Blackwell.

Bertalanffy, Ludwig von. 1950. "An Outline of General System Theory." *British Journal for the Philosophy of Science* 1, no. 2): 114–29.

———. 1951. "General System Theory: A New Approach to Unity of Science." *Human Biology* 23, no. 4: 303–61.

Bhambra, Gurminder K. 2007a. *Rethinking Modernity: Postcolonialism and the Sociological Imagination*. London: Palgrave Macmillan.

———. 2007b. "Sociology and Postcolonialism: Another 'Missing' Revolution?" *Sociology* 41, no. 5: 871–84.

———. 2014. *Connected Sociologies*. New York: Bloomsbury.

Bhambra, Gurminder K., and Ipek Demir, eds. 2009. *1968 in Retrospect: History, Theory, Alterity*. London: Palgrave Macmillan.

Billings, Linda. 2007. "Overview: Ideology, Advocacy, and Spaceflight—Evolution of a Cultural Narrative." In *Societal Impact of Spaceflight*, edited by Steven J. Dick and Roger D. Launius, 483–500. Washington, DC: NASA.

Blaut, James M. 1993. *The Colonizer's Model of the World: Geographical Diffusionism and Eurocentric History*. New York: Guilford Press.

Boy, J. D. 2015. "The Axial Age and the Problems of the Twentieth Century: Du Bois, Jaspers, and Universal History." *American Sociologist* 46, no. 2: 234–47.

Brenner, Neil. 1999. "Beyond State-Centrism? Space, Territoriality, and Geographical Scale in Globalization Studies." *Theory and Society* 28, no. 1: 39–78.

Burawoy, Michael. 2004. "Public Sociology: Contradictions, Dilemmas and Possibilities." *Social Forces* 82, no. 4: 1603–18.

———. 2005a. "The Return of the Repressed: Recovering the Public Face of US Sociology, One Hundred Years On." *Annals of the American Academy of Political and Social Science* 600, no. 1: 68–85.

———. 2005b. "For Public Sociology." *American Sociological Review* 70, no. 1: 4–28.

———. 2005c. "Facing an Unequal World: Challenges for a Global Sociology." In *Facing an Unequal World: Challenges for a Global Sociology*, edited by M. Burawoy, M. Chang, and M. Fey-yu Hsieh, 2005c. Taipei: Academia Sinica and International Sociological Association.

Castro-Gòmez Santiago. 2004. *La hybris del punto zero: Ciencia, raza e ilustraciòn en la Nueva Granada (1750–1816)*. Bogotá: Pontificia Universidad Javeriana/Instituto Pensar.

Chakrabarty, Dipesh. 2000. *Provincializing Europe: Postcolonial Thought and Historical Difference*. Princeton, NJ: Princeton University Press.

Chambers, Iain. 2015. *Location, Borders, and Beyond*. Naples: CreateSpace.

Chambers, Iain, and Lidia Curti, eds. 1996. *The Postcolonial Question: Common Skies, Divided Horizons*. New York: Routledge.

Chandler, David. 2009. "The Global Ideology: Rethinking the Politics of the 'Global Turn in IR." *International Relations* 23, no. 4: 530–47.

Connell, Raewyn. 1997. "Why Is Classical Theory Classical?" *American Journal of Sociology* 102, no. 6: 1511–57.

Coronil, Fernando. 2000. "Naturaleza del Poscolonialismo: del eurocentrismo al globocentrismo." In *La colonialidad del saber: eurocentrismo y ciencias sociales, Perspectivas latinoamericanas*, edited by Edgardo Lander, 87–111. Buenos Aires: CLACSO.

Cosgrove, Denis. 1994. "Contested Global Visions: One-World, Whole-Earth, and the Apollo Space Photographs." *Annals of the Association of the American Geographers* 84, no. 2: 270–94.

De Landa, Manuel. 2006. *A New Philosophy of Society: Assemblage Theory and Social Complexity*. New York: Bloomsbury.

Di Meglio, Mauro. 2004. "The Social Sciences and Alternative Disciplinary Models." In *Overcoming the Two Cultures: Science versus the Humanities in the Modern World-System*, edited by Immanuel Wallerstein and Richard E. Lee, 55–72. Boulder: Paradigm.

Dirlik, Arif. 1998. *The Postcolonial Aura: Third World Criticism in the Age of Global Capitalism*. Boulder: Westview Press.

Escobar, Arturo. 1995. *Encountering Development. The Making and Unmaking of the Third World.* Princeton, NJ: Princeton University Press.

Etzioni, Amitai. 1965. *Political Unification: A Comparative Study of Leaders and Forces*. New York: Holt, Rinehart and Winston.

Evans-Pritchard, Edward. 1951. *Social Anthropology*. London: Cohen and West.

Fox-Keller, Evelyn. 1985. *Reflections on Gender and Science*. New Haven, CT: Yale University Press.

———. 1992. *Secrets of Life/Secrets of Death: Essays on Language, Gender and Science*. New York: Routledge.

Galtung, Johan. 1996. "Rank and Social Integration: A Multidimensional Approach." In *Sociological Theories in Progress*, edited by. Joseph Berger, Morris Zelditch, and Bo Anderson. Boston: Houghton Mifflin.

Geppert, A. C. T. 2007. "Flights of Fancy: Outer Space and the European Imagination, 1923–1969." In *Societal Impact of Spaceflight*, edited by Steven J. Dick and Roger D. Launius, 585–600. Washington, DC: NASA.

Gilman, Nils. 2003. "From the European Past to the American Present." In *Mandarins of the Future: Modernization Theory in Cold War America*, edited by Nils Gilman, 24–71. Baltimore: Johns Hopkins University Press.

Go, Julian. 2014. "Occluding the Global: Analytic Bifurcation, Causal Scientism, and Alternatives in Historical Sociology." *Journal of Globalization Studies* 5, no. 1: 122–36.

Gregory, Derek. 1994. *Geographical Imaginations*. Cambridge, MA: Blackwell.

Grossberg, Lawrence. 1986. "On Postmodernism and Articulation an Interview with Stuart Hall. *Journal of Communication Inquiry* 10, no. 2: 45–60.

Habib, S. Irfan, and Dhruv Raina, eds. 1999. *Situating the History of Science: Dialogues with Joseph Needham*. New Delhi: Oxford University Press.

Haraway, Donna. 1988. "Situated Knowledges: The Science Question in Feminism and the Privilege of Partial Perspectives." *Feminist Studies* 14, no. 3: 575–99.

———. 1990. *Primate Visions: Gender, Race, and Nature in the World of Modern Science*. New York: Routledge.

———. 1991. *Simians, Cyborgs and Women: The Reinvention of Nature*. New York: Routledge.

Hart, Roger. 1999. "Beyond Science and Civilization: A Post-Needham Critique." *East Asian Science, Technology, and Medicine* 16: 88–114.

Harvey, David. 1982. *The Limits to Capital*. Oxford: Oxford University Press.

———. 1985. "The Geopolitics of Capitalism." *Social Relations and SpatialSstructure*, edited by Derek Gregory and John Urry, 128–63. London: Macmillan.

———. 2002. *Spaces of Capital: Towards a Critical Geography*. New York: Routledge.

———. 2010. *The Enigma of Capital and the Crises of Capitalism* Oxford: Oxford University Press.

Hobson, John M. 2004. *The Eastern Origins of Western Civilization*. Cambridge: Cambridge University Press.

———. 2012a. *The Eurocentric Conception of World Politics: Western International Theory, 1760–2010*. Cambridge: Cambridge University Press.

———. 2012b. "Global Dialogical History and the Challenge of Neo-Eurocentrism." *Asia, Europe and the Emergence of Modern Science*, edited by Arun Bala, 13–33. New York: Palgrave Macmillan.

Hopkins, Terence K., and Immanuel Wallerstein. *World-Systems Analysis: Theory and Methodology*. Beverly Hills: SAGE.

Inglis, David, and Roland Robertson. 2009. "Durkheim's Globality." In *Sociological Objects: Reconfigurations of Social Theory*, edited by Geoff Cooper, Andrew King, and Ruth Rettie. Farnham, UK: Ashgate.

Lagos, Gustavo. 1963. *International Stratification and Underdeveloped Countries*. Chapel Hill: University of North Carolina Press.

Magubane, Zine. 2005. "Overlapping Territories and Intertwined Histories: Historical Sociology's Global Imagination." In *Remaking Modernity: Politics, History, Sociology*, edited by Julia Adams, Elisabeth Clemens, and Ann Shola Orloff, 92–108. Durham, NC: Duke University Press.

Massey, Doreen. 1999. "Space-Time, 'Science' and the Relationship between Physical Geography and Human Geography." *Transactions of the Institute of British Geographers* 24, no. 3: 261–76.

———. 2005. *For Space*. London: SAGE.

Mbembe, J. Achille. 2003. "Necropolitics." *Public Culture* 15, no. 1: 11–40.

Merle, Marcel. 1987. *The Sociology of International Relations*. New York: Berg.

Mezzadra, Sandro, and Brett Neilson. 2013. *Border as Method, or, the Multiplication of Labor*. Durham, NC: Duke University Press.

Mignolo, Walter D. 2007a. "Delinking: The Rhetoric of Modernity, the Logic of Coloniality and the Grammar of De-coloniality." *Cultural Studies* 21, no. 2–3: 449–514.

———. 2007b. "Coloniality of Power and De-colonial Thinking. *Cultural Studies* 21, no. 2–3: 155–67.

———. 2014. "Decolonial Reflections on Hemispheric Partitions: The 'Western Hemisphere' in the Colonial Horizon of Modernity and the Irreversible Historical Shift to the 'Eastern Hemisphere.'" *Forum for Inter-American Research* 7, no. 3: 41–58.

Mitchell, Timothy. 2002. *Rule of Experts: Egypt, Techno-politics, Modernity*. Berkeley: University of California Press.

Moore, Wilbert. 1966. "Global Sociology: The World as a Singular System." *American Journal of Sociology* 71, no. 5: 475–82.

Nettl, John Peter, and Roland Robertson. 1968. *International Systems and the Modernization of Societies: The Formation of National Goals and Attitudes*. New York: Basic Books.

Palat, Ravi Arvind. 1996. "Fragmented Visions: Excavating the Future of Area Studies in a Post-American World." *Review (Fernand Braudel Center)* 19, no. 3: 269–315.

Parsons, Talcott. 1951. *The Social System*. New York: Free Press.

Parthasarathi, Prasannan. 2011. *Why Europe Grew Rich and Asia Did Not: Global Economic Divergence, 1600–1850*. Cambridge: Cambridge University Press.

Pomeranz, Kenneth. 2000. *The Great Divergence: China, Europe, and the Making of the Modern Economy*. Princeton, NJ: Princeton University Press.
Pratt, Mary Louise. 1992. *Imperial Eyes: Travel Writing and Transculturation*. London: Routledge.
Quijano, Aníbal. 1992. Quijano, A. (1992). Colonialidad y modernidad/racionali dad. *Perú Indígena*, *13*(29), 11–20.
Rahnema, Majid, and Victoria Bawtree, eds. 1997. *The Post-Development Reader*. London: Zed.
Raj, Kapil. 2013. "Beyond Postcolonialism . . . and Postpositivism: Circulation and the Global History of Science." *Isis* 104, no. 2: 337–47.
Rist, Gilbert. 2002. *The History of Development from Western Origins to Global Faith*. London: Zed.
Robertson, Roland. 1998. *Globalization: Social Theory and Global Culture*. London: SAGE.
———. 2001. "Globality." In *International Encyclopedia of Social and Behavioral Sciences*, edited by Neil J. Smelser and Paul B. Baltes, 6254–58. Oxford: Elsevier.
Rosenthal, Jean-Laurent, and Roy Bin Wong. 2011. *Before and Beyond Divergence: The Terms of Trade in Theory and Practice the Politics of Economic Change in China and Europe*. Cambridge: Cambridge University Press.
Rostow, Walt Whitman. 1950. "The Terms of Trade in Theory and Practice." *Economic History Review* 3, no. 1: 1–20.
———. 1951. "The Historical Analysis of the Terms of Trade." *Economic History Review* 4, no. 1: 53–76.
Sachs, Wolfgang, ed. 1992. *The Development Dictionary: A Guide to Knowledge as Power*. London: Zed.
Sassen, Saskia. 2011. *Territory, Authority, Rights: From Medieval to Global Assemblages*. Princeton, NJ: Princeton University Press.
Secord, James A. 2004. "Knowledge in Transit." *Isis* 95, no. 4: 654–72.
Seth, Sanjay. 2009. "Historical Sociology and Postcolonial Theory: Two Strategies for Challenging Eurocentrism." *International Political Sociology* 3, no. 3: 334–38.
Seth, Suman. 2009. "Putting Knowledge in Its Place: Science, Colonialism, and the Postcolonial." *Postcolonial Studies* 12, no. 4: 373–88.
Shahi, Deepeshikha, and Gennaro Ascione. 2016. "Rethinking the Absence of Post-Western International Relations Theory in India: 'Advaitic Monism' as an Alternative Epistemological Resource." *European Journal of International Relations* 22, no. 2: 313–34.
Spivak, G. C. 2003. *Death of a Discipline*. New York: Columbia University Press.
Steinmetz, George. 2005. "Introduction." In *The Politics of Method: Positivism and Its Epistemological Others*, edited by George Steinmetz, 1–56. Durham, NC: Duke University Press.
———. 2010. "Ideas in Exile: Refugees from Nazi Germany and the Failure to Transplant Historical Sociology into the United States." *International Journal of Politics, Culture, and Society* 23, no. 1: 1–27.
Tingyang, Zhao. 2005. *The Tianxia System: An Introduction to the Philosophy of a World Institution*. Nanjing: Jiangsu Jiaoyu Chubanshe.

Toye, John, and Richard Toye. 2004. *The UN and Global Political Economy: Trade, Finance, and Development*. Bloomington: Indiana University Press.

Wallerstein, Immanuel. 1976. *The Modern World-System I: Capitalist Agriculture and the Origins of the European World-Economy in the Sixteenth Century*. New York: Academic Press.

———. 1991. *Geopolitics and Geoculture: Essays on the Changing World-System (Studies in Modern Capitalism)*. New Haven, CT: Yale University Press.

———. 1996. *Open the Social Sciences: Report of the Gulbenkian Commission on the Restructuring of the Social Sciences*. Stanford, CA: Stanford University Press.

———. 1999. "States? Sovereignty? The Dilemmas of Capitalists in an Age of Transition." In *States and Sovereignty in Global Economy*, edited by David Alden Smith, David J. Sollinger, and Steven Topik, 20–34. New York: Routledge.

———. 2001. *Unthinking Social Science: The Limits of Nineteenth-Century Paradigms*. Philadelphia: Temple University Press.

Williams, Gregory P. 2013. "Special Contribution: Interview with Immanuel Wallerstein. Retrospective on the Origins of World-Systems Analysis." *Journal of World-Systems Research* 19, no. 2: 202–10.

Chapter 5

Conceptualization

The Operational Language of Theoretical Praxis

CROSS-CULTURAL DIALOGUE BETWEEN TRANSLATION AND TRANSLATABILITY

The tension between the global and the planetary designs the possibility of rethinking the world as a single yet multilayered spacetime of analysis (see chapter 4). Simultaneously, it raises the problem of *how* conceptualization should advance in order to cope with the asymmetrical power relations that materialize colonial history through heterarchies of class, gender, race, ethnicity, culture, knowledge, cosmology, and ecology, which shape long-term and large-scale processes of historical social change. New, silenced, or marginalized data and histories retrieved from the colonial archive put existing concepts in tension (see chapter 3). They serve the purpose of spatializing Western concepts toward the border of post-Western thinking.[1] They interpellate non-Western concepts that claim their own adequacy and potentially transform the parochial Eurocentric conceptual archive of global studies by reshaping its words, lemmas, and sintagmas according to what Inanna Hamati-Ataya (2022, xii) conceptualizes in terms of *parameters*: diversity, agency, and pluriversality.

When concepts draw from non-Western, Indigenous, or subaltern planetary knowledges, they inevitably bring to the fore the issue of translation. This aspect of concept formation needs a particular theoretical and practical care. The issue is not simply how to conceive the relation between concepts across different cultures, languages, and logics in order to render the vocabulary of social science more open and effective. Rather, it is about making the global an inclusive space without jeopardizing the possibility of its pluriversality by means of the essentialization of geohistorical clusters whose linguistic and ideational specificities would transmute into the same analytical rigidity that the cartography of area studies contributed to installing in the sociological imagination during the second half of the twentieth century under US world hegemony (Palat 1999).

Translation is not strictly a linguistic operation. It involves what the Southern Italian intellectual Antonio Gramsci theorized in terms of *translatability* during the eight years he spent in isolation inside the prisons of the Italian Fascist regime from 1926 to 1934. Gramsci distinguished translation (that is, the aspiration to produce semantic equivalence between two registers, idioms, or languages) from translatability (that is, the historical and social conditions providing the possibility for translation to take place; Gramsci [1939] 1975, 63). Gramsci suggested that even though cross-cultural translation may allow us to fully grasp the meaning of concepts and ideas from different geohistorical locations, either the levels of social stratification, or cultural contexts, or the changing historically determined conditions of translatability may render translation unable to reach its aim. In other words, even though the linguistic content can be accurately transferred, it does not mechanically fit with the historical, social, and cultural conditions of translatability (Rota 2020, 34). Gramsci conceived of translatability in space and time. He took issues with the relevance of mere translation, either for native speakers of the same language located in different epochs or for native speakers of different languages in the same era. He transmuted the linguistic problem of translation into the political possibility of translatability.

Gramsci's specific vantage point related to the aim of making the experience of the Soviet revolution readable in other potentially revolutionary contexts.[2] In these contexts, linguistic, cultural, social, and economic conditions profoundly differed from the original locations of enunciation of those same concepts, ideas, and theories he wanted to transfer both to refined intellectuals and to illiterate masses.[3] "This translatability" Gramsci (1975, 64) remarks "is certainly not 'perfect,' in all its details, even important ones (yet, what language is exactly translatable into another one? What single word is exactly translatable into another language?), but it actually is possible at its core." This permanent condition of discrepancy between translatability and untranslatability does not prevent Gramsci from displacing the problem of cross-cultural dialogue from the verbal level of semantic equivalence to the more relevant level of conceptual tools, mental structures, and social and historical contexts, which he considers the real dimensions where the conditions of possibility of ideational exchange locate. As Peter Thomas (2020, 13) has emphasized, Gramsci developed a nonessentialist theory of the reciprocal translatability of concepts, conceived not simply as knots in wider systems of signification but as conflicting or reinforcing forms of sociopolitical organization and action. For Gramsci, rather than translation being relevant to linguistic equivalence, translatability is the historical and social condition relevant to conceptualization. Translatability is the spacetime dimension where concept formation becomes operational *praxis*.

Conceptualization configures the concrete possibility of informing the way social change is conceivable according to new parameters such as different worldviews, nonhegemonic agencies, and pluriversal epistemologies, through linguistic operations whose words or lemmas work as conceptual sites of confrontation in the overlapping semantic fields of theory production. Therefore, cross-cultural dialogue assumes concept formation as a concrete theoretical *locus* of struggle, among other sites of negotiation and conflict where asymmetries of power materialize in *tropoi*. These *tropoi* are transient because their legitimacy is strictly derivative of the relative adequacy they enjoy in historically determined conditions of emergence and usage (Iveković 2010). Nonetheless, the cross-cultural translation of concepts remains mainly ignored as a specific task in most of the social sciences.

Contrary to this general inability of the social sciences to come to terms with the taken-for-granted protocols of concept formation, this issue has become immediately urgent in the field of the sociology of law and the international protection of human rights. Here, human rights as well as Indigenous rights continuously register definitional impasses that call for collective engagement into taxonomic operations, because concepts serve the need to codify processes, groups, and conditions through particular words that can become cornerstones for building jurisdictional architectures that concretely inform the life and histories of existing human beings. In the modern multicultural states of the postcolonial world shaped by war, displacement, eviction, and global migration, identity appears coded in religious, ethnic, or cultural terms; defined according to the position that the state from where the person arrives occupies in the shifting political scenario of the interstate system; or relegated to the socioeconomic logic of quota that institutions adopt according to the logic of the global market of the labor force. These approaches shape identity politics, citizenship, socioeconomic conditions, and cultural mediation. For this reason, from the angle of the decolonial intervention in the sociology of law, the possibility of cross-cultural dialogue in concept formation becomes methodologically relevant. Boaventura de Sousa Santos (2002, 48) explains that the process of exchange actively involves the formation of concepts across knowledges and cultures. And he draws from one available option that originates into the theology of liberation:[4]

> A diatopical hermeneutics is based on the idea that the *topoi* of an individual culture, no matter how strong they may be, are as incomplete as the culture itself. Such incompleteness is not visible from inside the culture itself, since aspiration to the totality induces taking *pars pro toto*. The objective of a

> diatopical hermeneutics is, therefore, not to achieve completeness—that being an unachievable goal—but, on the contrary, to raise consciousness of reciprocal incompleteness to its possible maximum engaging in the dialogue, as it were with one foot in one culture and the other in another, accounting for its diatopical character. A diatopical hermeneutics requires not only a different kind of knowledge, but also a different process of knowledge creation. It requires the production of a collective and participatory knowledge based on equal cognitive and emotional exchanges, *a knowledge-as-emancipation rather than knowledge-as-regulation.* (italics added)

This proposal expresses a shareable commitment and formulates it in an explicit manner. Nonetheless, the very last phrase raises disagreement from a methodological point of view: it is not necessarily true that knowledge-as-regulation is an alternative to knowledge-as-emancipation. Surely, it is true that the effort toward the elaboration of new concepts through cross-cultural dialogue requires participatory knowledge based on equality. Yet regulation is the space where methodology materializes. Regulation is precisely where the collective ability to create the conditions of conceptualization moves global studies toward equality, whereas equality is an objective to reach and not an illusory premise that hides the colonial Eurocentric history of the modern capitalist world. Making explicit the rules that regulate cross-cultural dialogue, translatability, and conceptualization aims at rendering these rules openly debatable rather than leaving concepts free to fluctuate across unequal cross-cultural *tropoi* whose power differentials mortify emancipatory theory and practice *a priori.*

Among these sites of conceptual struggle, one occupies a special place, since it functions as a basic epistemological category of translatability across different geohistorical and cultural locations: *relation.* Therefore, the issue of moving conceptualization from its Eurocentric sites of enunciation into the forming agenda of post-Western knowledge can be reformulated into the heuristic question: how to think, rethink, and unthink "relation"?

HERETIC/EROTIC ALLIANCES: FROM RELATIONS TO *VINCULI*

Aymara epistemology is a privileged locus of gnoseological effervescence in this regard. As Silvia Rivera Cusicanqui (2018) explains, there exist (at least) two Aymara "magic words" (*parabras magicas*) that enrich our planetary sociological imagination and operate toward the cocreation of an enlarged and more egalitarian conceptual archive for global studies: *ch'ixi* and *qhipnayra. Ch'ixi* is a concept that sheds light on the entire approach to Aymara epistemology in the context of the current debate over nonhegemonic forms of knowledge production. It is a term taken from geology and stonemasonry to describe the varying texture and color of rocks and minerals. This color is black and white at the same time: grey, which is white and not white at the same time; it is white and also black—that is, the product of juxtaposition—in small points or spots of opposed or contrasting colors. By analogic extension, *ch'ixi* includes natural combinations and recombinations of colors outside the mineral world, as well as beyond the original reference to black/white/grey. It adds two attributes to the planetary conceptual archive of global studies that are well positioned to mentally map alternative forms of critical human knowledge in terms of a *manchada* (spotted) and *abigarrada* (colorful) epistemological cartography. Conceptually, *ch'ixi* preserves the two opposites within the same figurative unity and it points to a semantic reference that exists outside the Western sociological imagination. It consists of an epistemological figure with which to elaborate an argument about the mixing of cultures, knowledges, logics, and worldviews that come together but retain their distinctive aspects. It expresses the parallel coexistence of multiplex differences that do not extinguish into each other.

In the theory of praxis, *ch'ixi* is a dialectic that does not culminate in a synthesis, analogously to what decolonial analectic reason does (as explained in chapter 2): it exists in permanent movement. Yet, beyond analectic reason, it entails a relational mode where the entities produced by the relation antagonize among themselves without dissolving the existing relation. *Ch'ixi* suggests two intertwined pathways. The first pathway aligns with those trends in global epistemics that consist in the possibility of moving outside the logical constraints of existing binaries such as white/black, north/south, Western/non-Western, male/female, human/animal. The second pathway consists in a form of relationality that does not necessitate either complementarity between the terms of the relation or the coincidence of the opposites: *ch'ixi* entails a relational mode wherein the entities produced by the relation antagonize among themselves and at the same time either cocreate themselves reciprocally or produce an unstable, ever-changing overall totality. These two paths are not straight perspectival lines, but rather configure unexpected geometries in motion that converge, intersect, and repeatedly diverge, enlarging the theoretical space of possibility for conceptual translatability that can span from hybridity to differentiation to irreconcilability in shifting combinations of these three alternatives: from the binary Aristotelian logic of the excluded middle, through the nondual logical possibility of the unexcluded middle, to the monist epistemology of what can be called the "included middle."

These three epistemological possibilities are not mutually exclusive. Rather, they materialize into a nonlinear chronotopical articulation that

Aymara language expresses through the second "magic word": *qhipnayra*. *Qhipnayra* literally means "past future." It rarely appears in isolation. It is more commonly spread within the ritual phrase *qhipnayr uñtasis sarnaqapxañani*, which is translatable as "looking to the future as to the past you need to walk in the present." Cusicanqui (2012, 96) analyzes this phrase with a hermeneutical approach:

> The contemporary experience commits us to the present—*aka pacha*—which in turn contains within it the seeds of the future that emerge from the depths of the past [*qhip nayr uñtasis sarnaqapxañani*]. The present is the setting for simultaneously modernizing and archaic impulses, of strategies to preserve the status quo and of others that signify revolt and renewal of the world: *Pachakuti*.

Qhipnayra places the past in the upcoming time of horizon. The past is what one can "see" in front of us while the future is obscure as something located behind our back; therefore, it enjoys a phantasmatic presence whose interrogation informs our perception of the present. The resonance with the Renaissance understanding of time is not merely formal; nor is it metaphorical—not only because their coalescence delegitimizes any narrative of progress and dethrones the epistemological ritual of modernity's temporality, around which the Western social sciences have built their unilateral approach to what knowledge is legitimate and what is not, but also because the recombination of past, present, and future into a shifting articulation of the single sintagma *future-past-present* discloses the vastness of the planetary conceptual archive to the possibilities of a new critical human knowledge.

Walter Mignolo and Catherine Walsh mobilize several nonhegemonic knowledges from the ancient Persian language to Andean Kechua in order to overcome the limits of the Western heuristics of relationality. Mignolo and Walsh (2018, 166) propose an all-encompassing understanding of relationality through the Persian noun *Runa*:

> *Runa* was and still is conceived in relation to and in *convivencia* (a literal translation would be "living-with-other-living-organisms," but the term is generally translated as "coexistence" or "conviviality") with huacas (deities, entities of the sacred sphere), sallqa (all living organisms), and the Apu (the tutelary spirit that inhabits the snowed peaks of the mountains). These organisms are all weaved together, for the metaphor of tejido (weaving) is commonly invoked to express conviviencia and *vincularidad* (translated as "relationality"). . . . Vincularidad is the awareness of the integral relation and interdependence amongst all living organisms (of which humans are only a part) with territory or land and the cosmos. It is a relation and interdependence in search of balance and harmony of life on the planet. As such, vincularidad/relationality unsettles the singular authoritativeness and universal character typically assumed and

portrayed in academic thought. Relationality/vincularidad seeks connections and correlations.

The slash here signifies a juxtaposition that does not form a new single concept out of the two words used but rather designs a space where the two used concepts overlap. At the same time, it leaves open two distinctive paths emanating from each of them. The slash symbolizes the colonial border that separates and connects different logics that are not mutually exclusive, yet never coincident or complementary.[5]

Nevertheless, the translation of *vincularidad* into "relationality" that Mignolo and Walsh propose is insufficient and superficial: it conceals under terminological juxtaposition what remains unheard in terms of translatability. A *vinculum* (from ancient Latin) is a tie, which is something more intense than a relation is. The semantic slippage from relationality to *vincularidad* creates an in-between space to be explored. The former suggests an aseptic, neutral condition of interdependence or connection, to be further qualified. Here "relationality and/or *vincularidad*" expresses a heuristic approach that is different from the way we have graphically expressed relation through the hyphen symbol (in chapter 4). Relationality refers to the Western conceptual archive. *Vincularidad* conjoins Indigenous knowledges and the constellation of marginalized Renaissance pantheistic, naturalistic, and animistic knowledges; they are all forms of knowledges that became subaltern throughout modernity: destroyed or relegated to primitive ecological phantasies. Conceptually, relation/*vinculum* invokes enhanced translation strategies across languages and logics that are able to enrich the conceptual lexicon available to the social sciences.

The lexicographic movement described herewith could appear as a circular one: from relationality to *vincularidad* to relationality. Yet relationality becomes epistemologically different: it is augmented by the exploration into the semantic field inhabited by the tensions translation enhances. It is not a circular movement, but rather a spiral. The transformation from the circle to the spiral happens if, and only if, the epistemological consequences transmute into the ability of thinking relations as inextricable from a single immaterial yet concrete force that translates relations into *vincula*: love.

In the context of methodological reasoning, the word *love* sounds inevitably pathetic. Instinctive awkwardness rises because of the sense of vacuum separating the rational endeavor of social thought from what Raymond Williams (1977) defined as the underlying structure of feelings of social thinking. In order to qualify *love* and subtract its inference from the common use to which modernity relegates it, Mignolo and Walsh (2018, 223) use the adjective *decolonial* as a strategy to bridge this gap in a consistent manner:

> Decolonial love implies it is enacted with dignified anger confronting the dismantling of the social fabric of civilizational tendencies that promote competition and war. Decolonial love moves in two simultaneous directions: one confronting and delinking from the meanings that the word love has in liberal and Christian discourses, both of them embedded in colonial matrix of power and the other, accepting that re-existence and building communalities of all kinds demands respect, listening, cooperation, and care. This is the direction that decolonial love is taking in rebuilding the principles and goals destroyed in the name of modernity and still being destroyed.

Decolonial love is the same inherent *vinculum* that was theorized by generations of scholars across the different cultures, languages, and societal formations since late antiquity in the premodern Mediterranean. It is the same concept that Giordano Bruno (2009) conceptualized in his fundamental and incomplete 1591 work *De vinculis in genere*. Here, Bruno defines *Eros* (love, in ancient Greek), as *vinculum vinculorum*: what connects all the connections, what relates all the relations, the tie of the ties. *Vincularidad* oscillates between composition and disconnection, between attraction and repulsion:

> All affections and bonds of the will are reduced to two, namely aversion and desire, or hatred and love. Yet hatred itself is reduced to love, whence it follows that the will's only bond is Eros. It has been proved that all other mental states are absolutely, fundamentally, and originally nothing other than love itself. For instance, envy is love of someone for oneself, tolerating neither superiority nor equality in the other person; the same thing applies to emulation. Indignation is love of virtue; modesty and fear *[verecundia, timor]* are none other than love of decency and of that which one fears. We can say the same of the other mental states. Hatred, therefore, is none other than love of the opposite kind, of the bad; likewise, anger is only a kind of love. As regards all those who are dedicated to philosophy or magic, it is fully apparent that *the highest bond, the most important and the most general [vinculum summum, praecipium et generalissimum]*, belongs to Eros: and that is why the Platonists called love the Great Demon, *daemon magnus* (Bruno, in Couliano 1987, 91).

For the Renaissance thinkers, Eros/love was not an ethical drive, yet the supreme principle of regulation of the relation between micro and macro cosmos in its multiple articulations. It consisted in the condition of possibility for both science and magic, where magic was understood as the operational possibility to intervene and transform ongoing processes scientifically understood, be they natural, historical, or social (Rossi 2006). This extended understanding of the connection between decolonial love and Renaissance magic through the transfiguration of the notion of relation into that of *vinculum* makes possible an unprecedented alliance between heretic and non-Western knowledges across colonial modernity toward the possibility of alternative, post-Western forms of human knowledge. Here, heresy should not be conceived as what dominant knowledge has taught us for centuries, that is, a doctrine that merely opposes the dominant one. Rather, it should be conceived as a political and theoretical strategy that consists in taking seriously the words spoken by power (Zito 1983): a constant process of dismantling, reconfiguring, transfiguring, and subverting the meaning of those words by fighting for the full recognition of such excluded, marginalized, silenced, yet existing, uncanny, living, embodied presences in order to claim the epistemological right to existence of the pluriversal historical connections and resonances.

THE TECHNIQUE OF SEMANTIC SPATIALIZATION: FROM CONCEPT TO INTENTION

The possibility of thinking relations in terms of *vinculi* has profound implications for concept formation. It immediately exposes the absence of neutrality that the coloniality of method is able to conceal, since every concept is driven by an inherent tension toward the social or historical reality it aims at representing, grasping, challenging, or silencing and distorting (see chapter 3). Yet a deeper epistemological investigation into such a tension is needed. The use of spatial metaphors to analyze the process of cross-cultural dialogue (as a tool to engage with the possibility of translatability in order to elaborate an open-ended protocol of concept formation) could remain a fuzzy, intuitively mental operation, or, alternatively, it can assume a more detailed shape and functional outline, as argued in what follows.

Mental operations consist in the ability to manipulate abstract notions, figures, or words, which operate within that complex and mysterious system called memory. Human mnemotechnics, from ancient civilizations to artificial intelligence and machine learning, adopts spatialization as an operational extension of the way memory naturally functions from living beings (both human and nonhuman) up to frontier computational techniques (Yates 1974; Maldonado 2005; Bermudez-Contreras, Clark, and Wilber 2020). The spatialization of concepts consists in locating meaning in semantic *loci* that are cocreated by the reciprocal interpellation of words into an imaginative set whose figurative or metaphysical characteristics can infinitely vary according to the imaginative power of the single individual, the cultural contexts of his or her concrete life, and many other variables. And even though such an infinite individual complexity cannot be transferred in its totality, it is still suitable for intersubjective communication and reciprocal interpretation. Chapter 3 has adopted this technique of spatialization in a scholastic manner in order to inform the design of a simple Cartesian diagram involving the four relevant approaches to concept formation currently used in the social sciences. Chapter 4 has connected the "global" as a unit of analysis to the "planetary" in order to explore the possibility of a conceptualization that extends within the space of dissonance between the former as a self-contained spacetime unity and the latter as a condition that ties historical and social subjectivities to the concrete processes of existence on this current cosmic spacetime location. The semantic dissonance between the global and the planetary is a double-bind to the semantic dissonance between relationality and *vincularidad*, that is, between relation and *vinculum*. In the imaginative space of concept formation, the sense of neutrality that "relation" conveys occupies a position that does not coincide with the position where *vinculum* is displaced by the distancing intervention that the connotation of love produces when the notions of attachment, responsibility, will, and intention further qualify relation and therefore transform its presumed neutrality. Such a space is a topological space, that is, it is meaningful regardless of any quantifiable distance: its value is heuristic rather than metric or essentialist. More precisely, the relation that a concept entails with the object of understanding, qualified by means of what it explicitly aims at engaging with or disengaging from, is a *vinculum*. A *vinculum* consists in a relation that a subject (collective or individual) intentionally establishes with an object of knowledge and the recursive tie that the object holds upon the subject of knowledge. Therefore, as far as the *vinculum* is concerned, subject and object are not fixed entities, nor one entirely resolved into the other. Now the scene is set to apply the strategy of spatialization, with a greater awareness, to the notion of *concept* itself. This operation is an exemplificative way to formalize the practice of cross-cultural translatability. Afterward, this strategy will be operationalized and applied to the concept of *capital*.

"CONCEPT" AND THE EIGHT STYLES OF CONCEPT FORMATION

The etymology of the word "concept" dates back to the fourteenth-century Latin word *conceptus*, which is the past participle of the verb *concipĕre*: "to conceive," in English, meaning both conceiving something immaterial like an idea and something material like a child. From antiquity until the fourteenth century, the Latin word currently in use to express the same notion was *intentio*, that is, "intention." The entire gnoseology from late antiquity to late medieval Scholasticism and beyond did not use "concept" but "intention." *Intentio* indicates both the act by which the subject tends toward the object of knowledge and the image or form of the object known inside the imagination of the knowing subject ("intentional species," in the terminology of late Scholasticism). In other words, it means simultaneously either the intellectual act tending to comprehend the object or the act of will tending to order action toward an aim. Such a meaning emerges from the translations of Aristotle's *Logic* from Arabic into Latin. In these medieval translations, "intention" corresponds to at least two Arabic terms: *ma'qūl*, which literally means "intelligible," and *ma'nā*, "meaning." The progressive semantic specialization of this term produced a differentiation from the Latin word *intentio*, which came to indicate the quantitative dimension of intensity. In the context of the Latin translation of Aristotle, particularly through Avicenna/Alī ibn Sīnā al-Balkhī al-Bukhārī's translations, intention enjoys a usage crucial for the problem of concept-formation.

Avicenna/Alī ibn Sīnā al-Balkhī al-Bukhārī uses *ma'nā* in two distinctive ways (Perler 2001). In his translation of Aristotle's *De Anima*, which started to circulate among Christian erudites after 1100 CE, "intention" indicates the nonsensible content of a sensible perception: for instance, the aggressiveness that the lamb perceives when it sees a wolf, a content that the lamb gets even though it is not specifically conveyed by a single sensorial perception, but rather conceived in its overall significance by the lamb's estimative faculty. Eduardo Kohn (2013, 8) refers to the same mechanism when he elaborates upon the possibility of transgressing the boundaries between human and nonhuman knowledge. The lamb perceives not only the wolf as the single instantiation of the icon of the wolf in general through its five senses plus its internal imaginative sense, but also by means of the perception of what is the *meaning* of it, that is, the fact that the wolf is a danger potentially threatening its life. This overall perception is thus an *index* to which an action or a set of actions correspond, such as, for instance, to run away, hide, or scream:

> These other modalities (in broad terms) are either "iconic" (involving signs that share likenesses with the things they represent) or "indexical" (involving signs that are in some way affected by or otherwise correlated with those things they represent). In addition to being symbolic creatures we humans share these other semiotic modalities with the rest of nonhuman biological life.

In the Latin translations of Avicenna/Alī ibn Sīnā al-Balkhī al-Bukhārī's translations and commentaries of Aristotle's *Logica* and *Metafisica*, *intentio* refers to either the universal intelligible form of a notion separated by its content perceivable through the senses and thinkable independently from them (*ma'qūl*) or the conceptual content of a notion that, since it would correspond to the ultimate essence of that thing, should be thought in absolute terms, beyond any quantitative determination, and therefore neither universal nor particular. The same position was held by Al-Farabi, who in his commentary on *De interpretatione* uses *ma'qūl* to translate the word *nòema* in Aristotle and maintains that logicians study concepts (*ma'qūl*) either with reference to external objects or with reference to the names given to those objects (Cova 2004).

Intentio acquired further meanings after the same works of Aristotle were translated and commented on by Averroes/Aḥmad ibn Rušd. His works began to circulate among the Latin-speaking intellectuals at the court of Frederick II in Sicily in the second half of the twelfth century. For him, the *intentio* is the content of knowledge whose formation is a by-product of all the different knowledge abilities: namely, the senses, imagination, fantasy, and intellect. This understanding is widely spread in Latin medieval Scholasticism. Aquinas engaged with Averroes/Aḥmad ibn Rušd's notion of *intentio* in the second half of the thirteenth century, in the doctrinal turmoil and ideological racialization I have analyzed in chapter 1. Aquinas refers to *intentio* as the end of the process of knowledge formation. This means that *intentio* is that through which knowledge occurs (*id quo intelligitur*) and not what is actually known (*id quod intelligitur*), that is, the object of knowledge. The known object is not located within the intellect as such, but only *intentionally*. The relevance of intention in the process of knowledge has further epistemological implications. Knowledge, in this sense, consists in the process through which humans make their understanding adequate to what is to be known: adequacy between intellect and thing (*adaequatio intellectus et rei*). Aquinas attributed this formula in Latin to the ninth-century Egyptian philosopher Isaac Israeli, but it actually derives from the Latin version of Avicenna/Alī ibn Sīnā al-Balkhī al-Bukhārī's translation of Aristotle's *Metaphysics*. Yet, in the original Arabic text, instead of *'aql* as "intellectus," there is *'aqd*, that is, "tie, link, nexus, vinculum." This makes explicit the intimate and necessary connection between knowledge and being, between epistemology and ontology: being is an act of knowledge and knowledge is an intentional relation to being. Modern philosophy cut off this tie since Descartes's *ego cogito*, thereby losing this relationality, or better, this *vincularidad*.

In the nineteenth and twentieth centuries, the European antipositivist tradition from Franz Brentano and Edmund Husserl to Martin Heidegger and Alfred Schutz followed an analogous path into the contribution of the Arabic tradition of epistemology in late medieval Latin Scholasticism, yet their research program was based on different premises and moved by different intentions, and it landed on different shores. Phenomenology was concerned with individual consciousness and was confronted with the challenge launched to sociology by the newly born social science of psychology (Wallerstein 1999). This means that phenomenology assumed the consciousness of the individual actor as the ultimate unit of analysis of social change and the way the individual makes sense of the world as the horizon of its *problematique* (Outhwaite 1983). It is not redundant to reaffirm that this "individual" with his life-world was the Western, white, male, Christian, middle-class subject uncritically projected to universally represent humanity as such. Rather than focusing on a subject acting and endowing its action with sense, Arabic Scholasticism, particularly after Averroes/Aḥmad ibn Rušd, was in fact concerned with *intentio* on a more-than-subjective, or collective, or epistemological dimension of knowledge production. Along such a narrow street, full of obstacles, censorship, marginalization, and oblivion, Giordano Bruno set his ultimate departure from the inner rigidities of Scholasticism epistemology. He assumed the transitional adequacy of whatever configuration in the hierarchy between forms, sources, and ways of knowledge and confronted directly the problem of intentionally forming concepts rather than the definition of what a concept is or should be.

In his most systematic and complex work on epistemology, the *Lampas Triginta Statuarum* (*The Lamp of the Thirty Statues*) written in 1591 and unknown until 1890, Bruno (2009, 939) keeps using exclusively *intentio*, even though the Latin word *conceptus* had already been in use for two centuries.

Haec quidem constat triginta statuis, in quibus triginta *intentiones* continentur, eo quo videbur modo explicandae: sunt quidem generals—ut esse debent—specialissimis autem specibus magis applicabiles.	Here presented are thirty statues, which hold thirty *concepts* that will have to be explained in the way that will appear more effective. These are—as it should be—general concepts, which can refer to the very special species more effectively than the categories that Archita, Aristotle, and Lullo had elaborated.

In the *Lampas*, intentions are associated to statues with manifold attributes, according to a sophisticated effort in making mnemotechnics available to nonspecialized readers, connecting the fundamental entities of the universe, such as Chaos, Light, and Shadow, to the constant production of living matter, up to the foundation of political and social life on earth. This entire living organism, with its infinite transformations, becomes accessible to human knowledge through the pluriversal generative power of intentions to operate in order to inform reality according to the recombination of different forces. As for Gramsci, Bruno's concepts are not merely ways of representation, but rather tools of operational praxis.

The etymology of "intention" is immediately understandable. This word is formed by the prefix *-in* and the word "tension." To put something in tension means to deform it, stressing its material disposition. More specifically, in-tension alludes to a sort of attachment that forces toward the self, that is, toward the subject producing the tension. Etymologically, intention is the underlying and deeper act of creating a tie, a *vinculum*. This figure of spatialization adds a further dimension that transforms the two-dimensional plan of semantic dissonances into a three-dimensional and further multidimensional plan, up to a *n*-dimensional space of thinking. Looking more closely into the etymology of the Latin substantive "concept," there emerges that the verb from which it derives discloses a deeper underlying universe of meaning. The Latin *concipĕre* means "to take together, to accept within." It is a by-product of the transliteration from *cumcapĕre*, which is composed by the prefix *cŭm*, "with," and the verb *capĕre*, "to take." To take, as a form of intention, is strictly tied with another word in Latin: *concupĕre*. *Concupĕre* is composed by *cŭm*, "with," and the verb *cupĕre*, "to desire"—the same root of the name Cupid, the Latin equivalent of the Greek Eros, that is, love. This example of the strategy applied to "concept" results in no lexicographic change. It is possible to keep using the word "concept" as in the first page of this book. Yet lexicologically, the same word conveys a greater awareness of the meanings that conceptualization activates and the extent to which concept formation involves the intention of intervening in the linguistic operations that shape knowledge production.

Bruno (2009, 933–34) proposes eight styles of concept formation, which I describe and interpret in what follows, preserving the awkwardness of their anachronistic lexicon in order to provoke the sociological imagination to transgress the disciplinary and epistemological barriers wherein hegemonic western modern thought contains it.

1. The first style operates through the disarticulation and decomposition of a whole into its elementary parts. It is specific to grammatology and its ability to distinguish among different genres of words and graphic signs. This style is particularly adequate for rhetorical and argumentative purposes, focusing upon the basic elements of discursive practices.
2. The second style proceeds by imposing a predetermined form upon a given object of knowledge. This means that the object becomes modeled as a figure: compressing or shaping a substance that could be modeled otherwise according to a different predetermined form, and therefore differently (in)formed. This style is associated with the analogical extension of consuetudinary taxonomies over new objects of knowledge.
3. The third style proceeds by juxtaposing and aggregating different parts around a single pivotal center according to the needs deriving from this center, which can be both material or spiritual. This style emulates the ability of thought that operates by attracting and recombining different parts around itself as a center and dissolves parts into unity.

4. The fourth style consists in combining multiplex parts and nonhomogeneous elements, as it happens in architecture or in mnemotechnics.
5. The fifth style works by thought subtraction of different parts from an amorphous whole. This mode is analogous to the elimination of a certain quantity of matter in a stone in order to stem a figure out of it.
6. The sixth style proceeds through different possible techniques of mixture. This is different from composition, because in this case the different parts merge into each other to form something new. This style is comparable to alchemy and medicine.
7. The seventh style operates by means of certain strategies that force the knowing subject (consciously or not) to form concepts according to another subject who actually controls the process of concept formation, so that whoever thinks of themselves as the main actor of the process does not realize that he or she is actually a means moved by somebody else.
8. The eighth, eventually, operates through contraposition. It makes visible relevant aspects of what is to be known by counterposing it to a substratum that is able to reflect its properties: in this way, it becomes possible to evoke infinite figures by projecting their reflexes into a unique mirror, and by orienting this mirror into different regions of the space of knowledge, concepts can be formed and transformed.

CAPITAL THROUGH THE MIRROR: THINGIFICATION, UNCOMMON, AND *MURI* [6]

A further step implies, as previously mentioned, the passage from this formal level to a more substantial one. The possibility of unthinking the concept of capital is explored here. The concept of capital in the canon of sociology remains Marxian in its fundamental aspects. Yet the canonization of the concept neglects its colonial formation from an epistemological rather than a historical point of view. A closer look at this formation exposes some of the limits inherent in the Eurocentric formation of Marx's concept of capital and brings into consideration some radical counter-hegemonic insights about slavery and indigeneity. The tensions that slavery and indigeneity produce within the concept of capital can be further coded through the Japanese concept of *muri*, at the borders of translatability.

Marx affirmed that capital is not a thing; capital is a social relation. As such, it points to a twofold constitutive outside: labor as not-capital and nature as not-capital. For this reason, slavery and indigeneity are necessary to decenter and reformulate the two entangled contradictions of capital: capital/labor and capital/nature. Bringing slavery back into the process of the formation of the concept of capital as a social relation creates a tension between the commodification of labor and the "thingification" of personhood. Bringing indigeneity back into the process of the formation of the concept of capital as a social relation creates a tension between the destruction of the common and the emergence of the *uncommon*.

Radical Black studies have shown that Marx did not expel slavery from the first contradiction of capital. Rather, he transmuted the slave into the recessive underside of the proletarian. The epistemological disavowal of slavery represents the foundational act of forceful silencing that enables the appearance of the Western white male wage worker on the stage of modern history and endows this historical figure with the role of outpost of the struggle of humanity for its emancipation from the chains of the capitalist mode of production. But the chains that Marx elevated to a metaphorical simulacrum of the captivity of the wage workers are in fact forged in the theoretical smithery of what Robbie Shilliam names the "slave analogy." Shilliam (2015a) shows that the condition of slavery provided Marx and Engels with an ineludible analytical trope since the time of their early concern with "scientifically" unfolding the hidden logic of capital.[7] The *Manifesto* could not have denounced exploitation suffered by European proletarians without Marx and Engels's continuous reference to the condition of slavery in antiquity and, *a fortiori*, without the enslaved Africans and the role their descendants played in the history of the Americas.

Whereas Marx saw the commodification of labor in industrial society as a privileged analytical locus, Aimé Césaire focused his own understanding of modern capitalism on slavery and its long-term social consequences:

> The core phenomenon to be addressed is not so much the alienation of the worker from the fruits of his/her labour power but rather, as Aimé Césaire puts it, the "thingification" (*chosification* in French) of personhood through enslavement and its lasting racial legacies. In other words, while the industrial factory system alienates labour power (and its results) from the labourer via the technology of waged work, plantation slavery alienates the entire body and labour power of the person via the technology of racialization. (Shilliam 2015a, 197)

Thinking from, with, and through the colonial Caribbean, Césaire first opposed thingification to commodification, in his 1955 *Discourse on Colonialism* (Césaire 2007). Achille Mbembe (2015) argues for the global relevance of thingification in the contemporary postcolonial world too: thingification is the logical premise and the primal force of global colonial capitalism as a whole. Reconfiguring the "first" contradiction through the conceptual and terminological lens of thingification calls for decentering exploitation and violence from the strict connection between performed work and remuneration to incorporate them into the multilayered, entangled dimensions that are essential to govern the relation between existence and the modes of social production, reproduction, and exchange on a worldly level. Once the colonial essence of modernity is exposed, the first contradiction becomes a broader and deeper instance of capital in the global world. It embodies complex and shifting combinations of racial technologies of discrimination and control within an articulated matrix of forms of social coercion, violence, and humiliation. The first contradiction refers to the drive of thingification (rather than merely commodification) toward the annihilation and mortification of the human (rather than only the accumulation of capital), and the resistance that humans (rather than mainly workers) oppose to dehumanization occurring within the concrete transient social *tropoi* where the biopolitics of thingification materialize. Thingification concerns fundamental theoretical dimensions of the detrimental effects of colonial capitalism upon human life that Marx's theory of labor value had underplayed.

Thingification bridges the first and second contradictions. As Arturo Escobar (2008, 93) explains, in fact, the second contradiction brings to the fore the conditions of production, insufficiently theorized by Marx but placed at the center of the inquiry by Karl Polanyi. A condition of production is defined as those factors that are not produced as commodities, that is, according to the law of value, even if they are treated as such; this includes those aspects that Polanyi called "fictitious commodities," such as land (nature), labor (human life), space, and many general and communal conditions of production.

Capital is inhabited by the idiosyncratic coexistence of two seemingly contradictory assertions: "labour is the father of wealth while land is its mother" and "the physical properties of commodities have nothing to do with their physical nature" (Marx, cited in Coronil 2000, 91). It follows that the materiality of commodities is inseparable from their capacity to produce and represent wealth: being the basic unit of wealth in capitalism, commodity form embodies both its natural form and its value form. This would suffice to recognize that the social groups involved in the production of wealth cannot be circumscribed to those involved in the dialectics of capital-labor (Coronil 2000).

These social groups are conceived mainly as an ethnic—or, alternatively, premodern or nonmodern—articulation of the peasantry. Indigeneity, which refers synthetically to vastly heterogeneous peoples, histories, and struggles, would thus manifest limitedly in the tactic resistance Indigenous communities oppose to environmental devastation. In Marxian terms, indigeneity would connote the effort to preserve alternative use-values of which Indigenous social organizations are bearers, as if the resistances against the dispossession of the commons embodied by indigeneity would be entirely determined by the power of capital as such to constantly produce social differences.

Conversely, taking seriously the potential of the irruption of indigenous subjecthood in the second contradiction turns out to be a broader theoretical issue. It prefigures a detour from what exceeds the dialectics of capital/nature to the borders of the logic of capital. For the way Indigenous communities tell their own histories about the destruction of nature, as well as the way they map the devastation of the territories they inhabit or even the detrimental effects of colonialism and capitalism over nonhuman beings that cohabit those same territories, is at odds with existing categories of sociological thinking. In this regard, Marisol De La Cadena (2015b, 3) recalls that colonization consisted not only in ecological devastation, but also in the annihilation of other worldviews about nature that did not conform with that of the colonizers: "A war waged against world-making practices that ignore the separation of entities into nature and culture—and the resistance to that war." De La Cadena (2015b, 3) maintains that the Indigenous resistance to annihilation is never extinguished, as its persistence over centuries proves that it exceeds destruction. Indigeneity, for her, refers to "more-than-human assemblages, both in the usual sense (i.e., that they may include humans and nonhumans), and in the sense that these categories (human and nonhuman, and therefore species) are also inadequate to grasp such compositions, which as said above, may not become through these categories." In order to clarify the relevance of this point for contemporary social theory, De La Cadena's argument is a counterpunctual intervention that exposes some limits of sociological thinking.

In their pathbreaking sociological conceptualization of commensuration, Wendy Nelson Espeland and Mitchell L. Stevens (1998) convincingly describe the act of commensuration as an enduring form of social power in the modern world as well as the fundamental grammar of capital. For Marx, they remark, capital manifests in the first instance as a drive toward making what exists as concrete social differences (qualities) commensurable through value, money, and abstract labor (quantities). For this reason, they describe radical social resistances in terms of incommensurability: "defining something as incommensurate is a special form of valuing. Incommensurables preclude trade-offs. An incommensurable category encompasses things that are defined as socially unique in a specific way. They are not to be expressed in terms of some other category of value" (Espeland and Stevens 1998, 326). For them, the environmental struggles of the Native American Yavapai people settled in Arizona is exemplificative of this social form of resistance. When the Yavapai's ancestral land was threatened by the project of a dam, the Yavapai people opposed the project and declared their land incommensurable against state and corporate logic:

> The rational decision models used by bureaucrats to evaluate the proposed dam required that the various components of the decision be made commensurate, including the cost and consequences associated with the forced resettlement of the Yavapai community. This way of representing Yavapai interests and expressing the value of their land was a contradiction of those values and of Yavapai identity. (Espeland and Stevens 1998, 327)

De La Cadena, similarly, takes as an example the environmental conflict in the northern Andean region of Peru. Here the project of a dam raises the resistance of the Indigenous community inhabiting the lagoon, which would dry because of the dam. De La Cadena (2015b, 6) maintains that "refusing to sell may also refuse the transformation of the entities into units of nature or the environment, for they are part of each other." Differently from Espeland and Stevens, she emphasizes that Indigenous people are not simply affirming that their land is incommensurable. Theirs is not a tactical response in the dialectics with capital, grounded in a traditional set of beliefs that does not allow for quantifying nature. Instead, Indigenous resistance is making visible a deeper epistemological awareness: the relation between capital and colonialism (and their agents), on the one hand, and indigeneity (and they as agents) on the other hand, irreversibly creates a new social reality that is entirely intelligible as neither commensurability that precedes the dispossession of a common nor the defense of nature as a sentient being; it exceeds both. This is evident when De La Cadena (2015b, 6) registers the voice of an iconic Indigenous peasant woman that is one among the so-called guardians of the lagoon: "The woman's refusal would thus enact locally an ecologized nature of interdependent entities that simultaneously coincides, differs, and even exceeds—also because it includes humans—the object that the state, the mining corporation, and environmentalists seek to translate into resources, whether for exploitation or to be defended."

The resistance to environmental devastation from the perspective of indigeneity is not limited to an opposition about the uses of nature. It is not entirely intelligible as the struggle to defend the commons against capital, importantly because it exceeds the grammar of capital. It shows that the power that capital holds to reduce social realities to its own logic depends also on the extent to which the relational nature of capital itself is concealed: being a social relation involving Indigenous resistance, the capital/nature contradiction is deformed by indigeneity as far as the relation involving Indigenous territory is concerned.

Moreover, what exceeds the grammar of capital is not a dialectical synthesis that simply posits a new social reality that can be made once again transparent to social theory by means of the categories of value, common, or commodification; it is rather a negative limit to knowledge: not a shared understanding, but the sharable awareness of a limit to understanding. De La Cadena (2015a, 63) designates the epistemological territory created by what resists destruction while simultaneously exceeding it, as the uncommon:

> Differences that appeared through what we shared were intriguingly obvious, for they were part of our similarities as well. But there was also a lot that made us uncommon to each other and that could not be explained through the analytics of race, ethnicity, and class; these were markers that the Turpos and I could talk about, sometimes in agreement and other times in disagreement. Instead, what made us mutually uncommon also exceeded our comprehension of each other; the difference thus presented was also radical to both of us.[8]

The uncommon that emerges from the tension between indigeneity and the second contradiction invites us to relocate conflicting understandings of nature into a more precarious, transient understanding of difference, an understanding that invokes less the ontological presence of alternative sets of assumptions about the world and more the relational contingent co-formation of knowledges about and within the world: "What emerges through it is not a 'mix' of nature and human. Being composed as humans with nature—if we maintain these categories of being—makes each more. *Entities emerge as materially specific to (and with!) the relation that inherently connects them*" (De La Cadena 2015b, 8, emphasis added). Indigeneity interrupts the dialectics between capital and nature, to set the uncommon as a limit to what can be made fully transparent to Western rationality through its own conceptual archive. As much as indigeneity places its epistemological constituency into the second contradiction, slavery places its epistemological constituency into the first contradiction.

Their interplay calls for disclosing Marx's trinity formula capital-labor-land to the relation it entails with what is "not-capital." The Japanese thinker Uno Kōzō, in the aftermath of World War II, analyzed the agrarian question in Japan. The outcomes of this analysis offer a methodological route along the path of the formation of the concept of capital in a post-Western approach. Uno questioned the assumption of the contradictory nature of the relation between capitalist social relations and preexisting noncapitalist social relations. Noncapitalist social relations were not always an impediment for capitalist development; in Marxian terms, they were not necessarily the notorious limits (not capital) that capital itself creates, which appear as barriers to overcome. Rather, what is considered not-capital can be analytically disarticulated into what opposes resistance to capital and what, instead, actively facilitates it:

> The rural village structure which had formed the social basis of the ancien régime was thus seemingly dismantled through violence, yet at the same time, this was also in fact an expression of the planned balancing and harmonization of capitalist production . . . the pastures, expanded to accommodate the goal of wool exports, offered raw materials to the domestic wool industry, and the peasantry, expelled from the land in precisely the same process, became the laboring proletariat, the force which spurred on the capitalist industrialization of the wool and other medieval industries, which were at that point still being managed and administered on the level of simple handicrafts. Thus the emerging proletariat was itself used as a powerful force of pressure in order to forcibly subordinate the existing artisans to capital. (Uno, in Walker 2012, 18)

Just as Quijano provoked a conceptual shift from the "colonial system" to "coloniality," Uno prefigured the possibility of not thinking in terms of the "feudal system" but rather in terms of "feudality" (*hôkensei*). Uno explains that

> the apparent existence of feudal relations in the countryside was not an indication that the actual full-blown feudal system remained on a partial basis, or that these relations were merely atrophied "remnants" but rather it indicated something much more complex: feudal relations or feudal "sentiments" were "maintained precisely as a sacrifice that enabled Japanese capitalism to develop without resolving the problems it itself posited." (quoted in Walker 2012, 29)

Noncapitalist relations provide the enabling conditions of possibility for the logic of capital to objectify itself: capital and noncapital reciprocally connect in a complex, multilayered relationship of mutual necessity but reciprocal noncoincidence, yet this process remains always incomplete. The transformative violence of capitalism pertains coextensively and originally to a violence that belongs also to the noncapitalist social relations themselves. It follows that the interactions, conflicts, and negotiations between existing social relations and capital are not adequately conceived in terms of alien, mutually exclusive, or ontologically irreconcilable historical formations. But then the analytical trope of the transition from the feudal to the capitalist mode of production (as we know it) morphs from a theoretical *problematique* into a problematic barrier for sociologically conceptualizing the relation between capitalist and noncapitalist social relations beyond a teleological mindset. Why? Marx was unequivocal about the fact that

> it would be impractical and wrong to arrange the economic categories in the order in which they "were the determining factors in the course of history. Their order of sequence is rather determined by the relation which they bear to each other in modern bourgeois society, and which is the exact opposite of what

> seems to be their natural order or the order of their historical development." (quoted in Sweezy 1970, 16)

Nonetheless, whereas Marx thought that once the transition to the capitalist mode of production has occurred, capitalist social relations irreversibly replace preexisting social relations forever, Uno thought otherwise: capital and noncapital are inherently relational, coconstitutive, coextensive and simultaneous.[9] Just as De La Cadena does, Uno places a strong theoretical emphasis on the generative nature of relations. Walker (2012, 30) explains Uno's understanding:

> The "leap" or "inversion" is precisely what creates the two sides. By inverting, reversing, leaping, or "passing through," a planar surface or single topological field in extension is retroactively split into two, made to appear double, so that there becomes "this side" and "that side," so that the historical process appears to be grounded on a set of uneven substances that pre-exist the moment when they are revealed. But prior to the moment of traversal, when a boundary or limit emerges that must be "passed through," the boundary or limit would merely be located as one moment of a single planar horizon, not something that marks the gap between two sides.

But even if one accepts that, in history, capitalist and noncapitalist relations reciprocally interpellate so that it becomes adequate to sociologically conceptualize them by giving priority to relations over formed entities, a problem remains: how to simultaneously conceive capital as a social relation that cannot historically preexist the connection it entails with what is external to it, on the one hand, and the logic of capital that, being capital's own inner integral rationality, has to necessarily preexist its own historical appearance, on the other hand. Uno answers this heuristic question by affirming that "[t]he starting-point of the systematic logic of political economy must always 'presuppose' (*voraussetzen*) something purely irrational as the ground of the rationality of the historical process, which will then be 'retrojected' back onto the moment of origin in order to once again 'presuppose' it as rational . . . the schema of capital must necessarily pre-exist its historical appearance" (quoted in Walker, 2012: 29).

Uno conceptualizes this impossibility as nihil of reason, a negative limit overlapping with the epistemological territory of the uncommon. But Uno entrusts the semantic designation of this uncommon to the Japanese word *muri*. *Muri* means impossibility but also inefficiency and waste, thereby evoking both a limit to the theorization of capital and its underside of irrecoverable loss. As Walker (2012, 17) notes, Uno "makes a kind of wager on the possibility of a certain excessive formalism as the only means available to us to 'express' the abstraction of the circuit process of capital." Uno's critique of Marx's logic of capital takes place at the abstract level of the schema of realization. Here the concept of *muri* deforms the crucial Marxian notion of unproductive consumption.[10] For Marx, unproductive consumption is consumption that is not oriented toward investment for profit by capitalists: in a broader sense, consumption that does not culminate in the reproduction of the means of production. While logically the self-valorization of capital presupposes the abstraction of a society made of only two antagonist classes, with the owners of the means of production orienting their consumption to investment and the workers consuming for their subsistence, historically—Marx concedes—the process of accumulation cannot exist if the schema of realization does not include the economic inefficiency and waste represented conceptually by unproductive consumption. Marx justified this circumstance by introducing an ad hoc hypothesis: a temporary status of exception.[11] But both historically and logically, this ad hoc hypothesis has proven a condition that is ineliminable and original rather than conjunctural and ancillary. Thus, the Marxian category of unproductive consumption formed a broad locus of further theoretical developments in social thought, ranging from Thorstein Veblen's (2005) conspicuous consumption to Henryk Grossman (1992) or Tony Cliff's (2003) theories of the centrality of war in capitalism.

Just as "labor" is not reducible to wage because it also involves the thingification of personhood, and "nature" is not reducible to land as a factor of production because it involves the annihilation of other understandings of nature, the overall outcome of several sociological understandings of unproductive consumption is that destruction and waste are not reducible to the significance they enjoy in Marxian political economy, for the conspicuous consumption of capital is not a zero-sum game where "the unproductive consumption of capital replaces it on one side, annihilates it on the other" (Marx 1993, 751); rather, the habit of consuming luxury goods involves material waste, social hierarchization, display of power, and cultural hegemony. And war is not reducible to a Keynesian variable where the production of the means of production couples with the production of the means of destruction, because it means both the destruction of value and the violent annihilation of the human.[12]

Muri exceeds unproductive consumption inasmuch as it offers a sociological conceptualization for those aspects of capitalist destruction that are not strictly confined within the destruction of value created by capital itself. Thinking with *muri* detaches destruction from the self-valorization of capital and its accumulation. It makes it possible to rethink destruction with a relative theoretical autonomy from accumulation, thereby creating the conceptual locus of destruction *per se*. Destruction *per se* is not the side effect of accumulation, because it displaces the alleged rationality of the self-contained logic of capital either from self-valorization through creative destruction aimed at reestablishing profitability, or from the self-destruction of its own material base to induce scarcity. Thus, destruction is not reducible to an ontological attribute of capital *in se*. Destruction *per se* connotes the reiterated co-formation of capital as a social relation that, because it is *per se* and not *in se*, it is actively co-formed by what is not capital. It follows that the logic of capital is unthinkable as fully rational in terms of accumulation, when its alleged rationality is subverted by the irrational drive to destruction *per se*. When launched beyond the epistemological barriers surrounding the theoretical core of capital, Marx's motto *Accumulation for accumulation's sake, production for production's sake!* resonates with a powerful echo that Eurocentrism had silenced: Destruction for destruction's sake!

The process of concept formation here explained throws three seeds: (1) The commodification of labor can be rethought in terms of the thingification of the human and humiliation of personhood; thingification is a condition of possibility of global colonial capitalist modernity as a whole rather than being circumscribed to the forms of "unfree" labor. (2) The destruction of nature involves the annihilation of alternative understandings of nature. But the radical resistance these alternative understandings enact interrupts the grammar of capital and displaces it into an uncommon epistemological territory: neither shared by, nor reducible to, one of the two sides of the colonial relation. (3) Capital as a social relation does not connote any historical entity called "capital"; rather, it denotes the irrational dimension of violence and destruction *per se* that capital as social relation entails across different social formations. Whereas Marx intended the movement from the concrete to the abstract in terms of temporary *reductio ad unum* of the conceptual complexity adequate to describe capital, the process of concept formation here proposed consists in complexifying the theoretical and semantic territory of capital, solicited by new decolonizing insights that offer alternative but not mutually exclusive views on the same processes that the concept of capital was originally designed to grasp. Thingification, the uncommon, and *muri* augment the heuristic power of the trinity formula but at the same time diminish the alleged "rationality" of the logic of capital while it remains connoted prevalently in terms of accumulation. Capital-land-labor can be reconceptualized with a hypostatic formula that makes explicit what has been disavowed: capital/destruction *per se*–labor/slavery–land/indigeneity.

Whereas Marx understood hypostatization as the fallacy of the reification of abstract notions, here hypostasis refers to the possibility of rearticulating in multiplex and heterogeneous forms the missing, silenced, hidden, and removed epistemological dimensions of capital. In this sense, capital as a social relation can be intentionally disclosed as a conception that shifts from its presumed integrity toward a plural understanding of the scattered, multiform ways through which the relations of violent annihilation and irreversible destruction reciprocally interpellate across different societal organizations, historical contexts, networks, and configurations of knowledge.

SIX PROCEDURAL DIRECTIVES

The tools for concept formation elaborated throughout the chapters of this book are thought of as an open-ended strategy from which multiple pathways derive. These pathways serve the purpose of orienting conceptualization in a procedural manner; therefore, they function as methodological directives. "Directive" expresses the intention to articulate a protocol of concept formation that enables active engagement with the concrete ability of deforming, informing, and transforming existing notions for historical social sciences, of creating concepts anew or thoughtfully dismissing existing concepts in use. Formalization involves six different procedural directives, but more can possibly emerge from further collective usage, testing, debate, and critique. These directives reciprocally interact in many ways and they are not mutually exclusive: they act like illustrative types, each of them coming together with one or more examples, which stand as the visible simulacra of viable concrete imaginative as well as applicative patterns of possibilities.

First Directive

The first procedural directive is genealogical. It pertains to the possibility of extending in space and time the genealogy of a concept. It sets out to produce a global cross-genealogy oriented toward looking into other civilizational and cultural conceptual archives. The aim is to find out if and how analogous conceptions exist and in what way they differ from those elaborated within European knowledge. This terminological analysis will put particular emphasis on the processes of construction and marginalization of otherness—that is, whatever does not conform to the colonizer's image of the world—which lies at the foundation of European-born notions. Its specific scope is to create a porous semantic field that works as a premise for the reciprocal interpellation of concepts across cultures, which allows alternative narratives, histories, and experiences, rather than analyzing the way notions relate or differ from each other. In this book, this directive was used in chapter 4 to elaborate on the concept of the *global*.

Second Directive

Following such a global cross-genealogy, the second directive is more strictly semantic. It consists in resignification. Resignification alludes to a specific semiotic process, where concepts are lifted from their usual contexts and relocated within new realms of understanding. This strategy opens up new paths to sociological imagination, and at the same time, it calls for further interventions to clarify and outline the aim and adequacy of such proposed semantic slippages, overlappings, and coming to terms with the discrepancies between ongoing global transformations and the provincial existing vocabulary devoted to their understanding (Ascione and Chambers 2016). The attempt to use *Asia* as method exemplifies this path. For instance, Fa-ti Fan (2016) tackles the crucial knot of the relation between histories and concepts drawn from a broad historiographical, rather than sociological, perspective. Fan underlines that the manner in which the birth and development of science is narrated is at the core of the European sociological self-understanding of modernity. This necessarily implies that the reconsideration of modern science inevitably involves a profound transformation in the basic understanding of the framework of modernity as regards the narrative and explanatory apparatus it deploys. Fan maps the vast and growing constellation of thick historiographical inquiries that in recent decades have provided different forms of refutation of the European master narrative of scientific modernity, its alleged superiority, and the mechanisms of its diffusion from the West to the Rest that Western historiography, even in its more self-critical versions, still tends to take for granted. In so doing, he elucidates how colonial and imperial histories of science agree, without necessarily overlapping, with postcolonial theory, inasmuch as they all construct interpretative models of the production of scientific knowledge that make it impossible to eschew the changing relations of power that contribute to determining whose "science" is to be considered more reliable and legitimate than another. In the context of knowledge transfer across civilizational borders, Fan interrogates the notion of "circulation," and he explains his dissatisfaction with it, given the degree of neutrality that circulation suggests, which does not do justice to the complex networks of power that can consent, but also interrupt or selectively allow movements of knowledges.

While Fan is skeptical about uncritical borrowing of terminologies across theoretical contexts, he proposes a broader strategy of resignification centered on the sintagma "Asia as method." Fan proposes to address the risks of overgeneralization and theoretical reification involved in the usage of the notion of "global" through a problematization of the issue of scale, as an antidote against Eurocentrism. "Shouldn't regions, therefore, be taken seriously, too?" he asks (Fan 2016). "Asia" here does not refer to a determined territorial or civilizational entity derived from the cartography of what James Blaut (1993) has identified as the "colonizer's model of the world." Rather, Fan explains why and to what extent "Asia as method is a critical and strategic regionalism that resists the global hegemony of Western modernity" (Fan 2016, 358).

Third Directive

The third directive is reconceptualization. It is the main, most synthetic, and most complex procedural directive. Reconceptualization can be oriented to enlarge the connotative space of the term as well as the historical-social dimensions it can legitimately claim to be referring to (Ascione and Chambers 2016). But, it should be noted, reconceptualization does not necessarily follow an incremental path. In fact, concepts can also become disempowered from reconceptualization and their adequacy, meaningfulness and scope thereby reduced. Bhambra (2016), for example, takes issue with hegemonic historical sociology, raising the problem of the analytical reductionism involved in the comparative method, grounded on ideal types and articulated via the nation-state. Bhambra shows why this methodological inadequacy is also theoretically illegitimate and analytically misleading to the extent that the concepts of *nation*, *state*, and *nation-state* that the social sciences inherited from Weber's sociology are all based upon a precise historical and epistemological premise. Namely:

> The failure to recognize prior global connections, or to regard them as substantively significant for modernity, is bound up with an elision of colonialism and empire as constitutive aspects of modernity's development. the elision of colonialism and empire as constitutive aspects of modernity's development. (Bhambra 2016, 336)

Rather than being blunt but still reliable, these methodological devices suffer from a generic inability to come to terms with entangled processes moving across national boundaries. This elision, Bhambra contests, is both historical and theoretical. Even though the state was narrowly conceptualized as a sociopolitical entity delineated by territorial boundaries, colonial relations actually connected the formation of the European nation-states, with their imperial and colonial areas of expansion overseas. Thus, the external/internal divide that provides the coherence of the mental representation of the concept of state alludes to situations altogether more fluid than social theory is often willing to admit. Bhambra focuses on the process of concept formation that led Weber to connote the state as a political, cultural, and legal institution in order to show that the inadequacy of our notion of the state does not derive from incomplete definitional or attributive procedures, nor from the wrong interpretations of historical occurrences.

The Eurocentric limits involved in the Weberian concept of the state arise from the epistemological architecture which generated and reproduced it. This architecture is organized around a particular logic of reciprocal legitimation between the interpretative schema of ideal types and empirical data drawn from the historical processes to be comprehended and explained. This reiterative legitimation is grounded in cultural and ideological colonialism that "precludes the possibility of establishing a general understanding based upon consideration of the different perspectives and inoculates each perspective from any criticism that taking another perspective seriously might engender" (Bhambra 2016, 338).

Bhambra underlines how the narrative and theoretical elision of connections is also the precondition for the construction of national identity involved in the Weberian notion of nation-states. The emergence of the political space of the German nation-state proceeds through the separation between the national "us" and the foreign "them." Here, the internal border pushed eastward by the Germanification of the eastern provinces is coextensive with the production of the external imperial and colonial border in Western Africa. An analogous process of nation-state formation during the same decades from the second half of the nineteenth century to World War II marks the Italian *Risorgimento* and the colonization of the south of the peninsula that ran together with the colonization of Libya and the so-called Horn of Africa (Lombardi-Diop and Romeo 2012). In the case of both the Italian and the German states, the institutional as well as rhetorical construction of national identity and the state apparatus has involved a profound process of silencing of the histories of imperialism, colonialism, and internal subalternization that were the foundational acts of the nation-state coming into being.

Bhambra suggests that the nation-state can be reconceptualized by including the missing colonial links not only within the historical narrative of the emergence of the nation-state and the public discourse of national identity. A further effort needs to be applied to reimagining the spatiotemporal and political boundaries of the nation-state in a radical manner. This means including the territorial and extraterritorial dimensions that connected the emergence of the European states with their own overseas areas of imperial and colonial expansion. In this manner, notions such as "citizenship" or "migrations" would assume a different and more inclusive meaning, and their significance could be mobilized to respond to the ongoing processes of worldly reconfiguration of regional and global political spaces.

Reconceptualization solicits conceptual polysemy. Against the well-established, territorialist, Weberian definition of the nation-state that prevails in historical sociology and provides the unit of analysis for comparative method, a decisively diverse conception can be opposed. The latter seeks to reconstruct the concept of nation-state on the basis of what Said (1979) called the "imagined cartographies" of postcolonial worlds, and the connected histories that make the world global, but not necessarily centered on Europe.

Fourth Directive

The fourth directive is taxonomic. Taxonomy, most of the time, is evitable. Very often, social theory indulges in taxonomy because of the pressures that capitalism puts on concept formation in the attempt to transform conceptualization in the production of academic branded terms to be sold, bought, grabbed, consumed, or imposed by the global market of scientific ideas, academic fashions, and intellectualistic simulacra. Nonetheless, when useful, taxonomy remains the most creative part in concept formation for the social sciences. This also implies radically confronting their own linguistic limits. In chapters 3 and 4 and in this one, several concepts, from *muri* to *Ubuntu* to *vinculum* to *ch'ixi*, coming from non-Western traditions, have been brought to the fore and their relevance argued in order to assess their conceptual and taxonomical value for global studies for forming a post-Western perspective. The concepts of *buen vivir* and *capitalocene* in the social sciences, for instance, are by-products of such creative taxonomical practice.

Fifth Directive

When resignification, reconceptualization, or taxonomy are effective, the objective of transforming and improving the conceptual vocabulary of the social sciences becomes achievable; in this case, the possible reiteration of the new meaning or concept through theoretical praxis relatively stabilizes relevance and multiplies usages, disclosing new and unforeseen paths. Then, the collective use of concepts through research and teaching produces the canonization of associated notions. When, instead, resignification or reconceptualization are not possible or effective, and taxonomical intervention is not even an option, the concept in question does not return to the status of legitimation it enjoyed before undergoing these procedures. It may appear increasingly inadequate and obsolete. As an example, the concept of *incorporation* that was pivotal in the main formulations of world-systems analysis as a way to grasp the process of colonization and the geographical expansion of the capitalist world economy at the global scale became obsolete and dismissible after the methodological critique of Eurocentric diffusionism, as shown in chapter 4.

Therefore, the fifth directive is dismissal. It relates to philology as a powerful politics of theory. Inadequacy and obsolescence need to be motivated through thought and debatable rationales as much as adequacy does. And the changing linguistic, political, and historical context for why inadequacy and obsolescence occur needs to be explained and the rationales argued so that the concept can be accurately stored: in the future, obsolescence and inadequacy can become anachronism, and anachronism may transform into a new, renewed, or different adequacy in another spacetime responding to other organizational needs. This thoughtful dismissal contributes to constructing a conceptual archive other than the Eurocentric one we inherited. The conceptual archive of the global social science will belong to all the different subjectivities and forms of knowledge that had participated in its collective process of knowledge production, with their respective understanding but also reciprocal irreducibility.

Sixth Directive

It follows that the sixth directive consists in living with untranslatability. It relates to communication in its deepest sense. It means assuming the working hypothesis that translation is not always possible. Untranslatability is more than a linguistic condition falling into the aim and scope of thick dictionaries devoted to this specific topic (Cassin et al. 2014). It is a remarkable space of generative tension. Untranslatability resonates with incommensurability as discussed above and overlaps with the concept of the *uncommon* from De La Cadena. The modern regime of translation is basically homolinguistic. It is a by-product of the emergence of the nation-state, and it presumes that every national society speaks the same language, against which the other languages and the human groups identifying with them are constructed as minorities. Before the affirmation of the nation-state during the nineteenth century, this condition was not the general rule in Europe either, since the elite had been proudly polyglot and the rest of the people easily used a variety of vernaculars (Mezzadra and Sakai 2021). Following Marx, the modern homolinguistic regime is the historical expression of the *vinculum* between translation and the production of value. Brett Neilson explains that in the *Grundrisse*, Marx parallels "translation and the role that money plays in facilitating the circulation of commodities and in making their universal exchange possible" (Neilson 2014, 121). Within what she calls "the political economy of signs," Lydia Liu connects the exchange of commodities with the exchange of signs (Liu 2014, 23). In this sense, untranslatability is an epistemological resource. As an example, Liu (2014) recalls a crucial episode that occurred during the elaboration of the Universal Declaration of Human Rights in 1948. Peng-chun Chang, the vice president of the United Nations Commission on Human Rights under the presidency of Eleanor Roosevelt, suggested that the Western commissaries sitting at her table take a six-month leave in order to get acquainted with Chinese philosophy and understand the commonalities, the differences, and the irreconcilabilities that the concept of *human* conceals beneath the surface of its presumed universal value. Chang noted, for instance, the distance between the notion of human that her Western colleagues championed and hers and that of other representatives of non-Western countries: the former was based on individualism; the latter, on collective identity aiming at communitarian rights (Liu 2014, 60). Chang's invitation remained unheard, and hence an opportunity for concept formation was lost.

Eventually, an equally cogent working hypothesis complements untranslatability: it consists in the opposite assumption that communication is always possible, even when conversation terminates in a cul-de-sac and exchange materializes in nothing but a pneumatic vacuum. For even when the space of impossibility speaks the language of conceptual silence, whereas worded concepts are expected to talk the language of reciprocal understanding, communication is not interrupted. It is just suspended: an interlocutory pause of indeterminacy, a generative silence to be accurately registered in the uninterrupted dialogue that flows among humans across the secret routes of the long-term and large-scale processes of planetary knowledge formation.

NOTES

1. The notion of spatialized historical concepts draws from Reinhart Koselleck's (2002) practice of conceptual history. Nonetheless, the problem of cross-cultural dialogue is absent in Koeselleck's approach.

2. Vladimir Lenin (1965) had anticipated this problem when he contested the 'The Equivalential Fallacy,' Lenin that is, the errors of those western European far leftists in the early 1920s who had thought they were presenting 'faithful' translations of the militancy of the Russian Revolution while completely misreading its significance. See Lenin (1965), 17–118. Lenin stated,

> at the Third Congress, in 1921, we adopted a resolution on the organizational structure of the Communist Parties and on the methods and content of their activities. The resolution is an excellent one, but it is almost entirely Russian, that is to say, everything in it is based on Russian conditions. This is its good point, but it is also its failing. It is its failing because I am sure that no foreigner can read it . . . it is too Russian . . . not because it is written in Russian—it has been excellently translated into all languages—but because . . . we have not learnt how to present our Russian experience to foreigners [in such a way that they might be able to] assimilate part of the Russian experience.

3. The same logic of subaltern politics and historiography was being adopted by Gramsci's contemporaries in Latin America, like José Carlos Mariátegui; it will be used as well in the last quarter of the twentieth century to rethink Gramsci by the Indian and the Latin American Subaltern Studies Group (Ascione 2009; Dufoix 2023).

4. Santos appropriates diatopic hermeneutics from theologian Raimon Panikkar to cope with issues of space. Analogously, Immanuel Wallerstein (2001, 155)

appropriated the notion of *Kairos* from the theologian Paul Tillich to cope with issues of time. Panikkar (1979, 49) calls it "[d]iatopical hermeneutics because the distance to be overcome is not merely temporal, within one broad tradition, but the gap existing between two human topoi, 'places' of understanding and self-understanding, between two—or more—cultures that have not developed their patterns of intelligibility. Diatopical hermeneutics stands for the thematic consideration of understanding the other without assuming that the other has the same basic self-understanding."

5. Border thinking as a gnoseological strategy was developed first by Mignolo (2000) on the basis of the analysis of the different linguistic languages colonial, Marxist, and Indigenous used in their rhetoric by the Zapatistas in Mexico during the 1990s.

6. Portions of this section have been previously published in *Sociology Vol.51*, No.1 as "Unthinking Capital: Conceptual and Terminological Landmarks," 2017.

7. Already before drafting the *Manifesto*, while in Brussels in 1846–1847, Marx (2001, 94–95) affirmed in *The Poverty of Philosophy* that

> direct slavery is just as much the pivot of bourgeois industry as machinery, credits, etc. Without slavery you have no cotton; without cotton you have no modern industry. It is slavery that has given the colonies their value; it is the colonies that have created world trade, and it is world trade that is the pre-condition of largescale industry. Thus slavery is an economic category of the greatest importance. Without slavery North America, the most progressive of countries, would be transformed into a patriarchal country. Wipe out North America from the map of the world, and you will have anarchy—the complete decay of modern commerce and civilisation. Cause slavery to disappear and you will have wiped America off the map of nations. Thus slavery, because it is an economic category, has always existed among the institutions of the peoples. Modern nations have been able only to disguise slavery in their own countries, but they have imposed it without disguise upon the New World.

8. Mariano and Nazario Turpo have been Indigenous leaders engaged in the Andean network of environmental struggles, as well as for the recognition of Indigenous rights.

9. Marx (1993, 489–514) makes explicit that the transition to the capitalist mode of production is irreversible since his preliminary writings to capital in the Gründrisse. Some afterthoughts on the cogency of this assumption, instead, merge only in his very last ethnological writings on non-Western societies. See Krader (1974).

10. For a general introduction to the role of unproductive consumption in Marxian political economy see Becker (1977).

11. In Marx's (1992, 530) words, "[b]ut *as things actually are*, the replacement of capitals invested in production depends to a large extent on the consumption capacity of the non-productive classes; while the consumption capacity of the workers is restricted partly by the laws governing wages and partly by the fact that they are employed at a profit for the capitalist class" (emphasis added). Elsewhere, Marx (1992, 667) claims that "[t]he capitalist mode of production, while on the one hand,

enforcing economy in each individual business, on the other hand, begets by its anarchical system of competition, the most outrageous squandering of labour power and of the social means of production, not to mention the creation of a vast number of employments, at present indispensable but in themselves are superfluous."

12. Nikolai Bukharin (1982 [1920], 52–53) wrote about destruction in the following terms: "a cannon cannot be transformed into an element of a new productive cycle; gunpowder explodes into thin air and does not reappear during the ensuing cycle . . . war is accompanied by a 'distorted,' regressive, negative character of the reproduction process." As Callinicos (2009, 58–63) notes, notwithstanding that both Grossman and Bukharin grasped some key dynamics in the relation between military expenditure, capital accumulation, and imperialism, their approach was discredited because its validity was tested against its (in)ability to predict the mechanisms of the fatal crisis of capitalism.

BIBLIOGRAPHY

Ascione, Gennaro. 2009. *A sud di nessun Sud: Postcolonialismo, movimenti anti-sistemici e studi decoloniali*. Bologna: Odoya.

Ascione, Gennaro, and Iain Chambers. 2016. "Global Historical Sociology: Theoretical and Methodological Issues—An Introduction." *Cultural Sociology* 10, no. 3: 301–16.

Bermudez-Contreras Edgar, Benjamin J. Clark, and Aaron Wilber. 2020. "The Neuroscience of Spatial Navigation and the Relationship to Artificial Intelligence." *Frontiers in Computational Neuroscience* 14: 63.

Becker James F. 1977. *Marxian Political Economy: An Outline*. Cambridge: Cambridge University Press.

Bhambra Gurminder. 2016. "Comparative Historical Sociology and the State: Problems of Method." *Cultural Sociology* 10, no. 3: 335–51.

Blaut, James M. 1993. *The Colonizer's Model of the World: Geographical Diffusionism and Eurocentric History*. New York: Guilford Press.

Bruno, Giordano. 2009. *Opere magiche*. Milano: Adelphi.

Callinicos, Alex. 2009. *Imperialism and Global Political Economy*. Cambridge, MA: Polity.

Cassin Barbara, Emily Apter, Jacques Lezra, and Michael Wood, eds. 2014. *Dictionary of Untranslatables: A Philosophical Lexicon*. Princeton, NJ: Princeton University Press.

Césaire, Aimé. 2007. *Discourse on Colonialism*. Princeton, NJ: Princeton University Press.

Cliff, Tony. 2003. *Marxist Theory after Trotsky: Selected Writings. Volume 3*. London: Bookmarks.

Coronil, Fernando. 2000. "Naturaleza del Poscolonialismo: del eurocentrismo al globcentrismo." In *La colonialidad del saber: eurocentrismo y ciencias sociales. Perspectivas latinoamericanas*, edited by Edgardo Lander, 87–111. Buenos Aires: CLACSO.

Cova, Luciano. 2004. "Intenzioni e intenzionalità. L'eredità del pensiero arabo nella Scolastica del XIII secolo." *Husserl in Laboratorio. Seminario Husserliano Permanente.* S. Cattaruzza, M. Sinico Editors, 97–120 Edizioni Università Di Trieste,.

Couliano, Ioan Petru. 1987. *Eros and Magic in the Renaissance.* Chicago: University of Chicago Press.

Cusicanqui, Silvia Rivera. 2012. "Ch'ixinakax utxiwa: A Reflection on the Practices and Discourses of Decolonization." *South Atlantic Quarterly* 111, no. 1: 95–109.

———. 2018. *Un mundo ch'ixi es posible. Ensayos desde un presente en crisis.* Buenos Aires: Tinta Limòn.

De La Cadena, Marisol. 2015a. *Earth Beings: Ecologies of Practices across Andean Worlds.* Durham, NC: Duke University Press.

———. 2015b. "Uncommoning Nature." *Eflux* 65: 1–8.

Dufoix, S. 2023. *Décolonial*, "Le mot est faible." Paris, Anamosa, coll.

Escobar, Arturo. 2008. *Territories of Difference: Place, Movements, Life, Redes.* Durham, NC: Duke University Press.

Espeland, Wendy Nelson, and Mitchell L. Stevens. 1998. "Commensuration as Social Process." *Annual Review of Sociology* 24: 313–43.

Fan, Fa-ti. 2016. "Modernity, Region, and Technoscience: One Small Cheer for Asia as Method." *Cultural Sociology* 10: 361–66.

Gramsci, Antonio. 1975. *Quaderni del carcere, Vol. 1. Il Materialismo storic e la filosofia di Benedetto Croce.* Turin: Giulio Einaudi Editore.

Grossman, Henryk. 1992. *The Law of Accumulation and Breakdown of Capitalism.* Edited and translated by Jairus Banaji. London: Pluto Press.

Hamati-Ataya, Inanna. 2022. "Thickening International Theory or Shrinking the Shagreen Skin?" *In Globalizing International Theory: The Problem with Western IR Theory and How to Overcome It*, edited by A. Layug and John M. Hobson, xi–xiv. London: Routledge.

Iveković, Rada. 2010. "The Watershed of Modernity: Translation and the Epistemological Revolution." *Inter-Asia Cultural Studies* 11, no. 1: 45–63.

Kohn, Eduardo. 2013. *How Forests Think: Toward an Anthropology Beyond the Human.* Oakland: University of California Press.

Koselleck, Reinhart. 2002. *The Practice of Conceptual History: Timing History, Spatializing Concepts.* Stanford, CA: Stanford University Press.

Krader Lawrence. 1974. *The Ethnological Notebooks of Karl Marx.* Assen: Van Gorcum and Comp BV.

Lenin, Vladimir Ilich. 1965. "Left-Wing Communist: An Infantile Disorder," in *Lenin Collected Works, Vol. 31*, Moscow: Progress Publishers.

Liu, Lydia H. 2014. "The Eventfulness of Translation: Temporality, Difference, and Competing Universals." *Translation: A Transdisciplinary Journal* 4: 147–70.

Lombardi-Diop, Cristina, and Caterina Romeo, eds. 2012. *Post-Colonial Italy: Challenging National Homogeneity.* London: Palgrave.

Maldonado, Tomàs. 2005. *Memoria e conoscenza: Sulle Sorti Del Sapere Nella Prospettiva Digitale.* Milano: Feltrinelli.

Marx, Karl. 1992. *Capital: A Critique of Political Economy.* 3 Vols. New York: Penguin.

———. 1993. *Gründrisse*. New York: Penguin.
———. 1995. *Capital: Volume III*. New York: International Publishers.
———. 2001. *The Poverty of Philosophy*. Chicago: Elbron.
Mbembe, J. Achille. 2003. "Necropolitics." *Public Culture* 15, no. 1: 11–40.
———. 2015. "Decolonizing Knowledge and the Question of the Archive." Available at: http://wiser.wits.ac.za/system/files/AchilleMbembeDecolonizingKnowledgeandtheQuestionoftheArchive.pdf (accessed 15 June 2023).
Mezzadra, S., and N. Sakai. 2021. "Introduction." *Translation: A Transdisciplinary Journal*, vol. 4, no. Spring, May 2021, 9–29,
Mignolo, Walter D. 2000. "The Many Faces of Cosmo-polis: Border Thinking and Critical Cosmopolitanism." *Public Culture* 12, no. 3: 721–48.
Mignolo, Walter D., and Catherine E. Walsh. 2018. *On Decoloniality: Concepts, Analytics, Praxis*. Durham, NC: Duke University Press.
Neilson, Brett. 2014. "Knowledge on the Move: Between Logistics and Translation." *Translation: A Transdisciplinary Journal* 4: 129–46.
Outhwaite, William. 1983. *Concept Formation in Social Science*. London: Routledge.
Palat, Ravi Arvind. 1999. "Fragmented Visions: Excavating the Future of Area Studies in a Post-American World." In *After the Disciplines: The Emergence of Cultural Studies*, edited by Michael Peters, 87–126. Westport, CT: Bergin & Garvey.
Panikkar, Raimon. 1979. *Myth, Faith and Hermeneutics*. New York: Paulist Press.
Perler, Dominik, ed. 2001. *Ancient and Medieval Theories of Intentionality*. Leiden: Brill.
Rossi, Paolo. 2006. *Il tempo dei maghi: Rinascimento e modernità*. Milano: Raffaello Cortina Editore.
Rota, Stefano. 2020. "Introduzione." In *La (in)traducibilità del mondo: Attraversamenti e confini della traduzione*, edited by Stefano Rota, 7–22. Verona: Ombre corte.
Said, Edward. 1979. *Imaginative Geography and Its Representations: Orientalizing the Oriental*. New York: Vintage.
Santos, Boaventura de Souza. 2002. "Toward a Multicultural Conception of Human Rights." In *Moral Imperialism: A Critical Anthology*, edited by Berta Esperanza Hernández-Truyol, 39–60. New York: New York University Press.
Shilliam, Robbie. 2012. "Forget English Freedom, Remember Atlantic Slavery: Common Law, Commercial Law and the Significance of Slavery for Classical Political Economy." *New Political Economy* 17, no. 5: 591–609.
———. 2015a. "Decolonizing the Manifesto: Communism and the Slave Analogy." In *The Cambridge Companion to the Communist Manifesto*, edited by Terrell Carver and James Farr, 195–213. Cambridge: Cambridge University Press.
———. 2015b. *The Black Pacific: Anti-Colonial Struggles and Oceanic Connections*. New York: Bloomsbury.
Sweezy, Paul M. 1970. *The Theory of Capitalist Development: Principles of Marxian Political Economy*. London: Dobson.
Thomas, Peter. 2020. "The Tasks of Translatability." *International Gramsci Journal* 3, no. 4: 5–30.
Veblen, Thorstein. 2005. *Conspicuous Consumption*. London: Penguin.

Walker, Gavin. 2012. "The World of Principle, or Pure Capitalism: Exteriority and Suspension in Uno Kōzō." *Journal of International Economic Studies* 26: 15–37.
Wallerstein, Immanuel. 1999. "The Heritage of Sociology, the Promise of Social Science Presidential Address, XIVth World Congress of Sociology, Montreal, 26 July 1998." *Current Sociology* 47, no. 1.
Williams, Raymond. 1977. *Marxism and Literature*. New York: Oxford University Press.
Yates, F. A. 1974. *The Art of Memory*. Chicago: University of Chicago Press.
Zito, George V. 1983. "Toward a Sociology of Heresy." *Sociological Analysis* 44, no. 2: 123–30.

Conclusion

Limits and Concerns

DEMOGRAPHY AND HEGEMONY

This book may underestimate the relevance of rapid demographic growth for the specific task of concept formation. It is a fact that a large part of the notions we uncritically use or critically discuss today to make sense of the world emerged with reference to a planetary human society that counted barely one billion persons at the beginning of the eighteenth century and has just reached eight billion.[1] Concept formation here relates to demographic geocultural change in qualitative terms but not directly to demographic growth in quantitative terms. It copes with demographic change only to the extent that the participation in the production of knowledge from non-Western geocultural locations can actually be read as an indirect indicator of the changing geography of world population, which steadily decreases in the West, particularly among the most privileged social strata, and grows everywhere else (Danna 2019). By extension, this is true also for the quantitative dimension of demographic change in gender relations, and more generally to the shifting configuration of social stratification along such lines as class and race. The relevance for the production of knowledge of those social groups or identities that historically occupy lower positions in the social hierarchies of the colonial modern world provoked many of the emerging issues this book addresses. Therefore, the intention to learn from subaltern gender, race, ethnicity, religion, cosmologies, languages, ecologies, and class positions in existing social relations drives the elaboration of the agenda for concept formation herewith. Nonetheless, while global demographic change enters this book indirectly as a qualitative parameter, what the French historian Fernand Braudel (1977) called "the weight of numbers" in historical social knowledge remains less defined. Therefore, a possible formulation for such a concern would be: is the unprecedented quantitative dimension of planetary demographic growth relevant to the concepts that global studies use or is called to elaborate to think the world exclusively in terms of the qualitative transformations I have outlined, or does the quantitative aspect of concept formation deserve more attention? The plausible answer to this question eludes me.

The second element is the concept of *hegemony*. I never address it directly. Throughout the book, I derivatively rely on an allusive notion of hegemony when I refer to nonhegemonic knowledges or antihegemonic stances. To be sure, in chapter 3 I clarify the way I use these terms. Yet the concept of hegemony requires a deeper understanding that engages with its changing historical meaning rather than merely with its capacity to grasp the transformations of power in the interstate system of international relations according to international theory or diplomatic history. This problem could be better formulated as follows: will the concept of hegemony remain adequate in, and after, the current systemic crisis provoking the current reconfiguration of global power? To sketch out a plausible answer, an interrogation into the semantic space of tension between *hegemony* and *dominance* comes to the fore. This is the crucial lesson from the genealogy of the word "hegemony" that global studies should take from the decolonizing intervention within Indian subaltern studies, made by means of their postcolonial reinterpretation of Gramsci (Guha 1997).

Hegemony connotes a certain degree of consensus, and the ways this consensus is built should not be taken for granted once and for all. It works through different kinds of rewards, and building an alternative or competing system of rewards may involve a shift in political and ethical values. Therefore, dominance without hegemony is a concrete option for global governance in the current crisis. Terence K. Hopkins (1990) wrote a short "note on the concept of hegemony" where he took issue with a way to look at hegemony through the glance of the different long-term temporalities and large-scale spatial organization of global power in the interstate system that remains substantially valid since the first reformulation of the original Gramscian notion that Robert Cox (1983, 170) proposed as a methodological device to reinterpret international relations historically: "In applying the concept of hegemony to world order, it becomes important to determine when a period of hegemony begins and when it ends. A period in which world hegemony has been established can be called hegemonic and one in which the dominance of a non-hegemonic kind prevails, non-hegemonic."

Hopkins (1990, 409) recalled that "hegemony has been defined as a cyclical pattern, a thrice-repeated preeminence of a primus inter pares or as an evolutionary pattern of stages." He criticized a certain degree of teleology in both the aforementioned definitions and suggested "a third possible conceptualization, one that uses the term to signify a historical 'moment.'" The problem, according to Hopkins, is that "what we're often weak at showing is what equally realistic historical alternatives to that which came to prevail ('succeeded') were thereby, or quite otherwise, eliminated."

What does this moment allow us to imagine for the future? If dominance without hegemony is an option to move from hegemony into world empire *manu militari*, it is also true that there are other concurrent possibilities available (Hopkins and Wallerstein 1996). One consists in a hegemonic transition analogous to the previous ones, with China apparently the most likely global power to take the lead (Arrighi 1999). A different option consists in a multipolar world where the geopolitical cartography of a few centers of power and resources overlaps with a geoeconomic map of regional spheres of influence. This scenario would represent an inversion of the increasing global integration that occurred throughout the last centuries and has been conceived in terms of globalization. Another not impossible scenario is a more radical version of this forced inversion of global integration that could lead to a split into a twofold geopolitical order where two distinctive macroaggregate entities are governed by alternative logics, in the last instance: one closer to an empire, where political authority governs over the logic of market efficiency and redistributes resources according to noneconomic organizational or military needs; the other, where the logic of capitalist accumulation predominates over all the other existing social forces or modes of production and distributions of wealth. The customary orientalist image of the capitalist West vis-à-vis the authoritarian east would not be necessarily foregone nor taken for granted. Analogously to the way multiple geopolitical entities coexisted and were interconnected in premodern times, the ties between these macroaggregates could exist and function in the form of logistics or even infrastructures without influencing the distinctive prevailing inner logic of organization (Abu-Lughod 1989), just as the commerce of luxury commodities or currencies between East and West did not actually do until the eighteenth century (Dussel 2000; Frank 1998).

Moreover, the concept of hegemony was designed according to the methodological significance of the nation-state as a global institution vis-à-vis ancient empires, even though both the Dutch and the British were actually integrated systems between a nation-state and its overseas empire. Will this notion apply to different political as well as demographic scenarios where entities such as China or India question *in se* and *per se* the concept of nation-state as it emerged in nineteenth-century Europe? Or might we envisage a future geopolitical order that functions without hegemony as we know it, rendering this concept obsolete and irrelevant to conceive an organizing principle in global power relation? Will hegemony, in time, preserve its meaningfulness to express the asymmetries of power between different human groups and their forms of knowledge production, located in unequal positions of the same social hierarchy?

This conundrum from the future-past is an interrogation that takes us beneath the semantic surface of the concept of hegemony. In ancient Greek, the word *hegemonikon* had a specific meaning in the field of medicine: "hearth." According to the first-century CE medical doctrine of Archigene of Apamea, from Syria, the *hegemonikon* was the cardiac "synthesizer" that is able to receive all the currents of information coming from all the senses (both external and internal): that is, from the five senses connecting with the outside and from the inner senses of imagination, intellect, and fantasy connecting with the inside. For the second-century Roman Claudio Galeno, whose doctrine is foundational of Western medicine, the *hegemonikon* was a twofold anatomic integrated system formed by the constant interaction of hearth and brain (Couliano 1987: 22–23). Does this etymological echo resonate with the modern idea that hegemony is a field of struggle to win hearts and minds? Or are the conceptual limits of hegemony as we know it in the social sciences secretly connected via etymology to the limits of modern Western medicine in relation to other possible non-Western or post-Western approaches to the relation between body and mind, health and illness, life and death, which are conceivable in nonbinary, nondualistic, or monist epistemological terms? At this moment, the answer eludes us.

NOTE

1. See United Nations World Population report at https://population.un.org/wpp/.

BIBLIOGRAPHY

Abu-Lughod Janet. 1993. *Before European Hegemony: The World-System A. D. 1250–1350*. London: Oxford University Press.

Braudel Fernand. 1997. *La dinamica del capitalismo*. Bologna: Il Mulino.

Couliano, Ioan Petru. 1987. *Eros and Magic in the Renaissance*. Chicago: University of Chicago Press.

Cox, Robert. 1983. "Gramsci, Hegemony and International Relations. An Essay in Method." *Millenium: Journal of International Studies* 12, no. 2: 162–75.

Danna Daniela. 2019. *Il peso dei numeri. Teoria e dinamiche della popolazione*. Trieste: Asterios.

Dussel, Enrique. 2004. "Modernity, European Empires, Colonialism and Capitalism." *Theologies and Cultures* 1, no. 2: 24–50.

Frank, Andre Gunder. 1998. *ReORIENT: Global Economy in the Asian Age*. Berkeley: University of California Press.

Guha, Ranajit. 1997. *Dominance without Hegemony: History and Power in Colonial India*. Cambridge, MA: Harvard University Press.
Hopkins, Terence, Kilbourne. 1990. "Note on the concept of hegemony." *Review*: *Journal of the Fernand Braudel Center*, 13: 409–411.

Index

Abbasid empire, 34–35, 41
abigarrada (colorful), 215
ab origine, 200
abstract, 185–89
Abstract Labor (Charabarty), 152–53
Abulafia, David, 47
Abu-Loghud, Janet, 36
Abū Ma'shar, 40, 94
Acharya, Amitav, 4, 5
Adas, Michael, 20
ad libitum, 175
Advaita, 2
Afrofuturism, 2
against nature (*contra natura*), 50
Agamben, Giorgio, 130, 139
agency: coloniality of method and, 184–85; power and, 191; in translatability, 211
Age of Exploration, 134
d'Alambert, Jean le Rond, 85
Albigensian Crusade, 45
Alexander the Great, 25, 91
All-under-Heaven, 152–53
Almagest (Ptolemy), 35
alterity, 101, 130; on Aristotle, 41; binarism and, 38; in China, 142; global and, 201, 202; with monstrosity, 134; racialization of, 11; teratology and, 142–43
Althusser, Louis, 23
American Sociological Association, 169, 180
Amin, Samir, 3–4, 5
amoxtlii, 84, 89
analessi, 105n3
Anievas, Alexander, 36
anima mundi, 78, 91
animism, 94, 101
anomie, 124
ante litteram, 46, 79, 168
Anthropocene, 182
anthropocentrism, 96, 138
anthropological egalitarianism, 94
antianthropocentrism, 94
anti-ethnocentrism, 5
anti-naturalism, 117
antispeciesism, 94
Apollo 8, 180
Apollo 17, 180–81
application, in TM, 155–56
Aquinas, Thomas, 28–29, 33, 41, 47–48; Aristotle and, 53–55; epistemology of, 118; Islam and, 48, 54–55; *pureza de sangre* and, 73; Scholasticism of, 48, 49, 53, 54–55, 56
Arabism, 29, 47–56
Arab thinking, 35
Argonauts, 78

Aristippo, Enrico, 40, 76
Aristotle, 22, 26; alterity on, 41; Aquinas and, 53–55; Augustine and, 31; Bruno and, 80; Christianity and, 28, 33, 40–41, 44, 49–51, 53, 54–55, 73–74, 90; Duhem on, 27; Enlightenment and, 90; epistemology of, 118; heterodoxy of, 55; ontology and epistemology and, 11; politics and, 47–56; racialization and, 34; translation of, 11
Arnauld, Antoine, 156
Arnoux, Mathieu, 42
Arrighi, Giovanni, 179, 203n10
Ars bene disponendi seriem plurimarum cogitationum, 156
articulation, 145–57, 166
Asad, Talal, 178
Ashcroft, Rachel, 77
The Ash Wednesday Supper (Bruno), 77–78
Asia, 236–37
assemblages, 12, 193–97
astrology, 2, 25, 40, 94–95, 103
astronomy, 35, 40, 84, 94–96, 98, 106n10
Atlantic piracy, 2
Augustine of Hippo, 28, 31–32, 33, 46, 118
Averroes (Ibn-Rushd), 35, 40, 41, 47–56, 80, 91
Avicenna, 40, 41
Axial Age, 23
Aymara, 2, 13, 101, 127, 214–16
Aztec, 103

Balibar, Étienne, 193–94, 196
Baltrušaitis, Jurgis, 102–3
Bandini, Domenico, 88
barbarians, 48, 89, 90, 116
Barkin, J. Samuel, 118
Bathensis, Adelardus, 40
Baumgarten, A. G., 57n2
Bayod, Jordi, 77
Bellarminio, Roberto, 98
bellatores (knights), 42
Bène, Amaury de, 50
Bennet, Tony, 165
Bennett, Andrew, 118
Benzoni, Gerolamo, 77
Berbers, 40
Bernal, Martin, 85
Bertalanffy, Ludwig von, 177
Bevir, Mark, 117
Bhambra, Gurminder K., 119, 122, 123–24, *126*, 169, 190, 191–92, 197, 198, 200, 237–38
Billings, Linda, 181
binarism, 35, 38, 90, 177
Biondo, Flavio, 88
Blake, Cecil, 85
Blanqui, Auguste, 92
Blaut, James, 166, 181–82, 236
Blue Marble, 180
Blum, Elisabeth, 75–76
Blumenberg, Hans, 56
Boethius, 35
Bonaventure, 41, 55
Boniface VIII (Pope), 47
borders, 12, 193–97, 242n6; double, 71–72, 105n6
borderscapes, 131, 137–38
Bourdieu, Pierre, 116
Braudel, Fernand, 71
Brenner, Neil, 171, 184
Bruno, Giordano, 10, 11, 63–105, 106n8, 140, 218; Aristippo and, 76; execution of, 84, 98; Inquisition and, 98; on modernity, 83–94
Buddhist monasteries, 25, 91
buen vivir, 121
Bukharin, Nikolai, 243n12
Burawoy, Michael, 169
Buzan, Barry, 4, 5
Byzantium, 45

cabalists, 25, 98
Cabezòn, José Ignacio, 38
Caliban (fictional character), 131–32, 134–37, 139–40, 143–45

Callinicos, Alex, 243n12
Canary Islands, 133
Canibal, 132–33
Les cannibales (Montaigne), 77
cannibalism, 77, 104, 132, 134, 139–40
capabilities, assemblages and, 195
capital, 13; endless accumulation of, 186; epistemology of, 234–35; Marx on, 225–27, 228, 230–32, 233, 234, 242n9, 242n11; *muri* and, 2, 232–35; thingification and, 232–35; translatability and, 220; uncommon and, 225–35
capitalism, 14, 24–25, 64; abstract-concrete and, 189; assemblages and, 196; epistemology of, 191; global and, 168; modernity and, 183; non-Western and, 130; power and, 185
Caribe, 132–33
Castilian language, 69, 71–73
Castro-Gómez, Santiago, 192–93
Cathars, 43, 46
cathdral schools (*scholae cahedrales*), 26
Cellarius, Christoph, 88
Césaire, Aimé, 226
CF. *See* criterial framework
Chakrabarty, Dipesh, 70, 105n5, 152–53, 192
Chambers, Iain, 193
Chandler, David, 171
Chang, Peng-chun, 240–41
chants (*mō teatea*), 148
Charles V, 71
China, 4, 52; First Opium War in, 165; House of Islam in, 43; Mongols in, 133; non-Western and, 130; political power of, 116; Qi on, 124–25; *Tianxia* on, 152–53
Chinese Rites, 37–38, 57n4
ch'ixi, 214–15
Chomsky, Noam, 146
Christianity, 2; Aristotle and, 28, 33, 40–41, 44, 49–51, 54–55, 73–74, 90; Chinese Rites and, 37–38, 57n4; coloniality of method and, 170; creation theology of, 79; ethnocentrism in, 55–56; Eurocentrism and, 37; global and, 181; Gregorian calendar and, 24; heterodoxy and, 91–92; historical social change in, 41–47; Islam and, 55; Jubilee of 1600 and, 84; in Middle Ages, 26; non-Western and, 129, 134; ontology and epistemology and, 11; pagans and, 89–90; racialization in, 28, 44–45, 52–53, 74; *Reconquista* and, 72, 105n6; in Renaissance, 89, 91–92; Scholasticism in, 26–29, 31–32; Scientific Revolution and, 20; in universities, 22. *See also specific topics and individuals*
Ciliberto, Michele, 84
circulation, 197–99, 236
classificatory, 122–23
clerks (*oratores*), 42
Cliff, Tony, 233
coherence, 173, 237; in CF, 125
colonialism, 3; abstract-concrete and, 189; abstract labor and, 153; in Americas, 14–15; as assemblage, 196; assemblages and, 196–97; familiarity and, 146, 147–48; global and, 166–67; of Italy, 238; modernity and, 64–66, 87; non-Western and, 128, 129, 130, 137, 140–41; of Portugal, 84, 85; reconceptualization of, 238. *See also* decolonization
coloniality of method, 196–97, 231; global and, 168–72; power and, 203n9
colorful (*abigarrada*), 215
color line, 131
Columbus, Christopher, 36, 72, 77, 78, 89, 132–33, 134
commensuration, 228–29
Commentarii (Ghiberti), 89
Comments on Aristotle's De Anima (Bruno), 80

commodification, 226–27, 234
Commune in Paris, 92
concept formation: data and classification for, 119–26, *126*; directives for, 235–41; eight styles of, 220–25; Eurocentrism and, 190; genealogy for, 235; globalization of, 5; holism for, 12; provincialization of, 6–10; semantic spatialization for, 13; TM of, 115–57; translatability and, 211–41. *See also specific topics*
Concept Formation in Social Science (Outhwaite), 8–9, 117
concept-to-concept, 126, 149
conceptual history, 1
concrete, 185–89
Condemnation, 38
The Confessions (Augustine), 46
conformality, 182
Confucianism, 33
connectedness, 12, 197–99
Connected Sociologies (Bhambra), 200
connected sociologies (CS), 125
Connell, Raewyn, 64, 167, 196
Constantinople, 26, 32, 45, 70, 75
contact, 198–99
contra natura (against nature), 50
contrapuntal, 65–66
Cooper, 116
Copernicus, Nicolaus, 94–95, 106n10
Coronil, Fernando, 193
Corpus Aristotelicum, 28, 31, 90
Corpus Hermeticum, 26
Cosgrove, Derek, 180–81
cosmology, 5, 29, 95, 118, 119, 211
cosmopolitanism, 36, 44, 47, 152–53
counterpoint, to modernity, 65–67
creationist theology, 79
Cremona, Gerardo da, 40
criterial framework (CF), 118–19, 122–23, 125, 126, *126*
critical globalization, 5, 12, 165
critical race, 5
critique, 139
Crusades, 26, 28, 44, 45, 46–47, 49, 50, 52
CS. *See* connected sociologies
Curti, Lidia, 193
Cusicanqui, Silvia Rivera, 100, 214–16
customs and protocols (*kanga*), 148
cyclical time, in Renaissance, 91–94
Cynocephali, 133–34

Daston, Lorraine, 142
De Anima (Aristotle), 40, 50, 53
De Coelo (Aristotle), 40
decolonization, 1, 190–93, 203n10; coloniality of method and, 168–72; in early modern reason, 68–83; in Enlightenment, 85; Eurocentrism and, 5; global and, 172–75; love and, 217–18; in Māori Renaissance, 15; modernization theories and, 172–75; planetary and, 201; in Renaissance, 63–105; after World War II, 12
Decolonizing Methodology (Smith, L.), 150
deep structure, 146
definition: meaning of, 9; in TM, 146–48
De Generatione (Aristotle), 40
dehumanization, 130, 141, 227
De immenso et innumerabilibus, seu de universo et mundis (Bruno), 79, 82, 84, 94
De Interpretatione (Aristotle), 90
De La Cadena, Marisol, 228, 229–30, 232, 240
De Landa, Manuel, 195
Deleuze, Gilles, 195
demarcation problem, 9
Democritus, 95, 106n10
De Mundo (Gundissalino), 40
Dendle, Peter J., 104
denial of coevalness, 128
depth, in CF, 125
De Revolutionibus Orbium Coelestium (Copernicus), 95

Descartes, René, 8, 22, 64, 67, 68, 82, 127, 194
Destructio destrucionum (Bruno), 80
developmentalism, 175, 203n3
De vinculis in genere (Bruno), 218
diatopic hermeneutics (DH), 119, 122, 123, 125, 126, *126*, 157n1, 242n5
differentiation, in CF, 125
diffusionism, of Eurocentrism, 166, 182–85, 200
directives, for concept formation, 235–41
Dirlik, Arif, 203n10
Discourse on Colonialism (Mbembe), 226–27
Discourse on the Method of Rightly Conducting One's Reason and of Seeking Truth in the Sciences (Descartes), 8
Discourse on the Sciences and Arts (Rousseau), 85
Discours préliminaire to the *Encyclopédie* (d'Alambert), 85
dismissal, 239–40
diversity, in translatability, 211
divine law (*lex divina*), 54
division of labor, 196
Dominicans, 22, 47–48, 54–55, 92. *See also* Bruno, Giordano
double border, 71–72, 105n6
double truth, 80
Drexciya, 140
dualism, 127, 138, 194
Du Bois, W. E. B., 131, 140, 167, 168, 192
Duhem, Pierre, 27
Durkheim, Émile, 64, 167, 196
Dussel, Enrique, 66, 67, 82

Earthrise, 180
Eastern Roman Empire, 26, 69
ego cogito ("I think"), 67, 82
ego conquero ("I conquer"), 67
Egypt, 25, 98
Eisenstadt, Shmuel, 21
Elements (Euclid), 35, 40
Elman, Benjamin, 37
empiricism, 8–9, 110
Engels, 226, 242n7
England, 47, 71, 72, 76–77
Enlightenment, 11; abstract labor of, 151; Aristotle and, 90; decolonization in, 85; epistemology after, 24; Middle Ages and, 88; Renaissance and, 57, 68, 70, 93–94, 101; Scottish, 86, 118
Epicureans, 75, 103
epistemic mapping, 101–2
epistemological *problematique*, 7
epistemological relativism, 1
epistemology: of Aymara, 214–16; of capital, 234–35; of capitalism, 191; of data, 119; defined, 27–28, 29; after Enlightenment, 24; ethnocentrism of, 19–20; Eurocentrism of, 21; of Māori, 150–51; of modernity, 191, 195; paradigms and, 10; of Renaissance, 13, 63–64, 90; teratology and, 64; in TM procedure, 149. *See also* ontology-epistemology-methodology
Erasmus, 82, 106n9
error Averrois, 50
Ersche, Christian, 125
Escobar, Arturo, 172, 227
Espeland, Wendy Nelson, 228–29
Essays (Montaigne), 77
essentialism, 5
eternal law (*lex aeterna*), 54
eternal return, 92
Ethica (Aristotle), 40
ethnocentrism, 3, 7, 15; in Christianity, 55–56; of epistemology, 19–20; global and, 166–67; non-Western and, 140
Euclid, 35, 40
Eurocentrism, 1, 2; abstract-concrete and, 189; abstract labor and, 153–53; Christianity and, 37; circulation and, 199; coloniality of method and,

169, 171; concept formation and, 5, 190; defined, 3–4; diffusionism of, 166, 182–85, 200; dimensions of, 57n3; of epistemology, 21; familiarity and, 146; global and, 165, 167; globalization in, 200; history and, 151–52; IRT and, 4, 5; modernity and, 64; Outwaite and, 9; reconceptualization in, 237; Renaissance and, 86–87; TM procedure and, 149; of universalism, 20; universalism in, 20, 57n3, 193
Evans-Pritchard, Edward, 177–78
experimentalism, 27
explananda, 201
explanans, 198
explanantes, 198

Fabian, Johannes, 128
faith, 31–34, 54; Aquinas on, 28–29; Augustine on, 28; in nominalism, 56
falsificationalist epistemology, 146
familiarity: in CF, 125; in definition, 146–48
Fan, Fa-ti, 61, 236–36
Fanon, Frantz, 192
Al-Farabi, 35, 54, 221–22
feminism, 2, 180, 203n12
Fernàndez Retamar, Roberto, 12, 131–37
Ferrier, James Frederick, 28, 29
feudality (*hôkensei*), 231
feudal mutation (*mutation féodale*), 42
Feyerabend, Paul K., 106n8, 146
field utility, in CF, 125
First Opium War, 165
Fisher, Karen, 148, 150
Florio, John, 77, 140
Fons memorabilium universi (*Source of Notable Information about the Universe*), 88
formalization: of global, 178; of nation-state, 175; in TM, 126, 149–54, 156–57
forma mentis, 188
Fortunio, Giovanni Francesco, 73
Foucault, Michel, 130
Fourth Crusade, 45, 49
Fox-Keller, Evelyn, 203n12
Franciscans, 22, 48, 50, 54–55, 133
Francis of Assisi, 133
Frank, André Gunther, 21
Frederick II, 13, 22, 47
from the mountains to the sea (*Ki uta ki tai*), 15, 150–51

Galileo Galilei, 97, 98
Gama, Vasco da, 36
Garcia Sanjuán, Alejandro, 105n6
Garin, Eugenio, 70, 72, 86–88, 90, 100–101, 105n4
genealogy: Chakrabarty on, 192; coloniality of method and, 169, 171–72; for concept formation, 235; in procedure of TM, 149
generalization, 141, 167
general systems theory (GST), 177, 181
genius loci, 77, 97
genocide, 2, 15, 99, 115, 130
genus, 30
geoculture, 64
geopolitics of knowledge, 4, 115–16, 128, 192–93, 202
Geppert, A. C. T., 180
Gerring, John: CF of, 118–19, 122–23, 125, 126, *126*; classification criteria of, 148
GF. *See* global flows
Al-Ghazali, 35
Ghiberti, Lorenzo, 89
Gilbert, William, 106n10
Gill, Barry, 21
Gillespie, Michael Allen, 49, 56
Gilman, Nils, 174
Ginés, Juan, 73
GK. *See* globalization of knowledge
Glissant, Édouard, 137
global: articulation of, 166; as assemblage, 196; capitalism and, 168; Christianity and, 181;

colonialism and, 166–67; coloniality of method and, 168–72; critical globalization and, 12; decolonization and, 172–75; ethnocentrism and, 166–67; Eurocentric diffusionism and, 182–85; Eurocentrism and, 165, 167; formalization of, 178; methodology for, 12; Middle Ages and, 195; modernity and, 168, 191; modernization theories and, 172–75, 200; nation-state and, 165; paradigms and, 165–68; planetary and, 12–13, 165, 199–203; system theory and, 176–82; in translatability, 211; as unit of analysis, 165–204
global flows (GF), 119, 125, *126*
globalization: coloniality of method and, 169; of concept formation, 5; critical, 5, 12, 165; in definition, 146; in Eurocentrism, 200; nation-state and, 195; in TM, 126, 156
globalization of knowledge (GK), 68, 125, 145, 148; formalization and, 156–57; inferential control and, 156; of Qi, 126; in TM formalization, 156, 157
globalization of sociology, 169, 178
Global South, 4, 129–30
Le Globe, 167
gnoseology, 57n2, 220
Gnosticism, 25–26, 127
Gnostics, 2
Go, Julian, 182
Gramsci, Antonio, 147, 212, 241n4
Granada, Miguel Angel, 82
Gran Khan, 133
Great Discoveries, 72–73
Great Divergence, 61
Gregorian calendar, 24
Gregory, Derek, 182
Grosfoguel, Ramon, 169–70, 203n9
Grossberg, Lawrence, 166
Grossman, Henryk, 233
Grundrisse (Marx), 240
GST. *See* general systems theory
Guamán Poma de Ayala, Guamán, 99
guardianship (*kaitiakitanga*), 148
Gundissalino, Domenico, 40
Gutenberg, Johannes, 24
Gypsies, 52, 84

habitus, 124
Hall, Stuart, 145–46, 166
Hamati-Ataya, Inanna, 211
Hamilton, Bernard, 45
Haraway, Donna, 192, 203n12
Harvey, David, 167, 185
Hegel, Georg Wilhelm Friedrich, 64, 127; idealism of, 22; integrated totality of, 188–89; *Phenomenology of the Spirit* by, 167–68; teleology of, 23
heliocentrism, 94, 95–96
Hempel, Carl Gustav, 186
Heng, Geraldine, 51–53
Herder, Johann Gottfried von, 86
heresy/heretics, 14, 44, 51–52; Augustine and, 46; Dominicans and, 92; of Galileo, 98; Inquisition and, 84; racialization of, 54; Renaissance and, 57
hermaphroditism, 104
hermeneutics, 9. *See also* diatopic hermeneutics
hermeticism, 25
heterodoxy, 14; of Aristotle, 55; Christianity and, 91–92; counterrevolution against, 27; of creation theology, 79; Gnosticism and Neoplatism and, 25; politics and, 47–56; racialization of, 44; Renaissance and, 57; translation and, 25
Hilgerdt, Folke, 172, 174
Hinduism, 25, 91, 95, 101
Historia del Mondo Nuovo (Benzoni), 77
Historia Medii Aevi (Cellarius), 88
historical epistemology, 1
historical materialism, of Marx, 167

histories-to-concept, 126
history: abstract labor of, 151–52; Eurocentrism and, 151–52; of Marx, 23; ontology-epistemology-methodology and, 24; resignification and, 236; in TM procedure, 149
history-as-eventuation, 123
The History of the Mongols We Call Tartars (*Istoria* Mongalorum quos nos Tartaros appellamus) (Pian del Carpine), 133–34
Hobson, John M., 21, 36, 38, 42–43, 183
Hodgson, Marshall, 38
hôkensei (feudality), 231
holism, 8; for concept formation, 12; Indigenous peoples and, 150; relationism and, 190; system theory and, 176–82
Holy Bible, printing of, 24
homosexuality, 50
Hopkins, Terence Kilbourne, 179–80, 183–89
House of Islam, 43
human, 13, 240; nation-state and, 140; nominalism and, 139. *See also* dehumanization
humanism, of Renaissance, 70, 100–105
Hume, David, 86, 110, 194
Hundred Years' War, 72
Hungary, 45
Huntington, Samuel, 21
hyperreal, 32, 70, 105nn5–6, 192

Ibn-Khaldun, Abd ar-Raḥmān ibn Muḥammad, 40
Ibn-Rushd (Averroes), 35, 40, 41, 47–56, 80, 91
Ibn-Sina, 35
"I conquer" (*ego conquero*), 67
idealism: of Hegel, 22; nominalism and, 97
ideal types, 123–24, 150, 237
imagined cartographies, 238
imperialism, 3
inclusion-relations, 186–87
incommensurability, 32, 90, 96, 106n8, 240
incorporation, 13, 185, 239
India, 4, 52; non-Western and, 130; numerology of, 98; political power of, 116; terms-of-trade with, 172–73. *See also* Hinduism
Las Indias de por acá (the Indies of this side of the world), 74
Indias italianas (Italian Indies), 74–75
the Indies of this side of the world (*Las Indias de por acá*), 74
Indigenous epistemologies, 2, 14
Indigenous peoples: capital and, 228–29; from Global South, 4; holism and, 150; non-Western and, 130; renaissance of, 101; statistics of, 121–22; uncommon and, 230; *vincularidad* and, 217
indio, 14
Indios, 74–75, 80, 84
Indipetae, 74
inferential control, in TM, 156
infidelitas, 55–56
infinite universe, 11, 94–100
Inglis, David, 167
Innocent III (Pope), 42–47, 49, 50
Inquisition, 14, 84, 98
integrated totality, of Hegel, 188–89
inter alia, 36, 94, 194
international relations theory (IRT), 169; Eurocentrism and, 4, 5; modernization theories and, 175
International Sociological Association, 169
internecine, 49
intersexuality, 104
Introduction to Astrology (Abū Ma'shar), 40
IRT. *See* international relations theory
Islamic clause, 38
Islam/Muslims, 2; Aquinas and, 48, 54–55; Christianity and, 55; creation theology of, 79; ontology and

epistemology and, 11; *Reconquista* and, 105n6; Scholasticism in, 26–27; translation and, 34
Istoria Mongalorum quos nos Tartaros appellamus (*The History of the Mongols We Call Tartars*) (Pian del Carpine), 133–34
Italian Indies (*Indias italianas*), 74–75
Italian Renaissance, 2, 11, 63, 68–76; Middle Ages in, 89; monstrosity in, 102–3. *See also* Bruno, Giordano
Italy: Castilian language in, 69, 71–73; colonialism of, 238; Jesuits in, 74–75; *Risorgimento* of, 238
"I think" (*ego cogito*), 67, 82

Al-Jabri, Mohammed Abed, 35
Jackson, Patrick, 117–18
Japan, 130
Jaspers, Karl, 23
Jesuits, 37, 74–75
Jews, 2, 52; cabalists, 25, 98; creation theology of, 79; *Reconquista* and, 72
Jordan, Chester, 32
Jubilee of 1600, 84
judicial astrology, 94

Kairos, 242n5
kaitiakitanga (guardianship), 148
kanga (customs and protocols), 148
Kant, Immanuel, 9, 22, 29, 64, 82, 127, 194
karakia (prayer and incantations), 148
Karsavin, Lev, 83
Kedar, Asaf, 117
Kepler, Johannes, 97–98, 106n10
Khan, Genghis, 43
al-Khwārizmī, 40
Al-Kindi, 35
Ki uta ki tai (from the mountains to the sea), 15, 150–51
knights (*bellatores*), 42
knowledge (*scientia*), 29
knowledge-as-emancipation, 214
knowledge-as-regulation, 214
Kohn, Eduardo, 137–38
Koselleck, Reinhart, 241n2
Kristeller, Paul Oskar, 100, 101
Kuhn, Thomas, 106n8

laboratores (laborers), 42
lacuna, 125
Lakatos, Imre, 12, 119, 143–45, 146
Larmore, Charles, 49
Las Casas, Bartolomé de, 73
Latin American Subaltern Studies Group, 65, 105n2
Latin Averroists, 41, 51, 80
Lazarsfeld, Paul, 180, 186
Leight, Joseph, 101–2
lemmas, 117
Lenin, Vladimir, 241n3
Leucippus, 95, 106n10
Levinas, Emmanuel, 66
lex aeterna (eternal law), 54
lex divina (divine law), 54
liberalism, 9, 177
liberation, 66, 83, 130, 213–14
licentia docendi (teaching license), 47
Linebaugh, Peter, 2
List, Friedrich, 173
Liu, Lydia, 240
Lives of the Artists (*Vite de' più eccellenti pittori scultori e architettori*) (Vasari), 89
Locke, John, 194
logica nova, 53
longue durée, 11, 19, 21, 23, 71, 127
love (*Eros*), 217–19

magic words (*parabras magicas*), 214
Magno, Alberto, 47
Magnubane, Zine, 180
Magyars, 45
maître à penser, 139–40
manchada (spotted), 215
Manifesto (Marx and Engels), 226, 242n7
Māori: epistemology of, 150–51; Renaissance of, 2, 15, 147–48

Mare Nostrum, 44
Mariátegui, José Carlos, 241n4
markets, 196
Marx, Karl, 64, 196, 240, 242n7; abstract labor of, 151; on capital, 225–27, 228, 230–32, 233, 234, 242n9, 242n11; Eurocentric diffusionism and, 184–85; historical materialism of, 167; history of, 23; methodology of, 188
Massey, Doreen, 197, 200
mātauranga, 147–48
Maya, 84
Mbembe, Achille, 130–31, 192, 226–27
McManus, Stuart Michael, 70
McMichael, Philip, 61, 203n7
medioevo, 88
Melissus, 106n10
Merle, Marcel, 167
Metamorphoses (Ovid), 103–4
metempsychosis, 91
Metereologica (Aristotle), 40
Methaphysica (Aristotle), 40, 41, 90
method of monster-barring, 119
"The Method of Political Economy" (Marx), 188
methodological formalization (MF), 123, 125, 126, 145, 148, 176
methodology, 7–8; for global, 12; of Marx, 188; of monstrosity, 12; neologisms for, 123; paradigms and, 10. *See also* ontology-epistemology-methodology
Mezzadra, Sandro, 193, 194
MF. *See* methodological formalization
Michie, Jonathan, 116
Middle Ages, 41; Christianity in, 26; cyclical time and, 94; Enlightenment and, 88; experimentalism in, 27; global and, 195; in Italian Renaissance, 89; Renaissance and, 85
Mignolo, Walter D., 63, 65–69, 71–73, 84, 86, 89, 193, 203n10, 216–18, 242n6; double border of, 71–72, 105n6
Mills, C. Wright, 140
Miranda (fictional character), 131–32, 134–36
Mittman, Asa Simon, 104
modernity: Bruno on, 83–94; capitalism and, 183; circulation and, 199; colonialism and, 64–66, 87; counterpoint to, 65–67; dualism and, 194; epistemology of, 191, 195; genocide of, 115; global and, 168, 191; non-Western and, 128, 130, 140; planetary and, 201; resignification and, 236; Scientific Revolution and, 86
modernization theories, 120–21; binarism of, 177; coloniality of method and, 170; decolonization and, 172–75; global and, 172–75, 200; IRT and, 175; replicability of, 175
modules, articulation of, 145–57
Moleti, Giuseppe, 98
Mongols, 34, 36, 43, 45, 52, 133
monism, 127
monstrosity: alterity with, 134; Lakatos on, 143–45; methodology of, 12; Renaissance of, 100–105; teratology and, 141–42; TM and, 143–45, 157
Montaigne, Michel de, 77, 139–40
Moore, Jason, 182, 183
Moore, Robert, 35–36
Moore, Wilbert E., 176, 177, 178–79
Moors, 52, 53, 71–72, 84
Morgan, Luke, 103–4
Morris, Meaghan, 166
mō teatea (chants), 148
Muhammad (Prophet), 42–43
Al-Muqaddima (Ibn-Khaldun), 40
muri, 2, 232–35
Murray, Christopher, 101–2
Muslims. *See* Islam
mutation féodale (feudal mutation), 42

Nahuatl, 84

Nardi, Bruno, 47
natio, 30
nationalism, 4
nation-state, 13; formalization of, 175; global and, 165; globalization and, 195; human and, 140; reconceptualization of, 237–38; in TM procedure, 154
naturalism, 117
nayri kati, 121–22
n-dimensional spacetime, 1, 4–5
Nebrija, 72, 73
necropolitics, 130–31, 192
negation, coloniality of method and, 170
Neilson, Brett, 193, 194
Neoclassicism, 102
neocolonalism, 3, 5
neologisms, 123, 124, 169
Neoplatonism, 25–26, 31, 41
Nepantla, 65
neutralization, coloniality of method and, 170
New Testament, printing of, 24
New World, 79, 80, 139
Nguni Bantu, 153
Nicole, Pierre, 156
Nietzsche, Friedrich, 92
Nisancioglu, Kerem, 36
nomadism, 40
nomen omen, 132
nominalism, 49; human and, 139; idealism and, 97; Scholasticism and, 56
nondualism, 94, 127
nonhuman semiosis, 2
non-Western: colonialism and, 128, 129, 130, 137, 140–41; dehumanization and, 141; dualism and, 138; ethnocentrism and, 140; familiarity and, 146–47; Global South and, 129–30; modernity and, 128, 130, 140; in TM, 127–45, 155, 156
Normans, 40
Le Nouveau Christianisme, 167
numerology, of India, 98

O'Brien, Patrick, 47, 56
ontology: of abstract, 189; liberalism and, 9; paradigms and, 10; relation and, 186–87
ontology-epistemology-methodology, 7, 11, 117–18; for abstract-concrete, 189; history and, 24; non-Western and, 127; power and, 24–25; racialization of, 22–23
oratores (clerks), 42
Organon (Aristotle), 53
Orientatlsim, 57n3, 179
Origen of Alexandria, 91–92, 93
Otherness, 146
Ouekumene, 38
Outhwaite, William, 8–10, 117
Ovid, 103–4

pagan-Islam-Christianity, 31–41
pagans, 28; barbarians and, 116; Christianity and, 89–90
Panikkar, Raimon, 123, 157n1, 242n5
Papi, Fulvio, 77
parabras magicas (magic words), 214
paradigms: to experimentalism, 27; global and, 165–68; Outhwaite on, 9–10; of transformational grammar, 146
parameters, in translatability, 211
Parentucelli, Tommaso, 100
Park, Katharine, 142
parsimony, in CF, 125
Parsons, Talcott, 177, 196
Parthasarathi, Prasannan, 61
particularism, 1, 10
part-whole, 187
past future (*qhipnayra*), 216
Pentateuch, 24
pepeha (tribal sayings), 148
Perkins, Franklin, 32–33
Persia: Abbasid empire in, 34–35, 41; Umayyad dynasty of, 34
perspicullum, 97–98
phenomenology, 222

Phenomenology of the Spirit (Hegel), 167–68
philautia, 77
Pian del Carpine, Giovanni da, 133–34
planetary: global and, 12–13, 165, 199–203; in translatability, 211
Plato, 26, 41
Platonism, 56
plenitudo potestatis, 46
pluralism, 187
pluriversality, in translatability, 211–12
point zero, 21, 193
Polanyi, Karl, 227
Polizeiwissenschaft, 116
polyphony, 65
polysemy, 123
Pomeranz, Kenneth, 203n11
Port-Royal Logic, 156
Portugal, 84, 85, 88
positivism, 5, 9, 146
postsecularism, 94
The Poverty of Philosophy (Marx), 242n7
power: agency and, 191; asymmetries of, 65, 190–93; borders and, 194; capitalism and, 185; coloniality of method and, 203n9; hierarchies of, 39–40; ontology-epistemology-methodology and, 24–25; translatability and, 214
Pratt, Mary Louise, 198–99
prayer and incantations (*karakia*), 148
Prebisch, Raul, 173
premodern epistemology, racialization of, 19–57
premodern pagans, 2
prima inter pares, 48
problematique, 5, 7; of Kant, 9–10; of Outhwaite, 10; of phenomenology, 222
procedure, in TM, 148–54
Proofs and Refutations (Lakatos), 143–45
properties, assemblages and, 195
Prospero (fictional character), 131–32, 134–37, 140
proverbs (*whakatauk ī*), 148
Provincializing Europe (Chakrabarty), 152–53
psychedelia, renaissance of, 101
Ptolemy, 35, 94
public life, in Renaissance, 92
pūr ākau (stories and narratives), 148
purez de sangre, 73

qhipnayra (past future), 216
Qi, Xiaoying, 119, 124–25, 126, *126*
queer methodologies of monstrosity, 2
La querelle des Anciens et des Modernes (Rousseau), 85
Quijano, Anibal, 75, 169, 203n9, 231
quod aliquem, 48

race, 30; Crusades and, 52
racialization: of alterity, 11; Aristotle and, 34; in Christianity, 28, 44–45, 52–53, 74; of heresy, 54; of heterodoxy, 44; of ontology-epistemology-methodology, 22–23; of premodern epistemology, 19–57; of Saracens, 52; thingification and, 226
racism, 30, 64
Raj, Kapil, 61, 198
Ramose, Mogobe, 153–54
rationalism, 9
realism, 9; liberalism and, 177
reconceptualization, 237–38
Reconquista, 71–72, 105n6
Rediker, Marcus, 2
reductio ad unum, 234
Reformation, 55
Regole grammaticali della volgar lingua (Fortunio), 73
regressio ad infinitum, 97
reincarnation, 56
reiteration, 64
relation, 186–87; assemblages and, 195, 196; borders and, 195

relationalism, 177, 190–93
relationality, 150, 215; *vincularidad* and, 216–17, 220
Renaissance, 11–12, 24; Aristotle/Christianity debate in, 73–74; astrology in, 94; Christianity in, 89, 91–92; cyclical time in, 91–94; decolonization in, 63–105; double border in, 71–72; England in, 76–77; Enlightenment and, 57, 68, 70, 93–94, 101; epistemology of, 13, 63–64, 90; Eurocentrism and, 86–87; financialization in, 72–73; heretic natural philosophy in, 2; hermetic astrology in, 2; humanism of, 70, 100–105; infinite universe in, 11, 94–100; love in, 218–19; of Māori, 2, 15, 147–48; Middle Ages and, 85; of monstrosity, 100–105; public life in, 92; Scholasticism and, 27, 101; Scientific Revolution in, 29–30; of Spain, 11, 63, 68, 70, 73; subterranean river to, 56–57; unconscious reading of, 71; *vincularidad* and, 217. *See also* Italian Renaissance
renovatio mundi (world renovation), 90
replicability, of modernization theories, 175
res cogitans, 194
res extensa, 194
resignification, 235–36
resonance, in CF, 125
resurrection, 91
return to the classics, 69
revelatio (revelation), 29
Revelation, 33
Ricci, Saverio, 83
Risorgimento, of Italy, 238
Rist, Gilbert, 172
Ritterhude, Konrad, 98
River (Fisher), 150
Robertson, Roland, 167, 169
Robertson, William, 86
Robinson, Cedric J., 21
Roman Empire, 25
Romantics, 63
Roosevelt, Eleanor, 240
Rostow, Walt Whitman, 173, 174
Rousseau, Jean-Jacques, 85
Runa, 216
Russia, 4, 116

Sacred Wood of Bomarzo, 103–4
sacrum sepolcrum, 46
Sahlins, Marshall, 134
Said, Edward, 65–66, 178, 238
Saint-Simon, Henri de, 167
Santos, Boaventura de Sousa, 123, 213–14; DH of, 119, 122, 125, 126, 242n5; diatopic hermeneutics of, *126*; Qi and, 125
Saracens, 52–53, 103
Sartori, Giovanni, 122
Sassen, Saskia, 195–96
Schlegel, Friedrich, 139
scholae cahedrales (cathdral schools), 26
Scholasticism, 24; of Aquinas, 48, 49, 53, 54–55, 56; Bruno, 80; in Christianity, 26–29, 31–32; *internecine* and, 49; nominalism and, 56; politics in late period of, 47–56; Renaissance and, 101
Schoppe, Kaspar, 98
scientia (knowledge), 29
Scientific Revolution, 20, 27, 29–30, 86, 198
Scoto, Michele, 40
Scottish Enlightenment, 86, 118
Second Renaissance, 71
secularization, 128
sedentarism, 40
semantic spatialization, 13, 219–20
Seth, Sanjay, 190–91
Seventh Crusade, 50
sexism, 64
Shakespeare, William, 12, 131–32, 134–37, 139–40
Shilliam, Robbie, 226

Sigieri of Brabante, 51
Singer, Hans, 172–73
situatedness, 13–15, 117, 192, 203n12
slavery, 226, 242n7
Smith, Linda Tuhiwai, 147, 150
Smith, Lisa, 150
Social Anthropology (Evans-Pritchard), 177–78
social cohesion, 196
sociology, of Weber, 22
sociology-as-structuration, 123
sociology of knowledge, 1
Sorokin, Pitirim, 173–74, 176
Source of Notable Information about the Universe (*Fons memorabilium universi*), 88
Spaccio della Bestia trionfante (Bruno), 77
Spain: Jesuits in, 74; *Reconquista* in, 71–72, 105n6; Renaissance of, 11, 63, 68, 70, 73
Spivak, Gayatri Chakravorty, 201
spotted (*manchada*), 215
Spruit, Leen, 93
Stagirites, 41, 53
Steinmetz, George, 176, 182
sterilization, coloniality of method and, 170
Stevens, Mitchell L., 228–29
stories and narratives (*pūr ākau*), 148
structural functionalism, 152–53, 177
studia humanitatis, 100
studium, 47
Sufficientiae (Avicenna), 40
Summa contra Gentiles (Aquinas), 55
symma theologiae (theological axiomatics), 53
synonymy, 123
system theory, 176–82

Tainos, 132–33
Taoism, 101, 127
Tarantino, Elisabetta, 78
Tartars, 45
taxonomy, 24, 239
teaching license (*licentia docendi*), 47
teleology, 23, 91
The Tempest (Shakespeare), 131–32, 134–37, 139–40
Tempière, Ètienne, 34, 55
temporality, 11
teratologic methodology (TM): application in, 155–56; of concept formation, 115–57; definition in, 146–48; formalization in, 126, 149–54, 156–57; inferential control in, 156; monstrosity and, 141–45; non-Western and, 127–45; procedural protocol for, 145–57; procedure in, 148–54
teratology, 12; alterity and, 142–43; epistemology and, 64; monstrosity and, 141–42
terms-of-trade, 172–73
Tertium non datur (Aristotle), 90
theological axiomatics (*symma theologiae*), 53
Theophilus, 92
theoretical utility, in CF, 125
thingification, capital and, 225–35
Thomas, Peter, 212–13
Thomism, 53
Tianxia, 2, 152–53, 181
Tillich, Paul, 242n5
Tiphys, 78
TM. *See* teratologic methodology
Toye, John, 172
Toye, Richard, 172
tractatus, 92
transfer of learning (*translatio studii*), 34
transformational grammar, 146, 157n2
translatability, 13, 211–41; capital and, 220; translation and, 212–13
translation, 2, 6, 32, 40, 97, 125, 156–57; of Aristotle, 11; heterodoxy and, 25; Islam and, 34; translatability and, 212–13
translatio studii (transfer of learning), 34

tribal sayings (*pepeha*), 148
tropoi, 213–14, 227
Truman, Harry S., 172
Turkey, 4
Turpo, Mariano, 242n8
Turpo, Nazario, 242n8
Tyndale, William, 24

ubuntu, 2, 153–54
Ubuntu (Ramose), 153–54
Umayyad dynasty, 34
uncommon, 225–35, 240
unconscious reading, of Renaissance, 71
unit of analysis, global as, 165–204
Universal Declaration of Human Rights, 240
universalism, 1, 10, 20, 57n3, 193
universities, 21–22
Uno Kōzō, 230–33
untranslatability, 240–41
urbis et orbis, 175
US hegemony, 176–82, 190

Valeriano, Antonio, 70
Vasari, Giorgio, 89
Veblen, Thorstein, 233
verstehen, 124
vicissitudine (vicissitude), 93
Vico, Gianbattista, 92
vincularidad, 216–17, 220
vinculum, 13, 217–18, 220, 240
Vite de' più eccellenti pittori scultori e architettori (*Lives of the Artists*) (Vasari), 89
voyages of discovery, 36
vuh, 84, 89

Walker, Gavin, 232–33
Wallerstein, Immanuel, 3–4, 5, 37, 41–42, 57n3, 169, 179–80, 182–83, 186, 189
Walsh, Catherine, 65, 216–18
Wang Hui, 40
Weber, Max, 10, 64, 117, 196, 237–38; Bhambra and, 123–24; generalization of, 167; sociology of, 22
Weisinger, Herbert, 87
Weltanschauung, 88, 147
Western code, 86
whakapapa, 148
whakatauk ī (proverbs), 148
William of Baglione, 55
Williams, Raymond, 217
world renovation (*renovatio mundi*), 90
world-system, 185–89, 203n8
World-Systems Analysis (Hopkins), 185–89
World War II, 87, 165, 170; decolonization after, 12; terms-of-trade in, 172–73

xenophobia, 51

Zhao Tingyang, 152–53
Zoroastrianism, 2, 25, 34, 127

About the Author

Gennaro Ascione is professor of sociology and the epistemologies of human sciences. He works on global historical sociology, science and modernity, global studies, non-Western epistemologies, social theory, methodology of social research, and decolonial and postcolonial theory at the Department of Human and Social Sciences, University of Naples "L'Orientale." He is cofounder of the global network of scholars Toward a Non-Hegemonic World Sociology (UNESCO e Fondation Maison des sciences de l'homme, Paris).